Springer Proceedings in Business and Economics

Springer Proceedings in Business and Economics brings the most current research presented at conferences and workshops to a global readership. The series features volumes (in electronic and print formats) of selected contributions from conferences in all areas of economics, business, management, and finance. In addition to an overall evaluation by the publisher of the topical interest, scientific quality, and timeliness of each volume, each contribution is refereed to standards comparable to those of leading journals, resulting in authoritative contributions to the respective fields. Springer's production and distribution infrastructure ensures rapid publication and wide circulation of the latest developments in the most compelling and promising areas of research today.

The editorial development of volumes may be managed using Springer Nature's innovative EquinOCS, a proven online conference proceedings submission, management and review system. This system is designed to ensure an efficient timeline for your publication, making Springer Proceedings in Business and Economics the premier series to publish your workshop or conference volume.

This book series is indexed in SCOPUS.

Luigi Paganetto
Editor

Economic Challenges for Europe After the Pandemic

Proceedings of the XXXII Villa Mondragone International Economic Seminar, Rome, Italy, 2021

Springer

Editor
Luigi Paganetto
Economics Foundation
University of Rome Tor Vergata
Rome, Roma, Italy

ISSN 2198-7246 ISSN 2198-7254 (electronic)
Springer Proceedings in Business and Economics
ISBN 978-3-031-10301-8 ISBN 978-3-031-10302-5 (eBook)
https://doi.org/10.1007/978-3-031-10302-5

This Springer imprint is published by the registered company Springer Nature Switzerland AG
The registered company address is: Gewerbestrasse 11, 6330 Cham, Switzerland

Contents

Contributors

Fabio Berzaghi Laboratory for Sciences of Climate and Environment (LSCE) - UMR, CEA/CNRS/UVSQ, Paris, France

Luigi Bonatti School of International Studies, University of Trento, Trento, Italy

Valentina Bonifacio Rome, Italy

Luis Brandao-Marques Rome, Italy

Nina Budina Rome, Italy

Ralph Chami International Monetary Fund, Washington, DC, USA

Lorenzo Codogno London School of Economics and Political Science, London, UK

Thomas Cosimano Blue Green Future, Falls Church, VA, USA

Balazs Csonto Rome, Italy

Philipp Engler Rome, Italy

Sonia Español-Jiménez Fundación Centro MERI, Castro, Chile

Giuseppe Ferrero Banca d'Italia, Rome, Italy

Chiara Fratto Rome, Italy

Connel Fullenkamp Duke University, Durham, NC, USA

Davide Furceri Rome, Italy

Marias H. Gestsson Department of Economics, University of Iceland, Reykjavík, Iceland

Deniz Igan Rome, Italy

Sergio Inferrera CompNet - The Competitiveness Research Network, Halle, Germany

Lorenza Alexandra Lorenzetti ALTIS, Università Cattolica del Sacro Cuore di Milano, Milan, Italy

Rui Mano Rome, Italy

Milton Marcondes Baleia Jubarte, Caravelas, Brazil

Franco Mosconi Jean Monnet Chair in 'The Economics of European Industry', University of Parma, Parma, Italy

Machiko Narita Rome, Italy

Murad Omoev Rome, Italy

Luigi Paganetto Economics Foundation, University of Rome Tor Vergata, Rome, Italy

Jose Palazzo Baleia Jubarte, Caravelas, Brazil

Gurnain Kaur Pasricha Rome, Italy

Massimiliano Pisani Banca d'Italia, Rome, Italy

Hélène Poirson Rome, Italy

Dominick Salvatore Fordham University, New York, NY, USA

Pasquale Lucio Scandizzo Rome, Italy

Martino Tasso Banca d'Italia, Rome, Italy

Paul van den Noord Amsterdam School of Economics, Amsterdam, The Netherlands

Gylfi Zoega Department of Economics, University of Iceland, Reykjavík, Iceland-Department of Mathematics, Economic and Statistics, Birkbeck College, University of London, London, UK

Creating an Epistemic Community: The Experience of the Villa Mondragone International Economic Seminar

Pasquale Lucio Scandizzo

1 The Themes of VIDMA as an Epistemic Community

As summarized in the contribution to the Paganetto & Scandizzo, 2020 conference by Paganetto and Scandizzo. One of the key themes of the Villa Mondragone Conference since its inception has been the determinants of economic development as endogenous growth, and, with a more recent emphasis, the problem of its sustainability (Scandizzo, 2019; Paganetto & Scandizzo, 2020). The foundation of a virtuous model of social development and realization of individual capabilities is not manifest knowledge, and many doubts persist on its constituents and durability. Creativity, both in the sense of cultural vitality and of entrepreneurial dynamism is a key ingredient, but its origin and persistence in modern society seems also elusive and somewhat mysterious. Institutional prowess, social virtues and altruism, together with qualities that do not seek but are ultimately their own reward also appear to be key to successful development over and beyond the often-narrow horizons of economic accomplishments (Phelps, 2015). At the same time, just as positive external effects, such as cooperation and joint knowledge, can promote growth beyond the limits of pure individual interests, so can negative external effects. These include private vices, like corruption and crimes, but also social failures, like growing income inequality and social injustice (Paganetto & Scandizzo, 2015, 2017). These may undermine the private bases of growth, by depressing factor productivity and agent's motivation for productive work. The lack of convergence among the different economies can therefore be explained by lacking or negative factors of endogenous development. Environmental externalities, such as greenhouse effects and other ecosystem changes may aggravate this

P. L. Scandizzo (✉)
Rome, Italy
e-mail: scandizzo@uniroma2.it

L. Paganetto (ed.), *Economic Challenges for Europe After the Pandemic*,
Springer Proceedings in Business and Economics,
https://doi.org/10.1007/978-3-031-10302-5_1

condition since they tend to be ignored by individual countries, as in the case of climate change. In this respect, the current pandemics has shown how dramatic can become the day of reckoning of global threats, when they become real and present dangers. The presence of negative endogenous factors can transform a condition of insufficient and low-quality economic development into a trap, from which it may be increasingly difficult to get out (Paganetto & Scandizzo, 2010). It is perhaps this trap that characterizes the present crisis of the world model of growth, and the conjectures of secular stagnation that some economists have elaborated to explain the slowdown of development and transformative innovation in many countries and in the world as a whole.

Is this trap the reason why growth is so anemic and productivity stagnating despite seemingly accelerating technological progress? (Paganetto & Scandizzo, 2015, 2016, 2018). More than a theme, this has been a leit motive for a wider debate of most of the more recent VM conferences and associated events during the years (Paganetto & Scandizzo 2016, 2017, 2018, 2020). Secular stagnation has been proposed as one of the hypotheses, as a major consequence of lacking major technological innovations. Technological cycles, however, and abrupt paradigm changes appear to be better candidates to explain the recurrence as well as the apparent faltering of long and continuous period's economic growth through sustained changes in total factor productivity (Paganetto & Scandizzo, 2010).

The role of technology in raising total factor productivity was, of course, essential in the industrial revolution, but, to a large extent, it was determinant only to establish the conditions for a spectacular increase in high-speed throughput, i.e. both in an increase in output and in a decrease in inputs per unit of time. In fact, most of the technological advances throughout the nineteenth and the twentieth century were of the incremental variety, both in the sense that they were perfecting discoveries which had already been known for long time (as was the case of the steam engine) and in the broader sense that they were feeding into revolutionary new forms of organization of the firm and of society itself, through mechanization, automation and other forms of vertical integration of technological processes.

The first economic revolution was based on the discovery and expansion of agricultural activities as a systematic exploitation of domesticated forms of plants and livestock and traced a road to growth whose reckoning is part of the present critical slowdown of growth and deterioration of the quality of development. It determined a development of the frontier of agricultural land, a process that came to proceed hand in hand with the process of urbanization. As in the industrial revolution, in the agricultural revolution throughput increased dramatically, by both increasing the intensity of production and by pushing outward the frontier of cultivation at the expense of forests, pastures and other forms of native destination of the environment. Productivity increases were, of course, the very product of systematic agriculture, through cultural practices, the management of water, the application of manure and other organic fertilizer and the selection of plants and livestock to improve performance. Compared to the industrial revolution, in fact, the role of technology for progress in agriculture has been and continues to be perhaps more crucial, since the organizational changes that can be achieved by lengthening the value chains are much more limited and entail higher economic and social transaction costs. The advancing Bioeconomy, which goes beyond agriculture in a more comprehensive governance of the ecosystem and of the biosphere as a whole is the new frontier of this development and a real hope to reach a sustainable equilibrium between nature and nurture (Scandizzo, 2009).

Anemic growth may also signal the prodrome of a third economic revolution in the 1980s or of a the never fully realized acceleration of productivity from ITC within the second economic revolution. According with several cyclical theories, peaks of economic prosperity are caused by waves of primary and secondary investments, stimulated by innovations, and followed by secondary technological changes and further investment (Scandizzo & Ventura, 2016). The inevitable slackening of the process, once the original momentum is lost, causes equally inevitable petering out of economic growth until another cluster of innovation materializes. In all cases, however, while endogenous growth appears to settle in during the change, the primary motion of the change appears somewhat mysterious, not fully endogenous and not fully exogenous, be it the technological shift at the basis of the "economic revolutions" or on an original and unexpected cluster of innovations that are described as the prime movers of a new science and technology paradigm. The production and use of energy in economic development, with the emerging overriding role of a green growth paradigm, may, however, be the missing link to explain the possible rise of the next cluster of disruptive innovations or, alternatively, the next inflection in the supply curve of new knowledge.

Yet another question on anemic growth concerns Europe, and its apparent difficulty not only to grow at a sustained rate, but even to keep up with its economic and political partners, face the challenge of China and the other emerging powers and provide a vision of economic and social progress to its citizens. As pointed out by many participants of the conference and related seminars, the problem of growth in the euro area is loaded with ambiguities, as a result of a fundamental misunderstanding. The misconception concerns the difference between the material well-being of the population, and the realization of the European Union.

What is the difference between mere economic growth and the pursuit of peace, justice and well-being through the political union of Europe? Everyone will agree with the obvious proposition that a larger set of goods and services available to a community is preferable to a smaller one. Growth in present and future consumption is therefore a fundamental criterion of efficiency, where the only yardstick is the importance ("utility") that society from time to time attributes to the various components of consumption. But here is the critical point, since this utility is dependent on the satisfaction of individual rights, namely the subjective and objective conditions of the social system considered. A theory of negative rights, such as that of the most representative neo-liberal philosophers, argues that individuals are inviolable moral spaces and that what must be preserved is respect for the rules by which individuals acquire resources and rights. Justice is therefore primarily dependent on procedures and legal certainty depends in a sense on a formalism that prevents the state from entering into the merits of the choices of the individual. Judged in this context, the historical events of the

European Union do not appear at all desperate. The market, the theater in which one plays the game of survival and economic selection under uncertainty, can only lead to inequalities. Income distribution, employment, transfers are more or less "right", only insofar as they contribute to ensure the efficiency of the system. Even inequalities, unemployment, poverty can therefore be justified if they are the inevitable by-products of economic development. The EU, in other words, should not be judged in *se ipsa*, but as part of the grand design of growth of the economic well-being of the countries that comprise it. Only if such a design causes a permanent underdevelopment of any area or ends up being a chain that prevents greater economic momentum, the EU will have to judge "unjust" its condition.

An opposite point of view, however, rests on the theory of positive rights, where the traditional concepts of well-being and utility are replaced by the concepts of "capability" and "functions". The realization of the ability of people to get into interactive relationships with the environment, "working" as consumers, workers, producers, friends, voters, citizens, etc., is, according to this theory, the real economic problem. The injustice of social conditions is the failure to achieve these capabilities, with effects that extend from material deprivation, unemployment, to anomie, i.e. a total divergence between ability and accomplishments (Phelps, 2015; Paganetto & Scandizzo, 2017, 2018). As a weak link in the production chain of the EU, Italy is the place where a gap between capacity and functions is consumed in more spectacular forms, as the country has already widely experienced in the past with its less developed Southern regions. In this context of progressive alienation and lack of positive accomplishments, the expectations created by the media, politics, culture from the participation to the European venture are continuously dashed, while, on the other hand, their failure equally continually creates new expectations of non-satisfaction, to be unemployed, poor, abandoned, forgotten. The two fundamental freedoms, which summarize negative and positive justice, are the freedom to act and the freedom to feel good, both in varying degrees negated by the lack of economic growth, not satisfied by a convergence towards the patterns of life of the richer part of Europe, by the collapse of the illusions fed by the overoptimistic and naïve original vision of the monetary union. The problem of Europe, in this regard, is distinct from the problem of Italy. For Europe, the challenge of the Union is to adopt the best policies to achieve the goals of justice, freedom and well-being, without indulging in the economistic temptations and, at the same time, without losing sight of the unification process. In this context, the economic policies prevailing before the pandemics (the so called stability and growth pact) can be legitimately criticized as a permanently restrictive fiscal policy, based on economic concerns on the weaker areas and the potential free riders, without a strategic vision of the common objectives. On the other hand, in view of the positive rights and freedom, the condition of Italy is essentially different from that of the Union as a whole. It is for those who want to embrace a moral philosophy of an active type that appears in all its seriousness the problem of the lack of development of Italy: first of all a problem of growth objectives and priorities, as well as identification of interventions. The main problem is a social context characterized by lack of institutions capable of producing and planning consent, with a national drama arising both from the shortcomings of positive rights, and the negative rights seeming to validate social inequalities.

Focus on the European growth anemics brings to the fore the fact that endogenous, knowledge-based growth may be lacking a crucial dimension for socially sustainable development. Globalization and shifting wealth, in fact, combined with biased technological progress threaten to undermine the social fabric of modern society as we know it, by polarizing labor markets in a continuing and ever-growing raise in inequality in income distribution, social status and inclusiveness (Paganetto & Scandizzo, 2003, 2018; Scandizzo and Pierleoni, 2018). These phenomena are part of a broader resource reallocation process within and across countries, resulting in greater demand for skills and a drive towards greater inequality. Accelerated high skill biased technological change, with the emergence of a fully digitalized, AI (artificially intelligence) driven economy, increases further the premium on highly qualified labor. These processes have been accentuated by the current pandemics in a more dramatic and extreme way, since the lockdowns have mostly hit the less qualified jobs in the manufacturing service sector, with fewer or null possibilities of developing new remote working modes and evolving models of distance labor. Further polarization has occurred between the higher level workers, who have continued and even intensified their activities, but have reduced consumption and accumulated savings, and lower level employees, small manufacturers and artisans, whose incomes have been shrinking because of the fall in demand.

However, the pandemic has also shown that declining public investment (Scandizzo & Napodano, 2010; Scandizzo & Tria, 2018; Scandizzo & Pierleoni, 2020) is linked to a critical lack of public goods and rather than means to an end, these goods should be considered an end themselves. In other words, rather than pursuing an elusive and abstract target of social well-being, it would be better to provide directly more public goods, like education, health services, unemployment protection.

Many of these considerations lead to reiterate one of the crucial questions raised by the conference: what can be considered "a good economy"? (Paganetto & Scandizzo, 2014). This theme echoes the three structural dilemmas of sustainable development that seem to escape the paradigm of the traditional governance: growing social injustice, individual loss of dignity and dynamism, progressive alienation from nature and nurture. These three problems have become more visible during the recent, and persistent, economic and financial crisis, and have somewhat exploded during the pandemics. The "Good Economy" is a broader concept of that encompasses the idea of a sharing prosperity but goes beyond the mere combination of growth and equality. As Paganetto and Scandizzo (2014) note, "the term "Good Economy" has recently entered into the language of economists through the work of E. Phelps, who adopts it to define what, in his view, is an innovative and dynamic system with inclusion, creativity, self-fulfillment, satisfaction and personal development". The "good economy" is thus a more just and sustainable economic system and has much in common with the concept of pre-distribution as it aims to implement economic policies to "build" sustainable forms of social justice, rather than to repair the injustices determined by the current mechanisms of competition and democracy. It follows John Rawl's ideas on social justice in denouncing the traditional welfare-state capitalism, which "… rejects the fair value of the political liberties, and while it has some concern for equality of opportunity, the policies necessary to achieve that are not followed. It permits very large inequalities in the ownership of real property (productive assets and natural resources) so that the control of the economy and much of political life rests in few hands".

2 Some Conclusions

This year VM conference comes at a critical moment where the world economy is still in shock, but a light at the end of the pandemic tunnel begins to shine. It is very difficult to predict even the broad lines of the recovery that will take place, and of the further crises that could appear on the scene to put it at risk, because of no quantitative evidence of similar historical events, except for distant and diverse narratives such as the Black Death and the Spanish flu. The most similar documented historical examples are the two world wars, with the enemy in the clothes of the virus, or vice versa, although there are profound economic differences between the two situations.

The Covid crisis has been a negative supply shock and, almost simultaneously, a demand shock, according to a model not comparable to that of the world wars that, although in different ways, also combined positive and negative supply and demand components. One of the biggest differences is the impact on employment, which is quite different in the case of a war and particularly worrying in the current situation. But the effect on assets is also totally different, because the war destroyed them, while the Covid crisis, in the presence of an ever-growing money supply, has created them out of nowhere, overestimating them in an unpredictable and worrying way. Another difference, perhaps even more profound, is the dual impact (the so-called decoupling) on the economy, with many sectors of services, from culture to tourism, but also in commerce and retail, hit to death and others not touched or even benefited by the crisis. Similarly, we are witnessing a dramatic decoupling around the world between the rich, who not only do not suffer from the crisis, but see the value of their assets grow disproportionately in increasingly exuberant financial markets, and the poor who suffer the consequences of unemployment and the crisis of small and medium-sized enterprises, which are also most affected by the primary and secondary effects of the crisis. Under these conditions, the fall in demand also implies an unprecedented accumulation of savings by lockdown consumers and an equally unprecedented loss of receipts from their non-suppliers. This effect, which leads to an increase in the stock of savings on the one hand and poverty on the other, is equivalent to a massive transfer of wealth. Apart from its iniquity, it is difficult to give an economic interpretation and to predict whether, how and when a sustainable balance between assets and incomes can be restored. In the more developed countries almost a quarter of households appear to be facing an improper tax that reduces their incomes and increases the wealth of the rest of the population. For the poorest countries, the situation is less clear, but the polarization between those who accumulate savings by abstaining from consumption in lockdowns and those who see their incomes fall is probably even greater. But this situation, which is in many ways paradoxical, causes further decoupling: that between public capital, where the process of accumulation, which has long been worryingly slowed down, and private capital. This decoupling also continues in the growing role that the state is acquiring in the economy as a result of the current crisis and even worsens, due to the growing weight of the cyclical component in monetary and fiscal policies.

Let us look at these policies. In many countries, different forms of quantitative easing have expanded the liquidity of the financial system through purchases of government bonds by central banks, and, in many cases, also through the purchase of private sector corporate bonds. This great monetary expansion was perhaps inevitable, and saved us from the depression, but it did not solve any structural problems, and rather aggravated the gap between public capital and private assets. It also carries long-term implications and creates several future macroeconomic risks, including a sudden correction in the prices of credit-inflated assets at extremely low interest rates and those of a season of explosive inflation of goods and services as economic activity picks up. Even on the optimistic assumption that future inflation will remain very low for an indefinite period, however, we must be concerned about the explosion of debt, which would instead be tempered by higher inflation.

Let us now consider the tax responses. In judging them, it is important to distinguish between those elements which have the nature of fiscal *stimulus* and those in the form of tax *relief*. The significance of the stimulus is that it corresponds to deliberate budgetary action through higher public spending, tax cuts, more generous social welfare benefits or payments to stimulate (we could say, resurrect) economic activity. Fiscal stimulus is aimed at the demand side of the economy and should work by increasing total spending to reverse an unexpected recession. On the contrary, tax relief is mainly directed at the supply side to stabilize production through tax breaks, although tax breaks can have secondary effects on demand that lead to future gains in output.

Before the current crisis, modern societies already seemed to be haunted by the ghost of missing growth. The inability to generate persistent growth had also been described as a set of scenarios of "secular stagnation", which could have been aggravated by fiscal policy and consolidation measures focusing on cuts in public investment spending. Before the pandemic, budgetary constraints had been particularly tight in the euro area due to the strict rules of the Stability and Growth Pact and further political reactions after the start of the euro crisis. In this context, although there is no data on previous experience for many aspects of the current situation, the conference and a series of related seminars appear to be instrumental in presenting some the latest developments in scientific research in economics and in suggesting some of the appropriate responses to the crisis and the broad outlines for policy actions. These studies, based on a set of theoretical insights, econometric estimates and cost-benefit analyses, suggest that public investment may be the best way out of the crisis, as long as public projects are efficient and carried out on a much larger scale than experienced or even suggested in the past.

As in the past years, the studies presented for this edition of the conference offer a robust combination of traditional methods of economic research with scientific applications based on information sciences and mathematical statistics. Contrary to conventional wisdom, they suggest the hypothesis that the decline in productive public services may be crucial in explaining the general decline in productivity growth and the trend towards stagnation which has recently affected many countries, and in which Italy has been the forerunner. Only a major revival of public capital, even in multi-national or transnational forms, can therefore save us from stagnation and respond to global challenges such as climate change, pandemics and the pervasive systemic risks of an increasingly hyper connected world.

An important and related issue, which figures prominently in the post Covid agenda, is thus how to prioritize and select the different forms of public capital to be provided and which investment programs to implement. This implies knowing how *public* capital affects economic systems, since there is some consensus that public capital represents the 'wheels', not the engine, of economic activity and that infrastructure investment, although necessary, alone is not sufficient to generate sustained increases in economic growth. This question represents the frontier of current research into economic policy and is essential to steer public capital expenditure towards more precise objectives of growth and sustainable development. Technological progress and the growing importance of global public goods also make other related issues particularly important for policymakers. These include further aspects of *how* public capital can influence economic growth in the new context of value chains and economic agents in a growing hyper-connected dimensions of global infrastructure: (i) the network interdependence of infrastructure services; (ii) infrastructure-related economies of scale, which attract enterprises and factors of production and, as a result, increase production; (iii) a new generation of "intelligent" public infrastructure incorporating technological progress and providing feedback to research and planning, (iv) the role of human and natural capital and the growing importance of the Bioeconomy as a major field of public capital provision, from biotechnology to the different forms of green and blue economy. Most of these effects are quantitatively unknown, but can be empirically measurable by monitoring the efficiency of new and old forms of public capital through cost-benefit and impact analysis of programs and projects if these practices themselves become part of public investment policies. In this respect, the crucial challenge facing economic research is the inherent difficulty of identifying changes clearly attributable to the different characteristics of public investment in macroeconomic data and also of following its dynamic effects over time.

References

Phelps, E. (2015). *Mass flourishing: How grassroots innovation created jobs, challenge, and change*. Princeton University Press.

Paganetto, L., & Scandizzo, P. L. (2020). Is globalization sustainable? In L. Paganetto (Ed.), *Capitalism, global change and sustainable development* (pp. 261–270). Springer.

Paganetto, L., & Scandizzo, P. L. (2018). Skill polarization and inequality: Are they real and inevitable? In L. Paganetto (Ed.), *Getting globalization right. Sustainability and inclusive growth in the post Brexit age* (pp. 37–54). Springer.

Paganetto, L., & Scandizzo, P. L. (2017). Innovation, inequality and growth. In L. Paganetto (Ed.), *Sustainable growth in the EU-challenges and solutions* (pp. 257–271). Springer.

Paganetto, L., & Scandizzo, P. L. (2016, May). Industrial policy, investment and green growth. In L. Paganetto (Ed.), *Stagnation versus growth in Europe. Capitalism in the 21st century* (pp. 87–106) Springer. ISBN 9783319269511.

Paganetto, L., & Scandizzo, P. L. (2015, June). Governance, moral and economic values. In L. Paganetto (Ed.), *Achieving dynamism in an anaemic Europe* (pp. 291–302). Springer. ISBN 9783319140995.

Paganetto, L., & Scandizzo, P. L. (2014, September). Policy prescriptions for good economy. In L. Paganetto (Ed.), *Wealth, income inequalities, and demography* (pp. 251–264). Springer.

Paganetto, L., & Scandizzo, P. L. (2010). Technology cycles and technology revolutions. In L. Paganetto (Ed.), *Global crisis and long term growth: A new capitalism ahead?* (pp. 157–169). McGraw-Hill.

Paganetto, L., & Scandizzo, P. L. (2003). The role of education and knowledge in endogenous growth. In L. Paganetto & E. S. Phelps (Eds.), *Finance, research, education and growth* (pp. 90–104). Palgrave Macmillan.

Scandizzo, P. L. (2019). Social capital, confidence and trust: The disillusionment from globalization and the search for sustainable and inclusive development background: Globalization and its discontents. In *Globalization, inclusion and sustainability in a global century*. Eurolink University Press.

Scandizzo, P. L., & Napodano, M. (2010). *Public investment management: Linking global trends to national experiences*. VDM Verlag.

Scandizzo, P. L., & Pierleoni, M. (2020). Short and long-run effects of public investment: Theoretical premises and empirical evidence. *Theoretical Economics Letters, 10*(04), 834–867.

Scandizzo, P. L., & Tria, G. (2018). Italy and a needed public investment boost: The demand and the supply side. *Journal of Global Economics, 4*(4).

Scandizzo, P. L., & Pierleoni, M. (2018). The distribution of wealth and real growth in Italy: A post-Keynesian perspective. *Economics, 7*(2), 34–46.

Scandizzo, P. L., & Ventura, M. (2016). Innovation and imitation as an interactive process. *Economics of Innovation and New Technology, 25*(8), 821–851.

Scandizzo, P. L. (2009). Science and technology in world agriculture: Narratives and discourses. *AgBioforum, 12*(1).

European Growth Prospects After Covid-19

Dominick Salvatore

1 Introduction

What are Europe's growth prospects after Covid-19? Will Europe grow more rapidly after the 2020 recession than after the 2009 recession? Will it match or surpass U.S. growth during this decade or will European growth be as anemic as in the previous decade?

This paper examines the reasons that European growth during this decade is likely to be faster than during the previous decade but not as fast as expected or hoped and still not match U.S. growth (which, itself, it may not be as fast as forecasted or anticipated in this decade).

2 Slow European Economic Recovery and Growth After the 2009 Recession

Table 1 shows that the 2020 Covid-19 recession was much deeper than the 2009 "great recession", except for Germany. Table 1 also shows that despite powerful traditional and non-traditional (QE) expansionary monetary and fiscal policies, the economic recovery and growth from 2010 to 2019 were slow in all advanced nations, averaging 2.1% in the United States, 1.4% in the EU-19 or Euro Area, 1.9% in the United Kingdom, 1.3% in Japan, and 2.3% in Canada.

Paper presented at the XXXII Edition of Villa Mondragone Conference, Rome, July 5–8, 2021

D. Salvatore (✉)
Fordham University, New York, NY, USA
e-mail: salvatore@fordham.edu

L. Paganetto (ed.), *Economic Challenges for Europe After the Pandemic*,
Springer Proceedings in Business and Economics,
https://doi.org/10.1007/978-3-031-10302-5_2

Table 1 Average annual % growth of real GDP in major advanced countries, 2009–2022

Nation/Area	Yearly average				
	2009	2010–2019	2020	2021[a]	2022[a]
USA	−2.8	2.1	−3.4	6.0	5.2
EU-19	−4.5	1.4	−6.3	5.0	4.3
Germany	−5.6	1.9	−4.6	3.1	4.6
France	−2.9	1.4	−8.0	6.3	3.9
Italy	−5.5	0.3	−8.9	5.8	4.2
Spain	−3.6	1.0	−10.8	5.7	6.4
U.K.	−4.3	1.9	−9.8	6.8	5.0
JAPAN	−5.4	1.3	−4.6	2.4	3.2
CANADA	−2.9	2.3	−5.3	5.7	4.9

Source: IMF, *World Economic Outlook*, October 2020/2021a
[a]Projections

Figure 1 and Tables 2 and 3 show that advanced nations used very powerful monetary and fiscal policies to combat the previous and the current recessions. Figure 1 shows that in March 2020 nominal policy rates approached zero in advanced economies (became negative in the Euro Area) and liquidity was also increased significantly. Tables 2 and 3 show that budget deficits and debts greatly increased in 2009 and 2020, especially in the United States.

In today's interdepended and high globalized world, the growth of Europe and the United States also depends on the growth of other large economies, Table 4 shows that the 2020 recession was much deeper than the previous one in the emerging markets in the G20 countries, except for Russia and Turkey, while China grew much less while India went from growth to deep recession.

3 The U.S. Has Grown Faster Than the EU and the Euro Area During the Past Two Decades

Figure 2 shows that taking the real GDP on the United States, the European Union (excluding Britain) and the Euro Area as 100 in 2000, the United States grew somewhat faster than the European Union and the Euro Area until 2011, but then the U.S. growth gap vis-à-vis Europe widened after 2011, especially with respect to the Euro Area. The Euro Area grew less than the European Union since some of the small European countries, not members of the Euro Area, grew faster than some Euro-Area members.

One important reasons for the U.S. growing more rapidly than Europe since 2000 and especially after the 2009 recession (and even more after the 2020 recession), is that the U.S. provided a more massive fiscal stimulus to its economy than Europe to overcome each of the last recessions. As indicated in Table 2, the U.S. budget deficit was more than double that of the Euro Area in most years since 2007, and it exceeded 13% of GDP in 2009 and nearly 15% in 2020 as compared 6.3% and 7.2%

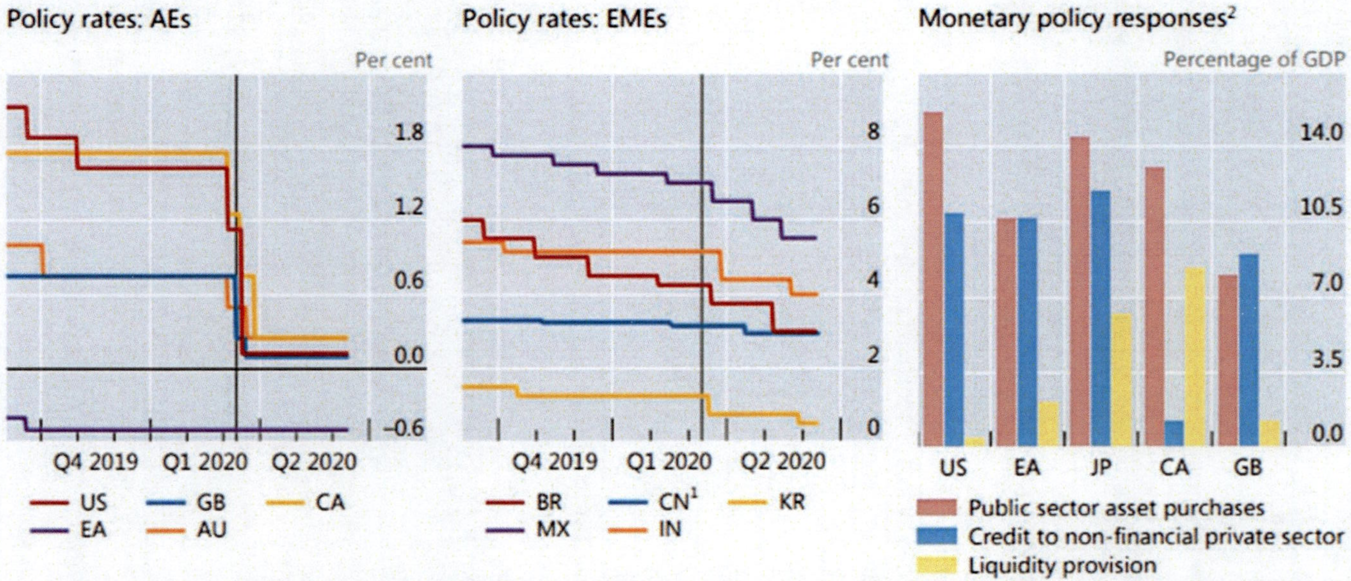

The vertical lines in the left-hand and centre panels indicate 11 March 2020 (coronavirus outbreak declared a pandemic by the World Health Organization).

[1] Medium-term lending facility, one-year rate. [2] Projected maximum support during March–December 2020, based on official announcements. See Cavallino and De Fiore (2020).

Fig. 1 Primary policy rates and monetary policy responses, Q4 2019 to Q2020

Table 2 Budget deficits as percentage of GDP in major advanced countries, 2007–2021

Nation/Area	2007	2009	2011	2015	2019	2020	2021[a]
USA	−2.9	−13.1	−9.7	−3.5	−5.7	−14.9	−10.8
Euro Area	−0.6	−6.3	−4.2	−2.0	−0.6	−7.2	−7.7
Germany	0.2	−3.2	−0.9	1.0	1.5	−4.3	−6.8
France	−2.5	−7.2	−5.2	−3.6	−3.1	−9.2	−8.9
Italy	−1.5	−5.3	−3.6	−2.6	−1.6	−9.5	−10.2
Spain	2.0	−11.0	−9.7	−5.2	−2.9	−11.0	−8.6
U.K.	−2.9	−10.2	−7.5	−4.5	−2.3	−12.5	−11.9
Japan	−2.1	−9.8	−9.4	−3.9	−3.1	−10.3	−9.0
Canada	118	−3.9	−3.3	−0.1	0.5	−10.9	−7.5

Source: IMF, *Fiscal Monitor*, October 2020/2021b
[a]Estimate

Table 3 Government debt as percentage of GDP in major advanced countries, 2007–2021

Nation/Area	2007	2009	2011	2015	2019	2020	2021[a]
United States	64.0	87.0	99.8	104.9	108.5	133.9	133.3
Euro Area	64.9	78.4	87.7	90.9	83.7	97.5	98.9
Germany	63.6	72.6	79.8	72.3	59.2	69.1	72.5
France	64.4	82.9	87.8	95.6	97.6	115.1	115.8
Italy	99.8	112.5	119.7	135.3	134.6	155.8	154.8
Spain	35.5	52.7	69.9	99.3	95.5	119.9	120.2
United Kingdom	42.2	64.1	80.1	86.7	85.2	104.5	108.5
Japan	183.0	201.0	221.9	228.4	235.4	254.1	256.9
Canada	66.8	79.3	81.8	91.2	86.8	117.5	109.9

Source: IMF, *Fiscal Monitor*, October 2020/2021b
[a]Estimate

Table 4 BRICS and other emerging markets in G20: percentage growth of real GDP, 2009–2022

Nation	2009	2010–2019	2020	2021[a]	2022[a]
China	9.2	7.6	2.3	8.0	5.6
India	8.5	6.9	−7.3	9.5	8.5
Russia	−7.8	1.9	−3.0	4.7	2.9
Brazil	−0.1	0.6	−4.1	5.2	1.5
S. Africa	−1.5	1.7	−6.4	5.0	2.2
Korea	0.7	3.3	0.9	4.3	3.3
Indonesia	4.7	5.5	−2.1	3.2	5.9
Mexico	−4.7	2.8	−8.3	6.2	4.0
Argentina	−5.9	1.4	−9.9	7.5	2.5
Turkey	−4.7	6.4	1.8	9.0	3.3
S. Arabia	−2.1	3.8	−4.1	2.8	4.8

Source: IMF, *World Economic Outlook*, October 2020/2021a
[a]Projections

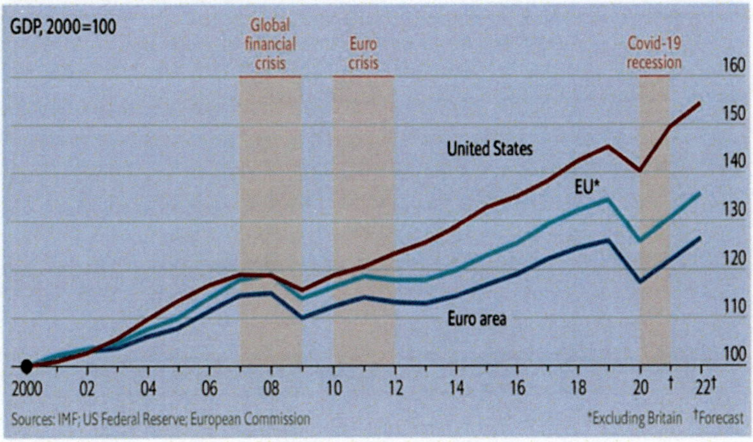

Fig. 2 The growth of the U.S., EU and Euro area since the year 2000. *Source*: *The Economist*, March 3, 2021. https://www.economist.com/finance-and-economics/2021/03/31/what-if-europes-fiscal-largesse-were-as-generous-as-americas

in the Euro Area! Table 3 shows that U.S. debt as percentage of GDP of 87% was only slightly higher than in the Euro Area in 2009, but it was almost 134% in 2020 while remaining below 100% in the Euro Area. Figure 1 shows that with a negative policy rate, traditional monetary policy was much stronger in the Euro Area than in the United States, but at that point traditional monetary policy had lost most of its efficacy (and U.S. non-traditional monetary policy was somewhat stronger in 2020).

Figure 3 shows that the massive $1.9 trillion fiscal stimulus that the U.S. provided its economy in March 2021 almost doubled the forecasted the U.S. growth rate for 2021, with significant positive spillover to other countries. Figure 4 then shows the IMF estimated the additional fiscal stimulus required by Europe to practically close its growth gap with the United States by 2022.

4 The Fundamental Reason Europe Grew Slower Than U.S. During Past Two Decades

Table 5 shows that the slower growth of real GDP in the Euro Area and the European Union in relation to the United States reflects Europe's slower growth of labor productivity and total factor productivity. The table shows that from 2000 to 2007, the average yearly growth of real GDP was 2.7% in the United States as compared with 2.3% in the Euro Area and 2.5% in the European Union of 27 (EU-27). From 2008 to 2019, comparable figures in percentages were, respectively, 1.8, 0.6 and 1.0. Thus, the growth of real GDP declined sharply in the United States, the Euro Area and EU-27 after 2007, but it remained lower in the Euro

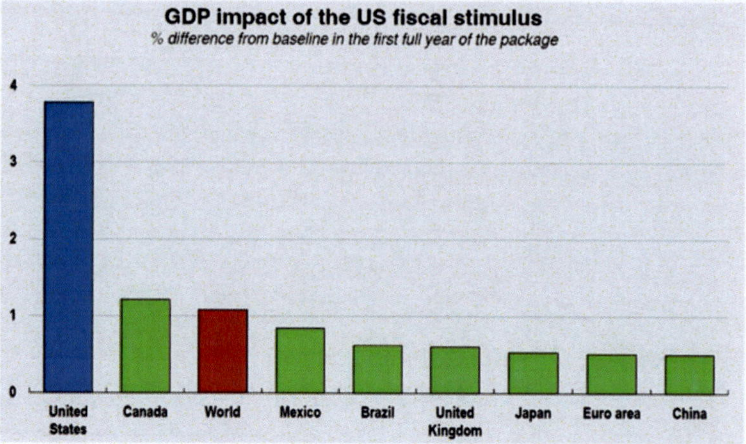

Fig. 3 Forecasted U.S. and world growth effect of the March 2021 U.S. Fiscal stimulus. *Source*: OECD, *Interim Economic Outlook*, 2021

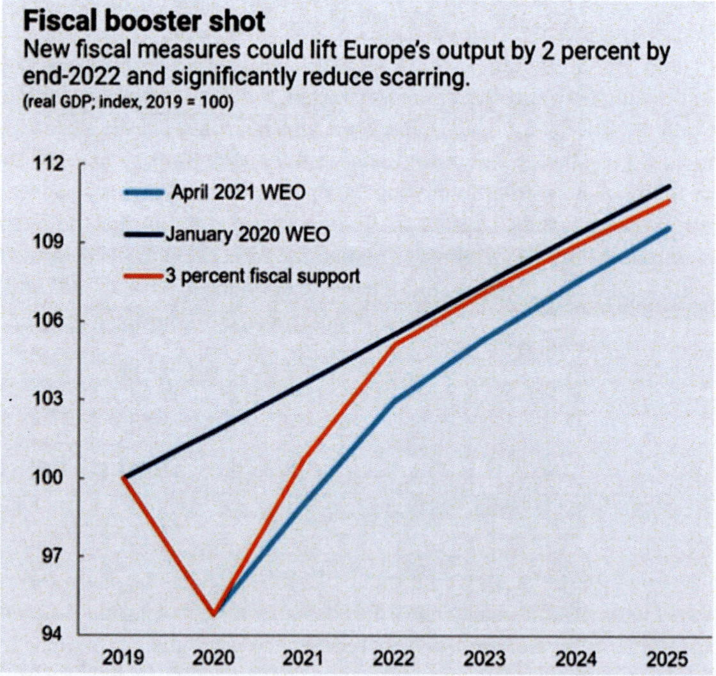

Fig. 4 Additional fiscal stimulus for Europe to close its growth gap with U.S. by 2022. *Source*: IMF, *Regional Economic Outlook*, April 2021c

Table 5 Average growth (%) of real GDP, labor productivity, and total factor productivity in the United States, Euro Area, and Europe Union of 27, 2000–2021

	United States	Euro Area	EU-27
Real GDP			
2000–2007	2.7	2.3	2.5
2008–2019	1.8	0.6	1.0
2019	2.3	1.5	1.9
2020	−3.4	−6.9	−6.3
2021 (Forecast)	6.0	4.5	4.7
Labor productivity			
2000–2007	2.2	1.3	1.9
2008–2019	1.2	0.6	1.0
2019	1.2	0.6	1.2
2020	2.6	1.0	0.2
2021 (Forecast)	2.3	0.8	1.6
Total factor productivity			
2000–2007	1.0	0.0	0.2
2008–2019	0.2	−0.2	−0.4
2019	0.7	−0.5	−0.2
2020	−0.6	−3.7	−3.8
2021 (Forecast)	2.5	1.3	1.6

Conference Board (2019 and 2021), *Total Economy Database*, New York (August)

Area and EU-27 than in the United States. Comparable figures (in percentages) for labor productivity growth were, respectively, 2.2, 1.3 and 1.9 for 2000–2007 and 1.2, 0.6, and 1.0 for 2008–2019. Even more importantly, the growth of total factor productivity (TFP—the increase in output over and above the increase in labor and capital used in production) were, respectively, 1.0, 0.0 and 0.2 for 2000–2007, and 0.2, −0.2 and − 0.4 for 2008–2019. The detailed data also shows that there were major differences in the growth of labor productivity and total factor productivity among the major Euro Area countries, Japan and the United States, but even Germany, the best performer of the Euro Area, did not perform as well as the United States.

The slow growth of labor productivity and total factor productivity in the Euro Area led to its low international competitiveness and growth of real GDP in relation to the United States. Most of the Europe's lower of international competitiveness has been attributed to overregulation and over-taxation, which discouraged innovations and reduced efficiency (Salvatore, 1998, 2004, 2015). An overview of the competitiveness problem that the Europe Area faces vis-à-vis the United States is summarized by the much lower ranking than the United States on the World Bank (2020) index on "Ease of Doing Business". The index includes the 12 specific measurements or indicators, among which: starting a business, getting construction permits, getting credit, protecting minority investors, enforcing contracts, and employing workers. The data shows that it was more than seven times easier to do business in the United States than in the Euro Area. The data also shows

Table 6 Ease of doing business and International Competitiveness for the G-7 Countries and Spain in 2020 (Indices 0–100)

Country	Ease of doing business	Intern. competitiveness
United States	84.0	89.6
United Kingdom	83.5	81.5
Germany	79.7	86.5
Canada	79.6	87.0
Japan	78.0	69.7
Spain	77.9	63.7
France	76.8	72.5
Italy	72.9	63.1

Source: World Bank (2020), *Ease of Doing Business*, Washington D.C. and IMD (2021), *International Competitiveness Yearbook,* Lausanne

that there is a high positive correlation between the ease of doing business in a nation and its international competitiveness, and finally that there is then a positive exponential correlation between the international competitiveness of the nation and its per capita GDP (see Salvatore, 2017). In other words, the easier it is to do business in a nation, the greater is its international competitiveness and the higher is its per capita income. Since the Euro Area ranks much lower than the United States in the ease of doing business, its international competitiveness is lower, and so is its real per capita income relative to the United States. Thus, the way for the Euro Area and Europe to increase its growth is by deregulating economic activities (i.e., making it easier to do business). This would increase international competitiveness and lead to higher real per capita income and growth.

Table 6 shows the latest data on doing business and international competitiveness of the G-7 countries and Spain in 2020. Indeed, the rank correlation between the ease of doing business and the international competitiveness for these largest advanced nations in 2020 was 83.3. Of course, correlation does not establish causality, but economic theory postulates (explains) how the lower ease of doing business leads to less international competitiveness of the nation—and how the latter leads to lower total labor productivity and total factor productivity, and hence to lower national growth.

5 Growth Prospects for Europe After the Pandemic

The EU has been worryingly aware its competitiveness and growth problems since 1990 and so in 2000 it launched the Lisbon Strategy or Agenda (European Council, 2000), with the specific aim of making Europe "the most competitive and the most knowledge-based economy in the world by 2010". The goal, however, was not achieved. To be sure, most nations of the world grew much more slowly in the 2000–2010 decade than in the previous decade after the global financial crisis, but as we have seen in Fig. 2, Europe grew more slowly than the United States, and so its growth gap with the United States persisted and even grew.

Because of this, the European Commission (2014) introduced the Europe 2020 agenda *Horizon 2020*. This was a seven-point program with nearly 80 billion euros in funding for making Europe "the best place in the world to innovate"—and also to increase industry's share of GDP from the 15% to 20% from 2014 to 2020. The EU subsequently introduced the Junker Investment Plan in December 2014, the Single Market Strategy in May 2015, and the Five Presidents' Report in July 2015—all aimed at increasing investments and innovations in the EU in order to increase its international competitiveness and speed up its growth.

All of these plans, however, seemed more statements of intentions and often led even to more regulations in the process of being implemented. In fact, as shown in Table 1, Europe's (and the U.S.) growth was rather anemic between 2020 and 2019 relative to the previous decade primarily because of the slowdown in the growth of labor productivity on both sides of the Atlantic, but also because of aging of population and the slowdown in the growth of international trade. Those growth-slowing factors or conditions persisted even before the pandemic (see Salvatore, 2020) and remain even today)—*and, it is in this context or background that the new EU programs to stimulate growth must evaluated in terms of their likely effectiveness and success.*

6 Programs to Stimulate European Growth and Deal with Climate Change

All European countries drew up plans to promote recovery from the pandemic recession, accelerate growth, and deal with the climate crisis. Although national plans and programs differed in detail, they all stressed digitalization of the economy and the green economy—as indicated in Fig. 5 (which shows the national plans for spending EU recovery funds submitted to the EU in April 2021 by the four largest countries). There were, of course, other national funds for these and other purposes, especially infrastructures, education, health, social inclusion, and welfare.

Investing technological innovation and digital transition by improving education and digital skills) is crucial in order to increase labor and total factor productivity (TFP). We know from growth theory that economic growth can be stimulated by increasing infrastructure investments and Total Factor Productivity (with more education, higher labor productivity, more R&D, and better regulations) and yet as I have written (2021) growth remained anemic over the past decade. Of course, most nations plan to redouble their efforts to stimulate labor productivity and TFP, especially now in order to recover from the recent deep recession by speeding the adoption of new and more productive technologies.

However, as pointed out by Acemoglu (2021), "The next phase of automation, relying as it does on AI and AI-powered machines such as self-driving cars, may

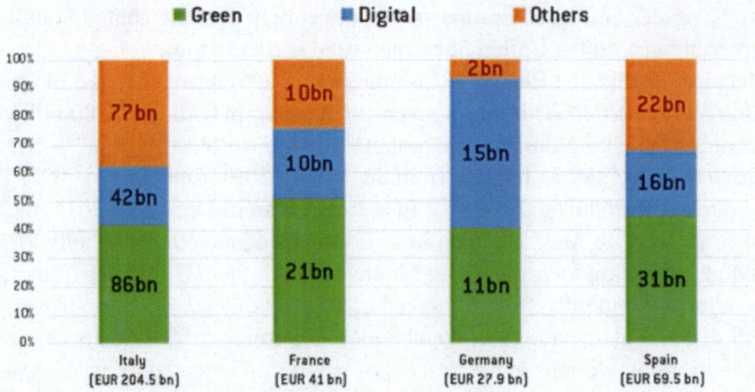

Fig. 5 Setting Europe's economic recovery in motion: plans for spending EU recovery funds submitted by the four largest countries. *Source*: Darvas and Tagliapietra (2021)

be even more disruptive, especially if it is not accompanied by other types of more labor-friendly technologies. This broad technological platform, with diverse applications and great promise, could help human productivity and usher in new human tasks and competencies in education, health care, engineering, manufacturing, and elsewhere. But it could also worsen job losses and economic disruption if applied exclusively for automation."

Furthermore, Dewan and Ernst (2020) point out that "The global pandemic caused millions of people to lose their jobs and is widening the gap between white-collar workers, who can work from home, and those who don't have the skills or resources to participate in a digitally-driven economy." We can add that more rapid application of new technologies, while they may increase labor productivity over the years, is now also seriously increasing inequalities within both advanced and developing nations, and between them.

In short, investing in technological innovation and digital transition is as crucial for stimulating future economic growth as it is to succeed. Europe tried this before without success and many of the same obstacles to growth remain and became even more intense, such as the more rapid aging of the population, the deeper and more serious international political and trade disagreements, and especially the more dramatic climate crisis (WTO Secretariat, 2020).

Turning to climate crisis, it is clear that time is running out to avoid a catastrophic climate change, the EU is stepping up its efforts to decarbonize Europe's economy. In fact, in October 2021 the EU launched its "Fit For 55" package of measures to cut carbon emissions 55% below 1990 levels by 2030, on the way to net zero at mid-century. Europe should be commended for taking the initiative and world leadership in undertaking this truly gigantic, but absolutely necessary, task.

But there are some major obstacles to carry the program out and achieve the "Fit For 55" goal.

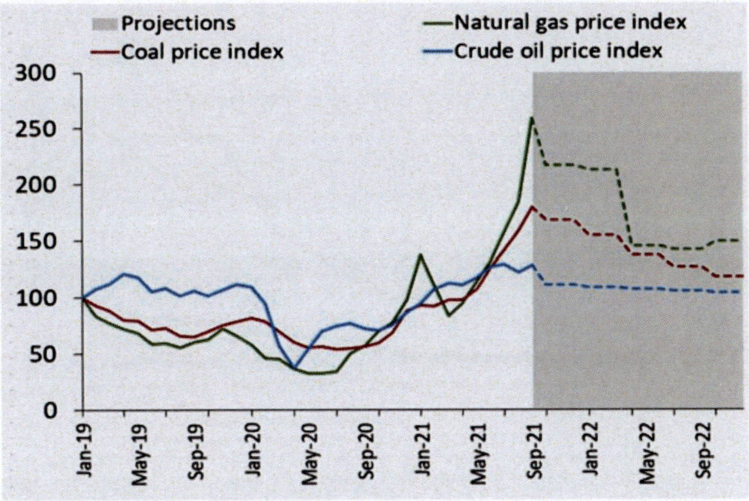

Fig. 6 Surging energy prices may not ease until next year (price indices: 1990 = 100). *Source*: IMF (2021d, July)

For one thing, trying for go from fossil fuel to green energy rather quickly is turning out to be extremely costly. As shown in Fig. 6, the price natural gas has more than doubled and the price of coal has increased by more than 50% in the first 9 months of 2021–even though the expectation is that these prices will moderate in 2022, this may not actually occur. In the meantime, costs of production and inflation are rising very rapidly, discouraging production and growth, and may lead central banks to raise interest rates, which may trigger a new financial crisis and recession (Institute of International Finance, 2020).

Then there is the problem of explicit free-riders and nations that will not honor their climate agreements. Figure 7 shows the dramatic extent by which CO_2 emissions by China and India have increased since 1990, while remaining constant in the United States and even declining in Europe and Eurasia. So, if some major polluters do not play their part or do not hold or respect to their commitment under climate agreements, they will nullify most of the efforts made by other nations and also gain a competitive advantage on other nations by having lower energy costs. For example, in 2021, China and India (now the world's two largest polluters) continued to build a large number of coal-fired power plants despite their promise to cut CO_2 emissions by 2030, thus jeopardizing both their decarbonization plans and global efforts to deal with the climate crisis (Standaert, 2021). Thus, while moving to a green economy is a must, it will lead to higher energy costs, at least in the short run, and it may it difficult for the world to achieve its climate goals.

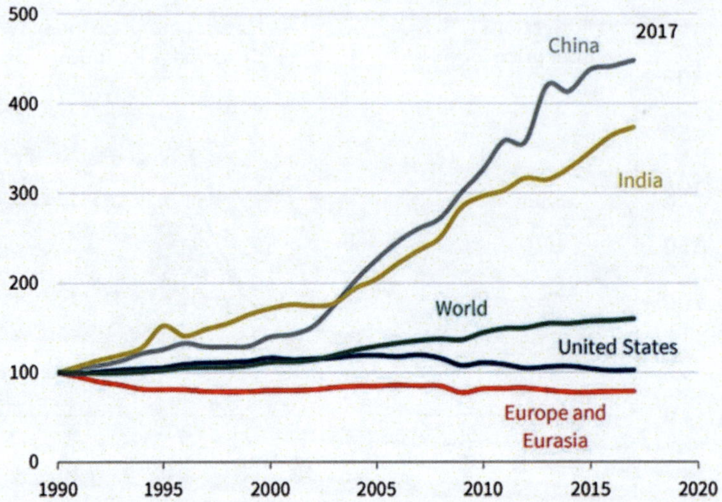

Fig. 7 Annual world carbon dioxide emissions, 1990–2017 (CO_2 emission index: 1990 = 100). *Source*: Council of Economic Advisors, Economic Report of the President, March, 2019

7 Concluding Remarks

In projecting economic world growth in this decade it is important to keep in mind that some of the factors responsible for anemic growth on both sides of the Atlantic (and also in most of the rest of the world) during the past decade are still operating in this decade (and some, such as the aging populations, is even accelerating).

It is true also that new technologies offer tremendous opportunities to increase labor and total factor productivity, but they may also prove more disruptive by also leading to more job losses and higher wage and income inequalities than in the past—and thus contribute less to economic growth than otherwise. In addition, while moving to a green economy is an existential must, that may be more costly and difficult to achieve than thought and contribute less to growth than commonly thought. Thus, future economic growth may be slower than expected and hoped.

Finally, future European growth may match or surpass U.S. growth in this decade, more as a result of slower U.S. growth to than as result of faster European growth than in the past!

References

Acemoglu, D. (2021). Remaking the post-Covid world. *Finance & Development*. (Spring).
Council of Economic Advisors. (2019). *Economic report of the president*. Washington D.C.
Conference Board. (2019/2021). *Total economy database*. New York (August).

Darvas, Z., & Tagliapietra, S. (2021, April 29). Setting Europe's economic recovery in motion: Plans for spending EU recovery funds submitted by the four largest countries. *Bruegel Post*.

Dewan, S., & Ernst, E. (2020). Rethinking the world. *Finance & Development* (Winter). https://www.imf.org/external/pubs/ft/fandd/2020/12/rethinking-the-world-of-work-dewan.htm

European Council. (2000). *The Lisbon strategy*. http://www.euractiv.com/future-eu/Lisbon-agenda/article-117510

European Commission. (2014). *Horizon 2020*. http://ec.europa.eu/programmes/horizon2020

IMD. (2021). *International competitiveness yearbook*. Lausanne.

IMF. (2020/2021a). *World economic outlook*. Washington, D.C. (October)

IMF. (2020/2021b). *Fiscal monitor*. Washington, D.C. (October)

IMF. (2021c, April). *Regional economic outlook*. Washington, D.C.

IMF. (2021d, July). *World economic outlook*. Washington, D.C.

Institute of International Finance. (2020, December). *Sustainable debt monitor: Up, up and away*.

OECD. (2020, December). *Turning hope into reality*. OECD Economic Outlook.

OECD. (2021). *Interim Economic Outlook*. Paris.

Salvatore, D. (1998). Europe's structural and competitiveness problems and the Euro. *The World Economy, 21*(2), 189–205.

Salvatore, D. (2004). Globalization, comparative advantage, and Europe's double competitive squeeze. *Global Economic Journal, 4*(1), 1–18.

Salvatore, D. (2015, May/June). Europe's Euro and competitiveness crises. *Journal of Policy Modeling, 3*, 445–449.

Salvatore, D. (2017, May). Europe's growth crisis: When and how will it end? *The World Economy, 5*, 836–848.

Salvatore, D. (2020, July/August). Growth and trade in the United States and the world economy. *Journal of Policy Modeling, 4*, 750–759.

Standaert, M. (2021, March 24). Despite pledges to cut emissions, China goes on a coal spree. *Yale Environment260*. https://e360.yale.edu/features/despite-pledges-to-cut-emissions-china-goes-on-a-coal-spree

The Economist. (2021, March 3). *What if Europe's fiscal largesse were as generous as America's?*https://www.economist.com/finance-and-economics/2021/03/31/what-if-europes-fiscal-largesse-were-as-generous-as-americas.

World Bank. (2020). *Ease of doing business*. Washington D.C.

WTO Secretariat. (2020, April 8). *Trade set to plunge as COVID-19 pandemic upends global economy*. https://www.wto.org/english/news_e/pres20_e/pr855_e.htm

Covid-19 and the Golden Rule of Social Distancing

Marias H. Gestsson and Gylfi Zoega

1 Introduction

There is every indication that the world will have to live with the COVID-19 virus in the future. New variants of the virus may prevent herd immunity from arising and reduce the effectiveness of vaccines. Vaccines will make the task easier, but they may not eliminate the need for other mitigating measures. Therefore, the virus may force countries to trade off economic activity against measures to curb the spread of the virus. In this paper, we ask about the appropriate level of social distancing aimed at reducing the infection rate in a steady-state equilibrium where the share of the population that is infected remains constant due to the constant entry of new variants of the virus through a country's borders. We will derive the optimal or golden rule steady-state value of social distancing that maximizes the welfare of each generation assuming the virus cannot be eliminated.

M. H. Gestsson
Department of Economics, University of Iceland, Reykjavik, Iceland
e-mail: marias@hi.is

G. Zoega (✉)
Department of Economics, University of Iceland, Reykjavik, Iceland

Department of Mathematics, Economics and Statistics, Birkbeck College, University of London, London, UK
e-mail: gz@hi.is

L. Paganetto (ed.), *Economic Challenges for Europe After the Pandemic*,
Springer Proceedings in Business and Economics,
https://doi.org/10.1007/978-3-031-10302-5_3

2 Literature

Several recent papers have incorporated economic trade-offs between infections and output within the SIR framework.[1] The papers by Glover et al. (2020), Hausmann and Schetter (2020) and Acemoglu et al. (2020) come closest to the present study.

Glover et al. (2020) show that social distancing involves a trade-off between the welfare of the old, who benefit through higher life expectancy, and the young, who lose because of lower output and consumption. The authors derive optimal social distancing of a utilitarian government that can redistribute across individuals at a cost. Optimal mitigation and redistribution policies interact and reflect a compromise between the preferred policy paths of the different groups.

Hausmann and Schetter (2020) show that while rich countries may want to sacrifice output to save their populations from the pandemic, poor countries can only reduce the level of transmission by increasing deaths from economic deprivation. In their model, households differ in their ability level. The trade-offs involve saving households from the pandemic or from dying from economic deprivation. If the government has fiscal space, such as the one that exists in richer countries, lump-sum fiscal transfers help alleviate the trade-off. Thus, optimal lockdowns are stricter for richer countries where there is more fiscal.

Acemoglu et al. (2020) consider differences in infection, hospitalization and fatality rates between groups, in particular between the young, the middle-aged and the old. They find that optimal policies involve different levels of lockdowns between groups, i.e., imposing stricter lockdowns on the most vulnerable group as well as limiting interaction between that group and the younger ones.

This paper differs from that of Acemoglu et al. in not allowing the authorities to impose different levels of social distancing on the young and the old nor preventing the young from visiting the old. As Hausmann and Schetter, we show that the social distancing should depend on income and as in the three papers it is the old who die during a pandemic. We differ in assuming a constant stream of new variants of the virus coming through the borders, which prevents herd immunity from arising and makes Covid-19 a permanent part of life.

3 Model

In this section, we derive the optimal level of social distancing. The question concerning the optimal level of social distancing is closely related to the golden rule literature that began with Ramsey (1928) on the optimal level of saving and was expanded in papers on the optimal level of research and the optimal level of education (see Phelps, 1966, 1968, among others). The state variable is limits on

[1] Such as Alvarez et al. (2020), Hall and Jones (2007), and Farboodi et al. (2020).

the spread of a pandemic and the associated mortality and the control variable is social distancing, which lowers output. The question is how much current output and consumption should be sacrificed in order to reduce the number of infections and deaths.

3.1 Demographics

Consider a model similar to that presented in Sect. III of Hall and Jones (2007) with the addition of explicitly taking into account the retirement age as in Gestsson and Zoega (2019). A non-pandemic economy consists of individuals who live for A years. The survival probabilities equal unity until age A is reached when death becomes a certainty. Individuals work until they reach the age of retirement R. Assume, for simplicity that one individual is born each unit of time and, hence, the population size is $N = A$, while the number of working (young) and retired (old) individuals are $N_w = R$ and $N_o = A - R$, respectively. It follows that $N = N_w + N_o$.

A pandemic is introduced in the economy by assuming that a pandemic decreases the number of old individuals compared to the non-pandemic economy above. Our infection dynamics differ from standard SIR models by assuming a constant inflow of infected people into a country. The number of infections then depend on the level of social distancing. We abstract from the role of herd new immunity by assuming the constant emergence of new variants entering the country. Our model describes the situation when new variants may constantly cause new waves of the pandemic.

The number of infected individuals is determined by the following first-order differential equation:

$$\dot{I} = [r - 1]\, I + Q$$

where r is the infection (or transmission) coefficient stating how many individuals an infected individual infects, I is the number of infected individuals and Q is the number of infected travellers coming into the country. We assume, for simplification, that each infected individual either recovers or dies immediately after the infection. Clearly, a steady state requires $r < 1$ but the elimination of the virus is not possible if $Q > 0$.

Although new variants make it impossible for vaccines to eliminate the pandemic, the vaccines are assumed to lower the rate of transmission r. The infection coefficient is assumed to be a function of social distancing s and the share of the population vaccinated v:

$$r = r\,(s, v) \tag{1}$$

such that an increase in social distancing reduces the coefficient at a decreasing rate, and an increase in the share of the population vaccinated reduces the coefficient while decreasing the effects of an increase in social distancing on lowering the coefficient:

$$\frac{\partial r}{\partial s} < 0, \frac{\partial^2 r}{\partial s^2} > 0, \frac{\partial r}{\partial v} < 0, \frac{\partial^2 r}{\partial s \partial v} > 0$$

The differential equation can therefore be written as:

$$\dot{I} = [r(s, v) - 1] I + Q$$

Assuming that $0 < r < 1$ such that a steady state for the number of infected individuals exists $\dot{I} = 0$, the number of infected individuals in steady state is

$$I = \frac{Q}{1 - r(s, v)} \tag{2}$$

The proportion of infected individuals surviving an infection is constant and equal to one for young individuals and h for old individuals, where $0 < h < 1$ and h is increasing in the available resources (medicine, health care staff etc.) for treating those infected :

$$h = \begin{cases} 1 & for \quad young \\ h(m) & \quad\quad old \end{cases} \tag{3}$$

where $\frac{\partial h}{\partial m} > 0$.

The probability of an individual being infected is the same for all individuals and, therefore, the number of infected young and old individuals is (due to the Law of large numbers):

$$I_w = \frac{N_w}{N} I = \frac{R}{A} I$$

$$I_o = \frac{N_o}{N} I = \frac{A - R}{A} I$$

and the number of infected individuals not surviving the infection is therefore zero for all young individuals and:

$$[1 - h(m)] I_o = [1 - h(m)] \frac{A - R}{A} I$$

for old individuals. The number of old individuals surviving the pandemic is therefore:

$$N_o - [1 - h(m)] I_o = [A - R] \left[1 - [1 - h(m)] \frac{I}{A} \right]$$

or, by using (2):

$$N_o - [1 - h(m)]\, I_o = [A - R]\left[1 - \frac{[1 - h(m)]\, q}{1 - r\,(s, v)}\right]$$

where $q = \frac{Q}{A} = \frac{Q}{N}$ is the number of infected travellers entering the country relative to its non-pandemic population. Therefore, in the presence of a pandemic, the number of old individuals in steady state can be written as:

$$\widetilde{N}_o = [A - R]\left[1 - \frac{[1 - h(m)]\, q}{1 - r\,(s, v)}\right] \quad (4)$$

Note that in the case of no infected travellers entering the country $Q = q = 0$, we have zero steady state infections $I = 0$ and that the number of old individuals equals non-pandemic number of old individuals $\widetilde{N}_o = N_o$.

For later use, we have:[2]

$$\frac{\partial \widetilde{N}_o}{\partial s} > 0,\ \frac{\partial \widetilde{N}_o}{\partial v} > 0,\ \frac{\partial \widetilde{N}_o}{\partial m} > 0,\ \frac{\partial \widetilde{N}_o}{\partial q} < 0$$

$$\frac{\partial^2 \widetilde{N}_o}{\partial s^2} < 0,\ \frac{\partial^2 \widetilde{N}_o}{\partial s \partial v} < 0,\ \frac{\partial^2 \widetilde{N}_o}{\partial s \partial m} < 0,\ \frac{\partial^2 \widetilde{N}_o}{\partial s \partial q} > 0$$

3.2 *Output*

Each young individual produces $y > 0$ at each point in time in the absence of social distancing and $y - \gamma G(s) > 0$ with social distancing. We write national output in the economy as:

$$N_w\,[y - \gamma G(s)]$$

where the $G(s)$ function is defined such that $G(0) = 0$, $G'(s) > 0$, and $\gamma > 0$ is a parameter indicating the importance of social contact in doing business in the economy. The parameter γ measures how sensitive output is to social distancing. Thus, economies that rely more heavily on producing services have higher γ. In what follows, γ is referred to as *service intensity* in the paper.

[2] See Appendix 1.

4 The Social Optimum

The social planner chooses between steady states with a balanced current account and strives to find the steady state that maximises welfare in terms of social distancing and consumption of the young and old. There arises a trade-off between consumption per capita and social distancing.

The economy-wide budget constraint is in balance at all points in time and equates the surplus output of the working-age cohorts and the consumption of the old:

$$N_w \left[y - \gamma G(s) - c_w\right] = \widetilde{N}_o c_o$$

or, by using (4) and that $N_w = R$:

$$R \left[y - \gamma G(s) - c_w\right] = [A - R] \left[1 - \frac{[1 - h(m)]\, q}{1 - r\,(s, v)}\right] c_o \tag{5}$$

An individual's utility from consumption is given by $u(c)$, which is assumed to be strictly positive, increasing and concave in consumption. The social planner's welfare objective can therefore be written as

$$W = N_w u\,(c_w) + \widetilde{N}_o u\,(c_o)$$

or, by using (4) and that $N_w = R$:

$$W = Ru\,(c_w) + [A - R] \left[1 - \frac{[1 - h(m)]\, q}{1 - r\,(s, v)}\right] u\,(c_o) \tag{6}$$

where c_w and c_o are the consumption of working and retired individuals, respectively. In essence, the social planner maximises the sum of utilities of all living generations at a point in time with respect to consumption and social distancing, considering that his decision affects both consumption of each individual as well as the survival probabilities of the old through the effect of social distancing on the rate of infection.

The maximization of this objective function with respect to the consumption of the young, the consumption of the old and social distancing subject to the budget constraint in (5) gives the social optimum. Note that the welfare function in (6) is strictly increasing in c_w, c_o and s. The budget constraint in (5) ensures that a maximum exists to the constrained maximization.[3]

[3] The second-order conditions for maximum are analysed in Appendix 2.

The Lagrangian for the maximization problem is (using (5, 6)):

$$\Gamma = Ru\left(c_w\right) + [A-R]\left[1-\tfrac{[1-h(m)]q}{1-r(s,v)}\right]u\left(c_o\right)$$
$$+\lambda\left[R\left[y-\gamma G(s)-c_w\right]-[A-R]\left[1-\tfrac{[1-h(m)]q}{1-r(s,v)}\right]c_o\right]$$

where λ is the Lagrange multiplier. Assuming an interior solution, the first-order conditions are:

$$u'\left(c_w\right) = \lambda \tag{7}$$

$$u'\left(c_o\right) = \lambda \tag{8}$$

$$-[A-R]\frac{[1-h(m)]q}{[1-r(s,v)]^2}\frac{\partial r}{\partial s}u\left(c_o\right)$$

$$=\lambda\left[R\gamma G'(s)-[A-R]\frac{[1-h(m)]q}{[1-r(s,v)]^2}\frac{\partial r}{\partial s}c_o\right] \tag{9}$$

The last condition is the budget constraint for the economy that sets total output net of consumption when young equal to the sum of consumption of the old:

$$R\left[y-\gamma G(s)-c_w\right]=[A-R]\left[1-\frac{[1-h(m)]q}{1-r(s,v)}\right]c_o \tag{10}$$

The conditions in (7, 8) imply that consumption when young and old are equal:

$$c_w = c_o \equiv c \tag{11}$$

Using (11), (7), (4) and that $N_w = R$ in (9) gives the optimal social distancing:

$$u(c)\frac{\partial\widetilde{N}_o}{\partial s} = u'(c)\left[N_w\gamma G'(s)+c\frac{\partial\widetilde{N}_o}{\partial s}\right] \tag{12}$$

This is our main result, which we call the *golden rule of social distancing*. The left-hand side shows the increased social welfare from social distancing in terms more old people surviving. The right-hand side shows the lost utility for the working-age individuals whose consumption is reduced due to lower output, because of social distancing, and the consumption of those who now survive. At the social optimum, the marginal benefit of increased social distancing is set equal to its marginal cost.

5 Comparative Statics

Since the second-order conditions for a maximum are fulfilled (see discussion above and Appendix 2), the conditions in (7)–(10) give the optimal steady state levels of consumption per individual when young and old c_w and c_o and social distancing s (and the Lagrange multiplier λ) as implicit functions of, among others, productivity y, service intensity γ, the share of the population vaccinated v, effectiveness of medical treatment m and the number of infected individuals entering the country as a proportion of non-pandemic population q.

Productivity in the production of goods and services y and service intensity of the economy γ affect the optimal level of social distancing s. The effect of increased productivity y is given by:[4]

$$\frac{\partial s}{\partial y} = \frac{N_w\left[N_w\gamma G'(s) + c_o\frac{\partial \widetilde{N}_o}{\partial s}\right]\left[u''(c)\right]^2}{\Psi} > 0 \tag{13}$$

where $\Psi > 0$ (see Appendix 3). The numerator is positive and hence the derivative is positive. Intuitively, an increase in productivity raises output and hence also consumption, higher consumption lowers the marginal utility of consumption and hence also the marginal cost of social distancing, which is the right-hand side of Eq. (12). This applies both to the negative effect of increased social distancing on output and the reduction in consumption needed to feed the increased number of surviving old individuals. It follows that a more productive economy should engage in more social distancing because the cost in terms of lower output and consumption is lower at the margin due to higher consumption.

The effect of increased service intensity of the economy γ is given by:[5]

$$\frac{\partial s}{\partial \gamma} = -\frac{\left[\begin{array}{c} N_w G(s)\left[N_w\gamma G'(s) + c\frac{\partial \widetilde{N}_o}{\partial s}\right]\left[u''(c)\right]^2 \\ - N_w u'(c)G'(s)\left[N_w + \widetilde{N}_o\right]u''(c) \end{array}\right]}{\Psi} < 0 \tag{14}$$

Intuitively, an increase in the service sector has the effect of increasing the marginal cost of social distancing since output falls more with social distancing in the service sector. It follows that the optimal or golden-rule level of social distancing is smaller in a service economy since it affects output more than in an economy that does not require proximity between staff and customers.

[4] See Appendix 3.

[5] Ibid.

The number of infected individuals entering the country q, the proportion of the population vaccinated v and the effectiveness of medical treatment m also affect the optimal level of social distancing s. The effect of increased life-saving ways of treating those infected m is given by:[6]

$$\frac{\partial s}{\partial m} = -\frac{\left[\begin{array}{c} c\frac{\partial \widetilde{N}_o}{\partial m}\left[N_w \gamma G'(s) + c\frac{\partial \widetilde{N}_o}{\partial s}\right]\left[u''(c)\right]^2 \\ + u'(c) N_w \gamma G'(s)\left[N_w + \widetilde{N}_o\right] u''(c)\frac{\frac{\partial^2 \widetilde{N}_o}{\partial s \partial m}}{\frac{\partial \widetilde{N}_o}{\partial s}} \end{array}\right]}{\Psi} < 0 \tag{15}$$

The intuition comes from the negative cross-partial derivative of s and m on the number of old individuals in Eq. (4). A higher m lowers the effect of a rise in s on the number of the old, hence the marginal benefit from raising s on the left-hand side of Eq. (12). The more old people survive infection because of better medical treatment, the smaller is the optimal level of social distancing. In the extreme, if the medication is a perfect cure, $h(m) = 1$, increasing social distancing has no effect on the life expectancy of the old and its optimal value should then be set equal to zero.

The effect of increased proportion of the population vaccinates v is very similar. The more people have been vaccinated, the fewer people each infected person is likely to infect, that is the lower the value of r. The derivative of social distancing with respect to v follows:[7]

$$\frac{\partial s}{\partial v} = -\frac{\left[\begin{array}{c} c\frac{\partial \widetilde{N}_o}{\partial v}\left[N_w \gamma G'(s) + c\frac{\partial \widetilde{N}_o}{\partial s}\right]\left[u''(c)\right]^2 \\ + u'(c) N_w \gamma G'(s)\left[N_w + \widetilde{N}_o\right] u''(c)\frac{\frac{\partial^2 \widetilde{N}_o}{\partial s \partial v}}{\frac{\partial \widetilde{N}_o}{\partial s}} \end{array}\right]}{\Psi} < 0 \tag{16}$$

The intuition is like that in Eq. (15). With more people vaccinated, each infected individual infects fewer other individuals so that the benefit of social distancing is smaller, that is the left-hand side of Eq. (12) is smaller.

Finally, the effect of increased number of infected travellers q is given by Eq. (17).[8] When more infected people enter the country, the benefit of social distancing goes up. Intuitively, more local people become infected when many infected enter the country, which increases the optimal level of social distancing. The higher is q, the larger is the marginal benefit of social distancing.

[6] Ibid.

[7] See Appendix 3.

[8] Ibid.

$$\frac{\partial s}{\partial q} = -\frac{\left[\begin{array}{c} c\frac{\partial \widetilde{N}_o}{\partial q}\left[N_w\gamma G'(s) + c\frac{\partial \widetilde{N}_o}{\partial s}\right][u''(c)]^2 \\ +u'(c)N_w\gamma G'(s)\left[N_w + \widetilde{N}_o\right]u''(c)\frac{\frac{\partial^2 \widetilde{N}_o}{\partial s \partial q}}{\frac{\partial \widetilde{N}_o}{\partial s}} \end{array}\right]}{\Psi} > 0 \tag{17}$$

This last effect highlights a trade-off between controlling the border to reduce the number of infected individuals entering a country, on the one hand, and social distancing within the country, on the other hand. The greater the inflow of infected people because of high levels of infections abroad and limited testing at the border has the effect of increasing the socially optimal level of social distancing within the country.

A rich country that borders a poor country faces the following problem. The golden rule social distancing is lower in the poor country due to the higher marginal cost of social distancing. The number of infected people in steady state is then higher in the poor country and so is the flow of infected individuals coming into the rich country, calling for increased social distancing in the rich country. It follows that output in the rich country falls due to the inflow of infected individuals coming from the poor country. This reasoning supports the case for rich countries sharing vaccines with poor countries. It also supports the continued use of international travel controls to stem the arrival of new variants of the virus after the population of the rich countries has been vaccinated.

6 A Look at the Data

Our model predicts that the level of social distancing within a country should be a positive function of output per capita and a negative function of the size of the service economy because the utility sacrificed through social distancing is decreasing in the former and increasing in the latter.

To explore whether countries are following our golden rule of social distancing, we use data for 37 countries.[9] The data include the number of cases by country by 27 June 2021: cumulative infections per million inhabitants (infect), cumulative deaths due to COVID-19 (deaths), GDP per capita in U.S. dollars (GDP); employment in the service sector as a share of total employment in percentages (ser) and a dummy variable for island economies (island).[10] Based on our model, we would expect GDP per capita to have a negative coefficient in both equations, service

[9] These are Australia, Austria, Belgium, Canada, Chile, Colombia, Czechia, Denmark, Estonia, Finland, France, Germany, Greece, Hungary, Iceland, Ireland, Israel, Italy, Japan, Latvia, Lithuania, Luxembourg, Mexico, Netherlands, New Zealand, Norway, Poland, Portugal, Slovakia, Slovenia, Spain, Switzerland, Turkey, the United Kingdom and the United States.

[10] See Appendix 4 for the sources of the data.

sector employment a positive coefficient, and the island dummy to have a negative coefficient because of a lower inflow of new infections. When we regress the number of infections (infect) per million individuals as a dependent variable on the explanatory variables we get these results:

$$infect = \underset{(2.7)}{140,734} + \underset{(2.2)}{0.77}\ GDP - \underset{(1.6)}{1400}\ ser - \underset{(5.0)}{64,244}\ island$$

$$R^2 = 0.48, F = 9.8$$

Output has a significant positive coefficient, in contrast to our model, and service employment a negative coefficient, also in contradiction of the model, but the island dummy has a significant negative coefficient as predicted by our model (islands have a lower value of q). Replacing the number of infections with the number of deaths gives:

$$deaths = \underset{(4.1)}{499} + \underset{(1.0)}{0.001}\ GDP - \underset{(2.7)}{5.4}\ ser - \underset{(3.9)}{118}\ island$$

$$R^2 = 0.45, F = 8.8$$

The pattern is the same as in the previous equation. In both equations we find limited support for our golden rule. The number of infections is rising in GDP per capita and falling in service employment. The lower number of infections and deaths in island economies is consistent with the effect of a lower q since controlling the inflow of new infections should be easier on islands.

7 Concluding Remarks

We have studied the choice of consumption and social distancing in a steady state when new variants of the virus constantly enter a country preventing herd immunity from arising. There is an optimal level of steady state social distancing where welfare is maximised. At this optimum, the marginal benefit in terms of the utility of consumption during an extended lifespan is set equal to the marginal cost in terms of lower output and consumption while working.

The analysis has several implications. First, a high-income country should engage in more social distancing than a low-income country because it can more easily afford the loss of output. Second, a service economy should do less social distancing because the cost in terms of lost output is greater. Vaccines and effective medications that reduce the transmission and mortality reduce the optimal level of social distancing. In contrast, open borders that facilitate the inflow of new infections increase the number of infections and deaths and the optimal level of social distancing. It also follows from our analysis that the severity of the pandemic and its effect on mortality will vary between nations. The pandemic will wreak havoc in poor countries where people work together in agriculture or services and share cramped quarters. The pandemic should be according to our golden rule, better contained in rich, industrialised countries, especially those where manufacturing is important.

The analysis points to possible frictions within and between countries due to the transmission of the virus between regions and countries. Low-income regions that specialize in services would like to relax social distancing earlier than the more affluent and industrialised regions. The same applies to countries. The level of social distancing should be lower in a poor country. This may force the more affluent countries to impose greater social distancing because of the number of new infections coming through the border from poorer countries. These externalities justify the provision of vaccines to poorer countries as well as continued international travel controls, even after the population of the rich countries has been vaccinated.

A.1 Appendices

A.1.1 Appendix 1

The derivatives are (from (1), (3) and (4)):

$$\frac{\partial \widetilde{N}_o}{\partial s} = -[A-R]\frac{[1-h(m)]\,q}{[1-r(s,v)]^2}\frac{\partial r}{\partial s} > 0$$

$$\frac{\partial \widetilde{N}_o}{\partial v} = -[A-R]\frac{[1-h(m)]\,q}{[1-r(s,v)]^2}\frac{\partial r}{\partial v} > 0$$

$$\frac{\partial \widetilde{N}_o}{\partial m} = [A-R]\frac{q}{1-r(s,v)}\frac{\partial h}{\partial m} > 0$$

$$\frac{\partial \widetilde{N}_o}{\partial q} = -[A-R]\frac{1-h(m)}{1-r(s,v)} < 0$$

$$\frac{\partial^2 \widetilde{N}_o}{\partial s^2} = -[A-R]\frac{[1-h(m)]\,q}{[1-r(s,v)]^2}\frac{\partial^2 r}{\partial s^2} - 2[A-R]\frac{[1-h(m)]\,q}{[1-r(s,v)]^3}\left[\frac{\partial r}{\partial s}\right]^2 < 0$$

$$\frac{\partial^2 \widetilde{N}_o}{\partial s \partial v} = -[A-R]\frac{[1-h(m)]\,q}{[1-r(s,v)]^2}\frac{\partial^2 r}{\partial s \partial v} - 2[A-R]\frac{[1-h(m)]\,q}{[1-r(s,v)]^3}\frac{\partial r}{\partial s}\frac{\partial r}{\partial v} < 0$$

$$\frac{\partial^2 \widetilde{N}_o}{\partial s \partial m} = [A - R] \frac{q}{[1 - r(s, v)]^2} \frac{\partial r}{\partial s} \frac{\partial h}{\partial m} < 0$$

$$\frac{\partial^2 \widetilde{N}_o}{\partial s \partial q} = -[A - R] \frac{1 - h(m)}{[1 - r(s, v)]^2} \frac{\partial r}{\partial s} > 0$$

A.1.2 Appendix 2

The first-order derivatives of the Lagrangian are (after using (4) and that $N_w = R$):

$$\frac{\partial \Gamma}{\partial \lambda} = N_w [y - \gamma G(s) - c_w] - \widetilde{N}_o c_o$$

$$\frac{\partial \Gamma}{\partial c_w} = N_w \left[u'(c_w) - \lambda\right]$$

$$\frac{\partial \Gamma}{\partial c_o} = \widetilde{N}_o \left[u'(c_o) - \lambda\right]$$

$$\frac{\partial \Gamma}{\partial s} = u(c_o) \frac{\partial \widetilde{N}_o}{\partial s} - \lambda \left[N_w \gamma G'(s) + c_o \frac{\partial \widetilde{N}_o}{\partial s} \right]$$

and the second-order derivatives are (after evaluating those at maximum and rewriting):

$$\frac{\partial^2 \Gamma}{\partial \lambda^2} = 0, \frac{\partial^2 \Gamma}{\partial \lambda \partial c_w} = -N_w, \frac{\partial^2 \Gamma}{\partial \lambda \partial c_o} = -\widetilde{N}_o, \frac{\partial^2 \Gamma}{\partial \lambda \partial s} = -\left[N_w \gamma G'(s) + c \frac{\partial \widetilde{N}_o}{\partial s} \right]$$
$$\frac{\partial^2 \Gamma}{\partial c_w^2} = N_w u''(c), \frac{\partial^2 \Gamma}{\partial c_w \partial c_o} = \frac{\partial^2 \Gamma}{\partial c_w \partial s} = 0$$

$$\frac{\partial^2 \Gamma}{\partial c_0^2} = \widetilde{N}_o u''(c), \frac{\partial^2 \Gamma}{\partial c_o \partial s} = 0$$

$$\frac{\partial^2 \Gamma}{\partial s^2} = \gamma N_w u'(c) G'(s) \left[\frac{\frac{\partial^2 \widetilde{N}_o}{\partial s^2}}{\frac{\partial \widetilde{N}_o}{\partial s}} - \frac{G''(s)}{G'(s)} \right]$$

Hence, for the first-order conditions being necessary and sufficient for a maximum, the following must hold (second order conditions using the bordered Hessian matrix):

$$-N_w\tilde{N}_o\left[N_w+\tilde{N}_o\right]u''(c)>0$$

which always holds, and:

$$-N_w\tilde{N}_o\left[\begin{array}{c}\left[N_w\gamma G'(s)+c_o\frac{\partial\tilde{N}_o}{\partial s}\right]^2\left[u''(c)\right]^2\\ +\Phi\left[N_w+\tilde{N}_o\right]u''(c)\end{array}\right]<0$$

where:

$$\Phi\equiv\gamma N_w u'(c)G'(s)\left[\frac{\frac{\partial^2\tilde{N}_o}{\partial s^2}}{\frac{\partial\tilde{N}_o}{\partial s}}-\frac{G''(s)}{G'(s)}\right]\gtreqless 0$$

For the second condition to hold it is necessary that:

$$\left[N_w\gamma G'(s)+c_o\frac{\partial\tilde{N}_o}{\partial s}\right]^2\left[u''(c)\right]^2+\Phi\left[N_w+\tilde{N}_o\right]u''(c)>0$$

Since the first term is positive and $\left[N_w+\tilde{N}_o\right]u''(c)<0$, this holds for all negative Φ and positive Φ such that

$$\Phi<-\frac{\left[N_w\gamma G'(s)+c_o\frac{\partial\tilde{N}_o}{\partial s}\right]^2u''(c)}{N_w+\tilde{N}_o}$$

or iff:

$$\gamma N_w u'(c)G'(s)\left[\frac{\frac{\partial^2\tilde{N}_o}{\partial s^2}}{\frac{\partial\tilde{N}_o}{\partial s}}-\frac{G''(s)}{G'(s)}\right]<-\frac{\left[N_w\gamma G'(s)+c_o\frac{\partial\tilde{N}_o}{\partial s}\right]^2u''(c)}{N_w+\tilde{N}_o.}$$

where the right hand side of the inequality is strictly positive. Since $\frac{\partial\tilde{N}_o}{\partial s}>0$, $\frac{\partial^2\tilde{N}_o}{\partial s^2}<0$, $\gamma N_w u^{'}(c)G^{'}(s)>0$ and $G^{'}(s)>0$ there clearly exist $G^{''}(s)\gtreqless 0$ ensuring that the second order conditions are fulfilled. We therefore conclude that the second condition holds, which is assumed in what follows.

A.1.3 Appendix 3

Taking the total difference of the first order conditions in (7)–(10) (after using (11) and (4)) with respect to the endogenous variables λ, c_w, c_o and s and the exogenous variables/parameters y, γ, m, q and v gives the following after collecting terms and rearranging:

$$u''(c)dc_w - d\lambda = 0$$

$$u''(c)dc_o - d\lambda = 0$$

$$-\left[N_w\gamma G'(s) + c\frac{\partial \widetilde{N}_o}{\partial s}\right]d\lambda + \Phi ds = N_w u'(c)G'(s)d\gamma$$

$$-u'(c)N_w\gamma G'(s)\frac{\frac{\partial^2 \widetilde{N}_o}{\partial s\partial m}}{\frac{\partial \widetilde{N}_o}{\partial s}}dm - u'(c)N_w\gamma G'(s)\frac{\frac{\partial^2 \widetilde{N}_o}{\partial s\partial q}}{\frac{\partial \widetilde{N}_o}{\partial s}}dq - u'(c)N_w\gamma G'(s)\frac{\frac{\partial^2 \widetilde{N}_o}{\partial s\partial v}}{\frac{\partial \widetilde{N}_o}{\partial s}}dv$$

$$-N_w dc_w - \widetilde{N}_o dc_o - \left[N_w\gamma G'(s) + c\frac{\partial \widetilde{N}_o}{\partial s}\right]ds$$

$$= -N_w dy + N_w G(s)d\gamma + c\frac{\partial \widetilde{N}_o}{\partial m}dm + c\frac{\partial \widetilde{N}_o}{\partial q}dq + c\frac{\partial \widetilde{N}_o}{\partial v}dv$$

Setting $d\gamma = dm = dq = dv = 0$ and dividing through each equation with dy gives four equations in four unknown variables, i. e. $\frac{\partial \lambda}{\partial y}$, $\frac{\partial c_w}{\partial y}$, $\frac{\partial c_o}{\partial y}$ and $\frac{\partial s}{\partial y}$:

$$u''(c)\frac{\partial c_w}{\partial y} - \frac{\partial \lambda}{\partial y} = 0$$

$$u''(c)\frac{\partial c_o}{\partial y} - \frac{\partial \lambda}{\partial y} = 0$$

$$-\left[N_w\gamma G'(s) + c\frac{\partial \widetilde{N}_o}{\partial s}\right]\frac{\partial \lambda}{\partial y} + \Phi\frac{\partial s}{\partial y} = 0$$

$$-N_w \frac{\partial c_w}{\partial y} - \widetilde{N}_o \frac{\partial c_o}{\partial y} - \left[N_w \gamma G'(s) + c \frac{\partial \widetilde{N}_o}{\partial s} \right] \frac{\partial s}{\partial y} = -N_w$$

Solving for $\frac{\partial s}{\partial y}$ gives:

$$\frac{\partial s}{\partial y} = \frac{N_w \left[N_w \gamma G'(s) + c_o \frac{\partial \widetilde{N}_o}{\partial s} \right] [u''(c)]^2}{\left[N_w \gamma G'(s) + c_o \frac{\partial \widetilde{N}_o}{\partial s} \right]^2 [u''(c)]^2 + \Phi \left[N_w + \widetilde{N}_o \right] u''(c)}$$

which gives (13). Similarly calculating $\frac{\partial s}{\partial \gamma}$, $\frac{\partial s}{\partial m}$, $\frac{\partial s}{\partial q}$ and $\frac{\partial s}{\partial v}$ gives (14)–(17). Note that the denominator in the derivatives:

$$\Psi \equiv \left[N_w \gamma G'(s) + c_o \frac{\partial \widetilde{N}_o}{\partial s} \right]^2 [u''(c)]^2 + \Phi \left[N_w + \widetilde{N}_o \right] u''(c)$$

is positive (see Appendix 2).

A.1.4 Appendix 4

Table A.1 The data and their sources

	Definition	Source	Link
Covid 19 cases	Cases of COVID-19 detected by 27 June 2021	Johns Hopkins Coronavirus Resource Center	COVID-19 Map–Johns Hopkins Coronavirus Resource Center (jhu.edu)
Service employment	Service employment as a share of total employment	The World Bank	World Development Indicators | DataBank (worldbank.org)
GDP per capita	GDP per capita in US dollars	OECD	https://stats.oecd.org/Index.aspx?DataSetCode = QNA#
Island dummy	Number one indicates an island	Google	https://www.google.com/maps

References

Acemoglu, D., Chernozhukov, V., Werning, I., & Whinston, M. D. (2020). *A multi-risk sir model with optimally targeted lockdown*. Cemmap working paper CWP14/20.

Alvarez, F. E., Argente, D., & Lippi, F. (2020). *A simple planning problem for Covid-19 Lockdown*. NBER Working Paper 26981.

Farboodi, M., Jarosch, G., & Shimer, R. (2020). *Internal and external effects of social distancing in a pandemic*. Working paper no. 2020-47. Becker Friedman Institute, University of Chicago.

Gestsson, M. H., & Zoega, G. (2019). The golden rule of longevity. *Macroeconomic Dynamics, 23*(1), 384–419.

Glover, A., Heathcote, J., Krueger, D., & Ríos-Rull, J.-V. (2020). *Controlling a pandemic*. NBER Working Paper No. 27046.

Hausmann, R., & Schetter, U. (2020). *Horrible trade-offs in a pandemic: Lockdowns, transfers, fiscal space, and compliance*. CID Faculty Working Paper No. 382.

Hall, R. E., & Jones, C. J. (2007). The value of life and the rise in health spending get access arrow. *The quarterly journal of economics, 122*(1), 39–72. https://doi.org/10.1162/qjec.122.1.39

Phelps, E. S. (1966). *Golden rules of economic growth*. W. W. Norton.

Phelps, E. S. (1968). Models of technical progress and the golden rule of research. *Review of Economic Studies, 33*, 133–146.

Ramsey, F. (1928). A mathematical theory of saving. *Economic Journal, 38*, 543–559.

The New European Industrial Policy and the Case of the 'Pharmaceuticals and Biotechnology' Industry

Franco Mosconi

1 Introduction

During the first two decades of the twenty-first century, industrial policy regained progressively its prominence on the European scene. But what kind of policy are we talking about? This paper tries to answer this question by looking at the approach that the EU—and, in particular, the European Commission—developed between 2002 and 2020.[1] In this context, the EU's 'new' industrial policy is one in which a central position is occupied by the increase of knowledge-based investments and the development of enabling technologies; these two priorities have become quite critical now that manufacturing has made a come-back and is reclaiming its vital role in advancing vibrant economic growth.

What comes to the surface is a picture in which the rhetorical recourse to *market failure* is nothing more than the simplest, and least controversial, method for justifying industrial policy. But if we look ahead to the next few years (decades), what is truly at stake is the place of European manufacturing within the new international division of labour, especially—let me say—in 'The Age of the Pandemic' (or, hopefully, after this Age).

[1] For a more comprehensive analysis of the 'new' European industrial policy, see: Mosconi (2015a) for the first decade (2002–2012) and Mosconi (2022) for the entire period (2002–2020); two extensive bibliographies are also published in these works (a chapter-book and monograph, respectively). In addition to European Commission's Communications examined over the period 2002–2020, there is also the latest one, a Communication from the European Commission (2021), aimed at 'updating the 2020 New Industrial Strategy'.

F. Mosconi (✉)
Jean Monnet Chair in 'The Economics of European Industry', University of Parma, Parma, Italy
e-mail: franco.mosconi@unipr.it

L. Paganetto (ed.), *Economic Challenges for Europe After the Pandemic*,
Springer Proceedings in Business and Economics,
https://doi.org/10.1007/978-3-031-10302-5_4

This paper is organized in the following manner. In Sect. 2 we briefly summarize what can be labelled the 'new' industrial policy. First (Sect. 2.1), we shed some light on the approach that has emerged from the economic literature thanks to the work of scholars such as Alexis Jacquemin and Dani Rodrik, to name just two. After that, the following Sect. 2.2 examines the so-called 'integrated approach' (i.e. both horizontal and vertical applications) to industrial policy developed by the European Commission from December 2002 until March 2020. We try, at the end of the Sect. 2.3, to better understand the current state of affairs at the EU level. Despite some new initiatives before the COVID-19 virus spread throughout Europe, the situation was still anchored to the preservation of the status quo in the sense that the interests of individual nation-states were always put first and foremost. Nevertheless, the spread of the pandemic and its terrible medical and socio-economic consequences have increased the desirability of implementing policies aimed at offering public goods to the EU level (e.g. vaccines). As a consequence, the framework is bound to change, and, in truth, it already has (e.g. NGEU, General escape clause, Temporary framework for State aid, SURE, etc.). In this vein, Sect. 3 discusses the case of one of the pillars of global R&D—'Pharmaceuticals and Biotechnology'—while Sect. 4 proposes a policy agenda capable of combining the business activities of new strategic firms with forward-looking public policies. Section 5 briefly concludes.

2 The New European Industrial Policy: An Overview

2.1 The Theoretical Background[2]

When one mentions the phrase 'industrial policy', the path immediately becomes difficult, and paradoxically, this is true even after the big crash of 2008. In fact, industrial policy always runs the risk of being treated like the 'ugly duckling' of Andersen's fairy tale, while other public policies—such as monetary policy, fiscal policy and the like—seem to be destined to a future of 'beautiful white swans'. At present, no one wants to deny the wisdom of central bankers or the virtues of a budget policy for keeping public finances in order. But going back to the fairy tale metaphor, the question arises: do things stand exactly this way today? Do they stand this way after all that has happened in the 2 years that followed September 2008 and had such a terrible impact on Western economies? Getting to the gist of the question: Is industrial policy wrong *per se*? Or is it not just about time to develop a new industrial policy at European level—as authoritative voices that we will discover along the way have underlined recently?

[2] '*The Jacquemin-Rodrik Synthesis*' has been originally developed in Mosconi (2012), and the Editorial Board of Polo Interregionale Jean Monnet has given the authorization for re-using a part of this essay.

Let's start from the persons and their ideas, and, in particular, let's begin with two prominent scholars: the late Alexis Jacquemin and Dani Rodrik. They both taught, and Professor Rodrik still does, in prestigious universities: Louvain-la-Neuve for the former and the John F. Kennedy School (Harvard University) the latter. Besides teaching and academic research, they both collaborated with important institutions: the European Commission headed by Jacques Delors in the case of the late Jacquemin; UNIDO and the World Bank in the case of Rodrik. They dealt extensively, and Rodrik still does, with industrial policy, without considering it wrong, useless or damaging at all.

In his seminal book from 1987—*The New Industrial Organization*—Jacquemin (1987) reserved the whole of the sixth and final chapter for industrial policy. The *leitmotiv* of the whole book is the contrast between 'market forces' and 'strategic behaviour'—a contrast that could not fail to have an impact on industrial policy choices. He argues that if 'for those who have full confidence in market mechanism the only real requirement is the existence of a healthy macroeconomic environment'; in contrast 'here is a whole tide of research questioning whether the market alone can efficiently accomplish selections leading to new industrial organizations'.

According to the author, the latter view leads us to the classic two arguments that justify an industrial policy: *(i)* 'the long list of so-called *market failures*' (e.g. the support for R&D in high-tech sectors) and *(ii)* 'the strategies that deliberately influence the transformation and the industrial reorganization of sectors, and nations'. This leads to his criticism of the domestic policies of Member States pursuing the creation of 'National Champions' and, at the same time, his proposal on the 'need to create a *concerted European industrial policy that will help overcome industry strategies along national lines*, to reduce the barriers among large national enterprises and to develop a large domestic European market for industrial applications' (emphasis added).

After Jacquemin's work (in the 80s) and a decade of silence on industrial policy (the 90s)—a policy area that fell victim both to its own past mistakes and the rise of a dominant ideology (i.e., the Washington Consensus)—we reach the 2000s. Halfway through the new decade, a couple of papers by Dani Rodrik shed light on what is really meant by industrial policy at the start of the twenty-first century. To avoid all misunderstandings, we can add the adjective 'new' to industrial policy to distinguish it from the industrial policy of the past, which focused on the 'picking the winners' and, more generally, on excessive public intervention (above all by the nation-state) in the economy, mainly through the state ownership of industrial and/or service enterprises and through all sort of state aid. The most commonly referred to of Rodrik's papers in the economic literature are those of (Rodrik, 2004, 2008), respectively entitled *Industrial Policy for the Twenty-First Century* and *Normalizing Industrial Policy*. In both papers the author illustrates the definition of industrial policy: 'I will use the term to denote policies that stimulate specific economic activities and promote structural change', and not only—he argues—in the manufacturing industry but also in all kinds of 'non-traditional activities' in agriculture or in the service sector.

Like Jacquemin, Rodrik, too, starts from a conventional point for industrial policy—that is, 'market failures' ('markets for credit, labor, products, and knowledge', he adds) and the need to deal with them. But once more, as with Jacquemin, there is something more in Rodrik's thought, something that leads him to state: 'The right model for industrial policy is not that of an autonomous government applying Pigovian taxes or subsidies but of strategic collaboration between the private sector and the government with the aim of uncovering where the most significant obstacles to restructuring lie and what type of interventions are most likely to remove them [...] It is innovation that enables restructuring and productivity growth'.

After the two papers mentioned above, Rodrik returned to the principles inspiring modern industrial policy in a debate promoted by *The Economist* in July 2010 with the title: 'This house believes that industrial policy always fails'. Among the most significant passages of the this debate between Rodrik and Josh Lerner (of the Harvard Business School, called to support the thesis of the British weekly) let me mention the following by Rodrik (2010): 'The essence of economic development is structural transformation, the rise of new industries to replace traditional ones. But this is not an easy or automatic process. It requires a mix of market forces and government support. If the government is too heavy-handed, it kills private entrepreneurship. If it is too standoffish, markets keep doing what they know how to do best, confining the country to its specialization in traditional, and low-productivity products'. Drawing on concepts he had already expressed in his papers from 2004 and 2007, Rodrik (2010) argues that it is not so much a question of asking ourselves 'whether' there should be an industrial policy, as a question of 'how' to organize it, manage it and assess its outcomes.[3]

2.2 The European Perspective

If the principles and objectives of what we have just labelled the 'new' industrial policy (in short, 'The Jacquemin-Rodrik Synthesi's[4]) are clear and shareable, the question of how it should be designed and implemented remains open. The EU should be considered as our natural point of reference in this area of policy for many reasons, among which we can mention at least two. First of all, since December 2002 the European Commission has started an important reflection on *Industrial Policy in an Enlarged Europe* (European Commission, 2002), which has gone on throughout the decade(s).

Second, the 'integrated approach' that has been developed by the European Commission in Brussels in communication after communication does certainly

[3] It is not meaningless to notice that, among the readers of *The Economist*, about three quarters of those (72% against 28%) agreed with Rodrik's view (Mosconi, 2015b).

[4] This point along with other stylized facts regarding the 'new' European industrial policy at large have been fully developed in Mosconi (2015b).

develop the 'horizontal' measures (to use the jargon of this policy area) that aim to make markets increasingly efficient by removing non-tariff barriers and excessive regulations; but it also focuses on 'vertical' applications—that is, on applications to certain industries/technological trajectories. Many industrial sectors and/or enabling technologies are mentioned in the documents the Commission issued between 2002 and 2021, and among them the most important are the research-intensive ones: biotechnology and life sciences, aeronautics and space technology, ICTs and digital transition, as well as the green economy and the ecological transition.

The European Commission is right when it places some R&D-intensive industries on a different plan: these are industries that need radical innovations—downright changes of paradigm—especially considering that the EU is lagging behind the United States in terms of technological advancements and in view of the new challenge coming from Asia and from the emerging countries in general (including, but not limited to, the famous BRICs). Today more than ever, all of these industries require a new industrial policy in the sense that we have tried to describe. In other words, a policy that 'overcomes industry strategies along national lines' thanks to negotiation at European level, and a policy that, thanks to a 'strategic cooperation' between the public and private sphere of the economy, is concerned above all with the provision of public goods for the productive sector. With respect to this, Rodrik (2004) points out that: 'Public labs and public R&D, health and infrastructural facilities, sanitary and phytosanitary standards, infrastructure, vocational and technical training can all be viewed as public goods required for enhancing technological capabilities. From this perspective, industrial policy is just good economic policy of the type that traditional, orthodox approaches prescribe'.

If the new paradigm is so clear, then where is the missing link in today's EU? In other words, why is it that after two decades of Brussels elaborating on the new industrial policy (2002–2021), the practice is still so distant from a really integrated and supranational approach? The answer has many facets:

(i) because the EU budget has remained essentially the same, with a substantial part (almost 40%) of it still destined to agriculture (CAP), despite changes made over the last two decades;
(ii) because this budget has not been thoroughly reformed, as the 'Sapir Report', *An Agenda for a Growing Europe* (Sapir et al., 2004) commissioned by President Romano Prodi had asked, with the creation of a 'Fund for economic growth' amounting to 45% of the total resources;
(iii) because the research and technology policy, while there are important EU programmes that deal with it, is mainly carried out by the single Member States, each with its own research system and its own laws for technological innovation (not to mention the further fragmentation of powers between central government and regions that occurs, for example, in Italy);
(iv) because after the big crisis of 2008 the rediscovery of 'Colbertism', timid in some countries and passionate in others, in more than one case has brought the risk of carrying out old-fashioned industrial policies; and

(v) because the creation of big European infrastructural networks—the 'Trans-European Networks' advocated by President Jacques Delors in his *White Paper* of 1993 (European Commission, 1993)—remained a dead letter for so many years.

All in all, this is exactly the opposite of the transfer to the supranational level of actions and instruments (R&D, TEN, etc.) that today are, by their very nature, a substantial part of the new industrial policy—a policy aiming at enhancing the competitiveness of the European industry.

2.3 The Next Generation EU (and Not Only): Toward a Change of Attitude

It was the arrival of COVID-19 in the early months of 2020 that would give the EU an external shock that was destined to profoundly reshape its status quo. The intent of this chapter does not allow us to examine the 1.8 billion euros package (1050 million from the new Multiannual Financial Framework plus 750 million euros from the Recovery Plan) approved during the summer of 2020 by the European Institutions. On the other hand, what absolutely needs to be examined in this setting is the EU's overall plan. When we look at the progressive implementation of the Next Generation EU in any given Member State,[5] the way in which each National Recovery and Resilience Plan is structured should not, in fact, make us lose sight of the overarching European programme. In other words, Italy's Recovery and Resilience Plan (MEF, 2021), well designed as it is, is (only) a part of the whole.[6] The whole is, naturally, the process of European integration, which not only must continue to develop, but more importantly must take a qualitative step forward.

The explosion of the pandemic in the winter of 2020 found the EU underprepared, and its first response was weak and largely insufficient; later on, though, the EU Institutions—each in its own way (the European Commission, the European Council, the ECB, the EIB)—approved important initiatives, many of which were entirely unheard of for the EU. Consider the suspension of the Stability Pact, the new procedures for government assistance and the SURE Fund for unemployment. The crowning achievement of this crescendo of initiatives would arrive with the decisions made about the Recovery Plan, which would subsequently be given the more appropriate name of Next Generation EU (NGEU).

---

[5] For an in-depth analysis of the chance offered by the PNRR (the Italian Plan), see the documents and reports published by the Fondazione Universitaria Economia Tor Vergata (2021) in the context of the initiative *Revitalizing Anaemic Europe* carried out by the Gruppo dei 20.

[6] All of the relevant documents (the National Plan, Assessment of the EU, etc.) for a better understanding of Italy's Recovery and Resilience Plan are available on the website of the European Commission: https://ec.europa.eu/info/business-economy-euro/recovery-coronavirus/recovery-and-resilience-facility/recovery-and-resilience-plan-italy_en

The NGEU (2021–2026) and the new multi-year EU budget (2021–2027), aside from the immensity of the funds, provide evidence of an institutional aspect that is worth highlighting, seeing as how—citing the Italian Plan (MEF, 2021, 9)—'the resources destined to the RFF, the most relevant item in the programme, are to be found through the issue of European bonds, leveraged by raising the upper limits of National Resources'.

We must ask: Have we entered the era of the 'Eurobonds', a topic that has always raised acrimonious debate, first within the CEE and then within the EU? It is not easy to answer this question in the sense that the very proposals for the issuance of European bonds that have been put forward over time (from the 1993 Delors White Paper on) are all different. The issuance of bonds to fund the NGEU and the consequent 'debt sharing' should therefore still be regarded as being partial (in their goals) and limited (in time), but they represent a sign of the times in the life of the EU-27.[7] The hope is that something fundamental is changing within all of the Member States in terms of their ways of understanding the concept of sovereignty and national interests. Faced by a negative event of global proportions like a pandemic, the conventional way of understanding this concept—the conviction that each State can make it on its own—has shown its limitations.

We must now bring together the various aspects that we have briefly summarized in this section. On the one hand, there is the evolution of the concept of industrial policy both within the economic literature and the activities of the European Commission. On the other, there is the shockwave that has run through the EU from the spread of COVID-19 and the necessary policy reaction at the EU level. The dynamics of the pharmaceutical and biotechnology Industry, on which we will focus our attention in the next section, represent a kind of *stress test* for understanding the state of the EU today.

3 The Pharmaceutical Industry: Pillar of Global and European R&D

3.1 The EU's R&D Scoreboard

The pharmaceutical industry, as emphasized in the economic literature, is widely recognized as one of the industrial sectors that, in the most developed countries, channels an important proportion of total R&D (Ganuza et al., 2009; González et al., 2016). In 2019, according to *The EU Industrial Investment Scoreboard*, which is published annually by the European Commission and Joint Research Centre

[7] We should keep in mind that the issuance of 'European' bonds has already been put into action for the SURE fund, one of the other EU initiatives enacted to confront the consequences of the pandemic, as mentioned above.

(2020),[8] 'Pharmaceutical and Biotechnology' companies invested an estimated 166.8 billion euros in R&D. In terms of so-called 'R&D intensity' (the ratio between research and development [R&D] investment and revenues), this means a remarkable 18–20% for pharmaceutical and biotech companies.

The company that spends the most in terms of R&D investment is Alphabet, Google's parent company, at a level of 23.2 billion euros. Usually, this scoreboard helps us understand a fundamental issue: how the EU is doing in comparison to its primary competitors (USA, China, Japan and others) in the most highly innovative sectors of the global economy. During the pandemic, however, with the fight against the virus and concern with mass vaccinations, the scorecard has lifted the veil on another big issue: the dynamics within the critically important pharmaceutical industry. This industry ('Pharmaceuticals and Biotechnology') is represented by numerous firms in the ranking, alongside businesses in other high-tech sectors, such as (we quote): 'Software & Computer Services', 'Technology Hardware & Equipment', 'Electronic & Electrical Equipment', 'Software & Computer', 'Automobiles & Parts'.

Seen from a European and an Italian point of view, the (big) issue becomes rather sensitive, considering the US-American successes in the discovery of the earliest vaccines against COVID-19: three out of four vaccines (of those approved by the European Medicines Agency as of this date) are US-American, although it must duly be noted that the creation of the first (by Pfizer) was significantly assisted by a German firm that had been created as a start-up in Mainz in 2008 (BioNTech). Moderna and Johnson & Johnson are both US-American, while the vaccine produced by AstraZeneca is European.

At this point, the question becomes: do the R&D investments detailed in the *Scoreboard* justify this result, especially in quantitative terms, or are there other factors at play here in the gap between the US and the EU? Within the rankings provided by the European Commission, we should focus on the top 100 firms—that is, the *Top 100* R&D investors in the world. Impressively, the 'Pharmaceuticals and Biotechnology' industry accounts for a full 23 firms within this elite group. Unsurprisingly, the world of ICTs has a larger number, but these firms are subdivided into many different specializations (hardware, software, etc.). This means that, at the cusp of the third decade of the twenty-first century, *Big Pharma* has proven itself to be one of the primary spenders in global research. The geographic spread of these 23 firms (or groups) brings our object of study—US-American leadership in the race toward a vaccine—into closer focus. In fact, ten of these are US-American, five from the EU, four from non-EU European nations and finally, four are Japanese. The following table displays their performances in greater detail (Table 1):

[8] The *Scoreboard* ranks the top 2500 businesses in the world in terms of R&D investment, and the most recent edition was published in December 2020 (based upon data through 31 December 2019). The full report is available at the following link: https://iri.jrc.ec.europa.eu/scoreboard/2020-eu-industrial-rd-investment-scoreboard

Table 1 Big Pharma and R&D

World rank (2500 top companies)	Company	Country	R&D 2019 (million euros)	Net sales (million euros)	R&D intensity (%)
9	ROCHE	Switzerland	10,753.2	56,511.3	19.0
10	JOHNSON & JOHNSON	US	10,107.7	73,045.2	13.8
13	MERCK US	US	8234.8	41,694.9	19.8
14	NOVARTIS	Switzerland	7713.2	44,940.4	17.2
15	GILEAD SCIENCES	US	7393.6	19,983.1	37.0
16	PFIZER	US	7373.2	46,065.5	16.0
23	SANOFI	France/EU	6015.0	36,126.0	16.7
25	BAYER	Germany/EU	5628.0	46,287.0	12.2
28	BRISTOL-MYERS	US	5373.9	23,273.1	23.1
29	GLAXOSMITHKLINE	UK	5068.0	39,425.2	12.9
30	ABBVIE	US	4813.1	29,611.9	16.3
31	ASTRAZENECA	UK	4795.3	21,705.5	22.1
45	TAKEDA PHARMACEUTICAL	Japan	4014.2	26,848.1	15.0
49	AMGEN	US	3663.9	20,795.8	17.6
53	ELI LILLY	US	3251.6	19,867.8	16.4
68	MERCK DE	Germany/EU	2268.0	16,152.0	14.0
76	ABBOTT LAB	US	2052.7	28,399.5	7.2
77	BIOGEN IDEC	US	2030.1	12,798.6	15.9
88	ASTELLAS PHARMA	Japan	1829.1	10,611.7	17.2
90	OTSUKA	Japan	1760.3	11,389.9	15.5
92	NOVO NORDISK	Denmark/EU	1722.1	16,270.1	10.6
99	DAIICHI SANKYO	Japan	1610.8	8009.1	20.1
100	ALLERGAN	Ireland/EU	1604.4	14,321.6	11.2

Source: Excerpt from European Commission & Joint Research Centre (2020)

Compared to the *Top 100*, Moderna—a firm founded in 2010 in the heart of the most important university city in the world, Boston—represents a truly special case. Moderna, Inc., is not on the list of the 'top 100' firms that we are using here, and not even among the next 200, coming in at only (so to speak) number 375 in the complete rankings of the 2500 firms in the EU document. But what matters is that, since being founded, it has specialized intensely in 'mRNA technology', and it boasts an incredible ratio between R&D spending (388.2 million euros) and revenues (53.6 million)—equal to 724.3%.

3.2 The Race for a Vaccine and the US–EU Gap

In our attempts to give a tentative answer to the question about the US–EU gap, we must now synthesize the data along the lines of macro-areas. The ten US-American *Big Pharma* firms invested 54.3 billion euros in R&D in 2019, compared to the 17.3 billion invested by the five EU firms (one French, two German, one Danish and one Irish) and the 28.3 billion invested by the four non-EU firms (two Swiss and two British, among which we find AstraZeneca, which the *Scoreboard* places within the UK). If we add up the EU and non-EU numbers to get the (theoretical) sum for 'Europe', we come to 45.5 billion euros, not far from the US-American figures.

But does it make any sense to do this addition? No, because the EU policies for combatting the pandemic—from vaccine-acquisition contracts (with their defects) to NGEU (with its opportunities), not to mention the suspension of the Stability and Growth Pact, etc.—only touch the 27 EU member states, just like the EU-wide programmes for supporting scientific and technological research, both public and private (i.e. Horizon) are only valid for member states. The distance between US and EU investments is thus indeed remarkable. We can try to repeat the exercise, this time doing the sum of revenues within the same macro-areas: 313 billion euros for the ten US-American firms compared to 128 billion for the five EU. This is rounded out by the 162 billion for the four non-EU firms, thanks especially to the two Swiss giants (Roche and Novartis).

This does not mean that there is a lack of excellence in the EU pharmaceutical industry; on the contrary, when we consider the therapeutic range covered by the products made by Sanofi and Bayer—the two largest in the EU—the opposite is true. This also remains the case when we look at the many excellent technological firms within the Italian pharmaceutical industry, which, as a whole, has a value of '34 billion euros in production' and 'is constantly investing more in R&D: 1.6 billion euros', according to the data published by Farmindustria. Importantly, this is a sector that is itself working on the development of its own vaccines. As of today, there are many European and Italian pharmaceutical companies that the European Commission, in agreement with national governments (in the case of Italy, the dossier is in the hands of the Ministry of Economic Development), engaging in the efforts to produce, within our borders and through licensing, the innumerable doses of the vaccine that are currently missing to make mass vaccination a reality.

4 A Fourfold Policy Agenda

Although we should not forget the positive signs within the EU pharmaceutical industry, it is nonetheless hard to avoid the impression that, from within the global perspective of the pandemic, we find ourselves facing what Ferruccio de Bortoli has called '*Small Pharma*: smaller is not sweeter when you have a pandemic' (L'Economia del Corriere della Sera, 8 March 2021). All things considered, the current situation has been stigmatized as 'a failure of the European pharmaceutical industry', to quote Romano Prodi (L'Economia, 8 March 2021). So, what is it that went wrong, or at the very least did not go the way we might have hoped? The numbers we have seen (the different levels of R&D spending and revenue from the pharmaceutical industry) on the opposite sides of the Atlantic explain a lot, but they do not explain everything. Perhaps part of the answer lies in bureaucratic realities (*lato sensu*) and in the rules of the game, so to speak.

We certainly have something to learn from the way in which the federal government of the United States and US-American pharmaceutical companies quickly developed a working relationship upon the arrival of the new coronavirus, a relationship that was solidified by the speed with which (conspicuous) public funds were made available for creating effective and safe vaccines in record time (faster than anything imaginable prior to 2020), all the while respecting the three fundamental clinical trials. We also have something to learn also from the US-American way of developing technological start-ups, which thrives on the virtuous circle of academic research, entrepreneurial activity and a financial system with an injection of venture capital and private equity funds. Even looking into our own house—the EU—we all have something to learn. Four points stand out:

(i) While he was economic advisor to Jacques Delors during the Delors Presidency of the European Commission, Alexis Jacquemin (1987, 179) once underlined '*the possibility of a concerted European industrial policy that will help overcome industry strategies along national lines, reduce barriers between national champions, and develop a large home European market for industrial applications*'. If this necessity was true then (in the mid-1980s), I believe that it is even more so today, with a larger EU following the expansion into Eastern Europe: it is now the largest single market in the world and offers the so-called 'level playing field' to its businesses upon which they can undertake long-term growth strategies.

(ii) The 'European Champions' are the natural result of these dynamics. In previous works on European industrial policy (Mosconi, 2015a, 2015b), I have classified these Champions into two types: those that can be formed along the line of Airbus and STMicroelectronics (through the collaboration of European governments who pool their state-owned assets in a specific industry), and those that are created by M&As in the market (integrating businesses that operate in the same core business, as in the recent cases of EssilorLuxottica and Stellantis). Leading technological start-ups must be nurtured alongside these Champions, making a special effort—now more than ever—in the field of

Table 2 The technological frontier

Technologies	EU: Important projects of common European Interest (IPCEI 2018–2021)	US: Supply chains—100 day review under President Biden's Executive Order 14017 (February–June 2021)
#1	Semiconductors	Semiconductor manufacturing and advanced packaging
#2	Batteries (two programmes)	Large capacity batteries
#3	Hydrogen	Critical minerals and materials
#4	. . .	Pharmaceuticals and advanced pharmaceutical ingredients (APIs)

Source: Author's elaboration on European Commission and White House official documents (2018–2021)

life sciences: the successes we mentioned above (i.e. BioNTech and Moderna) speak for themselves.

(iii) The tool for activating a supranational cooperation among EU nations already exists: these are the 'Important Project (s) of Common European Interest (IPCEI)'. Following its first project on semiconductors (December 2018) and two subsequent programmes for batteries (December 2019 and January 2021), there is currently a call for offers on the third project: hydrogen. It follows that life sciences should become fertile ground for a new EU-wide initiative. A comparison with the recent 'America's Supply Chains' initiative (The White House, 2021) is highly significant in this regard and can offer useful and forward-looking insights. Table 2 shows the three IPCEI developing at the EU level, and at the same time the four 'key products' at the centre of the President Biden's Executive Order 14017.[9]

(iv) As far as supranational cooperation goes, we should mention—from an institutional point of view—the creation of the European Health Emergency Preparedness and Response Authority (HERA), an institution that will theoretically be based on the model of the Biomedical Advanced Research and Development Authority (BARDA) in the US (Lo Turco, 2021). In the European Commission's words: 'The COVID-19 pandemic demonstrated the need for coordinated EU level action to respond to health emergencies. It revealed gaps in foresight, including demand/supply dimensions, preparedness and response tools. A European HERA is a central element for strengthening the European Health Union with better EU preparedness and response to serious cross-border

[9] In their *Introductory Note* to the President, Brian Deese (National Economic Council Director) and Jake Sullivan (National Security Advisor) write: 'It is our privilege to transmit to you the first set of reports that your Administration has developed pursuant to Executive Order 14017, "America's Supply Chains." The enclosed reports assess supply chains vulnerabilities across four key products that you directed your Administration to review within 100 days (. . .)' (White House, 2021, 4).

health threats, by enabling rapid availability, access and distribution of needed countermeasures.'[10]

5 Conclusion

The time to deliberately consider the role of the state in the economy during a pandemic seems to have truly arrived in the EU. This is especially true for industrial policy, which has always (as we mentioned at the beginning) been one of the most debated and controversial areas of public policy—a kind of 'ugly duckling' from the fairy tales.

There is a 'new' industrial policy that the European Commission—after taking into consideration developments in the economic literature—has developed over the last two decades but which has had trouble making its way into concrete action by the government of the EU-28 (now 27). This is the right time, then, to elude the grasp of the status quo and set our sights on greater supranational cooperation, especially in the field of *knowledge-based investments* (R&D, human capital, ICTs), which represent the backbone of an industrial policy that hopes to keep pace with the times in today's world.

Draghi (2014), in a commemoration of Tommaso Padoa-Schioppa, recalled the virtues of supranational cooperation in the field of 'structural reforms', following what had previously been done in the field of fiscal policy. Knowledge-based investments (or *technological policy*), representing the third side of the 'industrial policy triangle' (Cohen & Lorenzi, 2000),[11] must be woven into the concept of structural reforms to be carried out at the EU-level. Let's consider an important example that can give us, as Europeans, a just reason for hope. In fact, many lessons can be gleaned from the success story of CERN in Geneva, which represents an extraordinary example of the virtue of cooperation among many nations in a scientific field that is at the forefront of technological progress.[12] Here lies that crucial element of basic research where the necessary requirements in terms of capital—human, financial or technological—are often above and beyond the capabilities of single nation-states. Let's put it this way: at the beginning there was particle physics, and today there is—and will continue to be—medical and pharmaceutical research against all coronaviruses. Now is the time for something like the 'CERN of pharma and biomedical research' to be shaped. To conclude with

[10] See the European Commission's website: https://ec.europa.eu/info/law/better-regulation/have-your-say/initiatives/12870-European-Health-Emergency-Preparedness-and-Response-Authority-HERA-_en

[11] The two other sides are *competition policy* and commercial (*trade) policy*.

[12] Admittedly, this is not an Institution or an EU Agency in the narrow sense of the word (like a Parliament, Commission, Council, Court of Justice, etc.), but in its essence, it is a European institution.

a *reductio ad unum*, this is the ultimate significance of the four-fold policy agenda that we have outlined above.

References

Cohen, E., & Lorenzi, J. H. (2000). *Politiques industrielles pour l'Europe*. Conseil d'analyse économique, Rapport 26, La Documentation Française.

Draghi, M. (2014, July 9). *Memorial lecture in honour of Tommaso Padoa-Schioppa*. Speech by the President of the ECB. https://www.ecb.europa.eu/press/key/date/2014/html/sp140709_2.en.html

European Commission. (1993, December). *Growth, competitiveness, employment: The challenges and ways forward into the 21st century*. [White Paper]. COM(1993)700. European Commission.

European Commission. (2002, December). *Industrial policy in an enlarged Europe*. [White Paper] COM(2002) 714. European Commission.

European Commission. (2020, March). *A new industrial strategy for Europe*. [White Paper] COM(2020) 102. European Commission.

European Commission. (2021, May). *Updating the 2020 new industrial strategy: Building a stronger single market for Europe's recovery*. [White Paper] COM(2021) 350. European Commission.

European Commission & Joint Research Centre. (2020, December). *EU industrial & research and development scoreboard*. European Commission.

Fondazione Universitaria Economia Tor Vergata. (2021). *Revitalizing anaemic Europe*. [White Paper] "Gruppo dei 20". http://www-2019.fondazionetorvergataeconomia.it/gruppo-dei-20/

Ganuza, J. J., Llobet, G., & Domínguez, B. (2009). R&D in the pharmaceutical industry: A world of small innovations. *Management Science, 55*(4), 539–551.

González, P., Macho-Stadler, I., & Pérez-Castrillo, D. (2016). Private versus social incentives for pharmaceutical innovation. *Journal of Health Economics, 50*, 286–297.

Jacquemin, A. (1987). *The new industrial organization: Market forces and strategic behaviour*. MIT Press.

Lo Turco, A. (2021, April 9). *Vaccini anti-Covid: perché l'Europa ne produce pochi*. http://www.lavoce.info

Ministero dell'Economia e delle Finanze (MEF). (2021, April). *Piano Nazionale di Ripresa e Resilienza*. https://www.mef.gov.it/focus/Il-Piano-Nazionale-di-Ripresa-e-Resilienza-PNRR/

Mosconi, F. (2012, November). *The "Jacquemin-Rodrik" Synthesis and the design of a new European industrial policy, Pavia, polo interregionale di eccellenza Jean Monnet*. http://www.jeanmonnet-pv.it/Jean_Monnet_Centre_of_Excellence/publications_files/F_mosconi_jm_summary.pdf

Mosconi, F. (2015a). The new industrial policy in Europe a decade after (2002–2012). In M. Yülek (Ed.), *Economic planning and industrial policy in the globalizing economy. Concepts, experience and prospects* (pp. 207–238). Springer.

Mosconi, F. (2015b). The new European industrial policy. In *Global competitiveness and the manufacturing renaissance*. Routledge.

Mosconi, F. (2022, forthcoming). European industrial policy from 2000 to 2020. In: J.-C. Defraigne, J. Wouters, E. Traversa, & D. Zurstrassen (Eds.), EU industrial policy in the multipolar economy. Edward Elgar.

Rodrik, D. (2004). *Industrial policy for the twenty-first century*. HKS Working Paper No. RWP04–047. John F. Kennedy School of Government. https://www.hks.harvard.edu/publications/industrial-policy-twenty-first-century

Rodrik, D. (2008). *Normalizing industrial policy*. Commission on growth and development, Working Paper No. 3. https://drodrik.scholar.harvard.edu/publications/normalizing-industrial-policy

Rodrik, D. (2010, July 12–16). *Remarks as part of the economist debate*: *Industrial policy: This house believes that industrial policy always fails.* The Economist (online) (www.economist.com).

Sapir, A., Aghion, P., Bertola, S., Hellwig, M., Pisani-Ferry, J., Rosati, D., et al. (2004). *An agenda for a growing Europe: The Sapir report*. Oxford University Press.

White House. (2021, June). *Building resilient supply chains, revitalizing American manufacturing, and fostering broad-based growth.* 100-Day Reviews under Executive Order 14017. The White House. https://www.whitehouse.gov/wp-content/uploads/2021/06/100-day-supply-chain-review-report.pdf

Assessing Next Generation EU

Lorenzo Codogno and Paul van den Noord

1 Introduction

The magnitude of the Covid-19 shock to the European and global economics is unprecedented in post-war history, dwarfing the impact of the financial crisis that erupted a decade ago and that was already of historic significance.

The mechanisms through which the pandemic has affected the economy are multiple, including sharp increases in uncertainty, falls in certain strands of household consumption, the disruption of supply chains and the devastating impact of policies to stem the pandemic, such as social distancing, lockdowns and travel bans.

The recession after the financial crisis could also be described as the result of demand shocks stemming from a major deleveraging effort by households, governments, banks and businesses. The pandemic is affecting the economy both through demand and supply shocks striking at the same time.

The macroeconomic policy responses to mitigate the economic impact of the pandemic have been equally unprecedented, both in Europe and globally. In Europe, policy action at both the national and supranational levels involved state guarantees on bank loans, compensations for income losses for the most heavily affected

---

Lesson from COVID-19. A strong EU: Staying together in a new policy space. Edited by Luigi Paganetto, Tor Vergata University, Rome.

L. Codogno
London School of Economics and Political Science, London, UK
e-mail: l.codogno@lse.ac.uk

P. van den Noord (✉)
Amsterdam School of Economics, Amsterdam, Netherlands
e-mail: p.j.vandennoord@uva.nl

L. Paganetto (ed.), *Economic Challenges for Europe After the Pandemic*,
Springer Proceedings in Business and Economics,
https://doi.org/10.1007/978-3-031-10302-5_5

entrepreneurs and workers, and the postponement of tax collection. Alongside national fiscal policy relief, the pandemic prompted unprecedented action also at the EU level. Most significantly, the Covid-19 pandemic broke the taboo on a pan-European fiscal policy, with the package dubbed 'Next Generation EU' (Verwey et al., 2020). For the first time in the history of the EU, large scale bond issuance at the centre is used to finance top-down grants and loans to national governments.

The literature on the impact of the pandemic and the ensuing policy responses is rapidly expanding. Still, so far there has been no strong focus on estimating the pandemic's effect on the Eurozone economy. Its hallmark is the centralisation of monetary policy with an incomplete banking union and a large degree of fiscal policy autonomy (though subject to coordination). The vulnerabilities in this set-up are well known, including the risk that fiscal and banking distress can be mutually reinforcing and that a lack of fiscal capacity at the centre leads to an excessive (and politically contentious) reliance on monetary policy.

Many calls have been made for Eurozone reform, including the creation of a European safe asset to replace national sovereign bonds in their role as collateral for banks in repos and inter-bank loans (Alogoskoufis & Langfield, 2019; Bénassy-Quéré et al., 2018; Leandro & Zettelmeyer, 2018). Proposals have also been put forward to create a fiscal capacity at the centre of the euro area to finance deficit spending (Arnold et al., 2018). It is a version of the latter proposal that now appears to be materialising in response to the pandemic. However, the approach is ex post, ad hoc, and geared towards (politically contentious) fiscal transfers between Member States. The central tenet of the present paper is that now there is an opportunity to develop a framework for ex ante risk sharing which would contain the need for fiscal transfers. The creation of a safe asset, based on the new bonds issued by the EU in response to the pandemic, is a key element of this alternative proposal.

The paper is set up as follows. Section 2 briefly reviews the policies that have been adopted in the EU/Eurozone to mitigate the macroeconomic impact of the pandemic, including Next Generation EU. In Sect. 3 we develop the case for an alternative approach in which, at least in the Eurozone, ex-post risk-sharing (whereby the EU funds transfers to the most hard-hit countries) is replaced with a system of ex-ante risk-sharing built into the governance framework of the Eurozone—with an essential role for a single safe asset. In Sect. 4, we tentatively quantify the differences in impact responses between these two approaches in the face of the pandemic shock, using a stylised calibrated macroeconomic model for the Eurozone (reported in the Annex). Section 5 concludes the paper.

2 Policy Responses to Date

On 21 July 2020, the European Council adopted a 750bn euros package (around 7% of the EU's GDP) to allocate funding to governments in distress due to the pandemic. The novelty of the package is its financing, which is based on the issuance of EU bonds against the EU budget, with the debt servicing funded by (a slightly increased) EU budget. The programme contains the following elements:

1. The bulk of the fiscal expansion is provided in the form of grants and loans to Member States by the Recovery and Resiliency Facility (RRF) amounting to 312.5bn euros and 360bn euros, respectively, summing up to roughly 5% of the EU's GDP. While the exact parameters depend on GDP and unemployment in 2020–2021, the intention is to spread out the transfers over the 2021–2026 period, with the biggest part of the support going to those countries that have been hit the most by the crisis.
2. Alongside the RRF, Member States would receive 77.5bn euros in a range of other programmes, of which 47.5bn euros are for 'ReactEU' and 10bn euros for the 'Just Transition Fund'. All other programmes, which include Horizon Europe, InvestEU, Rural Development, RescEU, amount to 20bn euros.

This package came on the heels of the adoption by European Council of another set of measures in the spring of 2020 worth 540bn euros (around 5% of GDP), comprising up to 100bn euros for a European unemployment fund ("SURE"), 200bn euros worth of SME loans by the European Investment Bank (EIB) and a 240bn euros credit line made available by the European Stability Mechanism (ESM) for funding health-related expenditure (this latter so far not used). These amounts are envelopes, and not all the amounts may be taken up. This, in turn, came on top of massive national fiscal stimulus, with discretionary measures of about 4.5% of the EU's GDP.

As noted, the bulk of the funds are channelled through the Recovery and Resilience Facility. Each country has a right to claim a fraction of the total pot for grants and loans, based on a prior agreed formula relying on a set of objective indicators. Figure 1 depicts the original allocation of Next Generation EU funding throughout the Member States, broken down into grants and loans, although only part of the loans have so far been asked by countries. Figure 2 shows the estimated Next Generation EU cash flows over time, together with the cash flows from the European Commission's Support to mitigate Unemployment Risks in an Emergency (SURE) programme and the support from the European Stability Mechanism (ESM), if it is activated.

Next Generation EU is a commendable endeavour. It aims to lift public investment with a three-pronged objective: (i) boosting aggregate demand; (ii) supporting the most hard-hit countries in the pursuit of cohesion; and (iii) strengthening the economic growth potential of the Union (e.g. Verwey et al., 2020; European Commission, 2020a, 2020b; European Council, 2020). Indeed, Next Generation EU is about more than just supplementing demand in the short and medium run. It is the EU's 'Roosevelt moment' (Van den Noord, 2020), not only aiming to compensate the near-term collapse in demand, but also promoting deep structural reforms and reallocating resources to raise the economy's growth potential and achieve common policy objectives such as climate control.

It could be argued that it is more of a medium-term project and it has no ambition as a means of macroeconomic stabilisation. This latter function is left to national

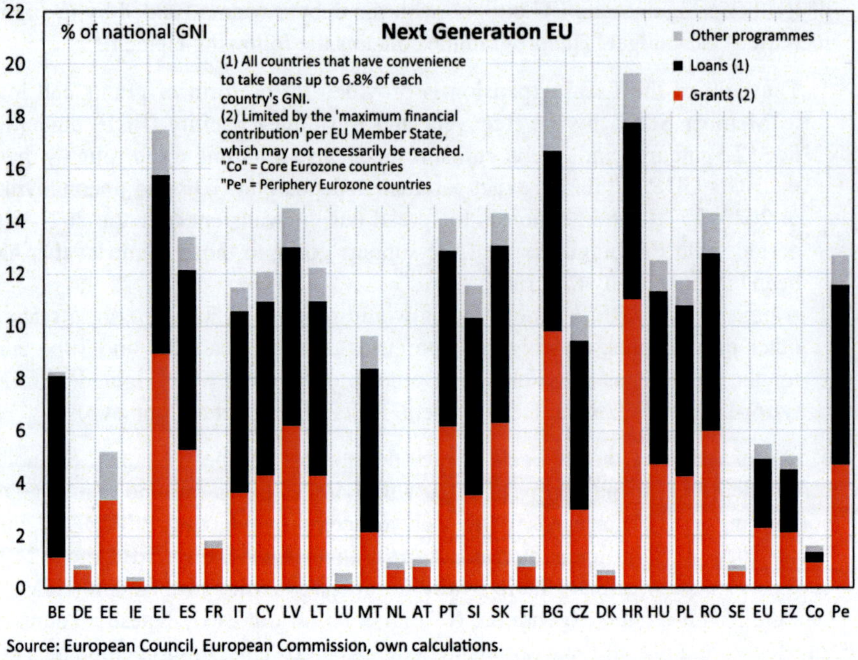

Fig. 1 Next Generation EU—allocation across Member States

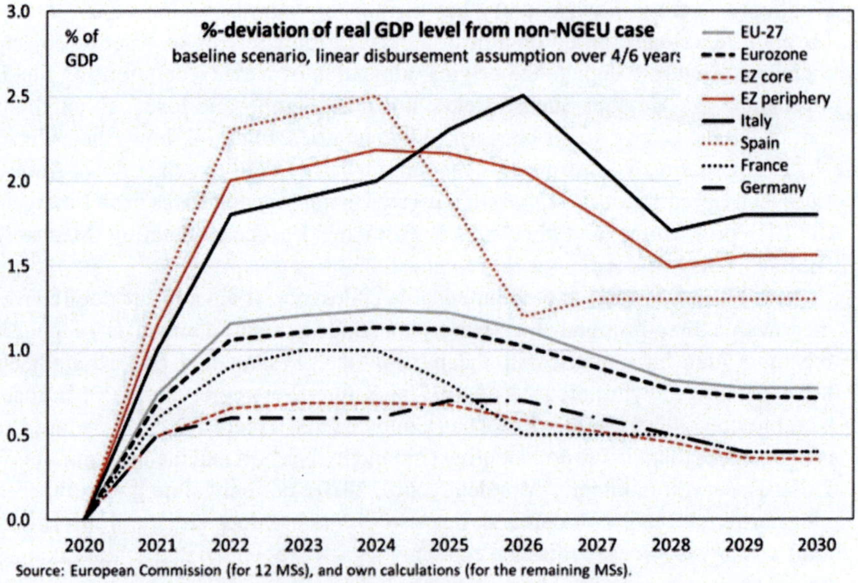

Fig. 2 Next Generation EU, estimated impact on GDP, baseline scenario

budgets instead and is helped by the suspension of budgetary rules. Yet, in the Recovery and Resilience Facility, the word 'Recovery' stands for macro stabilisation support, although not as timely as it would be desirable in the current circumstances.

The pandemic can be seen as an example *par excellence* of a common shock hitting the 'periphery' of the Eurozone asymmetrically more strongly than the 'core' in a context where the former was already more vulnerable than the latter. In such an environment, monetary policy can only partially absorb the shock, while debt sustainability concerns heavily constrained fiscal policy in the periphery. The standard policy prescription—reforms of product and labour markets in the pursuit of smooth adjustment, and fiscal consolidation to build up fiscal buffers—cannot be used to address the acute emergency either.

Against this backdrop, the New Generation EU approach appears as a rational response. Using conservative assumptions on the multiplier effects, the European Commission (Pfeiffer et al., 2021) shows an impact of about 1.2 pp. on the level of GDP by 2023, but it is twice as much for the Eurozone periphery (Fig. 2),[1] in the baseline scenario.

Yet, the approach is subject to several risks, which are common to most EU policy initiatives that rely on countries submitting their own plans (even when subject to coordination such as the European Semester), and of which some are acknowledged to have long plagued the effectiveness of EU projects (see Van den Noord, 2020):

- The additionality of the plans may turn out limited as countries use EU funds to finance existing projects or projects that would have been undertaken anyway. In that case, support funding can, at the most, limit the deficit/debt increase of countries with limited fiscal space, or simply represent cheap funding in the case of loans.
- Countries could shun the take-up of conditional loans, preferring grants and market loans without strings attached (Spain and other countries have decided not to ask for loans, for now). The latter are cheap even for the worst affected countries owing to the ECB's quantitative easing and the indirect effects of the common bond issuance of the EU package itself.
- Countries have limited administrative absorption capacity of projects: experience shows that money is left on the table because countries are unable to initiate adequate proposals which, at any rate, may clash with capacity constraints among private contractors or crowd out other viable activities.
- Countries may be tempted to channel EU funding to social transfers or tax cuts or to launch pet infrastructure projects that are not financially viable, which may result in a waste of resources.
- Spreading funds too thinly over small projects without a common strategy could lead to resources being misallocated or again wasted.

[1] Core includes Belgium, Germany, France, Netherlands, Austria, Finland, Luxembourg, Estonia and Ireland. All other Eurozone countries are included in the periphery.

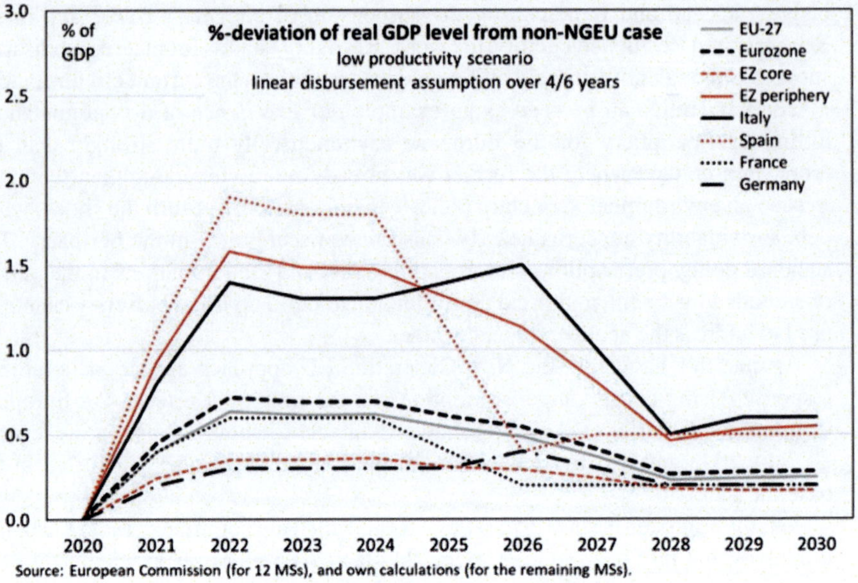

Fig. 3 Next Generation EU, GDP impact in the low-productivity scenario

The European Commission (Pfeiffer et al., 2021) presents also a 'low-productivity scenario' in which the near-term effect is almost as strong as in the baseline scenario, but it vanishes over the projection horizon as investment has a reduced capacity to increase the stock of productive capital (Fig. 3).

Because of the bottom-up planning and submission of projects, and the desire to leave ownership to the Member States, EU-wide projects are unlikely to be of sufficient weight. Therefore, the spillover effects inherent to large EU-wide infrastructure projects may be small as well (according to the same paper by the Commission, the spillover effect is about 0.35 percentage-points over 2021–2025 for the overall Eurozone). Sometimes, the scale of such investments may be too large for national administrations to handle on their own. Not only do individual countries fail to internalise positive spillovers, but they also find it inherently complicated to work together on large trans-border projects. In a way, the subsidiarity principle would argue for the top-down, rather than bottom-up, approach in the case of large infrastructure projects.

3 An Alternative Approach

All in all, Next Generation EU, in combination with the spring package and the national fiscal policies, looks set to provide major relief to absorb the pandemic shock, at least over the medium run, notwithstanding our reservations. But it comes with a price, which is of a political economy nature. Specifically, the policies currently in place rely to a large extent on ad hoc transfers from the core to the periphery via the EU budget. This is not something that can be easily replicated in future calamities—be they a next pandemic, a migration crisis or a climate catastrophe. Our alternative proposal laid out below, in contrast, being largely rules-based and relying on (ex-ante) risk-sharing so as to stem the 'doom loop', may be more sustainable. This is the primary motivation for our approach, which contains the following elements:

1. A 'safe asset' is issued at the Centre and underpinned by a stable revenue source, i.e. a proper central tax base or an obligation of national governments to secure a predictable revenue flow to the Centre. According to our proposal the amount issued should immediately reach at least 30–40% of the EU's GDP. Then, it is swapped at market prices for national sovereigns on the balance sheets of banks. It replaces national sovereign bonds in their role as collateral for banks in repos and inter-bank loans. Moreover, the safe asset enjoys exclusive eligibility for ECB asset purchases. It thus replaces national sovereign bonds on the ECB's balance sheet. To allow proper price discovery, a sizeable enough new issuance of the safe asset will precede the swap operation.
2. The safe asset receives seniority over national sovereign bonds. This also ensures that it is seen as an attractive investment for banks. The profit banks generate by the sale of sovereign bonds is allowed to be spread over several years. This is to smooth the transition to a bank business model that no longer relies on carry trades with sovereign bonds and to allow sufficient time for banks to achieve higher profitability from other sources. The swap operation would not imply any fiscal transfer. The ECB would enable banks to close in advance their financing operations to offset the selling of national sovereign bonds on their balance sheet.
3. Beyond the issuance of the safe asset to purchase national sovereigns, the role of the central fiscal capacity could be expanded to allow borrowing for the purposes of fiscal stabilisation policy. The ECB would be allowed to purchase the safe asset in the secondary market, as is already the case for debt issued by supranational EU agencies (such as the ESM). This would underpin the safe asset's role as a liquid, risk-free benchmark.

As noted, the total amount of safe assets needed to purchase national sovereigns in the hands of the ECB and on the balance sheets of the banks would be at least 30–40% of GDP. This implies that, on average over the cycle, the issuer of the safe asset would need a revenue flow roughly in the range of 0.5–1.0% of GDP, the bulk of it being covered by interest receipts on the national sovereigns owned at the Centre.

The additional issuance of the safe asset in bad times to fund deficit spending at the Centre depends on the depth of the slump. It could—according to the model simulation discussed below—be in the range of 5–10% of GDP in the current exceptional circumstances. If this were repaid over a period of 10 years, it would require an additional annual revenue flow to the Centre in the range of 0.5% and 1% of GDP, given that the yield would be low in today's conditions.

Aside from the stabilisation effects of this package (see below), the financial and policy landscape of the euro area would permanently improve. The replacement of national sovereigns with a safe asset on bank's balance sheets serves to break the 'doom loop' between the cost of bank funding and sovereign yields in the euro area 'periphery'. With the safe asset enjoying exclusive eligibility for the purposes of quantitative easing, the ECB would obtain a monetary policy instrument that does not interfere with national fiscal policies via national sovereign debt purchases. Moreover, as large amounts of national debt are swapped with safe European-level debt, the default risk at the national level is reduced, with fewer calls on rescue programmes.

4 A Numerical Comparison

We use a stylised macroeconomic model (see Annex) to compute the impact of the pandemic and policy responses thereupon over the medium run. The model distinguishes two economies, 'core' and 'periphery', with the latter prone to financial instability due to high public debt—much of it owned by local banks alongside loan books whose quality is (also) questionable. This gives rise to an adverse feedback loop between high public debt and weak banks, usually referred to as the 'doom loop'. Importantly, this mechanism gives rise to asymmetries in shock-responses, even in the case of a symmetric shock, with the 'periphery' more adversely hit. As explained in the Annex, the model parameters are calibrated on the basis of empirical findings in the mainstream literature and as such, not controversial. Even so, the model is necessarily a simplification of reality. Hence the numbers should not be taken as precise estimates but rather as broad indicators of the direction and order of magnitude of the effects.

In Sect. 4.1, we present the computed shock responses with regard to the actual policies (national and supranational) that were put in place in the Eurozone in the spring. We proceed in two steps, broadly reflecting the chronology of events. First, we look at the impact of the outbreak and both the national and pan-European responses which were shaped during the initial stages of the outbreak, including domestic fiscal stimulus, SURE, the ESM credit line as well as the ECB's monetary policy response. This is labelled as 'scenario I'. Next, we ship in Next Generation EU alongside the shocks and measures mentioned above, with the results marked 'scenario II'.

The thrust of the findings is that the initial policies embedded in scenario I fail to sufficiently mitigate the impact of the shock and that Next Generation EU, therefore, proves vital. However, as discussed in Sect. 4.2, better outcomes could be achieved by the approach laid out in Sect. 3 in which an alternative macroeconomic policy and governance framework is assumed, labelled 'Scenario III'. Specifically, in light of the discussion in Sect. 3 we assume (i) a single Eurobond to replace national bonds on banks' balance sheets so as to break the link between banking and sovereign distress, (ii) Eurozone fiscal capacity, including automatic stabilisers

Table 1 Impact-responses

Scenario	Actual policy		*III*	Scenario	Actual policy		*III*
	I	II	I	II			
Output (%)				*Primary deficit ratio (percentage-pts)*			
Core	−11.3	−4.2	−1.0	Core	8.2	4.4	2.9
Periphery	−16.6	−2.8	−2.9	Periphery	12.8	5.4	5.2
Aggregate	−13.9	−3.5	−1.9	Central	0.4	3.9	4.4
Inflation (%)				*Debt ratio (percentage-pts)*			
Core	−1.6	0.2	1.0	Core	14.7	6.8	6.5
Periphery	−4.5	2.4	2.3	Periphery	41.9	13.1	10.0
Aggregate	−3.1	1.3	1.7	Central	0.4	7.5	8.0
Yields (percentage-pts)				*Fiscal stance (percentage-pts)*			
Core	0.1	−0.1	0.3	Core	2.6	2.3	2.6
Periphery	6.4	0.8	1.6	Periphery	4.5	4.1	4.5
Central	3.2	−1.5	−1.0	Central	0.4	3.9	3.9
Bank credit (%)				*Monetary policy (percentage-pts)*			
Core	−12.1	−3.2	2.3	Policy rate	−0.3	−0.3	−0.3
Periphery	−48.7	−2.4	3.3	Asset purchase	24.6	24.6	12.3

Note: Scenarios refer to: I = National fiscal responses + SURE + monetary policy, II = I + 'Next Generation EU', III = Safe asset + permanent fiscal capacity

and discretionary (but rules-based) policy, and (iii) a new quantitative easing (QE) scheme that mandates the ECB to purchase Eurobonds (while national sovereigns lose QE eligibility and those still on the ECB's balance sheet are swapped for Eurobonds as well).

The results are reported in Table 1 and Figs. 4 and 5, which show the cumulative impact of the shocks or policies in the medium run relative to a steady-state baseline without shocks or changes in policy stances.

4.1 Actual Policy

The first column in Table 1, labelled 'I', shows the combined impact of the supply, demand and risk premium shocks attributed to the pandemic as well as the first set of policy responses. As explained in the Annex, the following exogenous impulses have been included:

1. The core and the periphery are hit by an adverse demand shock of respectively −10% and −15% of GDP and an adverse supply shock of respectively −5% and −7.5% of GDP. This is a crude gauge of the Covid-19 shock, but roughly in the ballpark of a recent estimate by Gomez-Pineda (2020). We also include a favorable risk premium shock of −200 bps in the core due to a flight to safety in

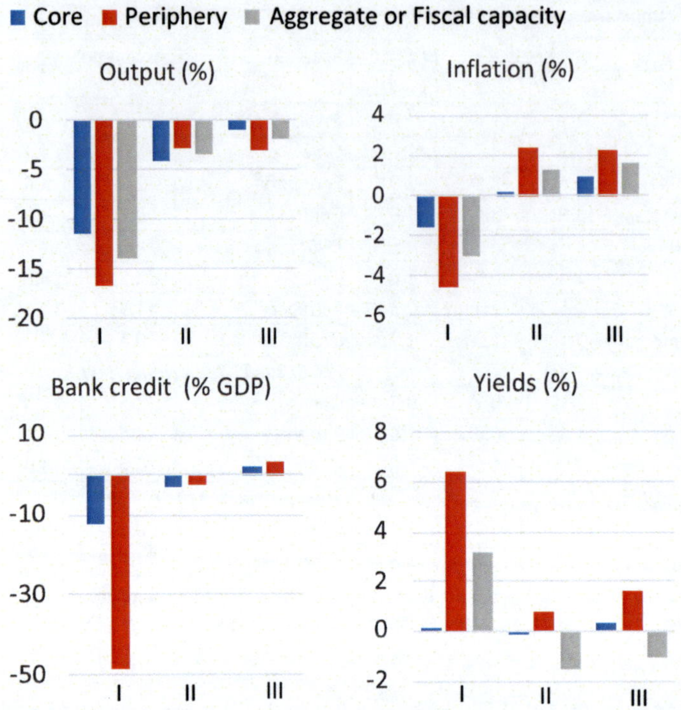

Fig. 4 Impact-responses of key macroeconomic variables

capital markets (this is aside from the endogenous change in the yield spread in response to the changes in debt positions embedded in the model).

2. Monetary policy stimulus consisting of a sustained 25 bp cut in the policy rate[2] and asset purchases amounting to 12.3% of GDP per annum sustained for 2 years.[3] We also assume an exogenous cut in the periphery sovereign yield by 200 bps, over and above the endogenous impact of the ECB's asset purchases, to reflect the availability of the new ESM credit line (even though this may never be used because of the stigma effect impacting the governments in office).
3. Domestic fiscal stimulus—gauged by an increase in the primary deficit—amounted to 6.2 percentage points of GDP in the core and 7.9 percentage points of GDP in the periphery.[4] Besides, we factor in the pan-EU measures adopted in

[2] This refers to the PELTROs which are available at a rate 25 bps below the REFI of −0.5%.

[3] This comprises the additional envelope of the Asset Purchase Programme (APP) of 120 billion euros adopted in March 2020 and the Pandemic Emergency Purchase Programme (PEPP) with an envelope of 1350 billion euros adopted in June 2020 (including an initial envelope of 750 billion euros adopted in March). Both are assumed to be extended by another year to a total of 2940 billion euros or 24.6% of 2019 GDP.

[4] Estimates based on Bruegel (2020), with some modifications.

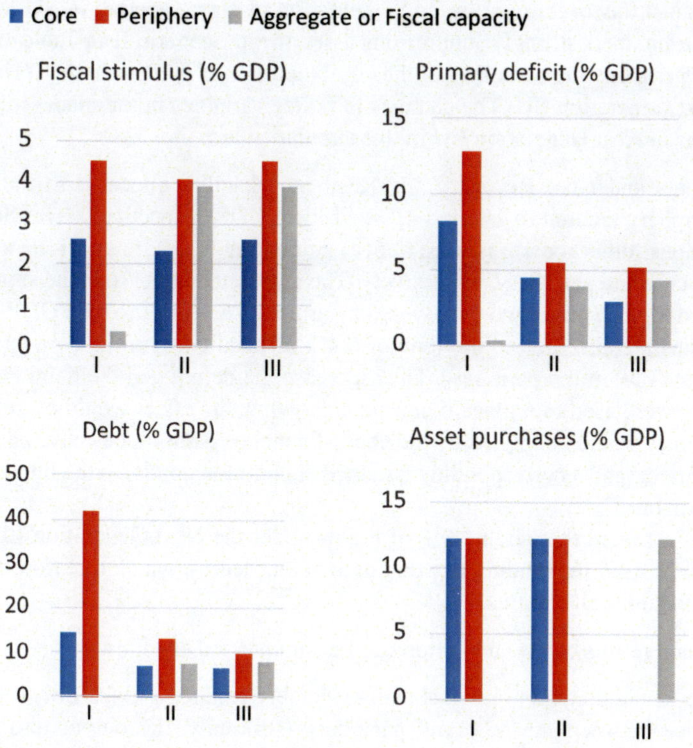

Fig. 5 Impact-responses of key policy variables

the spring, such as SURE, that involve fiscal stimulus of the order 0.9% of GDP (0.1 percentage points in the core and 1.9 percentage-points in the periphery).

The results indicate that the initial policy measures taken in the spring would not suffice to rein in the adverse impact of the pandemic to a satisfactory extent. The Eurozone's accumulated loss of real GDP would add up to almost 14%, with the core losing 11% and the periphery losing more than 16%. The periphery-core sovereign yield spread widens by an average of 630 bps, severely compromising the funding of periphery banks, as reflected in a near collapse of bank credit. Periphery sovereign debt would soar by over 40% of GDP.

If these numbers are anything to go by, the need for additional measures is clear. As Commission officials (Verwey et al., 2020) put it: "as impressive as these measures are, they will not be enough to ensure a rapid recovery and to avoid permanent damage to the EU economy", with "large negative second-round effects on investment, employment, growth and prosperity." Moreover, "beyond the short term, countries will unavoidably be left with significantly higher debt to be financed in the future—a particular challenge for countries that already had elevated debt and deficit levels before the pandemic struck."

Against this backdrop, the implementation of New Generation EU looks vital, and our numbers strongly support this assessment. Scenario II in Table 1 and Figs. 4 and 5 embody the outcomes of the combined sets of policies in the spring as well as Next Generation EU. The changes in policy variables in the model to gauge the policies in Next Generation EU in this simulation are:

1. Grants under the Recovery and Resilience Facility allocated to the core and periphery amount to 1% and 4.7% of local GDP, respectively. This adds to the various 'other measures' (see above) amounting to 0.25% and 1.1% of GDP in the core and periphery, respectively. The associated increase in the supranational (underlying) primary deficit would be around 3.5% of Eurozone GDP.
2. Loans are allocated to the tune of 0.4% of local GDP in the core and 6.8% of local GDP in the periphery. They increase the deficit and the debt. However, if they were used to replace domestic borrowing, the effect would be zero and the country would simply enjoy the cheap financing. Still, it does have an impact on EU debt (and a corresponding issuance of common bonds) to the tune of 3.5% of Eurozone GDP.
3. It is assumed that about 20% of grants under the Next Generation EU package will be used for funding existing national measures, which therefore reduce the national fiscal stimulus.

The main results of the simulation can be summarised as follows:

1. The accumulated output loss is considerably smaller (−3.5%), with less divergence between the core and periphery (strikingly, the output loss would be slightly smaller in the core than in the periphery). The yield spread would be neutralized, while bank credit would not shrink. The aggregate price level would show an increase as opposed to the deflationary impact in Scenario I.
2. On the fiscal side, we see the primary deficits at the national level increasing substantially by over 4% of GDP in the core and over 5% of GDP in the periphery. Yet, especially in the periphery, this is a much smaller increase than in Scenario I, which is helped by a more favorable macroeconomic environment, less prevalent automatic fiscal stabilisers and the use of transfers from the Centre to fund national programmes. The same holds for the public debt position. In Scenario I, the public debt ratios in the core and periphery soar, respectively, by almost 15% and 42% of GDP, but in Scenario II, these increases amount to only 7% and 13% of GDP. Meanwhile, public debt at the Centre in Scenario II would be 7.5% of Eurozone GDP instead of only less than 0.5% in Scenario I.

4.2 The Alternative Approach

Scenario III incorporates the impact of policies under the alternative approach discussed in Sect. 3. The computations are based on the following assumptions:

1. We maintain all national policy measures as well as the creation of the ESM credit line as assumed in Scenarios I and II. We also take the supranational fiscal stimulus (both loans and grants) on aggregate to be the same as in Scenario II, but instead with the fiscal stimulus used to fund pan-European (as opposed to national) programmes and projects. The rationale for this choice is to avoid crowding out national spending programmes and to stay in line with the subsidiarity principle, as discussed in Sect. 3. We also slash the ECB asset purchases by half.
2. Alongside discretionary fiscal expansion at the Centre, we assume supranational automatic fiscal stabilizers to cater for some horizontal redistribution. This could be the result of a centralised unemployment insurance or re-insurance scheme or the creation of a rules-based European buffer fund (see Van den Noord, 2020), for example. Specifically, we assume that for every 1 percentage point contraction in national GDP, there is an automatic transfer of 0.2 percentage-points of national GDP. This transfer replaces equivalent national automatic stabilsers to provide genuine fiscal relief.
3. We assume that a safe asset (the same common bond that is issued to raise money for fiscal stimulus at the Centre) is created and swapped for national sovereigns on banks' balance sheets to remove the bank-sovereign doom loop. We also assume that the safe asset has been made eligible for purchases by the ECB while national sovereigns lose this eligibility. Hence all asset purchases carried out by the ECB in this scenario refer to purchases of the safe asset.

The main results can be summarized as follows:

1. The aggregate stabilisation is slightly more potent than in Scenario II, though this is entirely attributable to the stabilisation of output in the core. This is not surprising given the absence of (discretionary) fiscal transfers to the periphery. Yet the periphery is not (much) worse off relative to Scenario II. On the other hand, the yield spread of the periphery widens somewhat relative to Scenario II, reflecting the absence of sovereign debt purchases by the ECB. Still, without affecting bank lending by much as the doom loop is now broken.
2. The fiscal-monetary policy mix has shifted towards the former, with the aggregate fiscal deficit at the Centre widening slightly more than in Scenario II—as the supra-national automatic stabilisers kick in—and the asset purchases halves. Since the ECB would purchase the common bond only, its yield is now disconnected from the national yields and falls relative to them. Even so, the total increase in government indebtedness (be it national or supranational) is not much different in Scenario III as compared to Scenario II. On the other hand, the supranational debt numbers reported in the table and figure refer to consolidated gross debt, which is without the purchases of national sovereign debt by the fiscal capacity at the centre and the issuance of supranational debt (the safe asset) to finance these purchases.

All in all, with a safe asset and a (partly rules-based) fiscal capacity, even more of the pandemic shock would be absorbed, with less quantitative easing needed.

Moreover, the asset purchases would be directed to the safe asset rather than national sovereigns and hence avoid the political conflict this could entail and the need to keep the purchases in check with the capital key. Even more importantly, there are no ad hoc transfers from the core to the periphery via the EU budget. The transfers that remain are rules-based, relying on the automatic stabilisers built in social security systems.

The current policy response could be seen as a second best, i.e. a less efficient way to respond to an economic shock, although still powerful, if not vital. But as noted, it cannot be easily repeated in the future without political economy setbacks. Therefore, it would be worthwhile to consider a more permanent macroeconomic stabilisation mechanism in the future along the lines of our proposal.

5 Conclusions

The EU/Eurozone policy response to the pandemic crisis is unprecedented and impressive, putting together monetary, fiscal and regulatory aspects/areas. The macroeconomic stabilisation role is implicitly given to monetary policy and national budgets, with Next Generation EU mostly focused on delivering investment projects and reforms that will increase resilience and enhance potential growth over time. In this paper, we argue that this policy response should be effective in mitigating the impact of the economic shock.

However, the EU fiscal package is one-off, will become effective with a delay, and relies on politically delicate fiscal transfers. An automatic mechanism based on a centralised fiscal capacity and a safe asset would have produced a better outcome in stabilising the economy, without any risk of the doom loop between the sovereigns and the banks, and without impinging on the ability of the central bank to manage monetary policy effectively.

Therefore, policymakers should consider moving from an ad hoc policy response to a more permanent mechanism in the future.

A.1 Annex: A Stylised Model

In an earlier paper (Codogno & van den Noord, 2019) we developed a model to examine how a new set of policy tools—in particular, a safe asset and fiscal capacity at the centre—could improve the resilience of the Eurozone economy to (symmetric or asymmetric) demand and supply shocks. In a subsequent paper (Codogno and Van den Noord, 2020), we extended this analysis to include financial risk-premium shocks stemming from, for example, deterioration of asset quality in periphery banks, political turmoil in the periphery or a fall in global risk appetite. This analysis necessitated a major extension of the model, to include explicit modelling of bond yields, bank lending and public debt dynamics. In the present paper, we have modified this model to capture the impact of the Covid-19 shock and its policy responses.

A.1.1 A.1 The Real Economy

The aggregate (log-linear) demand equations follow the standard Mundell-Fleming approach adapted to the features of a (closed) monetary union and are perfectly symmetric:

$$\begin{cases} y^d = \phi_1 l + \phi_2 \left(f + f^{€} + \ell + \ell^{€}\right) - \phi_3 \left(\pi - \pi^*\right) - \phi_4 \left(y - y^*\right) + \varepsilon^d \\ y^{*d} = \phi_1 l^* + \phi_2 \left(f^* + f^{*€} + \ell^* + \ell^{*€}\right) + \phi_3 \left(\pi - \pi^*\right) + \phi_4 \left(y - y^*\right) + \varepsilon^{*d} \end{cases} \quad (1)$$

where an asterisk (*) indicates the periphery, and variables without an asterisk refer to the core. Aggregate demand y^d and y^{*d} is determined by the supply of bank credit l and l^*, the fiscal stance—gauged by the primary government deficit f and f^*—and cross-border trade. The latter is a function of the inflation differential $\pi - \pi^*$ (a proxy for the real exchange rate) and the relative pace of economic growth $y - y^*$. In addition, we include the impact of fiscal policy conducted by the 'fiscal capacity', captured by its primary deficit as distributed to each block, denoted as $f^{€}$ and $f^{*€}$ as well as the impact of loans extended from the fiscal capacity to the national sovereigns ℓ and ℓ^*. Because these loans are below the line, they do not show up in the fiscal stance either at the centre or at the national level. However, they do have an impact on economic activity. For simplicity, the multipliers for national and supranational fiscal policy are assumed to be the same (i.e. ϕ_2). Finally, ε^d and ε^{*d} are demand shocks.

Aggregate supply y^s and y^{*s} is determined by the inflation 'surprises' $\pi - \pi^e$ and $\pi^* - \pi^{*e}$ relative to expectations (denoted by the superscript e) alongside exogenous supply shocks ε^s and ε^{*s}, via an inverted Phillips-curve:

$$\begin{cases} y^s = \left(\pi - \pi^e\right)/\omega + \varepsilon^s \\ y^{*s} = \left(\pi^* - \pi^{*e}\right)/\omega + \varepsilon^{*s} \end{cases} \quad (2)$$

Expected inflation is partly anchored in the official inflation target $\overline{\pi}^T$ and is partly backward looking and hence depends on actual domestic inflation:

$$\begin{cases} \pi^e = (1 - \eta)\,\overline{\pi}^T + \eta\pi \\ \pi^{*e} = (1 - \eta^*)\,\overline{\pi}^T + \eta^*\pi^* \end{cases} \quad (3)$$

Since all variables are defined as deviations from a steady state in which all shocks are nil, we may assume that $\overline{\pi}^T = 0$. We allow for the possibility of an asymmetry

Table 2 Numerical calibration

Real economy		Financial sector				Government sector	
		Bank credit		Bond yields			
ϕ_1	0.333	ξ_1	3.000	ϑ_1	0.500	τ	0.500
ϕ_2	0.800	ξ_2	0.130	ϑ_2	0.050	θ	0.250
ϕ_3	0.500	ξ_3	0.000	ϑ_3	0.230	χ	0.200
ϕ_4	0.500	ξ_1^*	3.000	ϑ_1^*	0.500	b_0	0.500
η	0.000	ξ_2^*	0.250	ϑ_2^*	0.100	b_0^*	1.300
η^*	0.500	ξ_3^*	4.500	ϑ_3^*	0.260	$b_0^€$	0.400
ω	0.250			σ_1	0.500		
				σ_2	0.075		

Sources: authors' calculations

in the formation of inflation expectations such that $\eta^* \geq \eta$, which means that potentially there could be greater inflation proneness in the periphery than in the core.

Finally, in equilibrium aggregate demand equals aggregate supply, hence:

$$\begin{cases} y^s = y^d = y \\ y^{*s} = y^{*d} = y^* \end{cases} \tag{4}$$

The numerical calibration of the parameters is displayed in Table 2. A crucial parameter is the fiscal multiplier ϕ_2. Mainstream estimates are of the order of 0.5, see for instance Baum et al. (2012) and Barrell et al. (2012), and we adopted this value in our earlier paper (Codogno and Van den Noord, 2020). However, as discussed in more detail in Van den Noord (2020), the magnitude of the fiscal multipliers depends inter alia on the cyclical position of the economy and whether or not a liquidity trap besets monetary policy. Therefore, we have augmented the multiplier to 0.8, crudely based on Batini et al. (2014).

With regard to the other parameters in the Eqs. (1)–(4) we resort to the calibration in Codogno & Van den Noord (2020). Specifically, for ϕ_1, capturing the impact of bank credit on the real economy (Antoshi et al., 2017) find for 39 European countries a 10% increase in bank credit to boost real GDP by 0.6–1%. However, Cappiello et al. (2010) find a much stronger effect for a panel of Eurozone members, with a 10% increase in credit leading to a 3.2% increase in real GDP. Accordingly, we adopt $\phi_1 = 0.333$. Estimates for the parameters that capture cross-border trade, comprising ϕ_3 for absorption and ϕ_4 for competitiveness, are based on Bayoumi et al. (2011) and ECB (2013), with $\phi_3 = \phi_4 = 0.5$.

For the parameter gauging the slope of the Phillips curve ω we again refer to Codogno and Van den Noord (2019), who—based on Ball et al. (2013) and Llaudes (2005)—assumed that $\omega = 0.25$. Finally, Van der Cruijsen and Demertzis (2009) find a strong dependence of inflation expectations on actual inflation in the periphery, but no such relationship in the core. Therefore, we will adopt as our baseline estimate $\eta = 0$ and $\eta^* = 0.5$.

A.1.2 A.2 The Financial Sector

A hallmark of the Eurozone predicament is the so-called 'doom loop' which refers to tensions in the sovereign debt market prompting a 'credit crunch', with the resulting economic slump feeding back into the sustainability of sovereign debt. The main channel through which tensions in sovereign debt markets affect the supply of bank credit is via the cost and the availability of wholesale funding for banks. Financial distress and the associated capital flight from the periphery to core sovereign debt raise the cost and cut the availability of funding for banks in the periphery.

It may be assumed that this source of vulnerability vanishes once Eurobonds, guaranteed by the joint sovereigns, become available. As the national sovereign will lose their eligibility for purchases by the ECB, and Eurobonds would be eligible instead, national sovereigns would become inherently riskier. It, therefore, makes sense that they would also lose their zero-risk weighting. Therefore, it is reasonable to assume that banks agree to swap their sovereign debt portfolio for Eurobonds, on a voluntary basis. As a result, sovereign debt distress, and the associated capital flight from the periphery to the core, no longer matters for the cost or availability of bank funding in the periphery.

Moreover, since all banks have access to the same safe asset, the Eurobond, central bank purchases can be assumed to induce banks to convert the additional (excess) reserves thus created into loans (unlike the current situation where banks keep the excess on their balance sheets as protection against loss of access to wholesale funding). This is known in the literature as the direct bank lending channel of quantitative easing. Evidence of this channel being effective at present in the Eurozone is weak, as banks in practice have been holding on to their excess reserves or used them to pay down external funding or (re-)purchase debt securities instead of providing credit to the economy (see Ryan & Whelan, 2019). However, this may change when banks are induced to hold Eurobonds in lieu of national sovereign bonds. As national sovereign bonds lose their zero-risk weighting, the scope for carry trades diminishes and, with the 'doom loop' broken, the need to hold on to excess reserves also diminishes, hence it looks plausible that a direct bank lending channel will open. There is indeed some empirical evidence that a direct bank lending channel is effective in cases where banks have access to a (national) safe bond, see Paludkiewicz (2018) for Germany, (Joyce & Salto, 2014) for the UK and Kandrac and Schlusche (2017) for the US.[1]

[1] To be fair, Rodnuansky and Darmouni (2017) find no evidence of a direct bank lending channel for the US (except for purchases of mortgage backed securities) and similarly Buttz et al. (2015)

These notions are embedded in the following stylised (log-linear) equations for bank credit measured as a percentage of nominal output, in which the periphery-core yield spread $r^* - r$ is included as a gauge of sovereign debt distress:

$$\begin{cases} l - (y + \pi) = -\xi_1 i + s\xi_2 q - (1 - s)\,\xi_3\,(r - r^*) + \lambda \\ l^* - (y^* + \pi^*) = -\xi_1^* i + s\xi_2^* q - (1 - s)\,\xi_3^*\,(r^* - r) + \lambda^* \end{cases} \tag{5}$$

and where λ and λ^* are exogenous shocks to the respective banking systems (credit crunch or credit boon). Moreover, q denotes the purchases of sovereign bonds by the ECB as a percentage of GDP, and i is the ECB's main policy rate (for simplicity we abstract from the distinction between the deposit and the repurchase rate, and s is a dummy variable which takes the value 1 if a Eurobond is created and which is nil otherwise. We expect that $\xi_1^* \geq \xi_1$, $\xi_2^* \geq \xi_2$ and $\xi_3^* \geq \xi_3$, so generally speaking the sensitivity of bank lending to monetary policy and financial market distress would be larger in the periphery than in the core. Note also that there is an asymmetry in the sense that the adverse effect of the yield spread on lending in the periphery has the opposite sign of the safe-haven effect on lending in the core, and that both tend to widen the differential.

This takes us to the determinants of the sovereign yield spread of the Eurozone periphery against the core $r^* - r$. There is burgeoning literature on the sovereign yield spread in the Eurozone, which is usually assumed to be driven by country-specific liquidity risk, country-specific default risk and the risk appetite of global investors (see, for instance, Codogno et al., 2003). The ratio of sovereign debt to GDP (alongside the fiscal deficit feeding into the debt ratio) is usually considered to be the main driver of country-specific default risk. As several studies have shown, the relationship between debt and spread can be strongly non-linear and dependent on global risk sentiment. With the outbreak of the global financial crisis, the perception of higher sovereign default risks produced a sharp increase in yield spreads, and even more so in countries whose initial debt ratio was comparatively high.

By contrast, as indicated inter alia by De Grauwe and Ji (2012), in developed economies with a federal/central government that issues debt in its 'own' currency, federal sovereign yields tend to incorporate liquidity and exchange rate risk premiums, but not a default risk premium. A Eurobond, issued by an appointed fiscal capacity with full democratic legitimacy, and which enjoys a joint guarantee by the national sovereigns, may be assumed to fit this description broadly. However, once a Eurobond exists, the national sovereigns would become more akin to state and local government debt in federal states, i.e. would still carry default risk premia (see Schuknecht et al., 2009). In fact, due to the joint guarantee (and assuming this guarantee is credible), national sovereign debt would become inherently riskier than

for the UK. Fatouh et al. (2019) even observe a decline in bank lending in the UK as large corporate borrowers turned to the corporate bond market were yields had fallen in response to QE (though arguably this is a demand effect and not a supply effect on bank loans).

at present, with their yields incorporating risk premia not only for national but also for supra-national public debt.

These features are reflected in the following set of equations for national and supranational yields:

$$\begin{cases} r = sr^{€} + (1-s)\left(\vartheta_1 i - \vartheta_2 q\right) + \vartheta_3\left(b + sb^{€}\right) + \rho \\ r^* = sr^{€} + (1-s)\left(\vartheta_1^* i - \vartheta_2^* q\right) + \vartheta_3^*\left(b^* + sb^{€}\right) + \rho^* \\ r^{€} = (1-s)\,\frac{1}{2}\left(r + r^*\right) + s\left(\sigma_1 i - \sigma_2 q + \rho^{€}\right) \end{cases} \quad (6)$$

where r, r^* and $r^{€}$ are the yields on core, periphery and supranational sovereign debt and b, b^* and $b^{€}$ denote the corresponding sovereign debt as a per cent of GDP. The variables ρ, ρ^* and $\rho^{€}$ are exogenous risk premium shocks. Moreover, q again denotes the purchases of sovereign bonds (regardless of the issuer) by the ECB, as a percentage of GDP, and i is again the ECB's primary policy rate. We expect $\vartheta_1^* \geq \vartheta_1$, $\vartheta_2^* \geq \vartheta_2$, $\vartheta_3^* \geq \vartheta_3$, so generally speaking periphery yields are the most sensitive to developments in sovereign debt and monetary policy. Let us recall that all variables (except for the dummy s) are defined in terms of deviations from a baseline in which all shock variables are nil. The idea is to leave these equations unchanged on the assumption that the yield of Eurobonds would follow the same pattern as ESM bonds, i.e. a weighted average of the underlying national sovereign bonds.

The numerical assumptions for the system of Eqs. (5) and (6) are again as much as possible based on the mainstream literature (see Table 1). For bank lending, Albertazzi et al. (2012) find for Italy (which we take to represent the periphery) an adverse effect of a 100 bps increase in the spread $r^* - r$ of the order of 3.5% for loans to NFCs and 6.0% for household loans. Given the relative weights of NFC and household loans, this implies that approximately $\xi_3^* = 4.5$. Based on the same study we adopt $\xi_1^* = 3.0$ for the impact of the policy rate on bank credit, although estimates were based on the peak of the government bond crisis and by now the sensitivity has decreased significantly. In the core, we assume the impact of the spread $r^* - r$ to be nil such that $\xi_3 = 0$, as suggested by Altavilla et al. (2016). For the impact of quantitative easing on bank lending we adopt $\xi_2^* = 0.25$, i.e. for every euro liquidity created on banks' balance sheets in the periphery through asset purchases, one-quarter is converted into bank loans. This is in line with findings for the United Kingdom reported by Joyce and Salto (2014). Our baseline assumption for the effectiveness of quantitative easing in the core is smaller than in the periphery, with $\xi_2 = 0.125$, to reflect the smaller holdings of sovereigns on banks' balance sheets.

The numerical calibration of the yield equations is based on De Santis (2016). Accordingly, we adopt for the impacts on yields of the policy rate $\vartheta_1 = \vartheta_2^* = 0.5$, with the impact thus less than proportional to reflect that tighter monetary policy now gets countries loser monetary policy later, so bond yields will not increase as much as policy rates. With regard to the impact of quantitative easing on sovereign yields we adopt $\vartheta_2 = 0.05$ and $\vartheta_2^* = 0.1$. This implies that for every 1% of GDP equivalent of asset purchases by the ECB, yields would drop by 5 bps in the core and by 10 bps in the periphery. Note that total asset purchases by the ECB to date have roughly amounted to around 25% of GDP, which according to the above estimates would have slashed yields by 100 bps in the core and 250 bps in the periphery. Finally, based on the same study, we adopt for the impact of the public debt ratio on the sovereign yields $\vartheta_3 = 0.23$ and $\vartheta_3^* = 0.26$.

Obviously, we do not know how the yield on Eurobonds will behave in response to monetary policy. Therefore, we will assume the impact of ECB asset purchases on the Eurobond yields to average that on the national sovereign yields when $s = 0$, so $\sigma_1 = 0.5$ and $\sigma_2 = 0.075$.

A.1.3 A.3 The Government Sector

The usual debt dynamics identities capture the evolution of the debt ratio to output at the national and supranational levels. We also allow for discretionary fiscal spending (grants) and loans at the centre to differ between the core and the periphery:

$$\begin{cases} b = b_0\left(\chi r - y - \pi\right) + f + \ell + \ell^{€} \\ b^* = b_0^*\left(\chi r^* - y^* - \pi^*\right) + f^* + \ell^* + \ell^{*€} \\ b^{€} = sb_0^{€}\left(\chi r^{€} - \overline{y} - \overline{\pi}\right) + \frac{1}{2}\left(f^{€} + \ell^{€} + f^{*€} + \ell^{*€}\right) \end{cases} \tag{7}$$

$$\begin{cases} f = -\left(\tau - s\theta\right) y + g,\ f^{€} = -s\theta y + g^{€} \\ f^* = -\left(\tau - s\theta\right) y^* + g^*,\ f^{€*} = -s\theta y^* + g^{*€} \end{cases} \tag{8}$$

where $\overline{\pi} = \frac{1}{2}\pi + \frac{1}{2}\pi^*$ and $\overline{y} = \frac{1}{2}y + \frac{1}{2}y^*$ and where g, g^*, $g^{€}$ and $g^{*€}$ denote the discretionary component of the respective deficits, ℓ and ℓ^* are loans from the national governments to the private sector, $\ell^{€}$ and $\ell^{*€}$ are loans from the centre national governments, and τ corresponds to the usual 'semi-elasticity' of the fiscal deficit with respect to output. In this specification, $s\theta$ takes a positive value when a supra-national fiscal capacity is created, and certain tax or spending programmes are reallocated to it, and nil otherwise. The primary deficit at the central level is simply the average $\overline{f}^{€} = \frac{1}{2}f^{€} + \frac{1}{2}f^{€*}$.

Let us recall that f, f^*, $f^{€}$ and $f^{*€}$ denote the respective primary deficits as a ratio to output that enters the system of aggregate demand Eq. (1) and that b_0, b_0^* and $sb_0^{€}$ are the respective 'initial' debt ratios, whereby we mean the prevailing debt ratios if none of the potential demand, supply or financial shocks occur (i.e. $\varepsilon^d = \varepsilon^{*d} = \varepsilon^s = \varepsilon^{*s} = \lambda = \lambda^* = \rho = \rho^* = 0$). As before, if $s = 0$ no Eurobonds are created, so $b^{€} = 0$. However, if $s = 1$, the debt ratio would change in response to variations in the relevant yields, economic growth and inflation alongside the conduct of fiscal policy at the centre. We make a simplifying assumption that a fraction χ of the changes in yields feed through in the implicit debt servicing cost, depending on the percentage of the total stock of debt that comes due each year. In the model simulations, it is assumed that $\chi = 0.2$.

The primary fiscal deficits $f, f^*, f^{€}$ and $f^{*€}$ are partly endogenous on account of 'automatic stabilisers' (e.g. variations in tax proceeds or social security outlays as a function of cyclical economic activity), so they comprise induced and discretionary components. For the numerical calibration of the automatic stabilisation effect, we refer to Van den Noord (2000) and Girouard and André (2005), which implies that $\tau = 0.5$. Furthermore, we assume that $b_0 = 50\%$, $b_0^* = 130\%$ and $b_0^{€} = 40\%$. This roughly corresponds to, respectively, the public debt to GDP ratios in Germany and Italy and the amount of Eurobonds that approximately needs to be issued to cover the purchases of national sovereigns on the balance sheets of the ECB and the banks as well as any additional purchases in the market needed to secure consistency with the capital key. As concerns the parameter θ we refer to Van den Noord (2020), who assumes that half of the automatic stabilisation effect would accrue to the centre, so if $\tau = 0.5$ then $\theta = 0.25$.

A.1.4 A.4 Shocks and Changes in Policy Variables

As discussed in the main text, three scenarios are computed. The exogenous changes assumed in each of these three scenarios are reported in Table 3 below. Specifically,

1. The dummy s takes a value 0 in Scenarios I and II and 1 in Scenario III.
2. In all three scenarios the same set of demand shocks ε^d and ε^{*d} and supply shocks ε^s and ε^{*s} are assumed as well as the same change in the policy rate i. Also, in all three scenarios the same exogenous risk premium shocks to sovereign yields ρ and ρ^* are incorporated to reflect a flight to safety effect on core yields and an offsetting (neutralising) effect of the ESM emergency facility on periphery yields.
3. The domestic fiscal shocks g are identical across the three scenarios except from a reduction in Scenario II to reflect the impact of grants from the centre used to replace deficit funding of domestic spending. The same holds for the domestic fiscal shock in the core g^*.
4. In Scenario I the increase in central public spending $g^{€}$ and $g^{*€}$ is modest, reflecting the first batch of EU programmes in the spring such as SURE. The sharp increases in these fiscal variables (especially in the periphery) in Scenario II reflect the grants provided under New Generation EU. The same holds for the increase in loans from the centre $\ell^{€}$ and $\ell^{*€}$ in Scenario II relative to Scenario I.
5. In Scenario III the aggregate amounts of grants and loans from the centre are the same in Scenario II, but the distribution across the core and symmetry is now symmetric, meaning that $g^{€} = g^{*€}$ and $\ell^{€} = \ell^{*€}$.

Table 3 Shocks and changes in policy variables

Scenario	Actual Policy		
	I	II	III
s	0	0	1
ε^d	−10.0	−10.0	10.0
ε^{*d}	−5.0	−5.0	−5.0
ε^s	−15.0	−15.0	15.0
ε^{*s}	−7.5	−7.5	−7.5
i	−0.25	−0.25	−0.25
q	24.6	24.6	12.3
ρ	−2.0	−2.0	−2.0
ρ^*	−2.0	−2.0	−2.0
g	2.60	2.34	2.60
g^*	4.50	4.05	4.50
$g^{€}$	0.35	1.60	3.88
$g^{*€}$	0.35	6.15	3.88
$\ell^{€}$	0.00	0.40	3.65
$\ell^{*€}$	0.00	6.90	3.65

Note: Scenarios refer to: I = National fiscal responses + SURE + monetary policy, II = I + 'Next Generation EU', III = Safe asset + permanent fiscal capacity

References

Albertazzi, U., Ropele, T., Sene, G., & Signoretti, F. M. (2012). *The impact of the sovereign debt crisis on the activity of Italian Banks*. Bank of Italy Occasional Papers 133.

Alogoskoufis, S., & Langfield, S. (2019, September). *Regulating the doom loop*, ECB working paper No 2313.

Altavilla, C., Pagano, M., & Simonelli, S. (2016, October). *Bank exposures and sovereign stress transmission*. European central bank working paper series 1969.

Antoshi, A., Arena, M., Gueorguiev, N., Lybek, T., Ralyea, J., & Yehoue, E. B. (2017). *Credit growth and economic recovery in Europe after the global financial crisis*. IMF working paper WP/17/256.

Arnold, N. et al. (2018). *A central fiscal stabilization capacity for the euro area*. IMF Staff Discussion Note 18/03.

Ball, L. M., Leigh, D., & Loungani, P. (2013). *Okun's law: Fit at 50?*. IMF working paper WP/13/10.

Barrell, R., Holland, D., & Hurst, I. (2012). Fiscal multipliers and prospects for consolidation. *OECD Journal: Economic Studies, 2012*(1), 71–102.

Batini, N., Eyraud, L., Forni, L., & Weber, A. (2014). *Fiscal multipliers: Size, determinants, and use in macroeconomic projections*. IMF technical notes and manuals, 14/04.

Baum, A., Poplawski-Ribeiro, M., & Weber, A. (2012). *Fiscal multipliers and the state of the economy*. IMF working paper WP/12/286.

Bayoumi, T., Harmsen, R., & Turunen, J. (2011). *Euro area export performance and competitiveness*. IMF working paper WP/11/140.

Bénassy-Quéré A., Brunnermeier, M., Enderlein, H., Farhi, E., Fratzscher, M., Fuest, C., Gourinchas, P.-O., Martin, P., Pisani-Ferry, J., Rey, H., Schnabel, I., Véron, N., di Mauro, B. W., &

Zettelmeyer, J. (2018, May). *Reconciling risk sharing with market discipline: A constructive approach to euro area reform*. CEPR Policy Insight No 91.
Bruegel. (2020). *The fiscal response to the economic fallout from the coronavirus*. Bruegel Datasets. https://www.bruegel.org/publications/datasets/covid-national-dataset/
Buttz, N., Churmz, R., McMahon, M., Morotzz, A., & Schanz, J. (2015, October). *QE and the bank lending channel in the United Kingdom*. Warwick Economics Research Paper Series 1073.
Cappiello, L., Kadareja, A., Soerensen, C. K., & Protopapa, M. (2010, January). *Do bank loans and credit standards have an effect on output? A panel approach for the euro area*. ECB Working Paper Series, No. 1150.
Codogno, L., Favero, C., & Missale, A. (2003). Yield spreads on EMU government bonds. *Economic Policy, 37*, 505–532.
Codogno, L., & van den Noord, P. J. (2019). The rationale for a safe asset and fiscal capacity for the Eurozone. In J. E. Castañeda, A. Roselli, & G. E. Wood (Eds.), *The economics of monetary unions: Past experiences and the Eurozone* (pp. 175–204). Routledge Studies in the European Economy.
Codogno, L., & van den Noord, P. J. (2020). Going fiscal? A stylised model with fiscal capacity and a Eurobond in the Eurozone. *Review of Economics and Finance, 19*, 54–72.
De Grauwe, P., & Ji, Y. (2012, January). *Mispricing of sovereign risk and multiple equilibria in the eurozone*. CEPS working document 361.
De Santis, R. A. (2016, July). *Impact of the asset purchase programme on Euro area government bond yields using market news*. ECB Working Paper Series 1939.
ECB. (2013, January). *Intra-Euro area trade linkages and external adjustment*. ECB monthly bulletin.
European Commission (2020a). *Identifying Europe's recovery needs*. Commission Staff Working Document SWD (2020) 98 final/2.
European Commission (2020b). *Guidance to Member States, Recovery and Resilience Plans*. Commission Staff Working Document, SWD (2020) 205 final.
European Council (2020). Conclusions. EUCO 10/20 CO EUR 8 CONCL 4.
Fatouh, M., Markose, S., & Giansate, S. (2019, March). The impact of quantitative easing on UK bank lending: Why banks do not lend to businesses? *Journal of Economic Behavior and Organization,* 3–10.
Girouard, N., & André, C. (2005). *Measuring cyclically–adjusted budget balances for OECD Countries*. OECD Economics Department Working Papers, No. 434.
Gomez-Pineda, J. G. (2020, July 30). *Growth forecasts and the Covid-19 recession they convey*. COVID Economics, CEPR, (40). https://cepr.org/content/covid-economics-vetted-and-real-time-papers-0
Joyce, M. A. S., & Salto, M. (2014). *Quantitative easing and bank lending: A panel data approach*. Bank of England Working Paper 504.
Kandrac, J., & Schlusche, B. (2017). *Quantitative easing and bank risk taking: Evidence from lending*. Finance and Economics Discussion Series 2017–125, Board of Governors of the Federal Reserve System (U.S.).
Leandro, Á., & Zettelmeyer, J. (2018, May). *Safety without tranches: Creating a 'real' safe asset for the Euro area*. CEPR Policy Insight No 93.
Llaudes, R. (2005, February). *The Phillips curve and long-term unemployment*. ECB Working Paper Series, No. 441.
Paludkiewicz, K. (2018). *Unconventional monetary policy, bank lending, and security holdings: The yield-induced portfolio rebalancing channel*. Deutsche Bundesbank Discussion Paper 22/2018.
Pfeiffer, P., Varga, J., & in't Veld, J. (2021, July). *Quantifying spillovers of next generation EU investment*. European Commission Discussion Paper no. 144.
Rodnyansky, A., & Darmouni, O. M. (2017). The effects of quantitative easing on bank lending behavior. *The Review of Financial Studies, 30*(11), 3858–3887.
Ryan, E., & Whelan, K. (2019). *Quantitative easing and the hot potato effect: Evidence from Euro area banks*. CEPR Discussion Paper 13499.

Schuknecht, L., von Hagen, J., & Wolswijk, G. (2009). Government risk premiums in the bond market: EMU and Canada. *European Journal of Political Economy, 25*, 371–384.

Van den Noord, P. J. (2000). *The size and role of automatic fiscal stabilisers in the 1990s and beyond*. OECD Economics Department Working Papers 230, OECD Publishing.

Van den Noord, P. J. (2020). Mimicking a buffer fund for the Eurozone. *World Economics Journal, 21*(2), 249–281. https://www.world-economics-journal.com/Journal/Papers/Mimicking%20a%20Buffer%20Fund%20for%20the%20Eurozone%20.details?ID=795

Van der Cruijsen, C., & Demertzis, M. (2009, December). *How anchored are inflation expectations in EMU countries?* DNB Working Paper, No. 235.

Verwey, M., Langedijk, S., & Kuenzel, R. (2020, June 9). *Next generation EU: A recovery plan for Europe*. VOX CEPR Policy Portal. OECD. https://voxeu.org/article/next-generation-eu-recovery-plan-europe

Globalization in Europe: Consequences for the Business Environment and Future Patterns in Light of Covid-19

Sergio Inferrera

1 Introduction

Globalization has always been a widely studied phenomenon, representing together with technological change the largest shock of the twenty-first century. In particular, at the end of the twentieth century and in the early 2000s the decline of trade costs, both in terms of reduced tariffs and technological progress, made it possible for firms in each part of the globe to exchange goods more easily (World Bank, 2020). The globalization process has been particularly fast in connecting agents of the economy across the entire world, accelerating incredibly before the Global Financial Crisis (Autor et al., 2013). This led to a dramatic increase in the trade in intermediate inputs: currently, more than two thirds of world's total trade is made up by trade in intermediate goods (OECD, 2020). However, after the Global Financial Crisis and the Sovereign Debt one, the level of integration of the global and European economy started declining, casting doubts on the chance of survival of globalization. The term *de-globalization* returned to be used in the aftermath of the latter crisis to indicate the process by virtue of which the degree of interconnectedness across countries diminished. Furthermore, tangible signs of de-globalization have arrived in the form of increased tariffs, trade wars, Brexit and the disruptions brought by the novel Covid-19.

The consequences of globalization on the economy have been largely discussed in the economic literature, with a lack of a clear consensus: whereas before the economic literature was more benign towards globalization highlighting its positive effects, either for the economy as a whole or for all its agents (both firms and

---

S. Inferrera (✉)
The Competitiveness Research Network, Milan, Italy
e-mail: Inferrera@comp-net.org

L. Paganetto (ed.), *Economic Challenges for Europe After the Pandemic*,
Springer Proceedings in Business and Economics,
https://doi.org/10.1007/978-3-031-10302-5_6

individuals), more recently globalization has been subject to a larger criticism highlighting its unintended consequences (Garcıa-Herrero and Tan, 2020).

In this paper, I contribute to this literature by focusing on globalization in the form of Global Value Chains (GVC), analyzing the consequences for the economy of an increased participation in international production networks. I focus both on a desirable outcome, that is the effect that globalization has on firms' productivity, and on an undesirable one, namely the effect on firms market power and market concentration. Furthermore, I contribute to the literature related to *de-globalization*, assessing the size of the trade shock brought by the Covid-19 pandemic hit the globalization process.

The remaining of this paper is organized as follows: Sect. 2 describes the literature concerning the effect of the Covid-19 pandemic, and the consequences of increased integration for the economy; Sect. 3 outlines the estimation strategy and discusses the results, as well as presenting the GVC-relate trade figures for 2020; finally, Sect. 4 concludes.

2 Literature Review

Amid the Covid-19 pandemic, plenty of studies aimed at explaining the economic impact of the crisis have emerged (see Shrestha et al. 2020 for an overview). In particular, much attention has been devoted by the literature to the role that globalization had in shaping the economic and health crisis. Globalization[1] has been highlighted as one of the main contributors of the current economic crisis for two main reasons:

- during the first wave of the pandemic, trade of medical supplies fell dramatically and most countries relied mainly on national companies to supply their citizens with the necessary medical devices (masks, gloves, hand sanitizing gel, etc.). This has been highlighted as a failure of globalization (Gereffi, 2020). Furthermore, globalization in the form of increased movement of people and trade across countries may have contributed to the physical spread of the virus (Masahisa and Nobuaki, 2020);
- disruptions along the value chains have been highlighted as an important factor in driving the negative effect that the pandemic has had on the business environment (Syverson and di Mauro, 2020). Di Nino and Veltri (2020) estimate that 25% of the drop in aggregate activity in the Euro Area is due to indirect propagation along the supply chains of the same region.

[1] Issues have been found in defining—and hence measuring—thoroughly globalization. To this aim, various indicators have been proposed starting from the interaction of various metrics, such as movement of goods (trade), people (migration) and of capital, but none has been recognized as systematically better than the others (Dreher et al., 2008). Here, I will focus on globalization in the form of trade of goods, in particular in the form of GVC.

A thorough assessment of the impact of the pandemic and the role that trade openness (*id est* globalization) has had on the economy has been conducted by Sforza and Steininger (2017). In their recent research, the authors highlight that the economic effects of a pandemic crucially depend on the extent to which countries are connected in global production networks. Exploiting the unique set-up provided by the Covid-19 pandemic, they study the diffusion of a global production shock along the supply chains and find that the economic crisis due to the pandemic led to an average 12.9% drop in GDP across countries. In their model, calibrated with 43 countries and 50 sectors with similar data to the ones I will use in Sect. 3, they show that linkages between countries account for a substantial share of the observed total income drop, on average 30% of the total across the countries. In addition to this, they provide evidence of the role of globalization in shaping the reaction of the business environment. They simulate the same model increasing current trade barriers by 100% points, in order to obtain a less integrated world. They find that on average the economic effects of the Covid-19 shock would have been only marginally worse in a closer economy, with an average drop of GDP of 13% across countries. All in all, the authors conclude that trade in the form of global production networks has two effects on the business environment: on the one hand, it allows consumers and firms to access products that otherwise would have been impossible to reach; on the other hand, it transmits the shocks along to the supply chain; the overall effect of any given shock (including the pandemic) depends on which of the two effects dominates, depending on the size of the shock and on the production structure of the economy. Hence, according to the authors, in a less globalized world the impact of the pandemic would have been roughly similar to the one we have currently experienced.

The evidence provided by Sforza and Steininger (2017) is of particular importance: the pandemic came during a period of crisis of globalization, casting doubts on its chances of surviving the pandemic.[2] Such concerns, however, are not shared by business leaders: in a usual survey conducted by the ECB (Maqui and Morris, 2020), when asked which would be the main long-term consequence of the pandemic, just shy of 10 % of the interviewed business leaders pointed to a crisis of globalization (or, *de-globalization*).

Rather than *de-globalization*, other research points towards a slowdown in globalization: Antràs (2020) finds little systematic evidence indicating that the world economy has already entered an era of *de-globalization*. Instead, he highlights that the observed slowdown in globalization is a natural consequence of its unsustainable increase rate experienced in the late twentieth century. He concludes that there are more signs of *slowbalization* rather than *de-globalization*. In particular, he argues that this is due to the resilience of firms' interlinks across the globe: he claims that establishing along international production networks requires some fixed and sunk costs and that only persistent shocks may change the production network. By

---

[2] For example, see experts' opinions expressed in this interview: Have We Reached Peak Globalization?, Bloomberg News, January 24, 2020.

studying the Global Financial Crisis, he provides evidence that the shock hit mainly the intensive and not the extensive margin of trade, concluding that a similar effect would be in place for the economic crisis due to the pandemic. Hence, the number of firms joining international production network should not be severely affected by the pandemic, signaling that globalization is just bound to slow its pace rather than ceasing to exist because of Covid-19.

A more pessimistic view is presented by Garcıa-Herrero and Tan (2020). The authors—coherently with a large amount of literature—find that after the global financial crisis there has been a slowing of global trade flows, arguing that the world entered an era of *de-globalization* because of this fall. The slowdown in trade flows is related not only to trade in goods, but even to trade in services and to the integration of GVC, that has also been steadily declining since the Global Financial Crisis. More importantly, the authors point towards the increasing tensions on trade between the US and China as the main responsible for the declining trends in globalization. President Trump's choices of increasing tariffs and establishing sanctions against China reinforced the post-GFC globalization trend, at least in terms of trade and GVC. However, the evidence presented in this paper is more in line with the idea of *slowbalization* rather than *de-globalization*: indeed, the authors actually find similar trends to the ones presented by Antràs (2020), but they drive different conclusions. This is due to the fact that, in their analysis, *de-globalization* trends are more evident in goods rather than capital movements. All in all, the evidence provided by the authors reinforced the view of *slowbalization*, since systematic evidence of *de-globalization* is not present neither in movement of goods, nor people, nor capital.

The evidence presented so far is of major importance: globalization in the form of increased trade and integration along the supply chains has been usually associated with several positive effects on the economy, hence a slowdown of the integration process could be dangerous. First and foremost, it is a well-established fact in the literature that firms that are able to export are on average more productive than domestic ones (Dhyne et al., 2015). Dhyne et al. (2015) find that the productivity premium of exporters is quite heterogeneous across European countries; on average, exporters have a labor productivity 20% larger than non-exporters in those countries. Similarly, Bernard et al. (2003) report the U.S. exporters' premium to be in the range 9–20% in labor productivity. Powell and Wagner (2021), on the other hand, argue that the premium is different along the entire distribution and actually find that it is positive at all productivity levels, but highest at the lowest quantiles. A similar result is found in CompNet (2020a), in which the authors find a positive and significant labor productivity premium for exporting firms in each quantile of the productivity distribution. This literature, of which the researches I presented constitute just some examples, is based on the seminal work by Melitz (2003) and Melitz and Ottaviano (2008), whose models show how the exposure to trade will induce only a handful of firms, namely the more productive, to engage in export activities while leaving less productive firms continue to produce only for the domestic market and forcing the least productive firms to exit. Among the exporters, too, plenty of empirical literature has shown that a large share of low productive exporters accounts for a negligible share of the overall sales abroad; on the other hand, only a few highly productive firms constitute the majority of exports (Mayer and Ottaviano, 2008). The latter firms typically engage into both exporting and importing activities (so called two-way-traders) and dominate GVC participation (CompNet, 2020a). For these firms, GVC participation represents a key channel of productivity gains: being a part of the international supply chains enables firms to achieve higher efficiency in the allocation of resources, wider variety and better quality (or cheaper) intermediate inputs, and enhanced technology transfers along the value chain. Altomonte et al. (2018) focus precisely on firms populating GVC and find that, during the period of surge of GVC, a positive effect of trade on growth was present through both productivity growth and capital deepening. For what concerns the channels through which this relation manifests itself, Chiacchio et al. (2018) investigate the way in which GVC participation can boost productivity. The authors find that, particularly in Central Eastern European countries, GVC act as a channel of technology transfer from parent firms to host economies and that technology-frontier firms are directly involved in GVC and exposed to new technology, while non-frontier firms mainly benefit from their participation in domestic production networks, as well as, to a lesser extent, from direct contact with parent companies.

Finally, an important strand of literature has been focusing on the unintended consequences of globalization, *id est* the social ones. Indeed, the sudden increase in the GVC participation across countries has impacted not only the economy by affecting firms' performances, but by affecting other agents, too. In a seminal paper Autor et al. (2013) instrument globalization through the well-known "China shock", that is, the sudden increase in import competition due to China. They analyze the impact that globalization has on local labor markets in the US, by focusing on the manufacturing sector because of the significant decline in the employment figures in this industry due to the competition with China. They find that an increase in import competition from China has had a negative impact on wages, labor force participation, and a positive one on unemployment; furthermore, import competition explains 25% of the decline in manufacturing employment. A more detailed description of the effect has been provided in a subsequent paper: the negative impact on wages has been larger for individuals already in the left tail of the wage distribution, making the globalization shock more costly for workers who were already worse-off before the shock (Autor et al., 2014). Hence, the impact of globalization has been uneven in the US. Furthermore, it has been shown that globalization has affected both the mental health and the political preferences of displaced workers in Europe: exploiting the China-shock, Colantone et al. (2019) explain in detail the mental health problems that are typically common for workers displaced by import competition, while Colantone and Stanig (2018a,b) show that globalization has had an important role in driving the rise of nationalism and Brexit.

This paper is related to all these strands of the literature: firstly, it outlines the productivity premia that firms joining GVC can enjoy, hence being related to the vast literature concerning the benefits of trade; in addition to this, this paper explains two additional unintended consequences of globalization, namely increasing market concentration and market power enjoyed by firms. However, whether rising concentration due to a more globalized world should be viewed as evidence of a weak competitive environment, or a reflection of more efficient market processes is still unclear and more research is needed to answer this question. Finally, this paper is related to the novel and growing literature regarding the Covid-19 pandemic impact on GVC.

3 The Empirical Analysis

The first part of this simple empirical analysis is aimed at estimating the elasticity of productivity to trade in GVC. Throughout this paper, I use the value of GVC-related trade value instead of the more classical GVC participation index as derived by Koopman et al. (2010). In particular, according to Borin and Mancini (2019a), I classify GVC-related trade as trade of goods that cross border more than once. The reason for this is simple: the figure of trade in GVC is often normalized to the value of total exports in order not to bias this measure for countries whose firms trade more, and hence are endowed with a larger figure for total exports. However, in a regression analysis through an appropriate structure of fixed effects, I can reach the same effect without losing variability in the independent variable. Indeed, the standard deviation and the variance for the GVC-related trade indicator are clearly larger in absolute value with respect to the GVC-participation index ones. Furthermore, even the ratio of the 95th percentile over the 5th is much larger for the GVC-value (the ratio is more than one thousand and a half) rather than for the GVC-participation index (the ratio is equal to almost three). Exploiting this larger variability, I am able to identify more precisely the coefficients I am interested in Wooldridge (2010).

One weakness of my study is that I do not have access to confidential firm-level information. Hence, my best effort in this paper is to rely onto the micro-aggregate approach (Lopez-Garcia & di Mauro, 2015) and conduct this analysis at higher aggregation levels, i.e. at the 2-digit sector-level or at the country one through the CompNet data.[3] However, the CompNet dataset does not have information on GVC participation of firms: since the dataset is micro-founded, data are taken from firms' balance sheets or from custom agencies, and therefore they do not provide information on firm-to-firm relationships. In order to create the dataset that includes the GVC values, I need to merge the CompNet data with another dataset, *id est* with the World Input-Output Database. This latter set of data is at the industry level, too, and hence I can merge it with the CompNet dataset.[4] This strategy is endangered by the very structure of the CompNet dataset: being a dataset built on micro-data it

[3] A detailed description of all the data employed in this study can be found in the appendix.

[4] The industry aggregations of the CompNet and WIOD dataset do not coincide precisely and hence some further aggregation is needed to perform an exact match of the two datasets. A detailed list of the 2-digit sectors available in the two datasets is available in the appendix.

does not contain values relative to the whole economy, but just idiosyncratic to the specific sample under scrutiny. Even if the sample is a representative one, it might not be entirely correct to merge it with other data sources that provide information relative to the whole economy. For example, this is the case with WIOD, the dataset that I use for the Input-Output tables. Fortunately, merging CompNet and WIOD is not a problematic procedure since CompNet implemented a weighting scheme in its protocol that makes its data fully comparable with other data sources related to the whole economy. Thanks to this, merging WIOD and CompNet is not a problematic procedure (Altomonte et al., 2018).

The first regression analysis will rely on the following equation:

$$y_{c,s,t} = \alpha + \beta\ GVC\ Index_{c,s,t} + X_{c,s,t} + \delta + \gamma + \lambda + \varepsilon_{c,s,t} \tag{1}$$

where GVC Index is the one identified by Borin and Mancini (2019b) in country c, sector s and year t and represents the value of production that cross more than one border (excluding the domestic value added directly absorbed by the importer); y the vector of each output variable in which I am interested in, including labor productivity, TFP and concentration level; X is a vector of control variables composed by the ratio of capital and intermediates to labor and total exports; δ is a vector of country fixed effects; γ is a vector of sector fixed effects; λ is a vector of time fixed effects; α is the constant term and finally ε is the error term in the regression. Table 11 presents some descriptive statistics for the main variables included in Eq. (1), that is, the average value of the distribution (at the country-sector-year level) and the standard deviation for the same distribution. I did not include the number of observations because it is roughly homogeneous across indicators, *id est* the country-sector pairs are similar across indicators and over time.

Clearly, Eq. (1) does not have any causal interpretation: disentangling the causal effect of involvement in international supply chains on the business environment is troublesome and sound identification strategies are needed, such as the one I will present later on. The coefficient β identified thanks to Eq. (1) will just represent an elasticity purged from the omitted variables that may bias the results. I will first present the results related to the elasticity of firm performances and concentration to GVC-trade.

In order to do so, I do not limit myself to analyze the overall figure of GVC-related trade, but I decompose total GVC-related trade as the sum of two items, domestic value added in third country exports (forward GVC) and foreign value added in own exports (backward GVC). In particular, always following the prescriptions of Borin and Mancini (2019b), I measure forward GVC trade as the exports in domestic value added absorbed by other countries than the direct importer; backward GVC integration, instead, is measured as the sum of the domestic double-counted value added and the foreign content in own value added. Intuitively, these two metrics measure the position in which the country-sector pair lies within the supply chain, whether more upstream (Forward GVC integration) or downstream (Backward GVC integration). I relate these metrics to the desired concentration measures, that is, the Herfindal-Hirschman Index (known

Table 1 Correlation (OLS-FE) of GVC trade by component on HHI and Mark up

	(1) HHI	(2) HHI	(3) HHI	(4) Mark up	(5) Mark up	(6) Mark up
Overall	−0.001			0.008***		
	(0.009)			(0.00292)		
Backward		−0.001			0.0104***	
		(0.009)			(0.003)	
Forward			−0.036***			0.011***
			(0.012)			(0.004)
M/L	0.001***	0.001***	0.001***	0.001***	0.001***	0.001***
	(0.000)	(0.000)	(0.00)	(0.00)	(0.00)	(0.00)
K/L	0.001***	0.001***	0.001***	0.001***	0.001***	0.001***
	(0.000)	(0.000)	(0.000)	(0.00)	(0.00)	(0.00)
Size	0.461***	0.461***	0.469***	−0.129***	−0.130***	−0.130***
	(0.028)	(0.028)	(0.029)	(0.009)	(0.009)	(0.009)
Constant	3.897***	3.894***	4.079***	1.426***	1.419***	1.422***
	(0.088)	(0.085)	(0.096)	(0.028)	(0.026)	(0.03)
Observations	3058	3054	3044	3052	3048	3038
R-squared	0.695	0.695	0.692	0.784	0.785	0.783

All the variables presented in the table are subject to logarithmic transformation. The list of countries and sector included are presented in the Appendix. Country, Sector and Year fixed effects are included in each regression. Robust Standard error in parentheses
*p< 0.1
**p< 0.05
***p<0.01

as HHI-index; Herfindahl 1950 and Hirschman 1980). This is the index used by the European Commission in the assessment of market concentration in the evaluation of mergers (see article 16 of the Mergers guidelines OJ C 31, 5.2.2004). Then, I relate them to mark-ups derived as in De Loecker and Warzynski (2012) assuming a Cobb-Douglas production function. This indicator serves to measure the market power that the average firm holds. Results for these models are presented in Table 1.[5]

The first three columns of Table 1 represent the models relating the concentration index to the GVC-related trade figures. All the models present the same control variables, *id est* the ratio of intermediate goods and capital to labor in order to control for changes in the mode of production, and the average firm size in a given sector, in addition to a full battery of fixed effects at the country, sector and year level. In the first three columns, it is possible to observe that GVC trade is negatively related to concentration levels, although the relation is not statistically significant. The only significant relation is with Forward GVC trade, that is, when upstream

[5] Please note that all the models presented here are fixed effect models, therefore each result needs to be interpreted as the increase (decrease) of y within a country-sector-year associated with the increase of x.

participation is larger the degree of concentration on the market diminishes. In addition to this, in absolute value, the relation with forward GVC trade is way larger than the ones for the other GVC indicators. Hence, country-sector pairs in which forward GVC trade is larger, *id est* in which firms that are embedded in international supply networks are placed relatively more upstream within the value chain, face a less concentrated business environment. Although a more robust identification strategy is needed to explain the mechanism driving this correlation, this may be due to international competition, possibly reducing firms' market share when the production is still far away from the final consumer. In the following section, however, I will show that this conclusion will be turned when exploiting the exogenous arm of GVC trade at the sector-level.

Notwithstanding this, columns (4), (5), and (6) show that larger involvement in international supply networks is associated with larger markups. The controls for these regressions are the same as the ones presented earlier. Here, it does not matter whether firms locate themselves upstream or downstream within the supply chain, since for each GVC indicator the relation with markups is significantly positive and of similar intensity. While it may seem counter-intuitive that Forward GVC trade is negatively correlated with concentration level and positively with markups, this does not endanger the quality of this result. Indeed, concentration and markups measure different things, namely, the extent to which market shares are hoarded by few or many firms and the average market power that they have. I provide a similar table to the one presented here in the Appendix (Table 12) analyzing labor productivity.

To test the heterogeneity of the elasticities along the distribution of firm-level indicators, I study the correlation of the GVC indicators with some specific percentiles of the dependent variable. While the structure of the CompNet dataset allows me to do this, I have to limit this analysis to the sectoral-aggregations that are equivalently present in both WIOD and in the CompNet dataset.[6] While in the earlier case I could aggregate myself the non-harmonized industries by taking the weighted average of the indicators of interest, with percentiles I cannot employ this strategy. Indeed, percentiles represent a firm-level figure and, being a singular point in the distribution, they cannot be aggregated. The following analysis, hence, will rely on a lower number of 2-digit industries. With this caveat in mind, Table 2 presents the result for the usual model with percentiles as dependent variables.

The first column of Table 2 displays the elasticity of several dependent variables, i.e. the top and bottom 10% and the median value of the markup and of the labor productivity distribution, estimated in a model with the usual controls and fixed effects. A larger involvement in GVC is correlated with a larger markup along the entire distribution, but the increase in the median value is particularly high. This means that the increase in the average value highlighted in Table 1 is not idiosyncratic to a particular *locus* of the distribution of markup. In other words, virtually every firm gains a degree of market power when in its industry a larger

[6] For example, the sector 10, 11 and 12 (Manufacture of respectively food, beverages and tobacco) are aggregated in only one figure in WIOD, they are separated in the CompNet dataset.

Table 2 Correlation (OLS-FE) of GVC trade by component on different percentiles of mark up and labor productivity distribution

	(1) Overall	(2) Forward	(3) Backward	Controls & FE	Obs.
Markup (p90)	0.0115**	0.0203***	0.0171***	Yes	2094
Markup (p50)	0.0190***	0.0293***	0.0224***	Yes	2098
Markup (p10)	0.0104***	0.0210***	0.0121***	Yes	2086
Lab. Productivity (p90)	0.0175***	0.0106	0.0212***	Yes	2102
Lab. Productivity (p50)	0.0107**	0.0129**	0.0129**	Yes	2102
Lab. Productivity (p10)	0.00782	0.0148**	0.0137**	Yes	2102
Lab. Productivity (sd)	0.024***	0.018***	0.031***	Yes	2098

All the variables presented in the table are subject to logarithmic transformation. Country, Sector and Year fixed effects are included in each regression. Control variables are: average firm size and ratio of capital and intermediates to labor. Robust standard error in parentheses
*$p< 0.1$
**$p< 0.05$
***$p<0.01$

involvement in GVC is present, with the firms in the central *locus* of the distribution accounting for the largest increase.

On the other hand, the positive correlation that is present between aggregate productivity and involvement in GVC is present mainly among the firms populating the right-hand side of the productivity distribution: Column (1) shows that the elasticity of the bottom 10% firms' labor productivity to overall GVC trade is not statistically significant. Moreover, the intensity of the elasticity is increasing along the productivity distribution: this is clearly evident in the overall GVC trade figure (Column (1)) and in the Backward one (Column (3)), that is, in the downstream market. This is not evident, however, in the upstream market (Column (2)), that is, in the one farther from final demand, in which all the elasticities are roughly similar. This simple evidence confirms the hypothesis that the bulk of the increase in labor productivity is driven by the best firms that grow more productive, whereas the rest lags behind. This is confirmed by using as a dependent variable the standard deviation of labor productivity (last row of Table 2), which shows how the distance between the best and the worst firms enlarges when involvement in GVC trade is higher.

3.1 Identification Strategy

In order to go beyond correlations, I use an instrumental variable approach in the spirit of Kummritz (2016). In particular, in order to isolate the exogenous variation in the GVC-related values, I exploit the indirect bilateral trade costs at the country-level and the distance in terms of upstreamness and downstreamness between different industries along the supply chain. Hence, the instrument will be composed by the interaction of these two components: (i) indirect bilateral trade costs in the spirit of Autor et al. (2013): the indirect trade cost is computed by averaging all the bilateral trade costs and excluding the country pair I am interested in; (ii) the distance between industries in terms of positioning along the supply chain.

The first component of the instrument theoretically relies on the work done through gravity structural models (see Johnson and Noguera 2017 and Noguera 2012), that highlights the importance of bilateral trade costs in determining value added trade flow. Following Kummritz (2016), I estimate the "indirect" trade costs by taking the weighted average of bilateral trade costs across all the countries in my sample, but more importantly excluding the country pair I am interested in. The trade cost measure will be weighted by the ratio of bilateral export flows to total exports of a country. To provide a concrete example, if I am interested in indirect trade costs between Italy and Germany, I will take the weighted average of all the Italian bilateral trade costs excluding the Italy-Germany pair, weighted by the ratio of each bilateral trade flow to total Italian export. The general formulation for this measure will be:

$$\bar{\tau}_{l,k} = \sum_{o} \tau_{l,o} * \frac{e_{l,o}}{\sum_{o} e_{l,o}} \tag{2}$$

where τ represents the trade cost metric, the subscript l identifies the reporting country (Italy, in my example), the subscript k the partner country (Germany, in my example), and the subscript o represents all the countries other than k and l. Clearly, to capture indirect trade costs and to have a relevant instrument for GVC, it is crucial that $k \neq l$. Note that for the sake of clarity I excluded from Eq. (2) the time subscript as all the variables presented are contemporaneous.

The data for trade costs are taken from the UNESCAP-World Bank Trade Cost Database, which estimates bilateral trade costs on the basis of the inverse form of the gravity model developed by Novy (2013). Note that the reason for which this instrumentation strategy is not sufficient is twofold: (i) trade costs are at the country-level while a more granular approach requires the GVC indicators to be at the industry-country level; (ii) furthermore, it may well be the case that trade costs themselves are endogenous. Here, the GVC structure of production equally allows for a simple solution.

Indeed, the second component of the instrument is the distance between the industries within the value chain. The position of industries along the supply chain measures how many steps it takes for a company active in that sector to reach the upstream firm or the downstream one. Not acknowledging this difference would imply that I assume the role of different industries to be the same within value chains, *id est* that all industries provide inputs to each industry within the production network. However, empirically this assumption has been proven to be wrong: according to the supply chain positioning literature (see for example Antràs and Chor 2013; Antràs et al. 2012 or Fally 2012) some industries act by and large as suppliers of intermediates while others are mainly customers for the same type of products. This idiosyncratic feature of each industry allows me to exploit the different relationships between industries as proxied by their distance along the supply chain. Intuitively, this distance affects the trade in value added between sector pairs: firms active in sectors relatively close are more likely to exchange goods, whereas firms upstream and downstream will need more steps to reach each other. Conceptually, this strategy follows the seminal work by Frankel and Romer (1999) that uses the geographical distance between two countries as an instrument for aggregated trade flows. However, this strategy is bounded to be at the country-level, and it would be appropriate for the research question of Kummritz (2016) that studies whether GVC-related trade causes an increase in GDP. On the other hand, this strategy alone is not well suited for studying neither productivity, that features a large heterogeneity even within narrowly defined sectors (CompNet, 2020a), nor for concentration levels, that widely differ between sectors for the presence of superstar firms (Bighelli et al., 2020). Exploiting this theoretical distance between industries allows me to use more granular, and hence better, data while using an identification approach very similar to a well studied one.

Furthermore, I depart from the strategy of Kummritz (2016) that interacts the index of upstreamness and downstreamness developed by Antràs et al. (2012) and Fally (2012), by using the more classical GVC position index developed by Koopman et al. (2010). This choice is motivated by the fact that by computing the upstreamness or downstreamness index I would make the assumption that the decision a firm takes when integrating along the supply chain is binary and unidirectional. That is, for each production stage companies make the integration decision only once, and this can be either backward or forward but not in both directions. This, however, is not desirable since the assumption that integration decisions are unidirectional is unrealistic (Del Prete and Rungi, 2020).

Hence, for each 2-digit industry I compute the GVC position index using the expression proposed by Koopman et al. (2010) at the sector-level, *id est*:

$$GVCPosition_{ir} = ln\left(1 + \frac{IVA_{ir}}{E_{ir}}\right) - ln\left(1 + \frac{FV_{ir}}{E_{ir}}\right) \tag{3}$$

Here, the "indirect value added exports" (henceforth, IVA) measures the Domestic Value Added embodied in intermediate exports used by the direct importer to produce goods for third countries; on the other hand, FV_{ir} measures the foreign value added used in exports, that is the value added from foreign countries embodied in own gross exports. In this case, the larger the value, the more upstream the country sector pair lies within a supply chain; on the contrary, if the second term dominates the equation, it means that the pair lies downstream.

Actually, by exploiting the fact that location measures such as downstreamness or upstreamness of an industry are very stable across countries (Antràs et al., 2012; Fally, 2012; Kummritz, 2016), I compute the index presented in Eq. (3) just for a (random) handful of countries.[7] The idea underlying this choice is that, for the position that firms take along the supply chain, the sector in which the company operates is more important than the country in which it establishes its registered office.

The resulting instrument, hence, will be given by the interaction of the indirect trade measure (Eq. (2)) and the inverse of the GVC position index (Eq. (3)). The measure will be at the country-sector level pair and it will be used to predict flows of exports in value added. Here, the idea is that this measure allows me to predict each element of an Inter-Country Input-Output table. However, following the methodology presented in Kummritz (2016), I use this instrument to predict the element of a matrix whose components are exports in value added and not intermediate and final consumption values as in more classical IO tables. To do so, I start by using the ICIO table from WIOD for each year and from there I take the estimated value added vector (V). The dimension of this vector will be *1xGN*, with G being the number of countries and N the number of sectors. I will then calculate the Leontief inverse (B) as prescribed by Borin and Mancini (2019b), which starts from the *GNxGN* matrix providing the industry flows including cross-border relationships (A). Finally, I will use the interaction between this vector and this matrix to calculate the value added origins of exports, by multiplying these two matrices with a GNxGN matrix whose diagonal I fill with each industry's exports (E), leaving empty any other cell. In matrix form, this will be: $VAE = V(I - A)^{-1}E$. Expanding the matrices, in a case of two countries *l* and *k* and two sectors *j* and *i*, I will have:

$$V(I-A)^{-1}E = \begin{pmatrix} v_{ik} & 0 & 0 & 0 \\ 0 & v_{jk} & 0 & 0 \\ 0 & 0 & v_{il} & 0 \\ 0 & 0 & 0 & v_{jl} \end{pmatrix} \begin{pmatrix} b^{ii}_{kk} & b^{ij}_{kk} & b^{ii}_{kl} & b^{ij}_{kl} \\ b^{ji}_{kk} & b^{jj}_{kk} & b^{ji}_{kl} & b^{jj}_{kl} \\ b^{ii}_{lk} & b^{ij}_{lk} & b^{ii}_{ll} & b^{ij}_{ll} \\ b^{ji}_{lk} & b^{jj}_{lk} & b^{ji}_{ll} & b^{jj}_{ll} \end{pmatrix}^{-1} \begin{pmatrix} e_{ik} & 0 & 0 & 0 \\ 0 & e_{jk} & 0 & 0 \\ 0 & 0 & e_{il} & 0 \\ 0 & 0 & 0 & e_{jl} \end{pmatrix} =$$

$$\begin{pmatrix} vae^{ii}_{kk} & vae^{ij}_{kk} & vae^{ii}_{kl} & vae^{ij}_{kl} \\ vae^{ji}_{kk} & vae^{jj}_{kk} & vae^{ji}_{kl} & vae^{jj}_{kl} \\ vae^{ii}_{lk} & vae^{ij}_{lk} & vae^{ii}_{ll} & vae^{ij}_{ll} \\ vae^{ji}_{lk} & vae^{jj}_{lk} & vae^{ji}_{ll} & vae^{jj}_{ll} \end{pmatrix} \text{ and } B = \begin{pmatrix} 1-a^{ii}_{kk} & -a^{ij}_{kk} & -a^{ii}_{kl} & -a^{ij}_{kl} \\ -a^{ji}_{kk} & 1-a^{jj}_{kk} & -a^{ji}_{kl} & -a^{jj}_{kl} \\ -a^{ii}_{lk} & -a^{ij}_{lk} & 1-a^{ii}_{ll} & -a^{ij}_{ll} \\ -a^{ji}_{lk} & -a^{jj}_{lk} & -a^{ji}_{ll} & 1-a^{jj}_{ll} \end{pmatrix}^{-1} \tag{4}$$

where $a^{(\cdot)}_{(\cdot)}$ is the share of inputs used in output. The elements of the $V(I - A)^{-1}E$ or *vae* matrix are the estimates for the country-industry level value added origins of each country-industry's exports. Each element of this matrix will be predicted using

[7] Since I focus on the European region, I randomly take a Southern region (Italy), a Northern one (Germany) and an Eastern one (Hungary).

the instrument given by using a linear approximation:

$$\hat{vae}_{jlik} = \alpha_0 + \beta_1\Big(\frac{\bar{\tau}_{lk}}{gvc\ position_{ij}}\Big) + \alpha_i + \alpha_k + \varepsilon_{jlik} \tag{5}$$

where α_i is a vector of sector fixed effect, while α_k is a vector of country fixed effect used to capture time-invariant characteristics. These are all the elements of the "zero" step used in this identification strategy. I combine the elements of this final matrix summing up the presented in (4) to obtain an estimate of GVC-related trade to be used in a classical 2SLS analysis.

In order to assess the validity of the instrument, I start by analyzing its relevance. As outlined in Angrist and Pischke (2008), with all types of instruments the first assumption to be assessed is whether the correlation between the instrumented variable and the instrument is large enough. The other assumption needed to infer a causal effect is the exclusion restriction, *id est* that the instrument influences the outcome (productivity and concentration) just through the independent variable, that is, GVC participation (see the Local Average Treatment Effect—LATE—theorem in Angrist and Pischke 2008). By virtue of these assumptions, the resulting estimator will measure the average causal response of the output variable to GVC participation. However, only the relevance assumption is empirically testable: I will do that by estimating model (5). Note that, in this case, I will estimate it over the whole time span available transforming the square matrices VAE and the IV one into two vectors. By doing this, I will have two vectors in which each of the respective entry indicates the value added in export (for the VAE vector) for a *country-sector x country-sector* group, while the other vector will feature the instrument value for the same group. The dimension of the vector will be given by the multiplication of the number of countries (G), sectors (N) and years (Y) (squared) that are available in my sample.

Table 3 presents the correlation coefficient of this model with an elasticity larger than one and shows its large significance, with an F-statistic well above any possible rule of thumb (Staiger and Stock, 1997). Hence, I can conclude that the instrument in the "step 0" is relevant and not weak. For what concerns the exclusion restriction, as mentioned above, it is not possible to test for the exogeneity of the instrument. The instrument is constructed at the country-industry level and country-time fixed effects can absorb any endogeneity that indirect trade costs might cause. At the same time, including time fixed effects allows me to avoid having results driven by time invariant characteristics of sectors. Hence, identification springs merely from the differential effect of the aggregated bilateral trade costs on particular industry pairs compared to other industry pairs. Exogeneity of productivity and concentration to this measure is a reasonable assumption, simply because the distance between industries is given by fixed technological processes.

Table 3 Correlation (OLS-FE) of bilateral Value Added with the instrument—(Step zero)

	(1)
	ln(VAE)
$\ln(\frac{\bar{\tau}}{\text{GVC position}})$	0.6869***
	(0.00033)
Constant	−3.339***
	(0.0039)
Country, sector, year FE	Yes
Observations	5,533,561
R-squared	0.8911
F(1,5532599)	4241175.33

Robust standard errors in parentheses
*p<0.1
**p<0.05
***p<0.01

3.2 Results

Using the instrument derived earlier, I inspect the role of involvement in international supply chains for the business environment. As earlier, I focus on all the components of the productivity Olley and Pakes decomposition (Olley and Pakes, 1996), the average mark-up enjoyed by firms at the sector-level and the degree of concentration in an industry. Before doing that, I run a first-stage regression, that is the "step one" of my empirical analysis. Indeed, after having built the value added matrix presented in Eq. (4) through the results coming from Eq. (5), I need to build the instrumented indicator for GVC trade. In Table 4, I present the correlation obtained by relating the fitted indicator to the actual overall GVC one. As in Kummritz (2016) I obtain a negative correlation coefficient, whose magnitude, although, is smaller in absolute value. The value of the F-statistic, which is useful to assess the relevance of the instrument, is well above any conventional rule of thumb (Staiger and Stock, 1997).

Then, I analyze the second stage of the 2SLS regression. These models differ partially from the ones presented in the earlier section (Tables 1 and 2), given that I do not include fixed effects at the sector-level here. By doing this, I allow the effect of GVC trade on the desired outcome to propagate across industries, therefore estimating the so-called "between-estimator". Hence, the coefficient presented in the following tables has to be interpreted as the difference across sectors in the desired outcome that is caused by a heterogeneous participation in international supply chains. Table 4 presents the first set of causal effects.

The second column of Table 4 shows the causal estimated effect of GVC trade on aggregate productivity at the industry-level. Here, I analyze the relation with firm performances by employing a productivity decomposition. Following Olley and Pakes (1996), I decomposed at the sector level the labor productivity into two components: (i) the unweighted average of labor productivity at the sector level, and

Table 4 IV estimation of the effect of GVC trade on various outcomes

	(1st stage) Overall	(2) Aggregate	(3) Within	(4) OP gap	(5) HHI	(6) Markup
IV overall	−0.285***					
	(0.047)					
$\widehat{\text{Overall}}$		0.117***	0.129***	1.730	0.250**	0.100***
		(0.04)	(0.0409)	(1.783)	(0.0976)	(0.031)
M/L	0.003***	0.001***	0.001***	0.0157***	−0.001***	0.001***
	(0.0002)	(0.0002)	(0.000)	(0.006)	(0.000)	(0.000)
K/L	−0.001***	0.001***	0.001***	−0.027***	0.001***	0.001***
	(0.000)	(0.00)	(0.00)	(0.002)	(0.000)	(0.000)
Avg. size	1.029***	−0.0752*	−0.145***	4.151**	0.437***	−0.210***
	(0.0432)	(0.043)	(0.04)	(1.89)	(0.103)	(0.033)
Constant	11.56	3.616***	3.552***	−6.052	3.178***	1.217***
	(1.18)	(0.194)	(0.195)	(8.501)	(0.466)	(0.15)
F-stat	37.04					
Observations	2889	2889	2889	2889	2891	2885
R-squared		0.716	0.734	0.328	0.305	0.450

All the variables presented in the table are subject to logarithmic transformation except for the OP Gap. The list of countries and sector included are presented in the Appendix. Country x Year fixed effects are included in each regression. Robust standard error in parentheses
*$p < 0.1$
**$p < 0.05$
***$p<0.01$

(ii) the covariance component that measures the extent to which more productive firms are larger. This latter term is known as OP-gap and, under the premise that is desirable that more productive firms should possess larger market shares, larger values of the OP-Gap indicate a higher level of allocative efficiency. Under this logic, changes in the OP-Gap reflect changes in the allocative efficiency or between-firm productivity within aggregation level. In contrast, changes in the unweighted term reflect changes in within-firm productivity (CompNet, 2020b).[8]

The effect is significantly positive and larger than the one identified in the OLS analysis (Table 12), suggesting that the OLS might be downward biased. Still, the OLS point estimate of the coefficient is in the right direction and downward biased in the case of all the terms of the labor productivity decomposition. However, the effect of internationalization on the allocative efficiency term of the productivity

[8] The models studying the OP gap are the only ones yet presented that have the dependent variable in levels instead of log. This is simply due to the fact that the covariance measure (covariance between productivity and market shares) can be either negative or positive. When it is negative, it shows that the allocation of production factors is not efficient, namely that less productive firms have larger market shares. By taking the logarithm of this measure, I would exclude all the negative values.

decomposition is positive but not significant, signaling that the only driver of aggregate productivity in this respect is the within-sector productivity. On the one hand, this is slightly surprising, given that in the literature the driver of increased aggregate productivity should be a reallocation of production factors across firms (Melitz, 2003; Melitz and Ottaviano, 2008). On the other hand, this result is relative to a specific set of firms involved in GVC-related trade, that form the most productive bulk of the exporting firms (CompNet, 2020a; Mayer and Ottaviano, 2008), as opposed to the findings of most literature that focus on the whole spectrum of exporting firm when analyzing the positive effect that trade should have on the OP-Gap. Hence, the relation between the OP gap and the GVC-related trade could be pushed downward, up until being not statistically significant.

In addition to this, another result that is qualitatively different with respect to the OLS one is presented in column (5) and is related to the concentration level (HHI index). In Table 1 the estimated coefficient of overall GVC-related trade on concentration level was negative and not significant; in Table 4 the situation is overturned, with an estimated positive and largely significant effect on the HHI-level. Hence, those sectors that are endowed with larger GVC-trade are—somehow surprisingly—more concentrated. Indeed, one may expect that those industries more involved in international supply networks face larger competition, due to a number of competitors that extends over national borders. However, this analysis leads to the rejection of this hypothesis, showing that larger participation in global supply chains leads to more market concentration.

Testing for the channels through which this relation springs would require more detailed data than the ones used in this analysis. However, a possible explanation for this is that larger concentration levels due to GVC come from the intersection of two elements: (i) firms that joined international production networks enjoy more market power, eventually leading to higher market concentration; (ii) firms involved in GVC are more efficient in their production, making it more difficult for new entrants to join the market and driving less efficient firms out of the market. Notwithstanding the fact that these possible explanation need further research to be confirmed, the evidence related to markups presented in Column (6) gives support to the first argument. Indeed, a positive effect of GVC-related trade is detected even for markups.

As earlier, I provide a distribution of the effect for markups and productivity.[9] Results are presented in Tables 5 and 6, respectively. From Table 5 it is possible to observe that the causal effect of involvement in international supply chains is larger for firms in the top percentiles of the markup distribution. The effect almost doubles from the 10th percentile to the median and almost doubles from the median to the 90th percentile. Hence, I can conclude that while the effect is present in the whole distribution of markup, it is stronger on its right tail. This conclusion is slightly different from the one presented in the OLS case, since there the impact

[9] Here, the same caveat of the results presented in Table 2 applies. The number of sectors used in this analysis is lower due to issues in the harmonization of different datasets.

Table 5 Correlation (IV-FE) of instrumented GVC trade on different percentiles of the Mark up distribution

	(1) Markup p90	(2) Markup p50	(3) Markup p10
$\widehat{\text{Overall}}$	0.370***	0.190**	0.104**
	(0.136)	(0.0761)	(0.0503)
M/L	0.001*	0.001***	0.001***
	(0.000)	(0.000)	(0.000)
K/L	0.001***	0.00	−0.001***
	(0.000)	(0.00)	(0.00)
Avg. size	−0.603***	−0.276***	−0.118**
	(0.162)	(0.0907)	(0.0594)
Constant	1.064**	0.685**	0.215
	(0.515)	(0.289)	(0.192)
N	1981	1981	1969
R-squared	0.899	0.897	0.733

All the variables presented in the table are subject to logarithmic transformation. The list of countries and sector included are presented in the Appendix. Country and Year fixed effects are included in each regression. Robust standard error in parentheses
*$p< 0.1$
**$p < 0.05$
***$p<0.01$

was symmetric and stronger in the median. Here, the results presented suggest that the rewards of GVC trade are uneven.

Then, Table 6 analyzes the distribution of the effect of GVC-related trade on the whole distribution of aggregate labor productivity. Here, again, the IV shows that the results presented in Table 2 estimated through an OLS suffer from a downward bias. As in the case of the markup presented in Table 5 the effect is increasing along the productivity distribution, even though it does not increase dramatically moving along the productivity density. The ratio between the estimated effect on the 90th percentile over the effect on the 10th percentile is slightly above 2, whereas the same ratio for the markup distribution equals 3.5. This evidence shows that the effect on the productivity distribution is less dispersed than the one on the markup.

In addition to this, column (4) shows that the dispersion of the productivity distribution—as proxied by the standard deviation—increases as a reaction to an increased participation in international supply chains. This means that in industries in which involvement in international supply networks is larger, the distance between the top and the bottom performing firms is higher. According to CompNet (2020a), this is a piece of good news for the business environment, since aggregate productivity is driven by a bulk of (top-performing) firms. Indeed, plenty of literature has underlined the importance of a handful of firms in driving aggregate trends: for instance, with US data Gabaix (2011) estimated that the business cycle movements of the largest 100 firms explain about one-third of the aggregate movements in output growth; in EU, Mayer and Ottaviano (2008) show that on

Table 6 Correlation (IV-FE) of instrumented GVC trade on different percentiles of the labor productivity distribution and standard deviation

	(1) Lab. prod p90	(2) Lab. prod p50	(3) Lab. prod p10	(4) Lab. prod sd
$\widehat{\text{Overall}}$	0.440***	0.211**	0.187**	0.628***
	(0.164)	(0.0903)	(0.0829)	(0.226)
M/L	−0.000	0.000	0.000	−0.000
	(0.000)	(0.000)	(0.000)	(0.000)
K/L	0.001***	0.001***	0.00	0.0019***
	(0.001)	(0.00)	(0.00)	(0.00)
Avg. Size	−0.518***	−0.163	−0.0476	−0.800***
	(0.193)	(0.107)	(0.0978)	(0.266)
Constant	3.323***	3.105***	2.256***	1.927**
	(0.629)	(0.347)	(0.319)	(0.867)
N	1985	1985	1985	1985
R-squared	0.973	0.701	0.852	0.925

All the variables presented in the table are subject to logarithmic transformation. The list of countries and sector included are presented in the Appendix. Country and Year fixed effects are included in each regression. Robust standard error in parentheses
*$p< 0.1$
**$p< 0.05$
***$p<0.01$

average the 'Happy Few' firms produce the bulk of output or of foreign sales; in China and India, Hsieh and Klenow (2009) that firms in the top decile are nearly five times productive as firms in the first decile.

3.3 *Robustness Checks and Limits of the Analysis*

In a nutshell, in the earlier section I found that increasing involvement in international production network causes a rise all over the distribution of production efficiency, as proxied by labor productivity, and in market power enjoyed by firms; moreover, as a reaction to increased market power, the concentration at the industry level will be higher, too. Clearly, this empirical analysis is subject to some problems. Firstly, it is based on micro-aggregated data that, although being the best possible option for cross-country comparison, do not allow me to exactly identify the effect for a firm of joining GVC; in addition to this, the lack of micro-data impedes the analysis of the mechanism through which the relation of productivity, market power and concentration with GVC participation manifest themselves. Finally, this analysis is not driven by a General Equilibrium model and hence it is a "Reduced Form" one. The issue with these kind of models is that—notwithstanding the amount of factors one can control for—the relations identified could be confounded by some unobservable trend, policy rule or expectations on that rule (Lucas Critique). In order to have a comprehensive view of the relations at play, one should build and then estimate a structural model that is able to explain thoroughly the mechanisms behind the empirical relationships estimated throughout this section. However, these flaws represent promising avenues to be pursued by future research.

Furthermore, I run some robustness checks to validate the results provided. In particular, I run the same regressions used in the earlier section, but employing different metrics: for productivity, I use TFP retrieved from a Cobb-Douglas production function estimated with an OLS and according to Wooldridge (2009), in order to control for the simultaneity bias. In addition to this, I employ both a production function based on revenues and one based on value added: while the latter should in principle be more appropriate to estimate TFP, in the data I am using value added is more noisy since it is retrieved by simply subtracting the value of intermediates from the turnover. Unfortunately, the metric used to measure intermediate costs accounts for several factors and hence it is more noisy and not well suited for cross-country comparison. Finally, for what concerns the concentration measure, I use the revenue share of the top 10 firms in a sector instead of the HHI index. Results are presented in Tables 13 and 14. The estimated models for aggregate TFP always show a positive point estimate that is in line in magnitude with the one presented in Table 4; for what concerns significance, however, only the TFP measures estimated with an OLS production function are significant. This is not cause for concern: the Wooldridge estimation of productivity is more volatile across countries given the data collection process of CompNet, hence this result is not troublesome. For what concerns the within term of the OP decomposition, the only model in line with the one presented in Table 4 is the one in column (5) of Table 14. All the others present point positive but not significant point estimates, different in magnitude from the coefficient identified in the main specification. This is more troublesome because the coefficient is not stable across different specifications, but when using a revenue based production function estimated through OLS (that returns the best TFP measure in these data) I obtain strikingly similar results to the main specification. Finally, the coefficient on allocative efficiency is always positive but larger in magnitude from what presented in Table 4. Furthermore, it is significant in 3 specifications out of five: this signals that when dealing with technological efficiency (TFP) rather than labor productivity, the reallocation mechanism is at work and pushed even further from increased GVC trade. On the other hand, for what concerns the relation between involvement in GVC trade and concentration—the main novelty of this paper—I find that the estimated coefficient in the robustness check is still positive and significant, but smaller in magnitude. This does not cause any concern because the dependent variables have different scales: the HHI is a sum of squared share, whereas the one used as a robustness is a share, hence the reduction in the point estimate is due to this difference.

3.4 The Future of Globalization

At the time of writing, the world is slowly emerging from one of its most challenging crisis. The Covid-19 pandemic has greatly influenced the economic activity of countries in several ways (see Syverson and di Mauro, 2020 for a review), one of which is globalization. Indeed, the pandemic came during a period of slowdown in globalization due to political frictions (e.g.: US-China trade war, Brexit) and, arguably, due to the reach of a peak in commercial interlinks between countries (Antràs, 2020). Participation in international supply chains has diminished recently and the pandemic possibly aggravated this situation by making the connections between firms along the supply chain more cumbersome, at least during 2020. Notwithstanding the gloomy situation, in a survey carried out within the ECB Economic Bulletin (issue 08/2020), when asked which long-lasting changes the pandemic has brought to the economic environment a large share of leading European firms answered that globalization is there to stay. Indeed, only slightly less than 10% of the surveyed leading companies answered that the pandemic will bring *de-globalization*, whereas this idea is more widespread in the public debate.

As mentioned earlier, one of the ways of measuring globalization is through trade. Particular attention has been devoted to trade in GVC as a proxy of globalization for two reasons: (i) gross trade measures are inaccurate because of double counting, *id est* goods and services exchanged across borders are increasingly counted more than once, making traditional trade measures less reliable (Borin and Mancini, 2019b; Koopman et al., 2010); (ii) trade within global production networks represent more than classical trade the essence of globalization, since companies from all over the world contribute to the production of one good or service. Unfortunately, measuring trade in GVC is a time-consuming process and it is not rare that official statistics become publicly available with huge time lags, whereas classic trade statistics are provided with smaller lags. For example, the whole analysis presented throughout Sect. 3 relies on the input-output tables provided by WIOD, which are available only up to 2014 (Timmer et al., 2015). Other projects publicly available provide similar tables, but the most recent one is published by the EORA project, which provides observations only up to 2015 (Lenzen et al., 2013). For these reasons, a thorough and up to date assessment of the state and the future of globalization—as proxied by trade in GVC—is impossible with official statistics.

Hence, economists rely on proxies to obtain up to date measures of trade and of involvement in GVC. The Covid-19 pandemic has accelerated the need for a real-time predictor of trade in order to promptly assess the changes in the trends that this massive shock has brought. Such a tool has been developed by Cerdeiro et al. (2020), that exploiting the massive amount of world seaborne trade[10] succeed in tracking in real-time and estimate trade volumes at the world, bilateral and within-country

[10] Hoffmann and Sirimanne (2017) estimate that over 80% of global merchandise trade by volume and more than 70% of its value can be traced to maritime transport.

levels. They do so by leveraging the maritime data from the Automatic Identification System (AIS), using raw data from the radio signals that the global vessel fleet emits for navigational safety purposes and providing a globally applicable end-to-end solution to transform raw AIS messages into economically meaningful, policy-relevant indicators of international trade through machine-learning techniques.

Exploiting this methodology, I can estimate the GVC arm of the gross export at the country-level, in order to assess whether the pandemic brought some serious disruptions along the supply chains in Europe, or whether the strong share of GVC participation by EU firms within the continent had the potential of sheltering those firms by severe global disruptions in supply chains (di Mauro et al., 2020). To do so, I retrieve the most recent (2015) indicator of GVC participation (estimated as in Borin and Mancini 2019b) through the EORA database. Then, by interacting this with the most up-to-date estimates of world seaborne trade I can obtain a gross measure of trade along international supply chains. I plot the results of this exercise for the European set of countries I used for the previous analysis in Figs. 1 and 2.

Figure 1 plots the moving average over 30 days of the estimated GVC-related trade as a share of the average trade volume from 2017 to 2019, following the methodology related to event studies presented in Cerdeiro et al. (2020). GVC-related trade has been subject to a huge shock in all of the four largest countries in

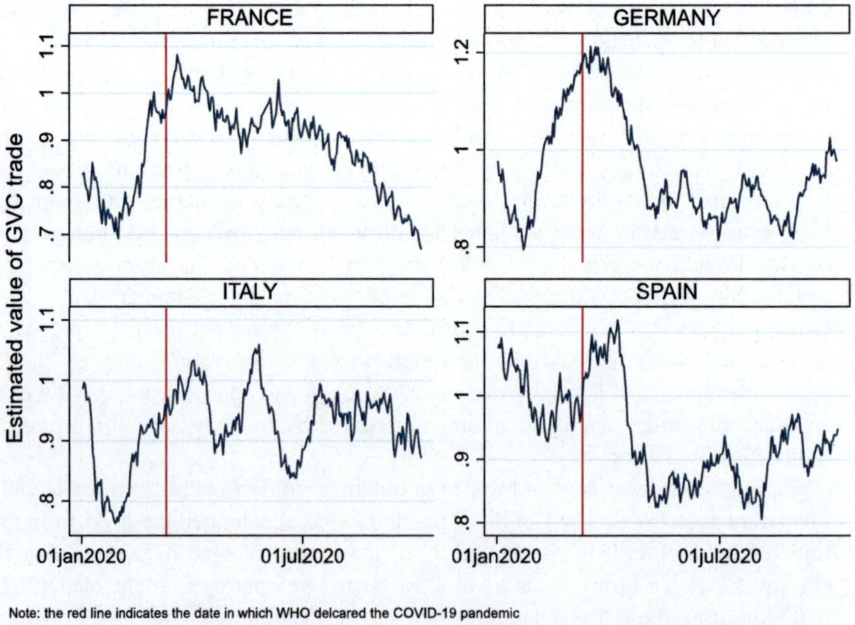

Fig. 1 Daily estimates of the GVC-related trade for selected countries (the 4 largest EU economies). Estimated value of GVC trade according to the Cerdeiro et al. 2020 methodology. The values for 2020 are presented as a share of the average GVC trade value from 2017–2019. This chart is available for a larger set of European countries in the appendix (Fig. 2)

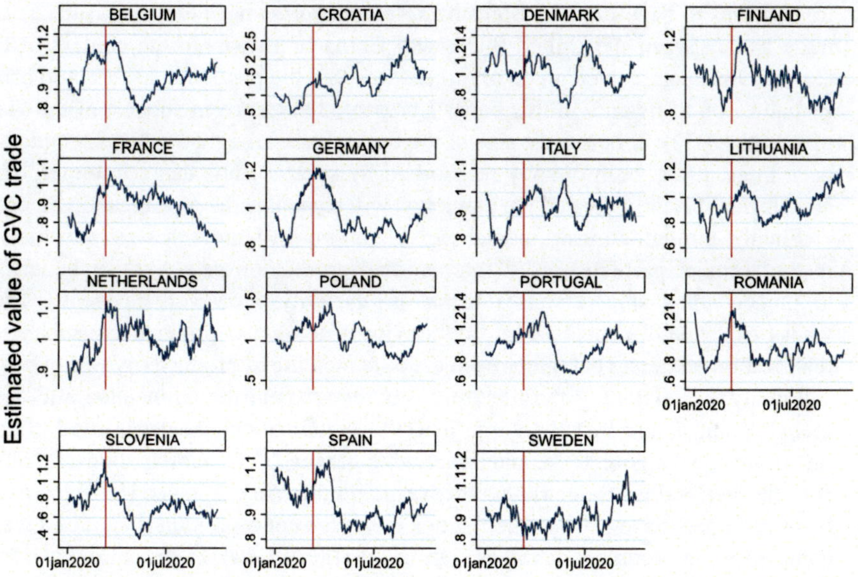

Note: the red line indicates the date in which WHO delcared the COVID-19 pandemic

Fig. 2 Estimated value of GVC trade according to the Cerdeiro et al. 2020 methodology.

EU, with Germany unsurprisingly being the most hit in this aspect by the pandemic. On the other hand, it is worth noticing that the country least hit on GVC is Italy, the European country in which the virus firstly spread and has been taking away most lives. Another fact worth noticing is that Germany is the only country that succeeded in returning back to the average 2017-19 GVC trade volumes, whether the other countries are still lagging behind. However, by looking at Fig. 2 it is not possible to detect any clear and common trend among European countries, mainly because participation in Global Value Chains differs greatly across countries in its composition (di Mauro et al., 2020). Hence, the effect of the Covid-19 pandemic on GVC trade is likely to be asymmetric across countries, depending mainly on countries' exposure to disruptions in international supply networks (Altomonte et al., 2020).

4 Concluding Remarks

The rise of globalization and of international supply chain trade was one of the most radical changes that the global economy has ever experienced. In the last years of the twentieth century and at the dawn of the new millennium, globalization has been increasing at an unsustainable pace (Antràs, 2020), whereas from the aftermath of the Global Financial Crisis until more recent days this increasing trend seems to have stopped. Signs of *de-globalization* have emerged, such as the trade war between the United States and China or Brexit. In the context of the Covid-19 pandemic, a common argument was that the pandemic itself could bring globalization to its end. In this paper I presented evidence in support of the view of Antràs (2020): although the size of the trade shock brought by the pandemic has been huge, it has been quickly reabsorbed by several European economies. This signals that it is unlikely that the pandemic will terminate the globalization process.

Finally, through an instrumental variable approach I show that globalization—in the form of participation in international production networks—is beneficial to the economy since it raises firms' productivity. However, differently from what I expected, the increase in productivity is not due to productivity-enhancing reallocation processes but rather from the pure increase of productivity within firms.

Finally, by relating to the literature concerned about the unintended effects of globalization, I find that the surge in GVC participation has detrimental effects on the economy, too: those industries with larger GVC participation are more concentrated and firms populating them enjoy more market power. However, more research is needed to clarify whether this increased concentration is sign of a weak competitive environment or rather sign of an efficient market structure rewarding the most efficient firms (Covarrubias et al., 2020).

In conclusion, these findings are relevant not only for the economic literature, but for policy as well: at the time of writing, the world is slowly emerging from the pandemic crisis and governments are trying to build plans for the recovery of their countries. Strengthening global production networks rather than incentivizing firms to reshore their production processes should be at the core of such plans.

Appendix

Data Sources

For this paper I used several data sources, exploiting micro-aggregated variables. In particular, I used the CompNet dataset, the World Input Output Database and the UN ESCAP dataset. This section is intended to briefly present each data source.

The CompNet dataset is the main product of the Competitive Research Network. It provides granular and micro-aggregated data overcoming the harmonization and confidentiality issues through the micro-distributed approach (Lopez-Garcia & di Mauro, 2015). The dataset presents data at the country, size, 2-digit sector and NUTS2 level. Tables 7 and 8 present the sample composition in terms of countries and industries. CompNet provides its dataset without ever accessing the micro-data, that are safely stored by the Data Providers and therefore avoiding confidentiality

Table 7 Countries available in the CompNet dataset. Note: Belgium, Italy, Spain and Switzerland data on trade variables are not available. For Czech Republic, Poland and Slovakia the only sample available is the one comprising firms with at least 20 employees.

Country	Country	Country	Country
Belgium	France	Netherlands	Slovenia
Croatia	Germany	Poland	Spain
Czech Republic	Hungary	Portugal	Sweden
Denmark	Italy	Romania	Switzerland
Finland	Lithuania	Slovakia	

Table 8 List of industries available in the CompNet dataset

Industry code	Industry code
10—Manufacture of food	47—Retail except motorvehicles
11—Manufacture of beverages	49—Land transport and via pipelines
12—Manufacture of tobacco	50—Water transport
13—Manufacture of textiles	51—Air transport
14—Manufacture of wearing apparel	52—Warehousing and support for transportation
15—Manufacture of leather and related	53—Postal and courier activities
16—Manufacture of wood, cork, straw and plaiting	55—Accommodation
17—Manufacture of paper products	56—Food and beverage services
18—Printing and reproduction of recorded media	58—Publishing
20—Manufacture of chemicals products	59—Multimedia services
21—Manufacture of basic pharmaceutical products	60—Programming and broadcasting activities
22—Manufacture of rubber and plastic	61—Telecommunications
23—Manufacture of non-metallic mineral products	62—Computer programming, consultancy et al.
24—Manufacture of basic metals	63—Information services
25—Manufacture of fabricated metal prod	68—Real Estate activities
26—Manufacture of computer, electronic, optical prod	69—Legal and accounting
27—Manufacture of electric equipment	70—Activities of head offices; consultancy
28—Manufacture of machinery and equipment n.e.c.	71—Architectural and engineering
29—Manufacture of motor vehicles, trailers	72—R&D
30—Manufacture of other transport equipment	73—Advertising and market research
31—Manufacture of furniture	74—Other professional, scientific activities
32—Other manufacturing	75—Veterinary activities
33—Repair and installation of machinery	77—Rental and leasing activities

(continued)

Table 8 (continued)

Industry code	Industry code
41—Construction of buildings	78—Employment activities
42—Civil engineering	79—Travel services
43—Specialised construction	80—Security services
45—Wholesale, retail and repair of motorvehicles	81—Services to buildings and landscap noisilye
46—Wholesale except motorvehicles	82—Office admin, office support

issues.[11] Notwithstanding this issue, harmonization of the raw variables is ensured by the CompNet research team, that works alongside the Data Providers to ensure the best data quality (CompNet, 2020b). The data collection process works in the following way: CompNet sends a harmonized data gathering protocol to collect and calculate various variables and indicators to several data providers (one for each of the 19 European countries in the dataset). The data gathering protocol computes the desired micro-aggregate indicators which are then sent back to the Scientific Staff of CompNet that subsequently builds the CompNet database from the micro-aggregate indicators. A particular feature of this dataset that I will exploit is that it collects joint distributions, i.e. conditional distributions of some variable given a specific condition, that can be either discrete or continuous.[12]

On the other hand, the World Input-Output Database (WIOD) is constituted by annual time-series of world input-output tables from 1995 to 2014. World Input-Output Tables and underlying data, cover 43 countries plus the fictional "Rest of the World" region, that comprises the residual countries of the world. Data for 56 sectors are classified according to the International Standard Industrial Classification revision 4 (ISIC Rev. 4). These tables have been constructed in a clear conceptual framework based on the system of national accounts. They are based on officially published input-output tables merged with national accounts data and international trade statistics (Timmer et al., 2015). A WIOT provides a comprehensive summary of all transactions in the global economy between industries and final users across countries. In addition to a national input-output table, imports are broken down according to the country and industry of origin in a WIOT in order to allow a user to retrieve domestic and foreign value added. Tables 9 and 10 provide the sample composition in terms of countries and industries present in the WIOD (Tables 9 and 10).

[11] Firm-level information is typically not available since it is confidential. Therefore, cross-country comparability is often hampered because data are stored by national statistical institutes. Often, the definition of variables may change, too.

[12] For example this means that I can compare the exporters' distribution of productivity with the one of domestic firms. This will help me in estimating productivity premia for firms engaged in international trade.

Table 9 List of countries available in the WIOD dataset

Country	Country	Country
Australia	United Kingdom	Norway
Austria	Greece	Poland
Belgium	Croatia	Portugal
Bulgaria	Hungary	Romania
Brazil	Indonesia	Rest of the World
Canada	India	Russia
Switzerland	Ireland	Slovakia
China	Italy	Slovenia
Cyprus	Japan	Sweden
Czech Republic	South Korea	Thailand
Germany	Lithuania	Turkey
Denmark	Luxembourg	Taiwan
Spain	Latvia	United States
Estonia	Mexico	
Finland	Malta	
France	Netherlands	

Table 10 List of industry codes available in the WIOD dataset. A more detailed description of the industry codes can be found here

ISIC Code					
A01	C19	C28	G45	J58	M71
A02	C20	C29	G46	J59-60	M72
A03	C21	C30	G47	J61	M73
B	C22	C31-32	H49	J62-63	M74-75
C10-C12	C23	C33	H50	K64	N
C13-C15	C24	D35	H51	K65	O84
C16	C25	E36	H52	K66	P85
C17	C26	E37-39	H53	L68	Q
C18	C27	F	I	M69-70	R-S
T	U				

Table 11 Descriptive statistics for the main variables of Eq. (1)

	Mean	SD
ln(HHI)	5.65	1.42
ln(Mark-up)	1.28	0.42
ln(aggregate labor productivity)	4.04	0.80
ln(within labor productivity)	3.90	0.83
OP Gap (covariance)	9.43	81.42
ln(GVC)	6.41	2.25
ln(Backward GVC)	5.76	2.37
ln(Forward GVC)	5.56	2.02

Table 12 Correlation (OLS-FE) of Backward and Forward GVC trade on OP decomposition of Labor productivity by component

	(1) Aggregate	(2) Aggregate	(3) Within	(4) Within	(5) OP gap	(6) OP gap
Backward	0.0231***		0.015***		0.955***	
	(0.00418)		(0.00396)		(0.231)	
Forward		0.022***		0.009*		1.093***
		(0.006)		(0.005)		(0.315)
M/L	0.001***	0.001***	0.001***	0.001***	−0.01**	-0.01**
	(0.00)	(0.00)	(0.00)	(0.00)	(0.004)	(0.004)
K/L	0.001***	0.001***	0.001***	0.001***	−0.041***	−0.04***
	(0.00)	(0.00)	(0.00)	(0.00)	(0.01)	(0.002)
Size	0.006	0.001	−0.01	−0.01	5.769***	5.80***
	(0.01)	(0.01)	(0.01)	(0.01)	(0.714)	(0.718)
Constant	3.804***	3.807***	3.771***	3.794***	−9.774***	−10.61***
	(0.038)	(0.043)	(0.036)	(0.040)	(2.12)	(2.383)
Observations	3052	3042	3052	3042	3052	3042
R-squared	0.854	0.853	0.880	0.879	0.479	0.479

All the variables presented in the table are subject to logarithmic transformation except for the OP Gap one. The list of countries and sector included are presented in the Appendix. Country, Sector and Year fixed effects are included in each regression. Robust standard error in parentheses
*$p< 0.1$
**$p< 0.05$
***$p<0.01$

Finally, bilateral trade costs data is taken from the UNESCAP-World Bank Trade Cost Database. It estimates bilateral trade costs on the basis of the model developed by Novy (2013), which estimates trade costs for each country pair using bilateral trade and gross national output. It collects information for over 200 countries, with observations ranging from 1995 to 2018. Through the methodology employed in retrieving the trade costs data, it gives a micro-founded comprehensive trade cost figure that includes both structural factors, such as geography, and policy measures, such as tariffs (Kummritz, 2016). Differences in economic size and endowments are not the only reason why some countries trade more than others: trade flows depend on many other factors that express the degree of separation between countries, such as the aforementioned geography and policy measure. A more detailed description of the database can be found in Arvis et al. (2013).

Table 13 Robustness checks. Effect of GVC trade on OP-decomposition components and revenue share of top 10 firms in a sector. The TFP components are based on a Cobb-Douglas production function with *Value Added* as dependent variable

	(1)	(2)	(3)	(4)	(5)	(6)	(7)
		WD			OLS		
	Aggregate	within	OP Gap	Aggregate	within	OP gap	Top 10 revenue share
$\widehat{\text{Overall}}$	0.0221	−0.00636	11.59***	0.152***	0.0566	9.842***	0.0337**
	(0.0457)	(0.0395)	(4.423)	(0.0488)	(0.0402)	(2.125)	(0.0156)
M/L	0.00172***	0.00142***	0.0858***	0.000429**	0.000568***	−0.0200***	−0.000145***
	(0.000165)	(0.000142)	(0.0159)	(0.000177)	(0.000146)	(0.00771)	(5.19e−05)
K/L	0.000371***	4.14e−05	0.0605***	−9.01e−05	−0.000333***	0.00966***	0.000106***
	(7.19e−05)	(6.21e−05)	(0.00696)	(7.65e−05)	(6.30e−05)	(0.00333)	(2.39e−05)
Avg. size	0.109**	0.0820*	6.778	−0.300***	−0.153***	−13.01***	0.0874***
	(0.0489)	(0.0423)	(4.737)	(0.0529)	(0.0436)	(2.306)	(0.0172)
Constant	4.340***	3.902***	10.33	3.288***	3.346***	−23.09**	0.00149
	(0.217)	(0.188)	(21.00)	(0.231)	(0.190)	(10.05)	(0.0736)
Observations	2884	2884	2884	2875	2875	2875	2691
R-squared	0.705	0.772	0.455	0.700	0.781	−0.262	0.346

All the variables presented in the table are subject to logarithmic transformation. The list of countries and sector included are presented in the Appendix. Country and Year fixed effects are included in each regression. Robust standard error in parentheses

*p < 0.1

**p < 0.05

***p <0.01

Table 14 Robustness checks. Effect of GVC trade on OP-decomposition components and revenue share of top 10 firms in a sector. The TFP components are based on a Cobb-Douglas production function with Turnover as dependent variable

	(1)	(2)	(3)	(4)	(5)	(6)
		WD			OLS	
	Aggregate	within	OP gap	Aggregate	within	OP gap
$\widehat{\text{GVC}}$ Overall	0.167	0.0934	6.698	0.273***	0.195***	7.417***
	(0.130)	(0.107)	(14.37)	(0.0752)	(0.0646)	(1.737)
M/L	0.00162***	0.00118***	0.244***	−0.00332***	−0.00300***	−0.0427***
	(0.0001)	(0.0004)	(0.0553)	(0.00027)	(0.00023)	(0.00626)
K/L	0.000552***	0.000260*	0.00784	0.000502***	0.000291***	0.00688**
	(0.000178)	(0.000147)	(0.0197)	(0.000117)	(0.000101)	(0.00270)
Avg. Size	−0.238*	−0.213*	−7.222	−0.477***	−0.373***	−9.391***
	(0.136)	(0.111)	(14.98)	(0.0816)	(0.0702)	(1.886)
Constant	2.908***	2.867***	389.0***	2.023***	2.134***	−20.58**
	(0.629)	(0.519)	(69.57)	(0.354)	(0.304)	(8.180)
Observations	2239	2242	2239	2839	2839	2839
R-squared	0.388	0.440	0.140	0.604	0.658	−0.344

All the variables presented in the table are subject to logarithmic transformation. The list of countries and sector included are presented in the Appendix. Country and Year fixed effects are included in each regression. Robust standard error in parentheses

*p < 0.1

**p < 0.05

***p <0.01

Additional Tables and Figures

Acknowledgments I am extremely grateful to Filippo di Mauro and Carlo Altomonte for useful comments. CompNet provided me with the data, and all the CompNet scientific team helped me to exploit better this rich dataset. All errors are my own.

References

Altomonte, C., Bonacorsi, L., & Colantone, I. (2018). Trade and growth in the age of global value chains (BAFFI CAREFIN Working Papers No. 1897). BAFFI CAREFIN, Centre for Applied Research on International Markets Banking Finance and Regulation, Università Bocconi, Milano, Italy.

Altomonte, C., Coali, A., & Ottaviano, G. I. P. (2020). Back to the future: The forward-looking consequences of covid-19 across eu regions. CompNet Policy Brief Series (10).

Angrist, J. D., & Pischke, J. (2008). *Mostly harmless econometrics: An empiricist's companion*. Princeton: Princeton University Press.

Antràs, P. (2020). *De-globalisation? Global Value Chains in the Post-covid-19 Age* (Tech. Rep.). National Bureau of Economic Research.

Antràs, P., & Chor, D. (2013). Organizing the global value chain. *Econometrica, 81*(6), 2127–2204.

Antràs, P., Chor, D., Fally, T., & Hillberry, R. (2012). Measuring the upstreamness of production and trade flows. *American Economic Review, 102* (3), 412–416. https://doi.org/1.1257/aer.102.3.412

Arvis, J.-F., Duval, Y., Shepherd, B., & Utoktham, C. (2013). Trade costs in the developing world: 1995–2010 (Policy Research Working Paper Series No. 6309). The World Bank. https://ideas.repec.org/p/wbk/wbrwps/6309.html

Altomonte, C., et al. "Assessing the reliability of the CompNet micro-aggregated dataset for policy analysis and research: coverage, representativeness and cross-EU countries comparability." The Competitiveness Research Network: available at www. comp-net. org (2018).

Autor, D. H., Dorn, D., & Hanson, G. H. (2013). The china syndrome: Local labor market effects of import competition in the united states. *American Economic Review, 103* (6), 2121–2168.

Autor, D. H., Dorn, D., Hanson, G. H., & Song, J. (2014). Trade Adjustment: Worker-Level Evidence. *The Quarterly Journal of Economics, 129* (4), 1799–1860.

Bernard, A. B., Eaton, J., Jensen, J. B., & Kortum, S. (2003). Plants and productivity in international trade. *American Economic Review, 93*(4), 1268–1290.

Bighelli, T., di Mauro, F., Melitz, M., & Mertens, M. (2020). Firm concentration and aggregate productivity. Firm Productivity Report (CompNet).

Borin, A., & Mancini, M. (2019a). Measuring what matters in global value chains and value-added trade. World Bank WP (8804).

Borin, A., & Mancini, M. (2019b). Measuring what matters in global value chains and value-added trade. The World Bank. https://doi.org/10.1596/1813-9450-8804

Cerdeiro, D. A., Komaromi, A., Liu, Y., & Saeed, M. (2020). *World Seaborne Trade in Real Time: A Proof of Concept for Building Ais-Based Nowcasts from Scratch* (Tech. Rep.). International Monetary Fund.

Chiacchio, F., Gradeva, K., & Lopez-Garcia, P. (2018). The post-crisis TFP growth slowdown in CEE countries: Exploring the role of global value chains. ECB Working Paper No. 2143.

Colantone, I., Crinò, R., & Ogliari, L. (2019). Globalization and mental distress. *Journal of International Economics, 119* (100), 181–207.

Colantone, I., & Stanig, P. (2018a). Global competition and brexit. *American Political Science Review, 112* (2), 201–218.

Colantone, I., & Stanig, P. (2018b). The trade origins of economic nationalism: Import competition and voting behavior in Western Europe. *American Journal of Political Science, 62* (4), 936–953.

CompNet (2020a). User Guide for the 7th Vintage CompNet Dataset. Accessible via: https://www.comp-net.org/data/7th-vintage/.

CompNet (2020b). The firm productivity report. Accessible via: https://www.comp-net.org/fileadmin/_compnet/user_upload/Documents/Productivity_Report_FINAL-.pdf

Covarrubias, M., Gutiérrez, G., & Philippon, T. (2020). From good to bad concentration? US industries over the past 30 years. *NBER Macroeconomics Annual, 34* (1), 1–46.

De Loecker, J., & Warzynski, F. (2012). Markups and firm-level export status. *American Economic Review, 102* (6), 2437–2471.

Del Prete, D., & Rungi, A. (2020). Backward and forward integration along global value chains. *Review of Industrial Organization, 57* (2), 263–283.

Dhyne, E., Berthou, A., Soares, A. C., Bugamelli, M., Cazacu, A.-M., Lalinsky T., Merikuüll, J., Harasztosi, P., Demian, C.-V., & Oropallo, F. (2015). Assessing European firms' exports and productivity distributions: The CompNet trade module (Working Paper Series). European Central Bank.

di Mauro, F., Altomonte, C., & Inferrera, S. (2020). Eu firms participation in gvc: Bliss or curse after covid? CompNet Policy Brief Series (9).

Di Nino, V., & Veltri, B. (2020). The viral effects of foreign trade and supply networks in the euro area (IWH-CompNet Discussion Papers No. 4/2020). Halle Institute for Economic Research (IWH).

Dreher, A., Gaston, N., & Martens, P (2008). Measuring globalisation. In *Gauging its consequences*. New York: Springer.

ECB. (2020). ECB economic bulletin (issue 08/2020).

Fally T. (2012). *Production staging: Measurement and facts* (pp. 155–168). Boulder: University of Colorado Boulder.

Frankel, J. A., & Romer, D. H. (1999). Does trade cause growth? *American Economic Review, 89* (3), 379–399.

Gabaix, X. (2011). The granular origins of aggregate fluctuations. *Econometrica, 79* (3), 733–772.

Garcıa-Herrero, A., & Tan, J. (2020). Deglobalisation in the context of United States-China decoupling. Policy Contribution, Issue n 21.

Gereffi, G. (2020). What does the covid-19 pandemic teach us about global value chains? The case of medical supplies. *Journal of International Business Policy, 3* (3), 287–301.

Herfindahl, O. (1950). Concentration in the U.S. Steel Industry, Dissertion. New York: Columbia University.

Hirschman, A. O. (1980). *National power and the structure of foreign trade* (vol. 105). Berkeley: University of California Press.

Hoffmann, J., & Sirimanne, S. (2017). Review of maritime transport. In United Nations Conference on Trade and Development

Hsieh, C.-T., & Klenow, P J. (2009). Misallocation and manufacturing TFP in China and India. *Quarterly Journal of Economics, 124* (4), 1403–1448.

Johnson, R. C., & Noguera, G. (2017). A portrait of trade in value-added over four decades. *Review of Economics and Statistics, 99* (5), 896–911.

Koopman, R., Powers, W., Wang, Z., & Wei, S.-J. (2010). Give credit where credit is due: Tracing value added in global production chains (Working Paper No. 16426). National Bureau of Economic Research.

Kummritz, V. (2016). *Do Global Value Chains Cause Industrial Development?* (Tech. Rep.). Centre for Trade and Economic Integration, The Graduate Institute.

Lenzen, M., Moran, D., Kanemoto, K., & Geschke, A. (2013). Building EORA: A global multi-region input–output database at high country and sector resolution. *Economic Systems Research, 25* (1), 20–49.

Lopez-Garcia, P., & di Mauro, F. (2015). Assessing European competitiveness : The new CompNet micro-based database (Working Paper Research No. 1764). European Central Bank.
Maqui, E., & Morris, R. (2020). The long-term effects of the pandemic: Insights from a survey of leading companies. Economic Bulletin Boxes, 8.
Masahisa, F., & Nobuaki, H. (2020). Globalization as civilizational progress and the covid-19 pandemic (Policy Discussion Papers (Japanese)). Research Institute of Economy Trade and Industry (RIETI).
Mayer, T., & Ottaviano, G. (2008). The happy few: The internationalisation of European firms. Intereconomics: Review of European Economic Policy.
Melitz, M. J. (2003). The impact of trade on intra-industry reallocations and aggregate industry productivity. *Econometrica, 71* (6), 1695–1725.
Melitz, M. J., & Ottaviano, G. I. P. (2008). Market size, trade, and productivity. *Review of Economic Studies, 75* (1), 295–316.
Noguera, G. (2012). Trade costs and gravity for gross and value added trade. Job Market Paper, Columbia University, 4.
Novy, D. (2013). Gravity redux: Measuring international trade costs with panel data. *Economic Inquiry, 51* (1), 101–121.
OECD. (2020). Trade policy implications of global value chains. OECD Trade Policy Brief.
Olley, G. S., & Pakes, A. (1996). The dynamics of productivity in the telecommunications equipment industry. *Econometrica, 64* (6), 1263–1297.
Powell, D., & Wagner, J. (2021). The exporter productivity premium along the productivity distribution: evidence from quantile regression with nonadditive firm fixed effects. In MICROECONOMETRIC STUDIES OF FIRMS'IMPORTS AND EXPORTS: Advanced Methods of Analysis and Evidence from German Enterprises 121–149.
Sforza, A., & Steininger, M. (2017) Globalization in the Time of COVID-19 (April 2020). CESifo Working Paper No. 8184. UNCTAD. Review of maritime transport. Flagship report.
Shrestha, N., Shad, M. Y., Ulvi, O., Khan, M. H., Karamehic-Muratovic, A., Nguyen, U.-S. D., Baghbanzadeh, M., Wardrup, R., Aghamohammadi, N., Cervantes, D., Nahiduzzaman, K. M., Zakig, R. A., & Haque, U. (2020). The impact of covid-19 on globalization. *One Health, 11*, 100180.
Staiger, D., & Stock, J. H. (1997). Instrumental variables regression with weak instruments. *Econometrica, 65* (3), 557–586.
Syverson, C., & di Mauro, F. (2020). The covid crisis and productivity growth (VoxEU.org 16 April 2020).
Timmer, M., Dietzenbacher, E., Los, B., Stehrer, R., & de Vries, G. (2015). An illustrated user guide to the world input–output database: The case of global automotive production. *Review of International Economics, 23* (3), 575–605.
Wooldridge, J. M. (2009). On estimating firm-level production functions using proxy variables to control for unobservables. *Economics Letters, 104* (3), 112–114.
Wooldridge, J. M. (2010). *Econometric Analysis of Cross Section and Panel Data* (vol. 1). Cambridge: The MIT Press.
World Bank. (2020). *World Development Report 2020: Trading for Development in the Age of Global Value Chains*. World Development report.

The Value of Nature to Our Health and Economic Well-Being: A Framework with Application to Elephants and Whales

Ralph Chami, Thomas Cosimano, Connel Fullenkamp, Fabio Berzaghi, Sonia Español-Jiménez, Milton Marcondes, and Jose Palazzo

1 Introduction

As the intense but relatively brief economic disruptions caused by the SARS-CoV-2 pandemic subside, Europe must resume its focus on longer-term economic challenges. Foremost among these is the need to avert climate disaster by limiting global temperature rise to less than 2 °C. In order to reach this goal, the European Union (EU) has committed itself to net-zero greenhouse gas emissions by the year 2050. Yet the long-term carbon strategy communicated by the EU (European Commission, 2018) projected that only 60% of this goal could be reached based on full implementation of EU climate-related legislation. Additional methods to further

R. Chami (✉)
International Monetary Fund, Washington, DC, USA

T. Cosimano
Blue Green Future, Falls Church, VA, USA

C. Fullenkamp
Duke University, Durham, NC, USA
e-mail: cfullenk@duke.edu

F. Berzaghi
Laboratory for Sciences of Climate and Environment (LSCE) - UMR, CEA/CNRS/UVSQ, Gif-sur-Yvette, France
e-mail: fabe@unitus.it

S. Español-Jiménez
Fundación Centro MERI, Castro, Chile
e-mail: sespanol@fundacionmeri.cl

M. Marcondes · J. Palazzo
Baleia Jubarte, Caravelas, Brazil
e-mail: milton.marcondes@baleiajubarte.org.br; jose.truda@baleiajubarte.org.br

L. Paganetto (ed.), *Economic Challenges for Europe After the Pandemic*,
Springer Proceedings in Business and Economics,
https://doi.org/10.1007/978-3-031-10302-5_7

limit greenhouse gas emissions or increase carbon capture have been proposed, but nearly all of these rely on technology—either scaling up existing technologies or developing new technologies.

A promising means of supplementing these efforts can be found in so-called Nature-based Solutions (NbS). Scientific research increasingly reveals that ecosystems and individual species contribute significantly to carbon capture. And to the extent that these same ecosystems and species have been greatly reduced in extent and number, an opportunity exists to augment carbon capture through concerted efforts to conserve and restore them. Although most people are aware of the role that trees can play in carbon capture, other habitats and species have the potential to capture similar quantities, and in some cases, much more. Many of these natural resources, moreover, such as salt marshes and kelp forests, are present in Europe.

Because NbS rely on conservation and restoration of nature, the case must be made to commit scarce resources to this approach. The fundamental question is whether the gains from enhanced carbon capture would be worth the significant investments of financial and human capital required to restore the carbon-capturing habitats and species to their former abundance. This, in turn, is essentially a question of valuation. But it has proven extremely difficult to value ecosystems and their services in ways that can convince policymakers and taxpayers that benefits exceed costs. A reliable way to value natural assets must be found well before the climate target is breached—and well before the dwindling natural resources are lost forever. Thus, solving the valuation problem is key to unlocking a potential source of carbon capture that could help Europe—and many other regions as well—attain their net-zero greenhouse gas or carbon-neutrality targets.

In most economic and financial contexts, the tools of valuation are used to make resource allocation or capital budgeting decisions. In these situations, the prior decision of whether to expend resources in order to reach an objective has already been made in favor of doing so, so that the purpose of valuation is to determine how best to deploy resources to attain the objective. For example, an individual's portfolio allocation problem, solved by applying models such as the Capital Asset Pricing Model or Arbitrage Pricing Theory, presumes that a household has already decided to smooth consumption over time or save toward goals such as starting a business.

In environmental economics, however, the tools of valuation are used not only to answer the allocation question, but also to motivate agents to answer the prior question—whether to expend any resources at all in pursuit of environmental objectives—affirmatively. As an example, The Economics of Ecosystems and Biodiversity (TEEB) initiative describes its goals in this way on its website (http://www.teebweb.org/about/the-initiative/):

> **The Economics of Ecosystems and Biodiversity** (TEEB) is a global initiative focused on **"making nature's values visible"**. Its principal objective is to mainstream the values of biodiversity and ecosystem services into decision-making at all levels. It aims to achieve this goal by following a structured approach to valuation that helps decision-makers ***recognize*** the wide range of benefits provided by ecosystems and biodiversity, ***demonstrate*** their

values in economic terms and, where appropriate, suggest how to ***capture*** those values in decision-making.

The National Research Council (2005, p. 2) describes the role of valuation in this way:

> Despite growing recognition of the importance of ecosystem functions and services, they are often taken for granted and overlooked in environmental decision-making. Thus, choices between the conservation and restoration of some ecosystems and the continuation and expansion of human activities in others have to be made with an enhanced recognition of this potential for conflict and of the value of ecosystem services.

These examples show that environmental economists explicitly employ valuation tools in an attempt to persuade individuals, businesses, and governments to expend resources on environmental protection and restoration. These attempts are necessary in order to overcome the significant disincentives to taking action associated with externalities and collective-action problems.

Because of these additional demands being placed on valuation tools by the environmental economics profession, it is sensible and necessary to reflect on whether the valuation tools and strategies currently being employed are effective at motivating people to commit their scarce resources to pursuing environmental protection and restoration. Unfortunately, it would be both very difficult and highly controversial to evaluate the impact of environmental valuation efforts on the amounts of resources (both financial and physical) expended in the pursuit of environmental protection and restoration. Nonetheless, it is probably fair to say that there is room for improvement. For example, since 1997 TEEB has produced estimates of the total value of ecosystem services provided by all of the planet's biomes. These estimates, which consistently produce a value larger than global GDP, do not appear to have catalyzed a wave of new investments in environmental protection and restoration.

It is still possible to evaluate the effectiveness of valuation methods and strategies in motivating environmental investments, however, by considering their characteristics rather than attempting to measure their impacts. One key characteristic is the ability of the information produced by the method to motivate or inspire people to take action. Several types of agents exist who use the information from environmental economics to make different types of decisions: individuals, business leaders, and policymakers. In order for a valuation method to be effective, each type of agent must find that the information produced by the method motivates them to take action. Although making judgments about the motivational power of a valuation method may at appear subjective, there is an extensive literature from economics, psychology, and marketing that we can draw from regarding attributes that make information persuasive or effective in provoking action.

This literature suggests that the motivational power of information comes from its ability to stimulate excitement or concern in the recipient. Information interacts with human emotions and cognitive biases to exert powerful influence over behavior and decision making. For example, Hesketh (2015) argues that information is persuasive when it enables people to satisfy important psychosocial needs, like the need to be loved. Crimmins (2016) discusses how information that works with people's cognitive biases, such as the many heuristics that humans use to make decisions, is more successful at motivating people to act than information that works against these biases.

In many contexts, the motivational power of information is the sole measure of its effectiveness. But people whose decisions are publicly scrutinized, such as policymakers and business leaders, place additional demands on the information they use, in order to withstand this scrutiny. These include many qualities such as accuracy, reliability, and replicability, but we summarize them in a criterion we call credibility. Credibility of information reflects the difficulty of doubting or disproving its truth or accuracy: the more difficult it is to doubt or disprove a piece of information, the more credible it is. This is important to policymakers and business leaders because they need to defend their decisions in the face of public scrutiny. If a decision is based on credible information—ideally, the best information available at the time—it is difficult to attack or fault.

In addition to being credible, and able to stimulate excitement or concern, valuation information must also be relatable. Relatability describes the extent to which information is expressed in terms that humans find relevant and useful. For example, from the point of view of businesses, relatable valuation information is helpful in identifying and evaluating feasible business opportunities. People find information on costs and benefits expressed in monetary terms to be useful for making decisions. On the other hand, they generally find imprecise, complex or abstract information difficult to relate to their objectives and hence a much weaker motivation for making decisions or taking action.

As an example of environmental information that performs well with respect to all three criteria, consider a television advertisement for the World Wildlife Fund (WWF) that was widely broadcast in early 2020, which had the purpose of encouraging donations to fund efforts to protect polar bears. It featured video sequences of mother polar bears and their offspring, while the voiceover in the advertisement discussed how climate change was causing the ice floes that polar bears depend on to vanish. The advertisement mentioned scientific studies, which viewers would find credible, but expressed the implications of the studies in simple, concrete, relatable terms that people could understand: the disappearance of ice floes and the polar bears that need them for survival. The advertisement also took advantage of the emotional impact created by the video images, and the brain's tendency to jump to conclusions, to create the impression of polar bears desperately searching for ice floes, stimulating the viewer's concern.

Although we are not suggesting that the WWF advertisement should be a template for environmental valuation, it nevertheless offers some lessons for improving the ability of environmental valuation to motivate the recipients and users of these valuations to take action. In particular, we argue that the criteria discussed above and the example of the WWF advertisement suggest that the following valuation strategy would be more successful at inspiring action than current valuation approaches:

- Use only market-based methods of valuation.

- Value individual resources rather than groups of disparate resources or ecosystems.

Valuations based on these two broad guidelines will perform well according to the criteria discussed above. Market-based methods of valuation will tend to have high levels of credibility, as long as the markets from which prices are obtained are relatively free of distortions, because of the confidence that free-market prices are fully reflective of all social costs and benefits and thus reveal the "truth" regarding how society values a good or service. They will also have high levels of relatability because they express values in monetary terms, and because they will naturally identify the markets that are relevant to a particular natural resource.

Estimating the value of individual resources will also support the credibility of the valuations, since the linkages from the resource to its value should be transparent. This approach is also highly relatable, since an individual resource and the market-valued services it provides are both concrete and specific. Valuing individual resources also has high potential to work with human emotions and cognitive biases in order to create concern or excitement. Although the term "charismatic megafauna" sometimes carries negative connotations because these species tend to draw attention away from other natural resources, it nonetheless acknowledges that individual resources can take advantage of humans' affinity and availability heuristics in order to arouse excitement and concern. And the surprise that an unexpectedly high valuation of an individual resource engenders can also strongly stimulate excitement or concern.

There is a cost to this approach to environmental valuation, which is the fact that it omits any non-market and non-use values and therefore does not capture the total economic value (TEV) of a natural resource. Our approach thus necessarily represents a conservative approach to valuation, which places lower bounds on the values of individual natural resources. We argue that this is a contribution of our method rather than a drawback. By including only those services to which market prices can be readily assigned, we remove as much subjectivity as possible from the estimated values. Valuation will always be as much art as science, in which human judgement plays a key role in identifying the determinants of value as well as in selecting and applying valuation models. But our approach removes unsupported claims and cheap talk from the critical step of assigning monetary values to the service flows or to the resource itself. Therefore, we argue that the estimates produced by our method are reliable and convincing starting points for public discussion regarding whether—and how much—to invest in environmental protection.[1]

Because our estimated values are lower bounds, they still allow for additional discussion about how the non-market-valued attributes of a particular natural resource should factor into the investment decision. We believe such discussions should always take place when making decisions about environmental protection

[1] See Lew (2015) for a discussion of criticisms of standard estimation methods.

investments. But if agreement cannot be reached about these difficult to measure sources of value, then the baseline monetary value provided by our estimates can still form a basis for constructive action, effectively preventing the perfect from becoming the enemy of the good.

In this paper, we outline a valuation procedure that follows the guidelines introduced above. Then we implement this valuation strategy on two resources—elephants and whales—to demonstrate its feasibility and its ability to produce valuations that people find more persuasive or motivational than existing methods and strategies. Part of the reason these resources were chosen is that new research has identified additional services, of significant market value, that are provided by these animals. Integrating these additional service flows into the values of whales and elephants is a further contribution of this paper.

The remainder of the paper is organized as follows. Section 2 develops the valuation model and the discusses its parameter requirements. Sections 3 and 4 apply the valuation procedure to African forest elephants and cetaceans (the nine great whales), respectively. Section 5 concludes.

2 A Valuation Framework for Natural Resources

Valuation of natural resources is an important area of research in the environmental economics literature. Although some benefits that flow from individual natural resources are traded and priced on markets, many if not most are not, and moreover, many natural resources produce only non-market-traded benefits. Thus, one focus of valuation research has been to use economic fundamentals such as preferences to estimate values for natural resources that cannot be fully valued by markets. One of the primary valuation benchmarks in this literature is willingness to pay (WTP), which is the amount that an individual would pay to enjoy a natural resource or contribute toward an effort to preserve it.

WTP is generally estimated using one of two methods.[2] Revealed preference methods utilize data on purchases to estimate hedonic pricing models, or data on other related expenditures, such as travel costs incurred, to estimate WTP. These methods are suitable for estimating the amount that people would pay to enjoy a natural resource. The opportunities to apply revealed preference models to natural resource valuation, however, have proven to be limited. Most natural resources are not purchased (or consumed) by their users, and other revealed preference approaches such as travel cost models are limited in the types of service flows (such as recreational flows) they can value.

The vast majority of studies that estimate WTP, therefore, use stated preference methods. As the name suggests, stated preference methods employ different types

[2] See Freeman (2004) for an extensive discussion of the methods used to estimate WTP. Lew (2015) also gives an extensive review of these methods and their applications to marine resources.

of surveys in which respondents state their willingness to pay taxes or fees that will be used to invest in specific natural resource preservation or enhancement programs. Stated preference methods are used to estimate public willingness to pay for individual conservation programs and for ranking competing programs. And for programs that aim to increase the population of a living resource, stated preference estimates could be interpreted as the value of an increase in the population. But they generally do not attempt to estimate the total values of specific natural resources.

Stated preference estimates of WTP tend to have lower credibility than market-based valuations, because the respondents to surveys are not generally required to pay the fees or taxes they claim they would pay. And it should not be forgotten that the valuations obtained are technically those of the programs proposed in the experiments rather than the resources to be protected by the programs.

In some cases, market valuation of individual resources may be possible as a consequence of quota or cap-and-trade systems designed to limit harvesting. For example, Costello et al. (2012) propose that the International Whaling Commission's whaling quotas be replaced by tradable harvesting rights. To the extent that such a market would be open to any willing purchaser, the resulting price would establish market values for whales that are more reflective of all of society's preferences. Such arrangements, however, presume that the case for preserving the resources has already been argued successfully, as reflected in the decision to implement a system of harvest limits. This method also begs the question of how to set the initial quotas and caps, which would presumably depend on the value assigned to the resource. And as in the case of revealed preference methods, only a very small subset of natural resources are harvested whole and could be valued in this way.

Most approaches to market valuation focus on the services produced by natural resources. These borrow the idea from financial economics that the value of a physical capital good is derived from the stream(s) of services that the good produces. Physical capital goods are created for the purpose of producing streams of services that have an explicit market value. Many natural resources also produce streams of services that are valuable to society, although this is not their primary goal or purpose. TEEB (2010) provides an overview of the types of services and the market-based methods of valuing them. While some services are priced in markets, such as ecotourism, other services provided by natural resources are regulatory services (such as predator or flood control) that are not directly priced in markets. Market values can be assigned to these services, however, by estimating what it would cost to replace them. Natural resources may also provide services that are inputs into the production of other goods and services to which market values can be assigned. Market values may be assigned to these factor-of-production services if the contribution of the natural resource to production can be estimated.

The valuation approach most similar to ours is embodied in the TEEB initiative as well as the Natural Capital Accounting method being developed by the U.K. Office of National Statistics (ONS) and Department for Environment, Food and Rural Affairs (Defra) (Philips, 2017). As in our approach, Natural Capital Accounting seeks to recognize and quantify the goods and service flows arising from natural resources, so that a monetary value may be placed on them. For example, Natural Capital Accounting recognizes regulatory services such as greenhouse gas sequestration and market-valued services such as ecotourism, both which are also essential to our valuation analysis.

The aims of Natural Capital Accounting, however, are not well suited to the valuation of individual natural assets. This approach takes ecosystems as its unit of analysis, focusing on the valuation of entire biomes or ecosystems rather than their individual constituents. This method has also emphasized biodiversity, an ecosystem characteristic which has proven difficult to integrate into the Natural Capital Accounting framework as well as difficult to quantify and value (CIEEM, 2019). Although there appear to be no theoretical obstacles to valuing individual natural resources using Natural Capital Accounting, no valuations of individual resources such as whales or elephants utilizing this framework have been published to date that we are aware of. To the extent that Natural Capital Accounting remains focused on valuing ecosystems, this approach does not perform well with respect to the relatability criterion. Biodiversity is too abstract, and ecosystems can be too large or too complex, to be helpful to individuals and businesses in making decisions. In addition, ecosystems do not appear to have a high ability to create excitement or concern, particularly in comparison to individual components of ecosystems.

Each of the above methods of valuation produces useful information for policymakers and the general public. But as our discussion indicates, none of them is well suited for estimating the value of individual natural resources. Therefore, we propose the following approach to natural resource valuation, which fills the need for this information. First, an individual natural resource is chosen. Then the services the resource produces are identified. These include only those services flowing from the natural resource that have been identified and measured in the academic and professional literature, and to which market values may be assigned.

Next, discounting is used to estimate the total market value of the services. The market value of an asset at any time is the discounted sum of the value of the services it is expected (or scheduled) to produce during all subsequent periods. Discounting the future values is necessary because these services are produced during many different future periods, and their value must be adjusted by the appropriate opportunity cost of waiting to receive these services. We initially assume for simplicity that only one type of service is produced by a physical capital asset. If we let $\boldsymbol{s}$ be the quantity of services produced, $\boldsymbol{p}$ be the market value (price) of these services, and $\boldsymbol{r}$ be the appropriate discount rate, then the value $\boldsymbol{V}$ of the physical capital asset is given by

$$V_t = \sum_{i=1}^{\infty} \frac{p_{t+i} s_{t+i}}{(1+r)^i}$$

This valuation equation is easily modified to accommodate multiple, distinct service streams because of the additivity of present values. If a physical capital good produces n distinct service streams with market prices $p_1, \ldots, p_n$, then the value of the capital good is given by

$$V_t = V_{1,t} + V_{2,t} + \cdots + V_{n,t} = \sum_{i=1}^{\infty} \frac{p_{1,t+i}s_{1,t+i} + p_{2,t+i}s_{2,t+i} + \cdots + p_{n,t+i}s_{n,t+i}}{(1+r)^i}$$

To summarize, the following procedure is used in this paper and can be used to estimate the money value of any individual natural resource:

1. **Identify the services produced by the resource.**
   (a) Verifiable estimates of the quantities of services produced must exist in the academic or professional literature.
   (b) If the quantity produced of a service is not measured in money, market prices must exist that can be sensibly assigned to the service.
2. **Project the market values of each service ($p_{j,t+i}s_{j,t+i}$) into the future.**
3. **Assign a discount rate appropriate to the natural resource and the service(s) produced.**
4. **Using the values projected in Step 2, calculate the value of the resource using the definition of V_t.**

The best way to demonstrate the utility of this approach—and to recognize the issues it raises—is to move directly to extended examples in which we apply the above procedure to estimate the values of natural resources. In the following sections, therefore, we apply our framework to value African forest elephants, and to value great whales found off the coasts of Brazil and Chile.

3 Applying the Framework to the Valuation of Forest Elephants in Africa

Our first application estimates the value of African forest elephants (*Loxodonta cyclotis,* Matschie, 1900), a sub-species of the African elephant (*Loxodonta africana,* Blumenbach, 1797). Forest elephants live in the rain forests of central and western Africa and are genetically and morphologically different from the ones inhabiting savannas. Further differences between savanna and forest elephants are their ecosystem engineering role. We focus on forest elephants as their ecosystem services (described below) have recently been quantified (Berzaghi et al., 2019).

3.1 Step 1: Identify the Services Produced by the Resource

Elephants produce several types of services that could be valued using market prices. First, in some places such as south- and southeast Asia, elephants are employed commercially as beasts of burden. Forest elephants are generally not used for this purpose. Elephants also undoubtedly generate ecotourism revenues, since they are one of the "big five" species that tourists wish to see when they visit African game preserves and parks. It is difficult to separate ecotourism revenues into those due specifically to elephants, however. Moreover, the majority of African ecotourism takes place in the savannahs rather than in the rainforests, where tourism is still underdeveloped. Because of these difficulties with measurement, we do not include these services in our elephant valuations.

On the other hand, forest elephants do produce carbon-capture services that can be valued. Elephants contribute to carbon capture and long-term storage in two ways. First, as large animals, elephants store nontrivial amounts of carbon on their bodies. Considering the average body mass of a mature forest elephant is 3000 kg (Grubb et al., 2000), we estimated that each individual body is composed of 24 percent carbon, or 720 kg (see methods).

Although an individual elephant will eventually die and the carbon carried on its body will be released back into the ecosystem or the atmosphere in the form of CO_2, a stable population of elephants will continually store some amount of carbon. We can therefore value the carbon currently stored on the bodies of the existing population of elephants as if it were sequestered, assuming that current populations are maintained. In addition, any permanent increase in the population (that is, increase to the equilibrium or steady-state population) implies that an additional amount of carbon can be added to the total amount sequestered in elephant bodies.

The second way in which African forest elephants sequester carbon is through their impact on the forest ecosystem. Large herbivores and megaherbivores are known to have significant impacts on their ecosystems, and by extension on the biogeochemical cycles taking place in these ecosystems. Recent research by Berzaghi et al. (2019) has shown that the activity of forest elephants contributes to the net accumulation of aboveground biomass (carbon) stored in trees. While moving through the forest and foraging for food, elephants reduce the density of trees smaller than 30 cm in diameter. This reduction in tree density changes light and water availability in the forest leading to an increase in the proportion and the average size of late-succession trees. Compared to other type of trees, late-succession trees are longer lived, require less light and water to survive, and become dominant once they reach the canopy. Late-successional trees store more carbon than other types of trees (given the same volume), so as their average size and abundance increase, there is a net increase in the amount of carbon stored in the forest.

3.2 Step 2: Project the Market Value of Services Provided into the Future

An important question that arises when valuing living organisms is how to model future populations. The services provided by future offspring can be a significant source of the current population's value, which implies that both over- and undervaluation are possible. In addition, the projected future population embeds assumptions about conservation and restoration that should be made transparent. Therefore, a population growth model is needed for each species. How population growth affects the production of services must also be specified.

In this paper, we project that future populations of both elephants and whales will grow from their current levels and eventually return to their estimated sizes before the advent of large-scale poaching and industrial whaling, respectively. We have two reasons for doing so. First, the current populations of elephants and whales are far below—on the order of ten percent of—their historical numbers. We argue that assuming a return to what scientists believe are their equilibrium populations strikes the right balance between over- and undervaluation. Second, estimates of the services provided by elephants and whales found in the literature are often based on the assumption of a return of the species to their previous population sizes.

We construct a model of population growth for elephants that utilizes data on birth rates, survival rates of calves and adults, ages at first reproduction, and intervals between births (Turkalo et al., 2017, 2018). A logistic function is used to model the birth rate, which converges to the death rate as the population reaches its steady-state value equivalent to the estimated pre-poaching population. Free parameters of the growth model are calibrated so that the initial numbers of births imply a constant ratio of births to population. Details of the construction of the population growth models are given in Appendix 1.

3.2.1 Carbon Capture and Sequestration Through Elephant Biomass

In order to value carbon capture, an estimate of the market price of this service is needed. The most developed markets for carbon capture deal in carbon dioxide rather than pure carbon, since these markets were created in order to limit carbon dioxide emissions from industrial production, power generation, and transportation. Thus, all estimates of carbon capture and sequestration must be converted to their CO_2 equivalent by multiplying the amount of carbon by 11/3. Although many carbon-trading markets exist globally, the most liquid is the European market ETS. We argue that this market provides the best estimate of the market price of carbon.

We estimate the value of carbon sequestration on elephant bodies by first calculating the amount of carbon sequestered by current and future elephant populations. Then the carbon is converted to its CO_2 equivalent and multiplied by the price of \$24.72 per tonne of CO_2.[3]

From above, the amount of carbon on the average elephant's body is 720 kg, which is multiplied by the current population of 100,000 individuals to obtain the starting amount of carbon sequestered. Additional carbon is sequestered each period equivalent to the change in elephant population implied by the growth model, multiplied by 720 kg. The amount of carbon on each elephant is equivalent to 720*11/3 = 2640 kg or 2.64 tonnes of carbon dioxide.

3.2.2 Carbon Capture and Sequestration Through Stimulating Forest AGB Increase

Our approach is to first value the carbon capture contributed by the current elephant population and then add the carbon sequestered by each additional elephant as the population increases. We assume that the changes made to the forest by elephant activity are permanent, so that the increase in carbon capture is effectively permanent.

Berzaghi et al. (2019) estimate that if forest elephant populations were to recover to their historic population, each forest elephant would stimulate a net increase in carbon capture in central African rain forests of 26 tonnes of C per hectare. Given the historic density of 0.5 elephants per km^2, this implies an actual increase in carbon capture of 13 tonnes of C per hectare. This increase in carbon capture will take place over a long period, however, for two reasons. The change in forest composition due to elephant activity will take decades to be completed, and the increase in the elephant population from their current number of approximately 100,000 individuals to their historic level of 1.1 million will require centuries to occur.

In order to make the carbon sequestration calculations simple and manageable, we make the following assumptions. First, we assume that the existing elephant population currently occupies only 200,000 km^2 of their historic range of 2.2 million km^2 at a population density of 0.5 elephants per km^2 (but see Maisels et al., 2013 as the current population is highly fragmented across central Africa). This enables us to estimate the current carbon sequestration services of the existing elephant population by assuming that these individuals have already increased carbon capture of forests by 13 tonnes per hectare in this area.

For each new cohort born, we assume that the cohort moves to an unoccupied portion of the forest elephants' historic range and lives there at a density of 0.5 elephants per km^2. The area of the plot occupied is therefore determined by the size of the cohort and the assumed population density of 0.5 elephants per km^2. On each

[3] The price of CO_2 per tonne is the average daily value during 2019 on the EU ETS. See https://markets.businessinsider.com/commodities/historical-prices/co2-european-emission-allowances/eur/1.1.2006_2.5.2020

newly occupied plot, we assume that the initial amount of carbon captured is 3.25 tonnes, and this increases due to the elephants' activity at a constant rate over the next 150 years until the full 13 tonnes per hectare is reached, which is equivalent to 9533 tonnes of carbon dioxide per km^2. Once the carbon capture has increased by 13 tonnes per hectare, the increment goes to zero so that no further services are contributed to the valuation by the cohort. The annual increments are multiplied by the price of carbon dioxide.

This assumed process of new cohorts settling unoccupied portions of the historic range and increasing carbon capture within these new settlements continues until the elephant population has grown to its pre-poaching population, at which time they will fully occupy their historic range. According to the parameters of the population growth model we developed, this will require about 9 centuries.

3.3 Step 3: Assign a Discount Rate Appropriate to the Natural Resource and the Service(s) Produced

According to financial economic theory, the discount rate used to value an asset consists of two components. The first is the risk-free interest rate, which is better understood as the return required to overcome human impatience and induce a person to wait for a future payment. The second component is a risk premium, which compensates the holder of an asset for the systematic or nondiversifiable risk that the asset incurs. The identifying feature of systematic risk is that it is common to many assets, making their payoffs fluctuate in concert. Thus, the most common measure of systematic risk is the covariance of an asset's payoff with the payoffs of other risky assets, such as the return to the market portfolio of assets.

Although the payoffs to a natural resource can be risky, this risk is not necessarily systematic. If the values of the streams of services provided by the resource do not exhibit significant covariance with other assets' payoffs, then the risk in the resource is idiosyncratic risk, which does not earn a risk premium. The flows of carbon-capture services from living adult elephants will remain roughly constant on a per-elephant basis, no matter how the payoffs from other assets fluctuate. Fluctuations in the quantities of these service streams come mainly from two sources. The first is expected population growth, which is likely to be uncorrelated with fluctuations in the payoffs from other assets. Unexpected fluctuations in services would primarily come from higher-than-average mortality among elephants. The events that cause unexpected mortality in elephants include poaching and disease. The occurrence of such events is likely to be uncorrelated with fluctuations in the payoffs from other assets.

The value of carbon-capture services produced by elephants can also vary because of fluctuations in the price of carbon. The most actively traded carbon market in the world currently is the EU's ETS market for carbon-dioxide emissions.

We obtained data on monthly closing prices of carbon emissions credits from this market and estimated a standard CAPM regression of the form

$$R_{CO2,t} - R_{f,t} = \alpha + \beta \left(R_{M,t} - R_{f,t}\right) + \varepsilon_t$$

where R_{CO2} is the monthly return on carbon emissions credits, R_f is the risk-free rate proxied by three-month U.S. Treasury bill yields, and R_M is the market return proxied by the monthly return on the S&P 500 equity index. Our estimate for the 2014–2019 period produced a positive but statistically insignificant coefficient. This implies that the price of carbon is not significantly correlated with other asset returns, suggesting that the appropriate discount rate for carbon-sequestration services is the long-term, risk-free rate.

Given that a long-term, risk-free discount rate is appropriate for valuing the benefits of elephants, the next question is how to estimate it in the context of environmental valuation. TEEB (2010) argues that the "impatience" component of the risk-free rate should be exactly zero, implying a near-zero risk-free rate when the effect of intertemporal substitution is taken into account. Philips (2017) uses the HM Green Book Social Discount rates, which decline from a top rate of 3.5 percent for periods up to 30 years, to a rate of 2.5 percent for periods up to 100 years but cautions that these rates tend to "overdiscount" the future, or are in other words too high. Professional investors commonly use the 10-year government bond yield as their estimate of the risk-free rate. Using the U.S. 10-year government bond rate and adjusting for inflation estimated via the GDP deflator, we obtain an average 10-year yield of approximately 2.65 percent over the 1954–2018 period. We choose two percent for the risk-free rate, since this reflects market evidence and the practices in the existing literature, but also lessens the likelihood that we are over discounting.

3.4 *Step 4: Using the Values Projected in Step 2, Calculate the Value of the Resource Using the Definition of V_t*

Present values were calculated using a 1000-year horizon. Using a starting population of 100,000 mature elephants, the future population path generated by the population growth model, and the other valuation parameters described above, we calculate a present value of carbon sequestration on elephant bodies of \$166 per individual.

The present value of carbon sequestration through an increase in carbon stored in AGB, however, is quite large. The total present value of this service is the sum of the contribution of the current elephants and the contribution from future generations of elephants.

$$\begin{aligned}\text{PV of Increased Forest Biomass} &= \$23.5656\text{ Billion} + \$152.7173\text{ Billion}\\ &= \$176.2829\text{ Billion.}\end{aligned}$$

Dividing this total value by the current population of elephants implies a value of $1,762,829 per elephant for this service. If we add the $166 for carbon sequestration on elephants' bodies, we obtain a total value of $1,762,995 per elephant.

3.5 *Discussion*

The result of this valuation demonstrates the potential of our approach to stimulate excitement, concern, and ultimately action. At over $1.75 million, the value of a single forest elephant is a striking number that is likely to gather significant attention, since people will want to know what exactly makes this creature so valuable. These inquiries will lead to further opportunities to educate the public about elephants' contributions to carbon capture and convince individuals to spend their resources on preservation of this species and its habitat. For example, a public relations campaign could be built around comparing the value of a live forest elephant capturing carbon—$1.75 million—to one that has been killed for its ivory, about $20,000 per tusk. Showing that the loss of a forest elephant implies the loss of valuable and important carbon sequestration services—which benefit humans—converts an intangible and remote psychic harm (the brutal and unnecessary death of a forest elephant) to a more direct and concrete harm to personal wellbeing (worsening consequences of climate change). We argue that this will significantly increase people's willingness to commit resources to elephant preservation and restoration.

This number should also generate interest among investors. Our valuation creates a "fundamentals" based estimate of the worth of a specific, tangible asset. This in turn creates a potential investment opportunity that is similar to the standard investment opportunities that financial professionals are familiar with. The challenge for investors is to devise instruments that would enable them to realize this potential value in terms of cash. Although this will be difficult, the size of the prize—over $176 billion total for the existing population of forest elephants—would undoubtedly attract many entrepreneurs and investment professionals who could profit either from taking an ownership stake in this investment or earning commissions from marketing this instrument to other investors.

4 Applying the Framework to the Valuation of Great Whales Frequenting the Brazilian and Chilean Coasts

This application considers great whales found off the coasts of Brazil and Chile. The great whales we include in our valuation are the nine large baleen whales (blue, bowhead, fin, minke, sei, right, humpback, gray and Bryde's), plus the sperm whale. Most but not all of these different species spend significant parts of the year off the coast of Brazil, and some are resident year-round. In the case of Chile, we consider only the blue whale due to data limitations. Whales make an interesting valuation case study because they produce several distinct services to which market values can be assigned, including services that recent research has helped to quantify.

As in the case of elephants, we project future populations by assuming that the populations of whales will eventually grow to reach their historical (pre-industrial-whaling) numbers. We construct a model of population growth for each whale species that utilizes data on birth rates, survival rates of calves and adults, ages at first reproduction, and intervals between births for each species of great whale. A logistic function is used to model the birth rate, which converges to the death rate as the population reaches its steady-state value. Free parameters of the growth model are calibrated so that the initial numbers of births imply a constant ratio of births to population. Details of the construction of the population growth models are given in Appendix 1.

4.1 Step 1: Identify the Services Produced by the Resource

Whales produce at least three services that society values and which have been measured by scientists and economists: ecotourism (whale watching), carbon capture, and fisheries enhancement. The carbon capture services can be further separated into the carbon captured in whale biomass, and the carbon captured by phytoplankton production that can be attributed to whale activities.

4.2 Step 2: Project the Market Value of Services Provided into the Future

4.2.1 Ecotourism (Whale Watching)

A benchmark estimate of the market value of whale-watching services can be obtained from the direct and indirect expenditures on whale watching worldwide. The International Fund for Animal Welfare estimated that whale watching tours generated $2.1 billion of expenditures in 2008, including both direct ticket sales and indirect expenditures generated by whale watching. At the time this estimate was made, many countries with the potential for whale watching had not developed this industry. Cisneros-Montemayor et al. (2010) estimate that the global whale-watching industry could generate up to $2.5 billion per year if fully developed. We assume that the current income flow from whale-watching is $2 billion.

We also argue that ecotourism revenues vary positively with whale biomass, so that as whale populations increase, ecotourism revenues will also increase. In particular, we assume that a return of whales to their pre-whaling populations will result in a doubling of global ecotourism revenues, to $4 billion annually. This

Table 1 Global whale populations

Species	Current population	Steady-state population	Carbon on body (tonnes)
Blue	5400	303,500	12.2692
Bowhead	26,000	110,000	4.4719
Bryde's	132,000	146,000	2.4359
Fin	110,000	763,000	6.7067
Gray	16,000	25,000	2.9262
Humpback	66,000	307,000	5.4842
Minke	704,000	928,000	0.4190
Right	14,500	124,000	6.0215
Sei	49,100	246,000	2.0493
Sperm	360,000	1,101,000	6.7125
Total	1,483,000	4,053,500	

projection is conservative in the sense that it allows for diminishing returns of services from whales. As shown in Table 1, if whales return to their pre-industrial whaling numbers, this is an average increase of over 173 percent in great whale populations for each species. Thus, an increase in services on the order of 100 percent would allow for significant diminishing marginal returns. In the case of ecotourism, the diminishing returns could be caused by lower novelty of watching whales, should whales become much more abundant.

4.2.2 Carbon Capture and Sequestration Through Whale Biomass

Because whales are some of the largest animals on earth, their bodies contain nontrivial amounts of carbon. The total amount of carbon captured by whale biomass over time can be decomposed into the carbon stored in the current population of whales, the carbon captured by future net additions to the whale population, and the carbon effectively sequestered by future whale falls.

The carbon captured in whale biomass has been calculated by Pershing et al. (2010) for various species of great whales. A stable population of whales will effectively sequester a quantity of carbon proportional to the number of individuals. Estimates of current whale populations are given by Smith et al. (2019), and are presented in Table 1, along with estimates of the pre-industrial whaling populations of each species, which are from Pershing et al. (2010), and Whitehead (2002). Table 1 also shows the amount of carbon sequestered on the body of the average whale by species. We estimate the value of the carbon currently sequestered on whale bodies by converting the carbon per body to its CO_2 equivalent, and then multiplying by the current population as well as the price of \$24.72 per tonne of CO_2. In addition, as the equilibrium population of whales increases, the net increase in the population will also create additional flux proportional to this increase. Our population growth model implies a time-varying increase in whale populations until they reach their long-run, steady-state equilibrium number.

Because whale falls (deaths in which the whale carcass falls to the ocean floor) effectively sequester carbon on the ocean floor, there is an additional annual flux in carbon sequestration equal to the annual number of whale falls multiplied by the carbon sequestered on the body of the particular species. The rate of whale falls lowers the rate of population growth used in our model, but the amount of carbon sequestered by these falls must be accounted separately from the carbon captured by the increases in population.

4.2.3 Carbon Capture and Sequestration Through Enhancement of Primary Production (Phytoplankton Fertilization)

Whales play an additional role in carbon capture and sequestration by promoting phytoplankton growth. Through their normal feeding behavior, which involves diving in search of food followed by resting and defecating at the ocean surface, whales transport nutrients upward through the water column in a process dubbed the "whale pump" (see for example Roman & McCarthy, 2010). In the Southern Ocean, whales transport needed iron to the ocean surface, where it leads to increased phytoplankton blooms. In addition to the whale pump, the migration behavior of whales also transports nutrients to areas where they are in limited supply. This process, dubbed the "whale conveyor" (Roman et al., 2014), transports nitrogen from high-latitude feeding areas to low-latitude calving areas, where availability of nitrogen limits phytoplankton growth.

Whales' contributions to phytoplankton growth in turn lead to increased capture and sequestration of carbon. Because phytoplankton currently capture the equivalent of 37 billion tonnes of carbon dioxide annually, a small percentage increase in the quantity of phytoplankton due to whale activity could result in large absolute contribution to carbon capture.

Several studies estimate the impact of the whale pump and whale conveyor on primary production. Lavery et al. (2010) estimates that the 12,000 sperm whales in the Southern Ocean export 400,000 tonnes of carbon annually through their impact on phytoplankton. Roman et al. (2014) estimate that the nitrogen transported by whales may increase primary production in whale calving areas by 15 percent. This large increase is a localized effect and is difficult to extrapolate to an impact on total primary production, however. On the other hand, Lavery et al. (2014) estimates that a return of the blue whale population to its pre-whaling level in the Southern Ocean would increase primary production by 0.23% in that body of water. Ratnarajah et al. (2016) estimate the impact of three whale species on primary production in the Southern Ocean. Mean estimates of the contributions of these species to primary production, assuming they return to their pre-whaling populations, sum up to nearly one percent of current primary production.

Given the limited number of studies and the variation in their estimates of whale impact on primary production, caution is warranted when using their results. Nonetheless, attributing one percent of current phytoplankton production to the current whale population appears, given the current state of the research, to be a reasonable initial estimate of the impact of whales on primary production.

We further argue that the amount of carbon capture services produced increases with whale populations. In particular, we assume that the quantities of services produced increase as whale biomass increases. We reason that whales' contributions to primary production should vary according to the quantity of feces produced, which we assume is positively related to biomass. The increase in primary production will in turn increase carbon capture by phytoplankton as well as further enrich fisheries, as we discuss below. Specifically, we project an increase on the order of one percent of global primary production due to whale activity, if whales were to return to their pre-whaling numbers. Because existing phytoplankton is estimated to capture ten billion tonnes of carbon annually (equivalent to 37 billion tonnes CO_2), this implies that whales currently stimulate the capture of 100 million tonnes of carbon (equivalent to 370 million tonnes CO_2) and will increase phytoplankton carbon capture by a further 100 million tonnes as their populations returns to pre-whaling levels. Again, we note that this projection allows for significant diminishing marginal returns of whale contribution to primary production.

4.2.4 Fisheries Enhancement

In addition to carbon capture, the increase in phytoplankton due to whale activity has also been shown to increase production throughout the marine food chain. We therefore attribute a portion of commercial fisheries income, one percent per year, to whale activities. This portion is equivalent to our estimate of whales' contribution to phytoplankton production. The UN's Food and Agriculture Organization (FAO) estimates that annual global fish production in 2018 was worth $401 billion (FAO, 2020), which was divided between $250 billion in aquaculture and $150 billion in traditional commercial fishing. Although much aquaculture takes place in ocean environments and therefore would potentially benefit from whale activity, we base our estimate on the value of traditional commercial fishing, which implies a value of $1.5 billion per year for the current annual service flow from fisheries enhancement. In addition, we project that whales' contributions to fisheries revenues increase from $1.5 billion to $3.0 billion per year as whale populations return to pre-whaling levels.

Using the population projections and the upper bounds on the increases in the three services described above, we then project the annual increases in the three services. We assume that the annual rate of increase $v_{i,t}$ in ecotourism, carbon capture through primary production, and fisheries enhancement services for each whale species i is equal to the ratio of the annual increase in the population, $N_{i,t} - N_{i,t-1}$ to the difference between the steady-state and current populations $N_{i,T} - N_{i,0}$: $v_{i,t} = \frac{N_{i,t}-N_{i,t-1}}{N_{i,T}-N_{i,0}}$.

The annual service flows of each service $j = 1, 2, 3$ from each species $i = 1, 2, \ldots, 10$ during each future year t are therefore equal to the initial flows multiplied by one plus the cumulative sum of the increases up to that year: $s_{i,j,t} = s_{i,j,0}\left(1 + \sum_{u=1}^{t} v_{i,u}\right)$.

4.3 Step 3: Assign a Discount Rate Appropriate to the Natural Resource and the Service(s) Produced

As in the case of service flows from elephants, we argue that the flows of carbon-capture and fisheries enhancement services from living adult whales will remain roughly constant on a per-whale basis, no matter how the payoffs from other assets fluctuate. Fluctuations in the quantities of these service streams come mainly from two sources. The first is expected population growth, which is likely to be uncorrelated with fluctuations in the payoffs from other assets. Unexpected fluctuations in services would primarily come from higher-than-average mortality among whales. The events that cause unexpected mortality in whales include ship strikes, entanglement in fishing lines, disease, and ingestion of plastics. The occurrence of such events is likely to be uncorrelated with fluctuations in the payoffs from other assets.

We have already argued that carbon prices do not exhibit systematic risk, so that the carbon sequestration services from whales should also be discounted at the risk-free rate. Ecotourism revenues, on the other hand, are probably at least somewhat correlated with the business cycle and hence with other asset returns. Likewise, the values of fisheries are probably also correlated somewhat with the business cycle. Thus, there is probably some systematic risk in the values of the service flows that whales produce. Sufficient data does not exist to enable estimation of the correlations of the returns on these service flows with the overall market return, however. We argue that the systematic risk component of the overall value of the services provided by whales is small, because the cyclicality of ecotourism and fisheries revenues are not expected to be very high, and because (as we show below) the majority of the value of the services provided by whales is associated with carbon capture, which should be discounted at the risk-free rate. Therefore, we conclude that the risk-free rate is a good first approximation of the appropriate discount rate.

4.4 Step 4: Using the Values Projected in Step 2, Calculate the Value of the Resource Using the Definition of V_t

The projected values constructed in Step 2 include the services produced by the entire world population of great whales. Therefore, the next step in valuing the whales off the coasts of Brazil and Chile is to assign the appropriate shares of global

Table 2 Whale populations in Brazil and Chile

Species	Current population	Steady-state population	Share of total whale biomass
Blue (Brazil)	64	3583	0.00015547
Blue (Chile)	760	57,000	0.00185364
Bowhead	0	0	0
Bryde's	1558	1723	0.00186513
Fin	1298	9007	0.00173128
Gray	0	0	0
Humpback	25,000	28,198	0.02725305
Minke	25,000	32,955	0.00208124
Right	800	6841	0.00103650
Sei	580	2904	0.00023615
Sperm	10,000	30,583	0.01334434

values to the local populations.[4] In principle, valuation of the whales in a particular area can begin by prorating the total value of each service produced by the fraction of total whale biomass present in local species. In the case of carbon sequestration on whale bodies, however, the value of this service can be constructed by applying the population growth models described in Step 2 to each local species.

In order to apply the population growth model to the whales off the coast of Brazil, we obtained or constructed estimates of both current and steady-state (pre-whaling) populations in this location. The Brazilian research organization Baleia Jubarte provided per-species estimates of current populations for minke, humpback, right, and sperm whales in Brazil.[5] Bowhead and gray whales are not present in Brazilian waters. Baleia Jubarte also estimated that the total number of blue, Bryde's, fin and sei whales present off the coast of Brazil is currently 3500 but did not provide estimates for each species. We allocated this total among the four species by assuming that the population of each of these four species in Brazilian waters is proportional to their current relative abundance in the world.

Estimates of pre-industrial whaling populations for each species present off the coast of Brazil were constructed by assuming that the steady-state levels reached by local populations will be proportional to their relative abundance in the global pre-industrial whaling population. The initial and steady-state population estimates are presented in Table 2.

The current local population estimates and data on the average biomass of each species were used to construct biomass weights w_i equal to the current biomass of each whale species found off the coast of Brazil, divided by total current great

[4] It is possible that the flows of services produced by whales vary by their location. But sufficient data does not yet exist to measure local variations in services produced, let alone test the hypothesis that migrating whales produce identical flows of services at each location they visit. Our estimates assume this hypothesis is true.

[5] See Appendix 2 for details on the sources of the estimates provided by Baleia Jubarte.

whale biomass: $w_i = \frac{b_i N_{i,0}^{Brazil}}{\sum_{i=1}^{10} b_i N_{i,0}}$ where N^{Brazil} denotes the local whale population in Brazilian waters. These weights were used to estimate each species' initial contribution to the flows of services from ecotourism and primary production. The weights are reported in Table 2.

The calculations for the population of blue whales off the coast of Chile were done in a similar way. Galletti Vernazzani et al. (2017) estimates that the current population of blue whales is between 570 and 760, and we assume that this represents one percent of the country's pre-industrial whaling population of blue whales. In order to keep the valuation as conservative as possible, we assume that the pre-whaling population is based on the lower current population estimate, or 57,000 blue whales, while the higher estimate of 760 is used for the current population. Doing so will lower the valuation of whales by reducing the present value of total services (the numerator of the per-whale value) and increasing the number of whales producing these services (the denominator of the per-whale value). The parameters of the population growth model used to estimate future blue whale populations in Chile are the same as those used for the Brazilian blue whales, with the exceptions of the starting and ending populations. A biomass weight used to estimate the Chilean blue whales' initial contribution to the flows of services from ecotourism and primary production was also constructed analogously to the biomass weights for the Brazilian whales.

As described above, the service flows from ecotourism, phytoplankton carbon capture, and fisheries enhancement are assumed to be proportional to each species' share of global whale biomass, reported in Table 2. The implied initial values for these services are reported in Table 3. The annual rates of increase in the production of ecotourism and phytoplankton-related services were then constructed for each species as described in Step 2. Similarly, estimates of carbon sequestered on the bodies of whales were constructed directly from local population forecasts, as described in Step 2. The value of the initial stock of carbon presently sequestered on the bodies of the Brazilian and Chilean whale populations is also reported in Table 3.

Annual service flows for each species were discounted and summed in order to estimate the total value of each species as well as the average values of individual whales. These are reported in Table 4.

The difference between the values of the Brazilian and Chilean blue whales is due to the difference in the ratios of starting to ending populations in the two countries. In the case of the Chilean blue whales, we are assuming that the starting population is a greater fraction of the steady-state population than for the Brazilian whales, which in turn implies an earlier acceleration of population growth in Chile, producing larger service flows that occur sooner, leading to a higher overall value of the services.

Table 3 Values of current service flows/stock of carbon

Species	Current values of annual service flows: Ecotourism	Phytoplankton Carbon capture	Fisheries enhancement	Value of stock: Carbon on body
Blue	$310,941	$1,421,994	$233,206	$74,754
Bowhead				
Bryde's	$3,730,269	$17,059,268	$2,797,702	$357,927
Fin	$3,462,555	$15,834,959	$2,596,917	$816,453
Gray				
Humpback	$54,506,095	$249,267,274	$40,879,571	$12,496,213
Minke	$4,162,488	$19,035,891	$3,121,866	$969,621
Right	$2,072,994	$9,480,217	$1,554,746	$456,281
Sei	$472,296	$2,159,906	$354,222	$111,226
Sperm	$26,688,674	$122,052,644	$20,016,506	$6,207,708
Totals (Brazil):	$95,406,313	$436,312,152	$71,554,736	$21,490,183
Blue (Chile)	$3,707,269	$16,954,085	$2,780,452	$845,183

Table 4 Present value of whales in Brazil and Chile

Species	Total value	Average per whale
Blue	$230,079,877	$3,609,454
Bowhead		
Bryde's	$3,573,801,371	$2,293,839
Minke	$4,129,486,080	$165,179
Fin	$2,862,258,915	$2,205,130
Gray		
Humpback	$52,191,344,148	$2,087,654
Right	$1,766,748,598	$2,208,436
Sei	$400,868,032	$691,634
Sperm	$22,282,689,815	$2,228,269
Total:	$87,437,276,836	
Blue (Chile)	$3,107,530,267	$4,088,856

4.5 Discussion

Although this exercise produces a wide range of values for the great whales from $165,000 for a Minke whale to $4 million for a blue whale, most of the whales have a value of about $2 million. We argue that, like the example of forest elephants, our estimated values of whales will generate excitement and concern among individuals and investors, for the same reasons as discussed above.

The whale valuations, however, incorporate services beyond carbon sequestration, namely ecotourism and fisheries enhancement. This is important because the flows from these services provide additional ways to use these valuations to promote action. As we show in Table 3, the values of the annual flows of services such as ecotourism and fisheries enhancement are significant. These amounts translate into economic activity and opportunity for local residents, which are both tangible and immediate benefits. Thus, quantifying these annual flows can be quite important in convincing important ecosystem stakeholders who interact directly and frequently with the resource to take actions to preserve or restore it.

5 Conclusion

In the introduction to this paper, we argue that our valuation strategy will be more effective at prompting action because it takes better advantage of humans' psychological tendencies. In this section, we also argue that our method will be more effective because it opens up new possibilities for action.

First, we argue that our valuation method will stimulate further research into the services produced by all natural resources and the value of these services to society. By demonstrating that individual resources such as elephants and whales can have significant value, our method will prompt efforts to identify and price the services produced by other individual resources—much as a profitable investment in one company leads investors to investigate the fundamentals of related companies in order to uncover hidden or overlooked value. Similarly, we believe that the demonstration effect arising from valuations of individual resources will stimulate additional interest in valuing the services flowing from entire ecosystems, using our framework.

Our valuation approach also facilitates a transformation in how people view natural resources, which in turn enables new approaches to conservation and restoration policies. The assignment of credible money values to individual natural resources, even if lower bounds, prompts society to view each natural resource as an agent that produces services with a marketable monetary value. This can lead to the legal recognition of the natural resource, not necessarily as a person, but nonetheless as an agent with rights (and obligations).[6] Chief among these can be the rights to legal protection against harm and to reasonable compensation for services rendered. This change is a foundation upon which to build a new generation of conservation and restoration policies. Because natural resources do not have the capacity to speak for themselves or defend themselves, guardians or advocates can be appointed to protect them and their interests, including the standing to initiate lawsuits on behalf of the resource.

One legal tool that our valuation method makes possible is the levying of economically appropriate and meaningful fines on agents who damage or destroy protected natural resources. These fines should be based on the values assigned to the resource. For example, a ship that strikes and kills a blue whale off the coast of Brazil should be fined the full value of the whale, or $3.6 million. The value could also be used to incentivize private monitoring of the (mis-)use of natural resources.

[6] New Zealand, for example, has recently recognized all animals as sentient beings.

Rewards linked to the values of whales could be paid to those who provide evidence leading to the successful prosecution of agents who harm or kill whales.

Similarly, our valuation of forest elephants can be used to establish penalties for poaching and incentives for monitoring that more nearly represent the true social costs and benefits of doing so. Turkalo et al. (2017)) estimated that poaching of elephants increases the mortality rate of elephants by 1.71 percentage points. The current population growth rate of 1.9% is conditional on the existence of poaching, so that removing poaching would increase the growth rate of elephants in African tropical forests to 3.62%. Under this higher growth rate of elephants, we repeated the same analysis of the three cases of elephants' contribution to tropical forest carbon stocks. When the higher population growth rate is used, the value of increased carbon capture in tropical forests increases to $375.2405 billion, or $3,752,405 per elephant. This means that poaching reduces the present value of the current 100,000 elephants by $198.9576 Billion or $1,989,576 per elephant.

The establishment of meaningful fines can stimulate private investment directed at protecting individuals and businesses from these penalties, but which simultaneously promotes the protection of natural resources. In other words, government-imposed penalties on the destruction of natural resources that are linked to the values of these resources can create markets for protecting them. For example, maritime insurers can develop whale-strike products that will compensate shippers for large fines incurred by ships that inadvertently harm whales. And insurers will doubtlessly wish to limit moral hazard-related losses by requiring the purchasers of insurance to take actions to avoid whale strikes, such as using goods or services that alert ship captains of whale proximity. This in turn provides incentives for private companies to improve existing methods of monitoring whales, or to invent better ones.

Credible valuations also justify the levying of user fees and license fees on those who enjoy or profit from natural resources. Such fees accomplish two complementary purposes. First, they give agents an incentive to stop overusing a resource, because doing so is no longer costless. In addition, the revenues from such fees can be earmarked for the financing of protection and restoration programs. As in the case of fines, the amounts of the user and license fees can be calibrated to the value of the services, so that they are effective in both curbing overuse and generating revenues. For example, significant user fees could be built into the prices of whale watching or elephant watching tours, or licensing fees on the companies that offer them (or both).

Moreover, imposing fees on the use of natural resources can also serve as a catalyst for private investment in conservation and restoration projects. A portion of fee revenues can provide impact investors, who seek both social and financial returns on their investments, the money component of return that up to now has largely been missing or nearly impossible to secure, due to lack of property rights. Such impact investing initiatives would be structured as public-private partnerships (PPPs) in which private-sector entities contribute management skills and technology to restoration projects, as well as the ability to recruit other private investors. PPPs could raise the initial capital required to start conservation and restoration projects from the private sector, based on the dual promises of improved protection for natural resources and future income flows from fee revenues. This would help establish natural resources as a new asset class for private investment, and also relieve governments of the burden of funding conservation projects from general tax revenues. This approach has great potential for protecting all resources, but particularly for resources like elephants that are illegally misused or destroyed, since PPPs would have a direct and strong incentive to protect their investments.

The potential gains discussed above also create incentives for international cooperation on conservation and restoration. Many natural resources are shared by countries, either because an immobile resource spans multiple countries' territories, or because a migratory resource visits multiple countries. The total value of a shared resource often depends on how well it is managed or protected by each of the countries sharing it. The value of a river in one country, for example, depends on how upstream countries managed their section of the river. The value that a resource provides to a particular country can be impaired or destroyed if the resource is misused in one of the other countries sharing it. Thus, if a particular country would like to assign value to a shared resource in order to stimulate private sector investment in its conservation and restoration, it will need other countries to commit to at least doing no harm to the resource.

On the other hand, the benefits of acting jointly to conserve and protect resources could be a strong incentive for more active cooperation. Countries could agree to coordinate the fines they levy on agents who misuse shared resources, and to share the proceeds from these fines. Governments could harmonize rules to create larger, single markets for protection of resources that would attract more private investment. Similarly, they could create international PPPs that would attract greater numbers of investors, who would be attracted by the more reliable promises of income flows due to larger user bases and uniform user and license fees across countries.

The policies described above will not necessarily result from the adoption of credible monetary valuations of individual natural resources, but it is difficult to imagine how such policies could develop without this foundation. Expert valuation of natural resources can—and indeed, we argue must—play the role that price discovery performs in markets for private goods and services.

Acknowledgement Berzaghi was supported by the European Union's Horizon 2020 research and innovation programme under the Marie Skłodowska-Curie grant number 845265.

Appendices

Appendix 1: Population Model

The populations of elephants and whales are based on a logistic model of births and an exponential model of the survival of living individuals. We assume each population follows the differential equation $\frac{dN(t)}{N(t)} = \nu(t)dt$ subject to an initial population $N(0)$, where $\nu(t)$ is the population growth rate. Following Karlin and

Taylor (1981 p. 420), the population under exponential growth rate ν leads to

$$N(t) = N(0)\exp\left[\int_0^t \nu(\tau)\, d\tau\right] \tag{1}$$

where N(0), the initial population of each species, is taken to be the number of elephants after poaching, and the number of whales after industrial whaling, respectively. N(T) is the steady-state population, for which we use the number of elephants before poaching and whales before industrial whaling.

Because we do not expect the populations of elephants or whales to grow indefinitely, we assume that $\nu(t) \to 0$ as $t \to \infty$. We also want to account for birth and deaths. As a result, we define $\hat{\nu}(t) = \nu(t) + c$, so that $\hat{\nu}(t)$ is the birth rate of whales or elephants, c is their constant instantaneous death rate, and $\nu(t)$ is the (net) growth rate of the population. Thus, $\hat{\nu}(t) \to c$ as $t \to \infty$.

These properties are captured by a logistic model for the birth rate such that

$$\hat{\nu}(t) = \begin{cases} \beta\left[1 - \frac{N(t)}{\alpha}\right] & for\ N(t) \le \frac{\alpha(\beta-c)}{\beta} \\ c & for\ N(t) > \frac{\alpha(\beta-c)}{\beta} \end{cases} \tag{2}$$

where $\frac{\alpha(\beta-c)}{\beta}$ is the level of population when the birth rate is equal to rate of death and the population growth rate is zero. As a result, $\frac{\alpha(\beta-c)}{\beta}$ is the steady state value of the population. For simplicity we set $\beta = \nu(0) + c$.

We know the survival rate S_a for mature elephants and whales over one year, so that the mortality rate c is given by the solution of

$$\int_0^1 e^{-ca}\, da = \frac{1}{c}\left(1 - e^{-c}\right) = S_a. \tag{3}$$

Substituting $\nu(t) = \hat{\nu}(t) - c$ and (2) into the differential equation $\frac{dN(t)}{N(t)} = \nu(t)dt$ for the growth rate of the population gives

$$\frac{dN(t)}{dt} = N(t)\,(\beta - c) - \beta\frac{N(t)^2}{\alpha}\ for\ N(t) \le \frac{\alpha\,(\beta - c)}{\beta}\ \text{and 0 otherwise.}$$

The solution to this ordinary differential equation is

$$N(t) = \frac{\alpha(\beta-c)\ N(0)}{\beta\ N(0)\left[1-e^{-(\beta-c)t}\right]+\alpha(\beta-c)e^{-(\beta-c)t}}\ for\ N(t) \le \frac{\alpha(\beta-c)}{\beta}\ \text{and 0 otherwise.} \tag{4}$$

As stated above, we use the post poaching or whaling population for N(0). The population converges to $N^* = \frac{\alpha(\beta-c)}{\beta}$, which we associate with the population before poaching or whaling. This means

$$\alpha = N(T)\frac{\beta}{(\beta - c)}.$$

Now we add a model of births that will be consistent with the above population model. We do so in order to be able to construct alternative scenarios in which we can show the impact of different birth and survival rates on future populations. We assume that births are always the same proportion b of population (which implies that births also follow the logistic model of population). This means $\nu(0)$ is the same for both population and births. If B(t) is the number of births, then

$$B(t) = bN(t) \Rightarrow \frac{B(0)}{B(T)} = \frac{N(0)}{N(T)} \Rightarrow B(T) = \frac{N(T)}{N(0)} B(0). \tag{5}$$

This implies from Eq. (1) that

$$\begin{aligned} bN(t) = bN(0)\exp\left[\textstyle\int_0^t \nu(\tau)\, d\tau\right] \Rightarrow B(t) = \\ B(0)\exp\left[\textstyle\int_0^t \nu(\tau)\, d\tau\right]. \end{aligned} \tag{6}$$

To complete the differential equation model we need to set B(0). We know the average number of births in the first year is $m = \frac{1}{IBI}$ for an average female, where IBI is the interval between births. Let AFR be age of first reproduction. Therefore, there are AFR years before a female born at time 0 can give birth at time AFR, so that the females born at time 0 mature in AFR years with survival chance of $S_{0AFR} = (So)^{AFR}$.

Let **O** be the oldest age of reproducing females. We assume the distribution of the ages of individuals is uniform across ages 0 to **O**. The number of female births (half the population) at time 0 is given by

$$\begin{aligned} B(AFR) &= \frac{O-AFR}{O}\,\frac{mN(AFR)}{2} \\ &= \frac{O-AFR}{O}\,\frac{mN(0)\left[\sum_{i=0}^{AFR-1} 0x\, S_o^{AFR-i}\, B(i) + \sum_{i=AFR}^{O} \frac{1}{O} S_a^i\right]}{2} \\ &= \frac{O-AFR}{2\,O^2} mN(0) \sum_{i=AFR}^{O} S_a^i \\ &= \frac{O-AFR}{2\,O^2} mN(0) S_a^{AFR} \sum_{i=AFR}^{O-AFR} S_a^i \\ &= \frac{O-AFR}{2\,O^2} mN(0) S_a^{AFR} \frac{1-S_a^{O-AFR}}{1-S_a} \end{aligned}$$

where Sa is the survival rate of adults. The female calves from ages 0 to AFR do not give birth, so that the first summation in the second equality is equal to zero and drops out.

We let B(AFR) be the number of births by mature females at the end of the initial period, so that

$$B(AFR) = B(0)\exp\left[\int_0^1 \nu(\tau)\,d\tau\right]$$
$$= \frac{O-AFR}{2\,O^2} mN(0)S_a^{AFR}\frac{1-S_a^{O-AFR}}{1-S_a}.$$

As a result, the initial number births by mature females is given by

$$B(0) = \frac{1}{\exp\left[\int_0^1 \nu(\tau)d\tau\right]}\frac{O-AFR}{2\,O^2} mN(0)S_a^{AFR}\frac{1-S_a^{O-AFR}}{1-S_a} = \frac{1}{\frac{1}{\nu}[e^{\nu}-1]}\frac{O-AFR}{2\,O^2} mN(0)S_a^{AFR}\frac{1-S_a^{O-AFR}}{1-S_a}. \tag{7}$$

Now that we have the initial births, we can solve the differential equation for births at any time. Because births are a constant fraction of population, the differential equation for births can be written as (see Eq. (6))

$$\frac{dB(t)}{dt} = \nu(t)B(t).$$

Also, since births are a constant share of population, we can rewrite (2) in terms of births:

$$\hat{\nu}(t) = \begin{cases} \beta\left[1 - \frac{B(t)}{\alpha_B}\right] & for\ B(t) \le \frac{\alpha_B(\beta-c)}{\beta} \\ c & for\ B(t) > \frac{\alpha_B(\beta-c)}{\beta} \end{cases} \tag{8}$$

where $\alpha_B = b\alpha$.

Substituting $\hat{\nu}(t) - c$ for $\nu(t)$, as well as the logistic model for $\hat{\nu}(t)$ in terms of births (8) into the differential equation for births above gives

$$\frac{dB(t)}{dt} = \begin{cases} B(t)\,(\beta - c) - \frac{\beta}{\alpha_B}B(t)^2 & for\ B(t) \le \frac{\alpha_B(\beta-c)}{\beta} \\ 0 & for\ B(t) > \frac{\alpha_B(\beta-c)}{\beta} \end{cases}. \tag{9}$$

This differential equation has the solution

$$B(t) = \frac{\alpha_B(\beta-c)B(0)}{\beta\ B(0)[1-e^{-(\beta-c)t}]+\alpha_B(\beta-c)e^{-(\beta-c)t}} \tag{10}$$
$for\ B(t) \le \frac{\alpha_B(\beta-c)}{\beta}$, and c otherwise.

Births net of deaths converge to 0 when $B(T) = \frac{\alpha_B(\beta - c)}{\beta}$.

$$\frac{\alpha_B\,(\beta - c)}{\beta} = B(T) \Rightarrow \alpha_B = \frac{\beta}{\beta - c} B(T).$$

We also know that the population and births grow at the same rate with initial ratio of $bN(t) = B(t)$, so that

$$\begin{aligned} N(t) &= \tfrac{1}{b} \tfrac{\alpha_B\ (\beta - c) B(0)}{\beta\ B(0)[1 - e^{-(\beta - c)t}] + \alpha_B(\beta - c) e^{-(\beta - c)t}} \\ for\ N(t) &\leq \tfrac{\alpha_B(\beta - c)}{b\beta}. \end{aligned} \tag{11}$$

Appendix 2: Valuation of Elephants in Central Africa Forest

This Appendix values forest elephants in Central Africa based on two services: (1) carbon capture on elephant bodies, and (2) increased carbon capture in trees. The quantities of each service produced per period depend on the elephant population. We use the same logistic model discussed in Appendix 1 to estimate the evolution of the elephant population. The parameter values for elephants are given in Table 5. We take these parameters from Turkalo et al. (2017, 2018). The population is currently 100,000, and we assume that the elephant population will stabilize at the pre poaching level of 1,100,000. The Central Africa forest covers an area of 2,200,000 km^2, which is about 44% of the size of the Amazon forest. Most of the Central African forests do not have elephants, so that the elephants can be spread over the current forest without changing the density of elephants per hectare.

AFR is age of first reproduction, O is oldest age of reproducing females, IBI is the interbirth interval, Sa is the survival rate of adult elephants, So is the survival rate of elephant calves, and $\nu(0)$ is the population growth rate.

We know the survival rate over 1 year $S_a = 0.9691$ for mature elephants, so that (3) yields a continuously compounded death rate of

$$c = 0.0631.$$

This means $\beta = \nu(0) + c$=0.019 + 0.0631= 0.0821.

Table 5 Parameters for population model for elephants

AFR	O	IBI	Sa	So	$\nu(0)$	Pop pre poaching	Current elephants
10	65	5.6	0.9691	0.97	0.019	1,100,000	100,000

Given these parameter values, the population of elephants following (4) with $\alpha = 4,753,552$ is given in the next graph.

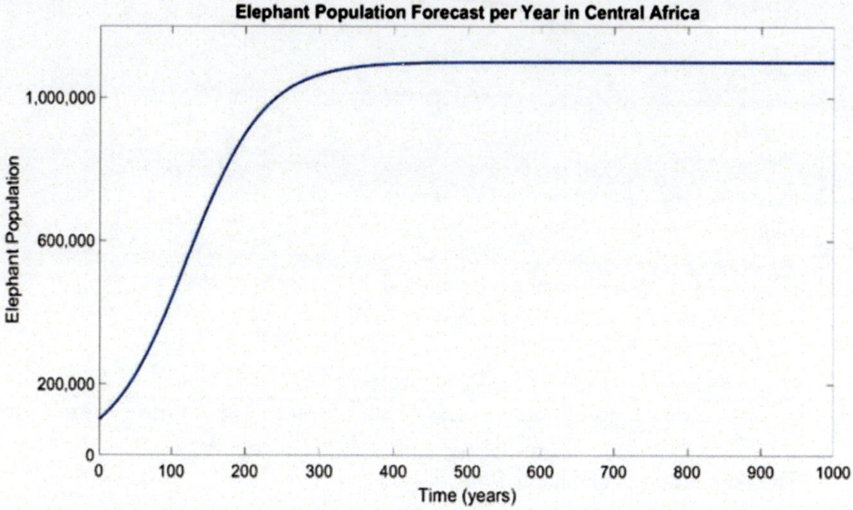

The birth of elephants following Eq. (8) starts at

$$B(10) = \frac{O - AFR}{2\,O^2} m N(0) S_a^{11} \frac{1 - S_a^{O-10}}{1 - S_a} = 2,259.$$

Consequently, the initial value of births, following Eq. (9), is given by

$$B(0) = 2,238.$$

Since the population of elephants grows to 11 times its initial size, the terminal births also increase by 11 times. Consequently, B(t) = 0.0348 N(t) for each time period, following Eq. (5). We use the solution to the logistic model for births (10) with parameter

$$\alpha_B = 106.3739.$$

This leads to the graph of elephant births over time in the next Figure.

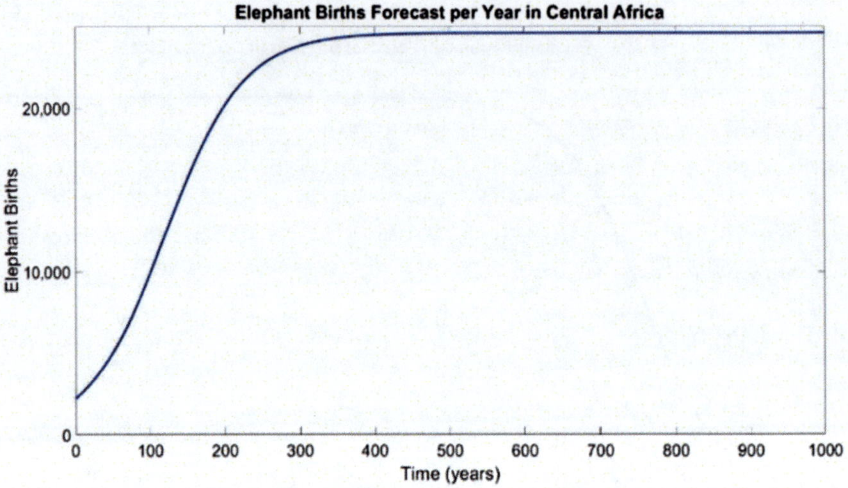

The population of elephants follows (11)

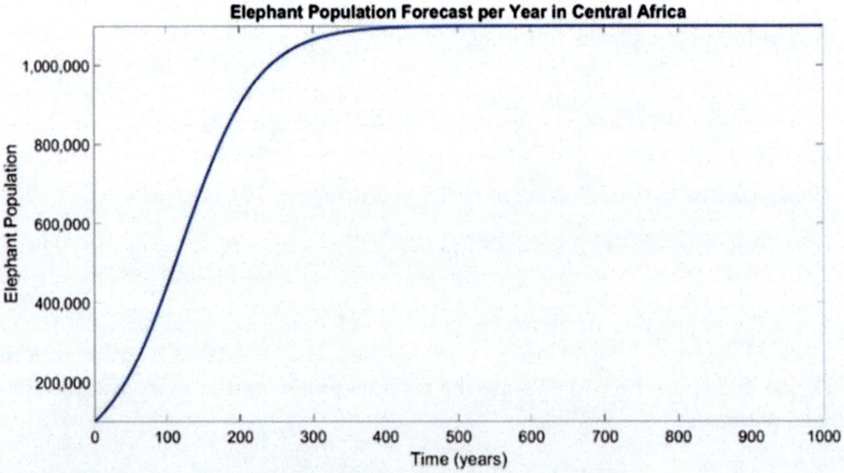

Carbon Capture in Elephant Bodies

Assuming an average body mass of 3000 kg (Grubb et al., 2000), of which 24% is carbon, we can calculate the CO_2 equivalent of the carbon captured in elephant bodies:

$$C = 0.24x3,000 = 720\ kg;\ CO_2 = \frac{11x720}{3}$$
$$= 2,640\ kg\ or\ 2.64\ metric\ tons.$$

The cash flow per year from increased carbon capture on bodies, CF(i) is equal to the increase in population multiplied by the CO_2 captured per body, multiplied by the price of carbon, $P_C = \$24.72$, so that for each species we have the market value for this service during period $t + i$

$$p_{1,t+i}\ s_{1,t+i} = P_C CO_2 [N(i) - N(i-1)] \text{ for i} > 0.$$

This corresponds to the increase in the value of carbon dioxide sequestration because of the increase in elephants.

Assuming a discount rate of r = 0.02, the present value of carbon content of 100,000 elephants is

$$V_{1,t} = PV\,(Body\ Carbon) = P_C CO_2 N(0) +$$

$$\sum_{i=1}^{\infty} \frac{P_C CO_2[N(i) - N(i-1)]}{(1+r)^i} = \$6,526,080 + \$10,059,942 = \$16,586,022.$$

This corresponds to a present value of carbon on an elephant's body of \$166.

Carbon Capture Enhancement Through Interaction with Tropical Forest

The historical elephant population was 1.1 million individuals spread over 2,200,000 km² of the central Africa tropical rain forest, implying an average density of 0.5 elephants/km² (Turkalo et al., 2017). At a density of 0.5 elephants per km^2, the carbon boosting effect of 0.5 elephants has been estimated at 13 metric tons (tonnes) per hectare. Since 1 km^2 = 100 hectares, the increase in carbon capture at a density of 1 elephant per km^2 is 13 * 2 * 100 = 2600 tonnes of carbon per km^2. The CO_2 equivalent is given by 2600 * 11/3=9533.33 tonnes. This calculation allows us to compute the increase in carbon capture based on the number of elephants.

We assume that as the elephant population increases, it will distribute itself among the African tropical forest in a way that maintains a density of 0.5 elephants/km^2. Therefore, as the population grows, elephants will expand their range maintaining an average density of 0.5 elephants/km^2. Thus, our calculations are based on maintaining the average effect of elephants per hectare while extending the elephant-occupied range.

The effect of elephants on CO_2 depends on how long the elephants are in a particular area of the forest. We begin with an initial plot of forest containing the currently existing 100,000 elephants (200,000 km^2) and assume that these elephants have been around long enough to increase carbon capture in this plot to its higher steady state. Consequently, $CO_2(0) = 9533$ tonnes per elephant on the initial plot.

The initial population of elephants N(0) = 100,000 occupies a plot of forest of 200,000 km^2 with a biomass of 953 million metric tons of CO_2. Thus, the initial 100,000 elephants produces carbon capture services worth \$23.5656 billion at the price of \$24.72 per metric ton of CO_2.

Now we consider how elephants affect carbon capture when they move to a currently unoccupied plot of land that is nonetheless within their historical range. Given that elephants had occupied these areas before, it is possible that the previous occupants had already enhanced the carbon capture in them and that some of this enhancement continues despite the lack of elephant activity.

Let C(0) be the initial CO_2 in a forest plot. We assume that it takes 200 years to reach the steady state of 9533 tonnes per elephant when C(0) starts at zero. In this case, the change is 9533/200 = 47.67 tonnes per year. We also assume that carbon is captured at this constant rate irrespective of the initial CO_2, i.e. C(0). Therefore, given an initial C(0), we can solve for the number of years to reach a CO_2 of 9533 metric tons per elephant using

$$Change = \frac{9533 - C(0)}{years} = 47.67.$$

Given the uncertainty about the initial carbon level on each re-occupied plot, we consider three cases:

1. Initial Carbon per hectare is one quarter of its maximum (3.25 tonnes) or C(0) = 9533/4 = 2383 tonnes per elephant. Elephant activity increases capture by 47.67 tonnes per year for 150 years.
2. Initial Carbon per hectare is one half of its maximum (6.5 tonnes) or C(0) = 9533/2 = 4767 tonnes per elephant. Elephant activity increases capture by 47.67 tonnes per year for 100 years.
3. Initial Carbon per hectare is 0 or C(0) = 0. Elephant activity increases capture by 47.67 tonnes per year for 200 years.

At time 1 there is an increase in population of N(1) - N(0), following the logistic population growth model for elephants. This new generation enters a plot of forest with biomass of C(0) tonnes per elephant and increases it to 9533 metric tons of CO_2 over 150, 100, and 200 years for cases 1, 2, and 3 respectively. The size of the plot is adjusted so that the density of elephants in the forest is maintained at 0.5 elephants/km^2.

At time 2, a new generation of elephants is born with size N(2) – N(1), which occupies a new plot and contributes to the growth of the biomass of the tropical forest as described above. We repeat this process for 1000 generations to ensure convergence of the elephant population to its steady state, at which point the total increase in carbon capture converges to zero.

Given the growth rate of carbon sequestration in the tropical forest for each generation, we can determine the value of the contribution of each generation of elephants. Assuming a price of carbon P_c = \$24.72 and an interest rate of 2%, the present value of each generation k's contribution to carbon capture in aboveground biomass, $V_{k,2,t}$, is given by $\frac{24.72*47.67*[N(k)-N(k-1)]}{.02}\left[1-\left(\frac{1}{1.02}\right)^Y\right]\left(\frac{1}{1.02}\right)^k$, where Y is the number of years corresponding to each case. Then the present value of each generation's contribution is summed to obtain the total present value of carbon capture by all future generations. The total present value of the biomass added to the tropical forest, $V_{2,t}$, is the sum of the contribution of the current elephants and the present value of the contributions from the future generations of elephants.

Results of these calculations are as follows:

$$\text{Case 1} : C(0) = 9533/4 = 2383 \text{ per elephant, } Y = 150 \text{ years.}$$

These calculations imply a present value of biomass added to the tropical forest by future generations of elephants of \$152.7173 billion. The total $V_{2,t}$ of forest biomass added by elephant activity = \$23.5656 billion + \$152.7173 billion = \$176.2829 billion.

This corresponds to a contribution to the biomass of the tropical forest worth \$1,762,829 per elephant. If we add the \$166 for the carbon on the body of the elephant, we obtain a total value of \$1,762,995 per elephant.

$$\text{Case 2} : C(0) = 9533/2 = 4767, Y = 100 \text{ years.}$$

Total $V_{2,t}$ of forest biomass added by elephant activity = \$23.5656 billion + \$113.1792 billion = \$136.7448 billion.

The contribution to the biomass of the tropical forest is worth \$1,367,448 per elephant.

$$\text{Case 3} : C(0) = 0.Y = 200 \text{ years.}$$

Total $V_{2,t}$ of forest biomass added by elephant activity = \$23.5656 billion + \$173.4365 billion = \$197.0021 billion.

The contribution to the biomass of the tropical forest is worth \$1,970,021 per elephant.

Our preferred case is case 1, since we believe that the impact of elephant activity has persisted, though elephants have been removed from much of their habitat for several decades, dramatically reducing their impact on these areas. Table 6 presents a sensitivity analysis showing how the total present value of carbon enhancement in each case depends on the number of years considered in the calculations. The present value of the elephants starts at \$43.8705 Billion in 50 years and increases to \$176.2222 Billion in 300 years. The last value is within \$0.0607 Billion or \$607 per elephant relative to the present value over 1000 years.

Table 6 Impact of years on present value of elephants (billion \$)

Years/cases	Case 1	Case 2	Case 3
50	\$43.8705	\$43.8705	\$43.8684
100	\$98.7666	\$98.7666	\$98.7587
150	\$149.5936	\$129.4208	\$149.5804
200	\$171.3928	\$135.7389	\$182.0976
300	\$176.2222	\$136.7378	\$196.6588

In Table 6 the first 100 years is the same since the same amount of carbon dioxide is being added each year. Starting at 150 years the amount is smaller, since the first generation is no longer adding to carbon dioxide under case 2.

The first 150 years are similar for Case 1 and Case 3, but the present values deviate over the next 50 years because the contribution of 47.67 tonnes per year of carbon dioxide lasts for 200 years for Case 3.

The Cost of Poaching

By Turkalo et al. (2017), poaching of elephants increases the mortality rate of elephants by 1.71 percent per year. The current growth rate of 1.9 percent is with poaching, so that removing poaching would increase the growth rate of elephants in African tropical forest to 3.62 percent. Using the higher growth rate of elephants, we carry out the same analysis of the elephants' contributions to carbon capture under each Case. Under Case 1, the V_t of elephant activity increases to $375.2405 billion or $3,752,405 per elephant. This implies that poaching reduces the present value of the current 100,000 elephants by $198.9516 billion, or $1,989,516 per elephant.

Appendix 3: Estimation of Whale Populations Off Brazil's Coast

Humpback whales: The Humpback Whale Institute (2015, unpublished data), estimated 17,000 humpbacks off the coast of Brazil in 2015. Wedekin et al. (2017) recorded a population increase of 12 percent per year between 2002 and 2011. Therefore, the most recent estimate, from Zerbini et al. (2019) of 25,000 humpbacks is consistent with previous findings.

Right whales: Groch et al. (2005) and Renault-Braga et al. (2018) present partial estimates of right whales off the coast of Brazil, but the numbers in these papers relate only to the South/Southeast of Brazil, although the species distribution is confirmed all the way to 12 degrees S. The estimate used in this paper is from a personal communication from Groch, K.R., head scientist of the Brazilian Right Whale Project. A report (Torres-Florez, 2020) presented to the IWC Scientific Committee includes the following comment:

> Population analyses and trends in abundance of Southern Brazil right whales are being carried out under a PhD thesis to be concluded in the end of May, 2020. The information will be available upon final approval of the thesis. IWC estimated 3,300 Southern Right whales in Western South Atlantic in 2009. In Brazil the population probably will be something between 500-900 animals.

Minke whales: Unfortunately for the two species of **minkes** (*B. acutorostrata* and *B. bonaerensis*), recent population estimates for Brazil do not exist. The IWC's most recent estimate was 515,000 minkes for the southern hemisphere in 2003/2004. Based on whaling data in Williamson (1975), da Rocha (1983), and de La Mare

(2014), and given that these species were always considered the most abundant, the same number estimated for humpbacks was used for Minke whales, assuming they would at least be as abundant as humpbacks.

Fin, Sei, Bryde's and Blue whales: Aerial surveys conducted in the Santos Basin (off Santa Catarina, Paraná, São Paulo and part of Rio de Janeiro States) recorded an estimated 2990 masticates (interval: 2038–4385); this area included the main range of these species for which records have been kept. Given that the aerial survey covered only a small part of the historic range, however, author (Palazzo) estimated a total population of 3500 individuals spread over the four species.

Sperm whales: Author's (Palazzo) calculations, based on frequent records (mostly unpublished) of sightings at the continental shelf edge.

Appendix 4: Valuation of Whales

We value whales based on four services: (1) carbon capture in whale bodies, (2) carbon capture through phytoplankton enhancement, (3) fisheries enhancement, and (4) ecotourism. As in the case of elephants, the quantities of each service produced per period by whales depend on whale populations. We use the same logistic model developed in Appendix 1 to estimate the evolution of whale populations. The growth model parameters are given in Table 7.[7] The populations before and after whaling are provided in Table 2 of the paper. In the discussion below, we use Brazilian Blue whales as our example.

First, we use the basic logistic model (1) and (2). From Table 7 we have $S_a = 0.9750$ for the Blue whale, which implies a continuous time mortality rate of c = 0.0509. As a result, $\beta = \nu(0) + c = 0.05 + 0.0509 = 0.1009$. The population of Brazilian Blue whales is given in the following Figure.

[7] The same parameters are used for Brazilian and Chilean blue whales except for the beginning and ending populations. See Table 2.

Table 7 Population parameters for each species of whales

Species	AFR	O	IBI	Sa	So	$\nu(0)$
Blue (Brazil)	11	65	2.5	0.9750	0.8190	0.05
Blue (Chile)	11	65	2.5	0.9750	0.8190	0.05
Bowhead	20	118	3.1	0.9800	0.8230	0.03
Bryde's	10	69	4	0.9900	0.8800	0.05
Fin	10	62	2.24	0.9600	0.8060	0.04
Gray	10	55	2	0.9500	0.7000	0.03
Humpback	6	55	2.36	0.9600	0.7600	0.05
Minke	8	51	1	0.9600	0.8060	0.09
Right	10	69	4	0.9900	0.8800	0.05
Sei	20	53	2.5	0.9600	0.8060	0.04
Sperm	12	59	5	0.9860	0.8280	0.03

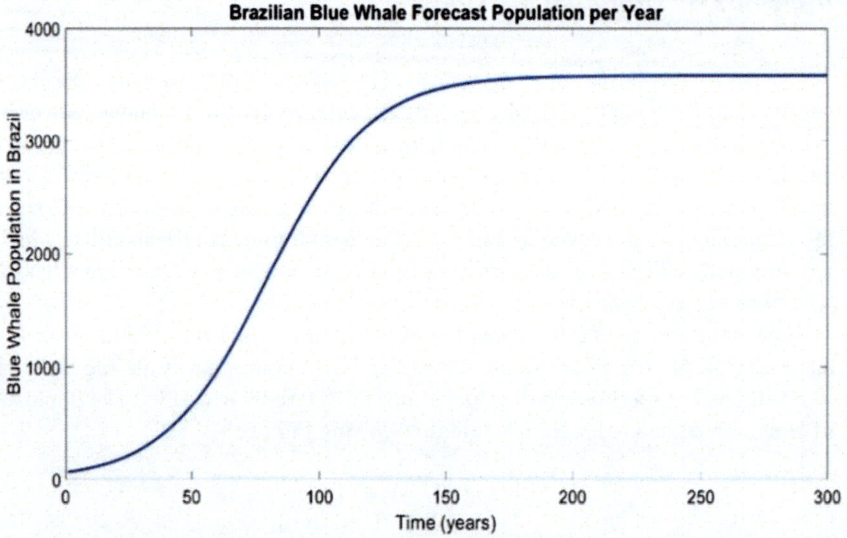

AFR is age of first reproduction, **O** is oldest age of reproducing females, IBI is the interbirth interval, Sa is the survival rate of adult Blue whales, So is the survival rate of Blue whale calves, and $\nu(0)$ is the population growth rate for Blue whales. The parameters come from Taylor, Chivers, Larese and Perrin (TCLP, 2007).

Next we examine the population of Brazilian Blue whales using the model of births and deaths, Eqs. (4)–(12). Suppose the survival rate is $s(a) = e^{-ca}$ where c is the continuously compounded mortality rate. Following TCLP (Table 1, first row), reproduced in Table 7 for the 11 species of whales, the interval between births for Blue whales IBI = 2.50. The average births over one year (see page 3, last paragraph TCLP) are m= $\frac{1}{IBI} = \frac{1}{2.50} = 0.4$. We know the number of births in the first year is m = 0.4 for an average female Blue whale. However, there are 11 years before a whale born at time 0 can give birth at time 11, so that the births at time 0 mature in 11 years with survival chance given by $S_{O11} = (So)^{11} = 0.1112$. We assume the distribution of the age of whales is uniform across ages 0 to **O**. The number of female births (half the population) at time 0 is given by (8), so that

$$B(11) = \frac{O - AFR}{2\,O^2} m N(0) S_a^{11} \frac{1 - S_a^{O-10}}{1 - S_a} = 3.6910.$$

We let B(11) be the number of female Blue whales at the end of the initial period, so that

$$B(11) = B(0)\exp\left[\int_0^1 \nu(\tau)\,d\tau\right] = 3.6910.$$

This implies that $\nu = 0.05$, which we assume is constant for the first year. As a result, we have from Eq. (9) that the initial number of mature females satisfies

$$B(0) = \frac{2,259}{\frac{1}{\nu}\left[e^{\nu} - 1\right]} = 3.5995.$$

By Eq. (10), the births converge to $\frac{\alpha_B(\beta - c_1)}{\beta}$ and $B(T) = \frac{3,583}{64} 3.5995 = 201.5$ with N(T) = 3,583.

$$\frac{\alpha_B\,(\beta - c)}{\beta} = 201.5 \Rightarrow \alpha_B = 201.5\frac{0.1009}{0.05} = 406.5.$$

The number of annual births over 300 years for Brazilian Blue whales are given in the following figure.

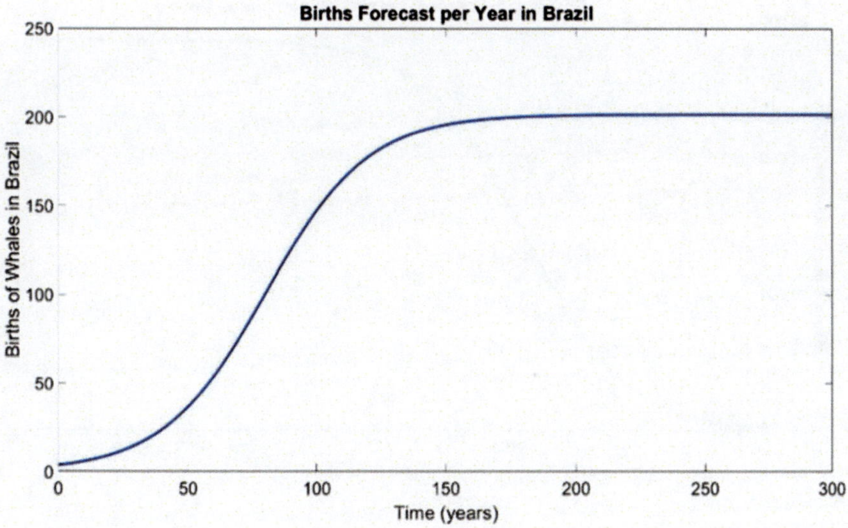

We also know that the population and births grow at the same rate with initial ratio, $b = 0.0562$, so that the total population implied by Eq. (12) is graphed in the next figure over 300 years for the Brazilian Blue whales.

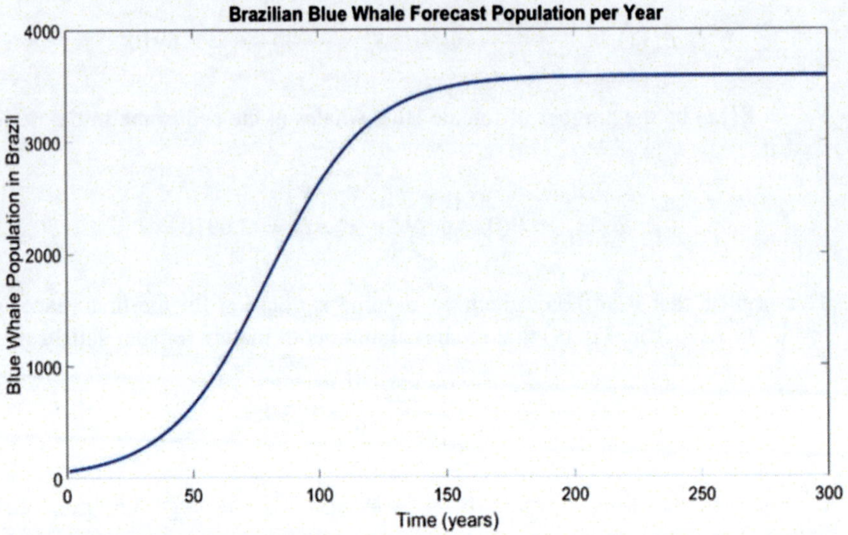

The Chilean population of Blue whales starts between 570 and 760, which is only 1% of the pre-whaling number of whales. As a result, we set the upper limit of Blue whales in Chile at N(T) = 57,000 based on the initial number of 570 whales. The next graph depicts the population of Blue whales in Chile using the same logistic model. The parameters for the Blue whales in Chile are the same as for the Brazilian whales in Table 7.

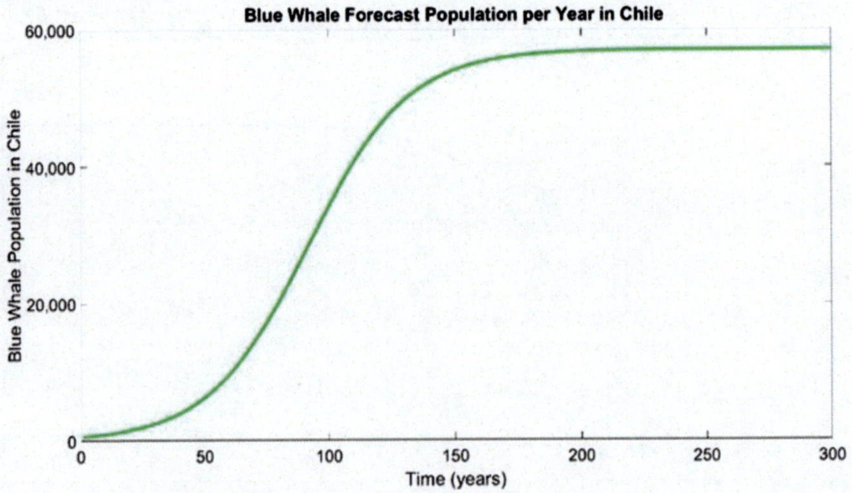

Table 8 Parameters for Weight of Each Species of Whales

Species	a	b	L (m)
Blue (Brazil)	0.000061	3.25	27
Blue (Chile)	0.000061	3.25	27
Bowhead	0.00255	2.916	16
Bryde's	0.0005	2.74	7
Fin	0.00025	2.9	23
Gray	0.0054	3.28	15
Humpback	0.00049	2.95	16
Minke	0.003188	2.31	7
Right	0.000348	3.08	16
Sei	0.001436	2.43	16
Sperm	0.000152	3.18	18.5

The values of a and b from Pershing et al. (2010)

Carbon Capture in Whale Bodies

The quantity of the carbon captured in the body of a mature whale is dependent on the biomass of the whale. The weight of Blue whales is given by

$$W = aL^b = 0.000061x\ [3.281\ x\ 27]^{3.25} = 130.0809 \text{ metric tons},$$

where a and b are parameters from Table 8. The weight is the same for the Chilean Blue whales, so that the carbon content (and carbon dioxide equivalent) is the same for Brazilian and Chilean Blue whales.

The first two parameters in Table 8 are for each species of whales. The length comes from Smith et al. (2019), Table 3, for each species.

The carbon dioxide content, in metric tons of CO_2 per Blue whale, is

$$CO_2 = 0.1048\ x\ W\ x\ 0.9\ x \tfrac{11}{3} = 0.1048\ x\ 130.0809\ \ x\ 0.9\ x \tfrac{11}{3}$$
$$= 44.9872 \text{ metric tons.}$$

The cash flow per year from increased carbon capture on bodies, CF(i), is equal to the increase in population multiplied by the CO_2 equivalent captured per body, multiplied by the price of carbon dioxide, $P_C = \$24.72$, so that for each species we have

$$p_{1,t+i}\ s_{1,t+i} = P_C CO_2\,[N(i) - N\,(i-1)] + P_C\ Fall\ N(i) \text{ for i} > 0.$$

The last term reflects the carbon content of whales that die and fall to the ocean floor, where $Fall = 1 - S_a$ per year and per whale.

Assuming a discount rate of r = 0.02, the present value of carbon captured by the bodies of the 64 Blue whales in Brazil is

$$\begin{aligned} V_{1,t} = PV\,(Body\ Carbon) &= P_C CO_2 N(0) + \sum\nolimits_{i=1}^{300} \tfrac{p_{1,t+i}\ s_{1,t+i}}{(1+r)^i} \\ &= \$74,754\,(845,183) + \$2,260,168\,(13,907,802) \\ &= \$2,334,922\,(14,752,985)\,. \end{aligned}$$

The present values for Chilean Blue whales are in parenthesis. These values are larger because of the larger population of Blue whales in Chile.

Phytoplankton Capture Enhancement

We now value the benefit of whale activity on phytoplankton, assuming that current whale populations are responsible for one percent of existing phytoplankton biomass, which captures the equivalent of 370 million metric tons of CO_2. We assume that as whales return to their pre-whaling populations, they stimulate an additional one percent increase in phytoplankton and therefore an additional one percent increase in carbon capture. We apportion this benefit according to the percentage of the total whale biomass accounted by each species, where these shares are reported in Table 2. For the 64 Brazilian Blue whales the biomass weight is 0.0001555 of the total population of whales in the world. This means that the Blue whales in Brazil currently account for the equivalent of 0.0001555 * 370 million = 57,524 metric tons of CO_2. The 760 Chilean Blue whales account for 0.001853 of the biomass of all whales in the world, which accounts for 685,845 metric tons of CO_2.

In each period the population of each species grows, so that the increase in capture each period by Blue whales in Brazil is given by

$$\begin{aligned} p_{2,t+i}\ s_{2,t+i} &= value\ of\ Phyto\ Capture_{Blue}\ per\ period(t) \\ &= \left[1 + \frac{\int_0^t dN(a)}{\int_0^T dN(a)}\right] x P_c\, 57,524 \\ &= \left[1 + \frac{N(t)-N(0)}{N(T)-N(0)}\right] x\ P_c\ x\ 57,524. \end{aligned}$$

Since we know the beginning and ending population as well as the population at each time, this can be easily calculated.[8] This value at time 0 is $P_c\ x\ 57,524$ and converges to $P_c\ x\ 2\ x\ 57,524$ at the steady state.

[8] In the second step we use the fundamental theorem from Calculus.

For Chilean Blue whales, we replace the 57,524 with 685,845 because of the larger population. Using an interest rate of r = 2% and a price of carbon dioxide of \$24.72, the present value of a one percent increase in phytoplankton from additional Blue whales in Brazilian waters is

$$V_{2,t} = PV\left(Phyto\ Capture_{Blue}\right)$$
$$= \int_0^T \left[1 + \frac{N_{Blue}(t) - N_{Blue}(0)}{N_{Blue}(T) - N_{Blue}(0)}\right] x P_C x\ 57,524\ x\ e^{-rt} dt$$
$$= \$164,714,579\ (1,916,963,736).$$

The present value of carbon capture from increased phytoplankton is \$164, 714.579 for Brazilian blue whales under continuous compounding.[9] The present value of the 570 Chilean Blue whales is \$1, 916, 963, 736.

Fisheries Enhancement

The total contribution to fisheries in the world is \$1.5 billion per year for all whales, which we assume increases by another one percent or an additional \$1.5 billion per year as whales return to their pre-whaling populations. Again, we apportion each species' contribution to increased fisheries according to its share of total whale biomass. This weight is 0.0001555 for Blue Brazilian whales, which implies a current flow of 0.0001555 * \$1.5 billion or \$233,206 per year. Each species' contribution to fisheries enhancement increases with its population so that

$$V_{3,t} = PV\left(Fish_{Blue}\right)$$
$$= \int_0^T \left[1 + \frac{N_{Blue}(t) - N_{Blue}(0)}{N_{Blue}(T) - N_{Blue}(0)}\right] x\$233,206\ x\ e^{-rt} dt$$
$$= \$27,013,018.$$

The present value of Brazilian Blue whales' contribution to fisheries is valued at \$27, 013, 018 using a 5% growth rate for Brazilian Blue whales. For 760 Chilean Blue whales, the present value of fisheries enhancement is \$314,380,041.

Ecotourism Revenues

Tourism from all whales is currently \$2.0 Billion per year, which we assume increases to \$4 billion per year as whales return to their pre-whaling populations. Once again the contributions are apportioned according to biomass weights, so that for Brazilian Blue whales we estimate the current contribution to ecotourism by 0.0001555 * \$2.0 billion, which is \$310,941. The contribution increases with its

[9] We approximate the integral by using summation over the T years and using discrete compounding.

population so that

$$V_{4,t} = PV\,(Tourism_{Blue})$$
$$= \int_0^T \left[1 + \frac{N_{Blue}(t) - N_{Blue}(0)}{N_{Blue}(T) - N_{Blue}(0)}\right] x\$310,941\,x\,e^{-rt}dt$$
$$= \$36,017,358.$$

The 760 Blue whales in Chile has a present value for tourism of $418,818,311.

In the Table below we summarize these results for the Brazilian Blue whale in column 2. The total value is $230,079,877 for 64 whales or $3,609,454 per Blue whale in Brazil. In Chile the total present value of the 760 Blue whales is $3,107,530,267 or $4,088,855.61 per Blue whale.

Present value	Brazilian blue whales	760 Chilean blue whales
Carbon Capture	$2, 334, 922	$14, 752, 985
Phyto Expansion	$164, 714, 579	$1,916,963,735
Fisheries	$27, 013, 018	$314,380,041
Tourism	$36, 017, 357	$418,818,311
Total	$230,079,877	$3,107,530,267

The values of the other great whales off the coast of Brazil are estimated in a similar way, using the corresponding parameters from Tables 2, 7, and 8.

References

Berzaghi, F., Longo, M., Ciais, P., Blake, S., Bretagnolle, F., Vieira, S., Scaranello, M., Scarascia-Mugnozza, G., & Doughty, C. E. (2019). Carbon stocks in central African forests enhanced by elephant disturbance. *Nature Geoscience, 1*. https://doi.org/10.1038/s41561-019-0395-6

CIEEM England Policy Group. (2019). *Natural capital and biodiversity: A briefing note for policy-makers*. Chartered Institute of Ecology and Environmental Management.

Cisneros-Montemayor, A. M., Sumaila, U. R., Kaschner, K., & Pauly, D. (2010). The global potential for whale watching. *Marine Policy, 34*, 1273–1278.

Costello, C., Gerber, L. R., & Gaines, S. (2012). A market approach to saving the whales. *Nature, 481*, 139–140.

Crimmins, J. C. (2016). *7 secrets of persuasion : leading-edge neuromarketing techniques to influence anyone*. Wayne, NJ: Career Press.

da Rocha, J. M. (1983). Revision of Brazilian whaling data. *Report of the International Whaling Commission, 33*, 419–427.

de la Mare, W. K. (2014). Estimating relative abundance of whales from historical Antarctic whaling records Canadian. *Journal of Fisheries and Aquatic Science, 71*, 106–119. https://doi.org/10.1139/cjfas-2013-0016

European Commission. (2018). *A clean planet for all: A European strategic long-term vision for a prosperous, modern, competitive and climate neutral economy*. European Commission Communication (COM(2018)773).

FAO (Food and Agriculture Organization). (2020). *The State of World Fisheries and Aquaculture 2020*. Sustainability in action.

Freeman, A. M. (2004). *The measurement of environmental and resource values* (2nd ed.). Resources for the Future.

Groch, K. R., Palazzo, J. T., Flores, P. A. C., Adler, F. R., & Fabian, M. E. (2005). Recent rapid increase in the right whale (Eubalaena australis) population off southern Brazil. *Latin American Journal of Aquatic Mammals., 4*(1), 41–47.

Grubb, P., Groves, C., Dudley, J., & Shoshani, J. (2000). Living African elephants belong to two species: Loxodonta africana (Blumenbach, 1797) and Loxodonta cyclotis (Matschie, 1900). *Elephant, 2*. https://doi.org/10.22237/elephant/1521732169

Hesketh, P. (2015). *Persuade : using the seven drivers of motivation to master influence and persuasion*. Chichester, West Sussex, UK: Capstone, Wiley.

Karlin, S., & Taylor, H. M. (1981). *A second course in stochastic processes*. Academic Press.

Lavery, T. J., Roundnew, B., Gill, P., Seymour, J., Seuront, L., Johnson, G., Mitchell, J. G., & Smetacek, V. (2010). Iron defecation by sperm whales stimulates carbon export in the Southern Ocean. *Proceedings of the Royal Society B, 277*, 3527–3531.

Lavery, T. J., Roundnew, B., Seymour, J., Mitchell, J. G., Smetacek, V., & Nicol, S. (2014). Whales sustain fisheries: Blue whales stimulate primary production in the Southern Ocean. *Marine Mammal Science, 30*(3), 888–904.

Lew, D. K. (2015). Willingness to pay for threatened and endangered marine species: A review of the literature and prospects for policy use. *Frontiers in Marine Science, 2*, 96.

Maisels, F., Strindberg, S., Blake, S., Wittemyer, G., Hart, J., Williamson, E. A., Abaa, R., Abitsi, G., Ambahe, R. D., Amsini, F., Bakabana, P. C., Hicks, T. C., Bayogo, R. E., Bechem, M., Beyers, R. L., Bezangoye, A. N., Boundja, P., Bout, N., Akou, M. E., ... Warren, Y. (2013). Devastating decline of forest elephants in Central Africa. *PLoS One, 8*, e59469. https://doi.org/10.1371/journal.pone.0059469

National Research Council. (2005). *Valuing ecosystem services: Toward better environmental decision-making*. The National Academies Press. https://doi.org/10.17226/11139

Pershing, A. J., Christensen, L. B., Record, N. R., Sherwood, G. D., & Stetson, P. B. (2010). The impact of whaling on the ocean carbon cycle: Why bigger was better. *PLoS ONE, 5*(8), e12444. https://doi.org/10.1371/journal.pone.0012444

Philips, J. (2017). *Principles of natural capital accounting*. U.K.

Ratnarajah, L., Melbourne-Thomas, J., Marzloff, M. P., Lannuzel, D., Miners, K. M., Chever, F., Nicol, S., & Bowie, A. R. (2016). A preliminary model of iron fertilisation by Baleen Whales and Antarctic Krill in the Southern Ocean: Sensitivity of primary productivity estimates to parameter uncertainty. *Ecological Modeling, 320*, 203–212.

Renault-Braga, E. P., Groch, K. R., de Carvalho Flores, P. A., Secchi, E. R., & Dalla-Rosa, L. (2018). Area usage estimation and spatiotemporal variability in distribution patterns of southern right whales, Eubalaena australis, of southern Brazil. *Marine Ecology., 2018*, e12506. https://doi.org/10.1111/maec.12506

Roman, J., & McCarthy, J. J. (2010). The whale pump: Marine mammals enhance primary productivity in a coastal Basin. *PLoS One, 5*(10), e13255. https://doi.org/10.1371/journal.pone.0013255

Roman, J., Estes, J. A., Morrisette, L., Smith, C., Costa, D., James McCarthy, J. B., Nation, S. N., Pershing, A., & Smetacek, V. (2014). Whales as marine ecosystem engineers. *Frontiers in Ecology and the Environment, 12*, 377–385.

Smith, C. R., Roman, J., & Nation, J. B. (2019). *A metapopulation model for whale-fall specialists: The largest whales are essential to prevent species extinctions*.

Taylor, B. L., Chivers, S. J., Larese, J., & Perrin, W. F. (2007). *Generation length and percent mature estimates for IUCN assessments of cetaceans, administrative report LJ-07-01 National Marine Fisheries Service*. Center.

TEEB. (2010). *The economics of ecosystems and biodiversity ecological and economic foundations*. Earthscan.

Torres-Florez, J. P. (2020). *IWC Western South Atlantic Southern Right Whale Conservation Management Plan –Progress Report April 2020*. International Whaling Commission.

Turkalo, A. K., Wrege, P. H., & Wittemyer, G. (2017). Slow intrinsic growth rate in forest elephants indicates recovery from poaching will require decades. *Journal of Applied Ecology, 54*, 153–159. https://doi.org/10.1111/1365-2664.12764

Turkalo, A. K., Wrege, P. H., & Wittemyer, G. (2018). Demography of a forest elephant population. *PLoS One, 13*. https://doi.org/10.1371/journal.pone.0192777

Vernazzani, G., Barbara, J. A., Jackson, E. C., Carlson, C. A., & Brownell, R. L. (2017). Estimates of abundance and trend of Chilean blue whales off Isla de Chiloé, Chile. *PLoS One, 12*(1), e0168646. https://doi.org/10.1371/journal.pone.0168646

Wedekin, L. L., Engel, M. H., Andriolo, A., Prado, P. I., Zerbini, A. N., Marcondes, M. M. C., Kinas, P. G., & Simões-Lopes, P. C. (2017). Running fast in the slow lane: Rapid population growth of humpback whales after exploitation. *Marine Ecology Progress Series, 575*, 195–206. https://doi.org/10.3354/meps12211

Whitehead, H. (2002). Estimates of the current global population size and historical trajectory for sperm whales. *Marine Ecology Progress Series, 242*, 295–304.

Williamson, G. A. (1975). Minke whales in Brazil. *Scientific Reports of the Whales Research Institute, 27*, 37–59.

Zerbini, A. N., Adams, G., Best, J., Clapham, P. J., Jackson, J. A., & Punt, A. E. (2019). Assessing the recovery of an Antarctic predator from historical exploitation. *Royal Society Open Science, 6*, 190368. https://doi.org/10.1098/rsos.190368

Public Policies and Long-Run Growth in a Model with Environmental Degradation

Luigi Bonatti and Lorenza Alexandra Lorenzetti

1 Introduction

The main purpose of this essay is to highlight the economic growth/environmental quality trade offs implied by the green policies implemented or under discussion in the advanced economies. Such assessment is particularly relevant in the face of the rather widespread rhetoric that, in order to make environmental policies more popular and appealing to the public opinion, does not just emphasize their benefits in terms of environmental sustainability and people's long-term well being, but even their alleged positive impact on economic growth. Therefore, the value added of the present essay lies in providing a stylized—but sufficiently rich—unified framework for analyzing the medium- and long-term effects of green policies on economic growth and human well being, under two alternative hypotheses concerning the possibility to offset the consequences of environmental degradation through the increasing utilization of manmade products and artifacts.

In more detail, we present a dynamic general equilibrium setup allowing for endogenous growth in the presence of optimizing agents. In this economy, production generates negative externalities, i.e. causes the emission of pollutants that accumulate in the air, water, or soil, with negative effects on individual well being, and investment in productive assets (physical & human & intangible capital) generates positive externalities, i.e. raises the overall productivity of the economy, thus allowing for unbounded GDP growth. The private sector of the economy

L. Bonatti (✉)
School of International Studies, University of Trento, Trento, Italy
e-mail: luigi.bonatti@unitn.it

L. A. Lorenzetti
ALTIS, Università Cattolica del Sacro Cuore di Milano, Milan, Italy
e-mail: lorenzaalexandra.lorenzetti@unicatt.it

L. Paganetto (ed.), *Economic Challenges for Europe After the Pandemic*,
Springer Proceedings in Business and Economics,
https://doi.org/10.1007/978-3-031-10302-5_8

consists of firms and households: the former decide how many workers to employ, and how much to invest in capital and in emission abatement capacity ("green technologies"), while the latter decide on how to allocate their income between consumption and saving, and their time between work and leisure. The government decides on green taxes on emissions, and on subsidies (negative taxes) to private investment in capital and in green technologies. In addition, the government must satisfy its intertemporal budget constraint but need not balance its budget every period (it can go into debt).

The two hypotheses mentioned above differ as to how the accumulation of pollutants affects human well being. Under the first hypothesis, there is no limit to the possibility for households to defend themselves against environmental degradation by using manmade products and artifacts, i.e. by increasing their "defensive expenditures", whereas according to the second hypothesis there is a threshold beyond which the adverse effects of the accumulation of pollutants—such as greenhouse gases—cannot be offset by devoting increasing quantities of output to this scope, thus making possible a climate catastrophe. Notice that this hypothesis is consistent with the prevailing scientific consensus concerning the long-term effects of global warming.

Under both hypotheses, we compare the laissez-faire path of the economy, i.e. the equilibrium trajectory in the absence of any government intervention, to the socially optimal path by deriving the balanced growth path (BGP) of the economy. Then, we check whether the latter can be decentralized by using the three policy instruments available to the government (taxes on pollutant emissions, subsidies to investment in capital and subsidies to investment in green technologies).

Essential starting point for the recent literature on growth and the environment is Nordhaus's (1994) dynamic integrated model of climate and the economy (the DICE model). DICE combines the Ramsey growth model with equations governing emissions and climate change. However, differently than the model presented here, it does not account for endogenous growth, and it does not specify a market structure and generic climate policies, thus focusing only on the social planner's optimal plan.

Subsequent integrated models of climate and the economy, such as Dietz and Stern (2015) and Bretschger and Karydas (2019), allow for endogenous growth by assuming that damage from a changing climate falls on capital accumulation, and not only on gross output at a particular point in time as in the DICE model.

Also in our essay endogenous growth is driven by knowledge spillovers from the accumulation of capital by firms, but—differently from the models mentioned above (and as in Uzawa, 2003; Acemoglu et al., 2012)—pollution damages enter households' utility. Indeed, we model the idea that people's well being crucially depends on the possibility to combine manmade products bought on the market with commons—primarily, environmental and social assets—and that this is the main channel whereby environmental degradation can affect the evolution of the economy. Among others, indeed, individual choices that are fundamental for shaping the economy's long-term trajectory, such as those on how much and what to consume or on how to allocate one's total time, are deeply influenced by the possibility to have access to some basic commons and by their quality.

Under this respect, the present essay gives substance to the distinction between adaptation, i.e., "anticipating the adverse effects of climate change and taking appropriate action to prevent or minimise the damage they can cause, or taking advantage of opportunities that may arise", and mitigation, i.e., "making the impacts of climate change less severe by preventing or reducing the emission of greenhouse gases (GHG) into the atmosphere". In fact, one of the conclusions of the literature dealing with this distinction[1] is that adaptation tends to impose negative externalities on others (individuals, groups of people or countries), thus becoming 'maladaptation', defined as "action taken ostensibly to avoid or reduce vulnerability to climate change that impacts adversely on, or increases the vulnerability of other systems, sectors or social groups" (Barnett & O'Neill, 2010, p. 211). The model presented here, indeed, moves along the same lines as Bartolini and Bonatti (2002, 2003, 2008), which show how under laissez faire the possibility of using private goods and services as substitutes for environmental and social commons that are deteriorating because of the increase in production and consumption can become an engine of GDP growth, by creating a vicious circle of more production and more degradation.

However, differently than in Bartolini and Bonatti (2002, 2003, 2008), we recognize here that dealing with climate change one should also account for the possibility—deemed very likely by the overwhelming majority of scientists studying global warming—that there is a point beyond which the effects of environmental degradation cannot be compensated by an increasing use of manmade products and artifacts. The implications of the existence of such point are studied also by Acemoglu et al. (2012), who illustrate how—at least when the 'dirty' production technology and the 'clean' production technology are substitutes—a temporary subsidy to the development of the latter can avoid an environmental disaster. Our conclusion is more pessimistic: whenever there is a tipping point beyond which the effects of environmental degradation cannot be offset by increasing quantities of output, there are circumstances in which laissez faire leads to an environmental catastrophe, and it is socially optimal to have unbounded economic growth only in the special case in which the increase in abatement capacity (the progress of green technologies) can stabilize the stock of pollutants in an ever growing economy.

The rest of the essay is organized as follows: Sect. 2 presents and discusses the model, Sect. 3 analyzes the balanced growth path characterizing the economy when it is always possible to offset the negative effects of environmental degradation on human well being by devoting increasing quantities of output to this scope, Sect. 4 analyzes the balanced growth path characterizing the economy if such compensation is not possible once that the concentration of pollutants goes beyond a certain threshold, Sect. 5 concludes.

[1] For a synthetic review of this literature, see Schumacher (2019).

2 The Basic Model

We study a market economy where production generates negative externalities, i.e. causes the emission of pollutants that accumulate in the air, water, or soil, with negative effects on human well-being, and where investment in productive assets (physical & human & intangible capital) generates positive externalities, i.e. raises the overall productivity of the economy, thus allowing for unbounded growth. In this economy, the private sector consists of firms, that decide on the utilization of labor and invest both in capital and in improving their emission abatement technologies ("green technologies"), and households, that decide on how to allocate their income between consumption and saving, and their time between leisure and labor. A public authority ("the government") decides on green taxes on emissions, and on subsidies (negative taxes) to private investment in capital and in green technologies. The government must satisfy its intertemporal budget constraint but need not balance its budget every period (it can go into debt).

Markets are perfectly competitive, time is discrete, and the time horizon is infinite. There is no source of random disturbances and agents' expectations are rational (i.e., they are consistent with the true processes followed by the relevant variables), thus implying perfect foresight.

2.1 Production

In the economy there is a large number (normalized to be one) of identical firms. In each period t, the representative firm produces the non-storable good Y_t (the numeraire of the system, whose price is set to be one) according to the following technology:

$$Y_t = A_t K_t^{\alpha} L_t^{1-\alpha} 0 < \alpha < 1, \tag{1}$$

where K_t and L_t are, respectively, the labor input and the capital stock used to produce Y_t, and A_t is a variable measuring the state of technology of the firm, i.e., its total factor productivity.

2.2 Total Factor Productivity

We assume that total factor productivity is a positive function of the capital installed in the economy:[2]

$$A_t = K_t^{1-\alpha}. \tag{2}$$

This assumption combines the idea that some learning-by-doing takes place whenever a firm utilizes its capital stock and the idea that knowledge and productivity gains spill over across all firms (see Barro & Sala-i-Martin, 1995). Therefore, in accordance with Frankel (1962), it is supposed that although A_t is endogenous to the economy, each firm takes it as given, since a single firm's decisions have only a negligible impact on the aggregate stock of capital.[3]

2.3 Emissions

In each period t, the representative firm generates polluting emissions E_t that are proportional to its output:

$$E_t = e\left(Z_t\right) Y_t, e' < 0, \tag{3}$$

where the factor of proportionality is a decreasing function of Z_t, that is the installed abatement capacity of the representative firm (its "abatement capital"). It is assumed that the functional form of $e(Z_t)$ is

$$e\left(Z_t\right) = Z_t^{-\varphi}, \varphi > 0. \tag{4}$$

The stock of pollutants, S_t, moves over time according to the following linear difference equation:[4]

$$S_{t+1} = E_t + \left(1 - \delta_S\right) S_t, \quad 0 \leq \delta_S < 1, \tag{5}$$

[2] Consistently with this formal set-up, one can interpret technological progress as labor augmenting.

[3] This amounts to say that technological progress is endogenous to the economy, although it is an unintended by-products of firms' capital investment rather than the result of purposive R&D efforts.

[4] Interpreting S_t as the CO_2 concentration in the atmosphere at time t, our equation simplifies the formal treatment of the carbon cycle contained in the RICE/DICE model, in which three CO_2 reservoirs are considered: the atmosphere, the biosphere and upper layers of the ocean, and the deep ocean (for a discussion see Hassler & Krusell, 2018).

where δ_S is the rate of absorption, the fraction of pollutants that is absorbed by the environment (atmosphere, oceans, soil . . .) in each period. It should be stressed that the emissions of any single firm have only a negligible impact on the stock of pollutants.

2.4 *Firms' Profits*

At time t, the net profit (cash flow) of the representative firm, π_t, is given by:

$$\pi_t = Y_t - W_t L_t - B_t (1 + r_t) - \tau_t E_t, \tag{6}$$

where W_t is the wage paid to each unit of labor, L_t are the units of labor employed by the representative firm, $B_t \geq 0$ are the bonds with maturity in period t issued in t-1 by the representative firm to finance its investment in that period, r_t is the one-period market rate of interest, and $\tau_t \geq 0$ is the tax per unit of emissions that the firm must pay to the government.

2.5 *Firms' Investment*

The capital stock installed by the representative firm evolves according to

$$K_{t+1} = I_{kt} + (1 - \delta_k) K_t, 0 \leq \delta_k \leq 1, \;\; K_0 \text{ given}, \tag{7}$$

where I_{kt} is gross capital investment in period t and δ_k is a depreciation parameter.

The abatement capacity installed by the representative firm evolves according to

$$Z_{t+1} = I_{zt} + Z_t, \; Z_0 \text{ given}, \tag{8}$$

where I_{zt} is investment in green technologies in period t. Notice that the firm's abatement capacity does not depreciate: once a firm improves its abatement technology, the latter is not subject to downgrading (improving this technology is "building on the shoulders of the giants").

Firms finance their investment by going into debt:

$$I_{kt} (1 - v_t) + I_{zt} (1 - b_t) \leq B_{t+1}, \; 0 \leq v_t < 1, 0 \leq b_t < 1, \tag{9}$$

where v_t (b_t) is the fraction of the firms' investment expenditure in capital (green technology) that is subsidized by the government in period t.

2.6 Firms' Profit Maximization

In each t, firms decide on $\{L_{t+j}\}_{j=0}^{\infty}$, $\{I_{kt+j}\}_{j=0}^{\infty}$ and $\{I_{zt+j}\}_{j=0}^{\infty}$ subject to (7)–(9) in order to maximize their discounted sequence of net profits

$$\sum_{j=0}^{\infty} \frac{\pi_{t+j}}{\prod_{h=1}^{j}(1+r_{t+h})}, \tag{10}$$

where $\prod_{h=1}^{0}(1+r_{t+h}) = 1$.

2.7 Dynastic Families

For simplicity and without loss of generality, it is assumed that the large number (normalized to be one) of identical households is fixed, and that each of them takes account of the welfare and resources of their actual and prospective descendants. Hence, following Barro and Sala-i-Martin (1995), this intergenerational interaction is modeled by imagining that the current generation maximizes utility and incorporates a budget constraint over an infinite future. That is, although individuals have finite lives, the model considers immortal extended families ("dynasties"). Again for simplicity and without loss of generality, it is assumed that all households—being the firms' owners—are entitled to receive an equal share of the firms' net profits.[5]

2.8 Households' Utility

As in Acemoglu et al. (2012), we assume that environmental quality directly affects utility. In particular, the period utility function of the representative household, $U(C_t, S_t, L_t)$, is given by a weighted average of the utility that it draws from the consumption of the produced good, critically depending on the state of the environment, and the utility that it draws from leisure:

$$U(C_t, S_t, L_t) = \sigma \frac{[x(C_t, S_t)]^{1-\theta}}{1-\theta} + (1-\sigma)\frac{(N-L_t)^{1-\vartheta}}{1-\vartheta},$$
$$0 < \sigma < 1, x_c > 0, x_s < 0, x_{cs} < 0, \theta \geq 0, \vartheta \geq 0, N > 0, \tag{11}$$

where C_t are the units of good Y_t consumed by the representative household and N is the time endowment of the representative household (hence, $N\text{-}L_t$ are the units of time that each household devotes to leisure). The function $x(C_t, S_t)$ can

[5] As in Barro and Sala-i-Martin (1995, p. 120), we assume that the firms' net cash flow is paid out as dividends to the shareholders.

be interpreted as a household production function, which dictates the way whereby the consumer good and the environmental quality can combine for generating the services from which individuals draw utility. Notice that it is increasing in C_t and decreasing in the stock of pollutants S_t, and it is such that $U_{cs} < 0$ for $0 < \theta < 1$ and $U_{cs} > 0$ for $\theta > 1$.This allows both for the possibility that environmental degradation makes consumption less valuable to the households (whenever $U_{cs} < 0$), or alternatively for the possibility that it makes consumption more valuable to them (whenever $U_{cs} > 0$). The former case reflects situations where there is some complementarity between environmental quality and consumption (a fall in environmental quality would make people want to consume less), while the latter case reflects situations where there is some substitutability between them (a fall in environmental quality would make people want to consume more, which is typical of those situations where people react to environmental degradation by increasing their defensive expenditures).[6]

2.9 Households' Production Functions

We study the trajectory of the economy under two hypotheses about the functional form of the household production function:

$$x\,(C_t, S_t) = \frac{C_t}{S_t} \tag{12a}$$

or alternatively

$$x\,(C_t, S_t) = C_t\left(\frac{M}{S_t} - 1\right),\ M > 0. \tag{12b}$$

The household production function given by Eq. (12a) is consistent with the hypothesis that the households can always preserve their well being in the face of environmental degradation by using increasing quantity of produced goods. In contrast, Eq. (12b) applies to the hypothesis that the accumulation of pollutants can reach a threshold M beyond which efforts to compensate or offset the damage they cause to people's well being by using more manmade products are vain.[7] It is

[6] As defined by Leipert, "*Defensive expenditures comprise those economic activities by which we defend ourselves against the unwanted side effects (negative external effects) of our aggregate production and consumption. They are understood as expenditures to cure, neutralize, eliminate, avoid, and anticipate burdens on and damage to the environment (and living conditions in general) caused by the economic process in industrial countries.*" (Leipert & Pulselli, 2008, p. 154).

[7] One could argue that, if we want to model the effects of global warming on human well being, it would be more appropriate to insert the earth's global average temperature in Eq. (12b) instead of the stock of pollutants S_t, that in this context can be approximated by the concentration of

apparent that Eq. (12b) captures what may happen according to most scientists as a consequence of global warming, namely that catastrophic consequences for human well-being are likely to occur if the accumulation of CO_2 in the earth atmosphere—and the consequent increase in average temperature—exceeds a certain critical level.[8]

2.10 Households' Intertemporal Problem

In each period, the households decide on how to allocate their income between consumption and saving (spent for buying corporate and government bonds), and their time between leisure and labor. Thus, the problem of the representative household amounts to deciding a contingency plan for C_t, L_t, B_{t+1} and G_{t+1} in order to maximize the discounted sequence of utilities

$$\sum_{j=0}^{\infty} \gamma^j U\left(C_{t+j}, S_{t+j}, L_{t+j}\right), \ 0 < \gamma < 1, \tag{13}$$

subject to

$$B_{t+1} + G_{t+1} + C_t \leq (1 + r_t)\,(B_t + G_t) + \pi_t + W_t L_t, \ B_0 \text{ and } G_0 \text{ given}, \tag{14}$$

where γ is a time-preference parameter and $G_t \geq 0$ are the bonds with maturity in period t issued in t-1 by the government.[9]

2.11 Government

The government takes into account the optimizing behavior of firms and households, and in each period it decides a contingency plan for τ_t, v_t and b_t in order to maximize (13) subject to its period budget constraint

$$(1 + r_t)\,G_t + v_t I_{kt} + b_t I_{zt} \leq G_{t+1} + \tau_t E_t, \tag{15}$$

CO_2 in the atmosphere. However, an acceptable approximation to the relation linking the global average temperature to CO_2 is that the temperature increase over any time period is proportional to the accumulated emissions of CO_2 over the same period, with the proportionality factor that is independent of the length of the time period and of previous emissions (see Matthews et al., 2009). Thus, considering that the relationship between pollution stock (CO_2 concentration) and temperature is approximately linear, one may omit to introduce a separate variable for temperature (see Bretschger & Karydas, 2019).

[8] It goes without saying that any calibration of the model with real world data has to deal with the uncertainty surrounding all the parameters values; in particular, this applies to the tipping point M, whose existence is not recognized by all the scholars on climate change.

[9] The households' budget constraint (14) implicitly assumes the existence of a non-arbitrage condition that equalizes the rate of return on the corporate bonds and the rate of return on the government bonds.

and to its intertemporal budget constraint (no-Ponzi condition)

$$G_t + \sum_{j=0}^{\infty} \frac{(v_{t+j} I_{kt+j} + b_{t+j} I_{zt+j})}{\prod_{h=1}^{j} (1 + r_{t+h})} \leq \sum_{j=0}^{\infty} \frac{\tau_{t+j} E_{t+j}}{\prod_{h=1}^{j} (1 + r_{t+h})} \quad (16)$$

where $\prod_{h=1}^{0} (1 + r_{t+h}) = 1$.

2.12 Market Equilibrium

Equilibrium in the good market implies

$$I_{kt} + I_{zt} + C_t = Y_t. \quad (17)$$

Equilibrium in the labor market implies

$$L_t^s = L_t^d, \quad (18)$$

where L_t^s are the units of labor supplied by the households and L_t^d are the units of labor demanded by the firms.

Equilibrium in the market for corporate bonds implies

$$B_t^s = B_t^d, \quad (19)$$

where B_t^s are the bonds issued by the firms and B_t^d are the corporate bonds demanded by the households.

Equilibrium in the market for government bonds implies

$$G_t^s = G_t^d, \quad (20)$$

where G_t^s are the bonds issued by the government and G_t^d are the government bonds demanded by the households.

3 The Economy's Balanced Growth Path When $x(C_t, S_t) = \frac{C_t}{S_t}$

3.1 The Laissez-Faire Path

Assuming no government intervention amounts to set $\tau_t = v_t = b_t = 0\ \forall t$, $G_0 = 0$. In this case, firms have no incentive to reduce their emissions and invest in abatement technologies ($I_{zt} = 0\ \forall t$, entailing $Z_t = Z_0\ \forall t$), and also their investment in capital is sub-optimally low because they have no incentive to take into account the positive externalities that this investment activity generates for the entire economy. Under these circumstances, one can derive the "laissez-faire" equilibrium path of the economy,[10] which is governed by the following two difference equations in L_t and $s_t \equiv S_t/K_t$:

$$s_{t+1}\,(1 + g_{kt}) - Z_0^{-\varphi} L_t^{1-\alpha} - (1 - \delta_s)\, s_t = 0, \quad Z_0 \text{ given}, \tag{21}$$

$$\frac{\gamma}{s_{t+1}}\left(\frac{s_{t+1}}{c_{t+1}}\right)^{\theta}\left(\alpha L_{t+1}^{1-\alpha} + 1 - \delta_k\right) - \frac{(1 + g_{kt})}{s_t}\left(\frac{s_t}{c_t}\right)^{\theta} = 0, \tag{22}$$

where $g_{kt} \equiv \frac{K_{t+1}-K_t}{K_t} = L_{t+1}^{1-\alpha} - \delta_k - c\,(s_t, L_t)$ and $c_t \equiv C_t/K_t = c\,(s_t, L_t) = \left[\frac{s_t^{\theta-1}(1-\alpha)\sigma(N-L_t)^{\vartheta}}{(1-\sigma)L_t^{\alpha}}\right]^{\frac{1}{\theta}}$.

Along a balanced growth path (BGP), $L_{t+1} = L_t = L^{LF}$ and $s_{t+1} = s_t = s^{LF}$, entailing $g_{kt+1} = g_{kt} = g_k^{LF} \gtreqless 0$ and $c_{t+1} = c_t = c^{LF}$. Moreover, along a BGP, $Z^{LF} = Z_0$, $g_Z^{LF} = 0$, $g_Y^{LF} = g_C^{LF} = g_S^{LF} = g_K^{LF}$, where $g_{zt} \equiv \frac{Z_{t+1}-Z_t}{Z_t}$, $g_{Yt} \equiv \frac{Y_{t+1}-Y_t}{Y_t}$, $g_{ct} \equiv \frac{C_{t+1}-C_t}{C_t}$ and $g_{st} \equiv \frac{S_{t+1}-S_t}{S_t}$.

Notice that along a BGP, (i) the stock of pollutants, S_t, and the stock of productive assets, K_t, grow at the same rate, and (ii) one may have unbounded growth ($g_Y^{LF} = g_C^{LF} = g_S^{LF} = g_K^{LF} > 0$). This allows us to state the following proposition:

Proposition 1 *If the household production function is given by Eq. (12a), that is, if it is always possible to offset the harm that environmental degradation causes on people's well being by an increased use of manmade products, GDP growth can go on forever under laissez faire in spite of the growing environmental damage due to production. In this case, (i) laissez faire is consistent with unbounded growth, (ii) environmental degradation has never catastrophic effects on human well being, and (iii) human well being remains constant along the BGP.*[11]

3.2 The Socially Optimal Path

Suppose that there is a central planner with full control over the allocation of all resources (people's time included) which maximizes (13). From the solution of the planner's problem (see the Appendix), one can derive the optimal path of the

[10] All derivations are available on request from the authors.

[11] Since, along the BGP, consumption and the stock of pollutants grow at the same rate, while leisure is constant.

economy, which is governed by the following four difference equations in K_t, S_t, L_t and Z_t:

$$K_t\left(L_t^{1-\alpha}+1-\delta_k\right)-K_{t+1}+Z_t-Z_{t+1}-C_t=0,\ K_0 \text{ and } Z_0 \text{ given,} \tag{23}$$

$$S_{t+1}-\frac{K_tL_t^{1-\alpha}}{Z_t^{\varphi}}-(1-\delta_s)S_t=0,\ S_0 \text{ given,} \tag{24}$$

$$\frac{\gamma\sigma(1-\delta_k)}{S_{t+1}^{1-\theta}C_{t+1}^{\theta}}+\frac{\gamma(1-\sigma)L_{t+1}}{(1-\alpha)K_{t+1}(N-L_{t+1})^{\vartheta}}-\frac{\sigma}{S_t^{1-\theta}C_t^{\theta}}=0, \tag{25}$$

$$\frac{\gamma\sigma C_{t+1}^{1-\theta}}{S_{t+1}^{2-\theta}}+\frac{\gamma\sigma(1-\delta_s)Z_{t+1}^{\varphi}}{S_{t+1}^{1-\theta}C_{t+1}^{\theta}}-\frac{\gamma(1-\sigma)(1-\delta_s)Z_{t+1}^{\varphi}L_{t+1}^{\alpha}}{(1-\alpha)K_{t+1}(N-L_{t+1})^{\vartheta}}-\frac{\sigma Z_t^{\varphi}}{S_t^{1-\theta}C_t^{\theta}}+\frac{(1-\sigma)Z_t^{\varphi}L_t^{\alpha}}{(1-\alpha)K_t(N-L_{t+1})^{\vartheta}}=0, \tag{26}$$

where $C_t=C(K_t,S_t,L_t,Z_t)=\left[\frac{S_t^{\theta-1}(1-\alpha)\sigma(N-L_t)^{\vartheta}}{(1-\sigma)L_t\left(\varphi Z_t^{-1}+K_t^{-1}\right)}\left(\frac{\varphi K_tL_t^{1-\alpha}}{Z_t}+\delta_K\right)\right]^{\frac{1}{\theta}}$.

In the general case in which $\theta\neq 1$, i.e., in the case in which the preferences for the combination of consumer good and environmental quality from which households draw utility, $x(C_t, S_t)$, are **not** logarithmic, a BGP is characterized by $K_{t+1}=K_t=K^{OP}$, $S_{t+1}=S_t=S^{OP}$, $L_{t+1}=L_t=L^{OP}$ and $Z_{t+1}=Z_t=Z^{OP}$, entailing $g_Y^{OP}=g_c^{OP}=g_s^{OP}=g_k^{OP}=g_z^{OP}=0$. Hence, the following proposition holds:

Proposition 2 *If the household production function is given by Eq. (12a) and $\theta\neq 1$, a socially optimal path (i.e., the path along which a benevolent planner with full command of resource allocation would lead the economy) has a steady state where GDP growth—together with the accumulation of both capital and pollutants—ceases, differently than under laissez faire, where the economy can exhibit unbounded growth.*

The intuition behind Proposition 2 is that under laissez faire the economic agents have no incentive to invest in abatement capacity and tend to protect themselves (and their descendants) from environmental degradation by using more manmade products, thus feeding economic growth, while a benevolent planner invests in abatement capacity, thus stopping both environmental degradation and the need to produce more and work harder in order to compensate for this degradation.

In the special case in which $\theta=1$, i.e., in the case in which the preferences for $x(C_t, S_t)$, are logarithmic, the Eqs. (23)–(26) governing the optimal path of the economy can be rewritten as a system of four difference equations in L_t, $z_t \equiv Z_t/K_t$, g_{kt} and g_{st}:

$$L_t^{1-\alpha} + 1 - \delta_k + z_t - (1 + g_{kt})(1 + z_{t+1}) - f(L_t, z_t) = 0,\ z_0 \text{ given}, \tag{27}$$

$$(1 + g_{kt}) - \left[(1 + g_{st}) \left(\frac{z_{t+1}}{z_t}\right)^{\varphi} \left(\frac{g_{st+1} + \delta_s}{g_{st} + \delta_s}\right) \left(\frac{L_t}{L_{t+1}}\right)^{1-\alpha}\right]^{\frac{1}{1-\varphi}} = 0, \tag{28}$$

$$\frac{\gamma\sigma(1 - \delta_k)}{f(L_{t+1}, z_{t+1})} + \frac{\gamma(1 - \sigma) L_{t+1}}{(1 - \alpha)(N - L_{t+1})^{\vartheta}} - \frac{\sigma(1 + g_{kt})}{f(L_t, z_t)} = 0, \tag{29}$$

$$\begin{aligned} \gamma\sigma &+ \frac{\gamma\sigma(1-\delta_s)L_{t+1}^{1-\alpha}}{(g_{st+1}+\delta_s) f(L_{t+1}, z_{t+1})} - \frac{\gamma(1-\sigma)(1-\delta_s)L_{t+1}}{(1-\alpha)(g_{st+1}+\delta_s)(N-L_{t+1})^{\vartheta}} - \frac{\sigma L_t^{1-\alpha}(1+g_{st})}{(g_{st}+\delta_s) f(L_t, z_t)} \\ &+ \frac{(1-\sigma)L_t(1+g_{st})}{(1-\alpha)(g_{st}+\delta_s)(N-L_t)^{\vartheta}} = 0, \end{aligned} \tag{30}$$

where $c_t \equiv C_t/K_t = f(L_t, z_t) = \frac{(1-\alpha)\sigma(N-L_t)^{\vartheta}}{(1-\sigma)L_t\left(\varphi z_t^{-1}+1\right)} \left(\frac{\varphi L_t^{1-\alpha}}{z_t} + \delta_K\right)$.

In this case, along a BGP, $L_{t+1} = L_t = L^{OP}$, $z_{t+1} = z_t = z^{OP}$, $g_{kt+1} = g_{kt} = g_k^{OP} \gtreqless 0$, $g_{st+1} = g_{st} = g_s^{OP} = \left(1 + g_k^{OP}\right)^{1-\varphi} - 1$ and $g_Y^{OP} = g_c^{OP} = g_k^{OP}$. Notice that $g_Y^{OP} = g_c^{OP} = g_k^{OP} > 0$ entails $g_s^{OP} < g_Y^{OP} = g_c^{OP} = g_k^{OP}$, thus allowing us to state Proposition 3:

Proposition 3 *If the household production function is given by Eq. (12a) and $\theta = 1$ (implying that the marginal utility of consumption is not affected by environmental degradation), it can be socially optimal to have unbounded GDP growth, since investment in abatement capital can lead the stock of pollutants to grow at a rate permanently lower than the rate of GDP growth, thus allowing the households' well being to increase limitless along a BGP.*

This optimistic long-term conclusion associated to the case of logarithmic preferences is reinforced if $\varphi > 1$, i.e., if the elasticity of emissions with respect to abatement capital is larger than one: whenever improvements in the firms' abatement capacity bring about strong reductions in emissions per unit of output, an optimal BGP can be characterized by both an ever increasing GDP and a declining stock of pollutants.

3.3 The "Green-Policy" Path

Decentralizing the socially optimal path can in principle be achieved by a public authority ("the government") levying taxes on emissions and subsidizing investment. We define "green-policy" path the trajectory along which the economy moves whenever the government utilizes its policy instruments (green taxes on emissions and subsidies to private investment in capital and in green technologies). The "green-policy" path is governed by the following Eqs. (23, 24),

$$\frac{\gamma S_{t+1}^{\theta-1}}{C_{t+1}^{\theta}}\left[\frac{\alpha L_{t+1}^{1-\alpha}\left(1-\tau_{t+1}Z_{t+1}^{-\varphi}\right)+(1-\delta_k)(1-v_{t+1})}{1-v_t}\right]-\frac{S_t^{\theta-1}}{C_t^{\theta}}=0,\ S_0 \text{ and } Z_0 \text{ given,} \tag{31}$$

$$\begin{aligned} &D_{t+1}+\tau_t Z_t^{-\varphi}K_t L_t^{1-\alpha}-b_t\left(Z_{t+1}-Z_t\right)-v_t\left[K_{t+1}-(1-\delta_k)K_t\right]- \\ &-D_t\left[\frac{\alpha L_t^{1-\alpha}\left(1-\tau_t Z_t^{-\varphi}\right)+(1-\delta_k)(1-v_t)}{1-v_{t-1}}\right]=0,\ D_0 \text{ and } K_0 \text{ given,}\end{aligned} \tag{32}$$

$$\left[\frac{\alpha L_t^{1-\alpha}\left(1-\tau_t Z_t^{-\varphi}\right)+(1-\delta_k)(1-v_t)}{1-v_{t-1}}\right]-\left[\frac{\varphi\tau_t Z_t^{-\varphi-1}L_t^{1-\alpha}K_t+1-b_t}{1-b_{t-1}}\right]=0, \tag{33}$$

where $C_t = C\left(K_t, S_t, L_t, Z_t\right) = \left[\frac{(1-\alpha)\sigma K_t(N-L_t)^{\vartheta}\left(1-\tau_t Z_t^{-\varphi}\right)}{S_t^{1-\theta}(1-\sigma)L_t^{\alpha}}\right]^{\frac{1}{\theta}}$, and the evolution of τ_t, v_t and b_t is determined by the government's policy rule.

The optimal policy rule, i.e., the policy rule driving the economy along a socially optimal path, is the following:
(i) $\tau_t^* = Z_t^{\varphi}\left[1-L_t^{\alpha-1}\left(\varphi z_t^{-1}L_t^{1-\alpha}+\delta_k\right)\left(\varphi z_t^{-1}+1\right)^{-1}\right]$ $\forall t$, (ii) $v_t^* = 1\text{-}\alpha$ $\forall t$ and (iii) $b_t^* = 0$ $\forall t$. The optimal policy rule is feasible if and only if it is consistent with $D_t/Y_t \rightarrow F$ as $t \rightarrow \infty$, where F is a finite constant (public debt must be sustainable).

The optimal rule corrects the negative externality associated to the firms' production activities by taxing the emission of pollutants at rate τ_t^*, and the positive externality generated by private investment in productive assets by subsidizing it at rate v_t^*. Once that both these market inefficiencies are corrected, private investment in green technologies is at its socially optimal level without the need of public subsidies supporting it ($b_t^* = 0$). This differs from Acemoglu et al. (2012), where there is a sharp distinction between dirty and clean production technologies, and the optimal public policy discourages research aimed at improving the productivity of the former not only by levying a tax on emissions but also by subsidizing the latter.[12] In contrast, in our framework improvements in abatement technologies can make all productive activities cleaner, and optimal public policy encourages these improvements only by taxing emissions, while at the same time it subsidizes investment in productive assets.

Given the optimal policy rule, the five difference Eqs. (23, 24, 31–33) in K_t, S_t, L_t, Z_t and D_t fully characterize the "green-policy" path of the economy, and Proposition 2 holds: in the general case where $\theta \neq 1$, differently than under laissez-faire, the adoption of the optimal policy rule prevents the economy from exhibiting unbounded GDP growth.

If the optimal policy rule is not feasible, one should consider other policy rules. A simple—but suboptimal—alternative policy rule amounts to keep constant the fraction of GDP paid to the government as emission tax, and the fractions of private investment in productive assets and in green technologies that are paid by the government: (i) $\tau_t = hZ_t^{\varphi} \forall t$, $0 \leq h < 1$ (total emission taxes are a fixed fraction h of GDP), (ii) $v_t = v \; \forall \; t$, $0 \leq v < 1$, and (iii) $b_t = b \; \forall \; t$, $0 \leq b < 1$. Again, policy parameters h, b and v must be such that $D_t/Y_t \rightarrow F$ as $t \rightarrow \infty$. Notice that also with the adoption of this suboptimal rule the five difference Eqs. (23), (24), (31–33) in K_t, S_t, L_t, Z_t and D_t fully characterize the "green-policy" path of the economy, which does not exhibit unbounded growth in the general case where $\theta \neq 1$.

In the special case in which $\theta = 1$, Eqs. (23), (24), (31–33) can be rewritten as Eq. (28),

$$L_t^{1-\alpha} + 1 - \delta_k + z_t - (1 + g_{kt})(1 + z_{t+1}) - n\left(L_t, \tau_t Z_t^{-\varphi}\right) = 0, \; z_0 \text{ and } Z_0 \text{ given,} \tag{34}$$

$$\frac{\gamma\sigma\left[\alpha L_{t+1}^{1-\alpha}\left(1 - \tau_{t+1}Z_{t+1}^{-\varphi}\right) + (1 - \delta_k)(1 - v_{t+1})\right]}{n\left(L_{t+1}, \tau_{t+1}Z_{t+1}^{-\varphi}\right)(1 - v_t)} - \frac{\sigma(1 + g_{kt})}{n\left(L_t, \tau_t Z_t^{-\varphi}\right)} = 0, \tag{35}$$

$$\begin{aligned}(1 + g_{kt})\, d_{t+1} + \tau_t Z_t^{-\varphi} L_t^{1-\alpha} - b_t\left[(1 + g_{kt})\, z_{t+1} - z_t\right] - v_t\left(g_{kt} + \delta_k\right) - \\ - d_t\left[\frac{\alpha L_t^{1-\alpha}\left(1 - \tau_t Z_t^{-\varphi}\right) + (1 - \delta_k)(1 - v_t)}{1 - v_{t-1}}\right] = 0, \; d_t \equiv D_t/K_t, \; d_0 \text{ given,}\end{aligned} \tag{36}$$

[12] In general, as pointed out by Golosov et al. (2014), it is far from clear that there should be a favorable treatment of green R&D in the presence of an optimal emission tax, which is justified in Acemoglu et al. (2012) by assuming a built-in path dependence that over time would lead to a disaster, motivating early efforts to switch alternatives.

$$\left[\frac{\alpha L_t^{1-\alpha}\left(1-\tau_t Z_t^{-\varphi}\right)+(1-\delta_k)(1-v_t)}{1-v_{t-1}}\right]-\left[\frac{\varphi\tau_t Z_t^{-\varphi}L_t^{1-\alpha}z_t^{-1}+1-b_t}{1-b_{t-1}}\right]=0, \tag{37}$$

where $c_t \equiv C_t/K_t = n\left(L_t, \tau_t Z_t^{-\varphi}\right) = \frac{(1-\alpha)\sigma(N-L_t)^{\vartheta}\left(1-\tau_t Z_t^{-\varphi}\right)}{(1-\sigma)L_t^{\alpha}}$.

Supposing that the government adopts the policy rules outlined above, the five difference Eqs. (28), (34)–(37) in L_t, g_{st}, g_{kt}, z_t and d_t fully characterize the equilibrium path of the economy when $\theta = 1$. In this special case, Proposition 3 holds: the adoption of the optimal policy rule is consistent with unbounded GDP growth.

3.4 Numerical Example 1

Assume the following parameter values: $\alpha = 0.25$; $\gamma = 0.92$; $\theta = 1$; $\vartheta = 1$; $\sigma = 0.5$; $N = 1.5500971$; $\varphi = 0.3405566$; $\delta_k = 0.1$; $\delta_s = 0.3160914$. Given these values, the BGP values obtained under laissez faire are the following:

$$L^{LF} = 0.7211987;\ c^{LF} = 0.6746038;\ Z^{LF} = Z_0;\ g_z^{LF} = 0;\ s^{LF} = 2.4147692 Z_0^{-0.3405566};$$

$$g_Y^{LF} = g_k^{LF} = g_c^{LF} = g_s^{LF} = 0.0079986;$$

$$\begin{aligned} U^{LF} &= 0.5\ln\left(\frac{c^{LF}}{s^{LF}}\right) + 0.5\ln\left(N - L^{LF}\right),\\ &= 0.5\left[0.3405566\ln\left(Z_0\right) - 1.2752334\right] + 0.5(-0.1876476)\\ &= 0.1702783\ln(Z_0) - 0.7314455, \end{aligned}$$

where $c_t \equiv C_t/K_t$, $s_t \equiv S_t/K_t$, $g_{Yt} \equiv \frac{Y_{t+1}-Y_t}{Y_t}$, $g_{Ct} \equiv \frac{C_{t+1}-C_t}{C_t}$ and $g_{zt} \equiv \frac{Z_{t+1}-Z_t}{Z_t}$.

Given the same parameter values, the BGP values obtained when the economy follows its optimal path are the following:

$$\begin{aligned} &L^{OP} = 0.4000807;\ c^{OP} = 0.4030493;\ s^{OP} = 1.5914684\left(Z^{OP}\right)^{-0.3405566};\\ &z^{OP} = 1.2379469;\ g_Y^{OP} = g_k^{OP} = g_c^{OP} = g_s^{OP} = g_z^{OP} = 0;\\ &U^{OP} = 0.5\ln\left(\frac{c^{OP}}{s^{OP}}\right) + 0.5\ln\left(N - L^{OP}\right) =\\ &0.5\left[0.3405566\ln\left(Z^{OP}\right) - 1.3733535\right] + 0.5(0.1397762)\\ &\quad = 0.1702783\ln\left(Z^{OP}\right) - 0.6167886. \end{aligned}$$

Supposing that the government adopts the optimal policy rule, along the BGP total emission taxes as a fraction of GDP are $\tau^{OP}(Z^{OP})^{-0.3405566} = 0.6283538$, and $d^{OP} = 2.772569$.

Comparing the laissez-faire BGP to the socially optimal BGP, one can check that $g_Y^{LF} > g_Y^{OP}$ and $L^{LF} > L^{OP}$, while $U^{OP} > U^{LF}$ (where $Z^{OP} \geq Z_0$). Hence,

Proposition 4 *Whenever the household production function is given by Eq. (12a) and θ=1, numerical examples show that in the long-run GDP growth is higher along a laissez-faire path than along a socially optimal path, while people enjoy more leisure and well-being along the latter.*

4 The Economy's Balanced Growth Path When $x\,(C_t, S_t) = C_t\left(\frac{M}{S_t} - 1\right)$

4.1 The Laissez-Faire Path

Whenever the households' production function is given by Eq (12b), the "laissez-faire" equilibrium path is governed by the following three difference equations in L_t, K_t and S_t:

$$K_t\left(L_t^{1-\alpha} + 1 - \delta_k\right) - K_{t+1} - C\,(K_t, S_t, L_t) = 0,\ K_0 \text{ and } S_0 \text{ given,} \tag{38}$$

$$S_{t+1} - Z_0^{-\varphi}K_tL_t^{1-\alpha} - (1 - \delta_s)\,S_t = 0,\ Z_0 \text{ given,} \tag{39}$$

$$\gamma C_{t+1}^{-1}\left[C_{t+1}\left(\frac{M}{S_{t+1}} - 1\right)\right]^{1-\theta}\left(\alpha L_{t+1}^{1-\alpha} + 1 - \delta_k\right) - C_t^{-1}\left[C_t\left(\frac{M}{S_t} - 1\right)\right]^{1-\theta} = 0, \tag{40}$$

where $C_t = C\,(K_t, S_t, L_t) = \left(\frac{M}{S_t} - 1\right)^{\frac{1-\theta}{\theta}}\left[\frac{K_t(1-\alpha)\sigma(N-L_t)^{\vartheta}}{(1-\sigma)L_t^{\alpha}}\right]^{\frac{1}{\theta}}$.

In the general case in which $\theta \neq 1$, a BGP is characterized by $L_{t+1} = L_t = L^{LF}$, $K_{t+1} = K_t = K^{LF}$, and $S_{t+1} = S_t = S^{LF}$, entailing $g_Y^{LF} = g_c^{LF} = g_s^{LF} = g_k^{LF} = g_z^{LF} = 0$. Hence, the following proposition holds:

Proposition 5 *If the household production function is given by Eq. (12b) and θ≠1, the laissez-faire path has a steady state where GDP growth—together with the accumulation of both capital and pollutants—ceases, differently than the laissez-faire path when the household production function is given by Eq. (12a), which can exhibit unbounded growth even if θ≠1 (see Proposition 1).*

If the marginal utility of consuming manmade products is not any longer positive once that the stock of pollutants surpasses a certain threshold, there is no incentive for households to go on accumulating wealth in a scenario of progressive environmental degradation. Hence, even under laissez faire, in general one cannot have unbounded GDP growth whenever the adverse effects of the accumulation of pollutants on people's well being cannot be compensated by devoting increasing quantities of output to this scope. However, in the special case in which $\theta=1$, the marginal utility of consuming manmade products is not affected by the stock of pollutants ($U_{cs}=0$), and unbounded growth is possible even when the household production function is given by Eq. (12b). In this special case, indeed, the laissez-faire equilibrium path of the economy is governed by the following two difference equations in L_t and $s_t \equiv S_t/K_t$: (21) and

$$\frac{\gamma}{c_{t+1}}\left(\alpha L_{t+1}^{1-\alpha}+1-\delta_k\right)-\frac{(1+g_{kt})}{c_t}=0, \tag{41}$$

where $g_{kt} \equiv \frac{K_{t+1}-K_t}{K_t} = L_{t+1}^{1-\alpha}-\delta_k-f(L_t)$ and $c_t \equiv C_t/K_t = f(L_t) = \frac{(1-\alpha)\sigma(N-L_t)^{\vartheta}}{(1-\sigma)L_t^{\alpha}}$.

Thus, in the special case in which $\theta=1$, a BGP is characterized by $L_{t+1}=L_t=L^{LF}$, $s_{t+1}=s_t=s^{LF}$, $Z^{LF}=Z_0$ and $g_z^{LF}=0$. Moreover, along a BGP one may have unbounded growth $\left(g_Y^{LF}=g_c^{LF}=g_s^{LF}=g_k^{LF}>0\right)$. This allows us to state the following proposition:

Proposition 6 *If the household production function is given by Eq. (12b) and $\theta=1$, laissez faire can lead to a "climate catastrophe" by determining unbounded growth, which—in the absence of any incentive in invest in green technology—drives S_t (the stock of pollutants, e.g. the amount of CO_2 in the atmosphere) to overpass its maximum compatible with life on earth, thus precipitating the collapse of individual's well being ($U^{LF}\to-\infty$ as $t=\to\infty$).*

4.2 The Socially Optimal Path

The optimal path is governed by the following four difference equations in K_t, S_t, L_t and Z_t: Eqs. (23), (24),

$$\frac{\gamma\sigma(1-\delta_k)}{C_{t+1}^{\theta}}\left(\frac{M}{S_{t+1}}-1\right)^{1-\theta}+\frac{\gamma(1-\sigma)L_{t+1}}{(1-\alpha)K_{t+1}(N-L_{t+1})^{\vartheta}}-\frac{\sigma}{C_t^{\theta}}\left(\frac{M}{S_t}-1\right)^{1-\theta}=0, \tag{42}$$

$$\frac{\gamma\sigma MC_{t+1}^{1-\theta}}{S_{t+1}^{2}}\left(\frac{M}{S_{t+1}}-1\right)^{-\theta}+\frac{\gamma\sigma(1-\delta_s)Z_{t+1}^{\varphi}}{C_{t+1}^{\theta}}\left(\frac{M}{S_{t+1}}-1\right)^{1-\theta}-\frac{\gamma(1-\sigma)(1-\delta_s)Z_{t+1}^{\varphi}L_{t+1}^{\alpha}}{(1-\alpha)K_{t+1}(N-L_{t+1})^{\vartheta}}-$$
$$-\frac{\sigma Z_t^{\varphi}}{C_t^{\theta}}\left(\frac{M}{S_t}-1\right)^{1-\theta}+\frac{(1-\sigma)Z_t^{\varphi}L_t^{\alpha}}{(1-\alpha)K_t(N-L_{t+1})^{\vartheta}}=0, \tag{43}$$

where $C_t = C\,(K_t, S_t, L_t, Z_t) = \left[\left(\frac{M}{S_t}-1\right)^{1-\theta}\frac{(1-\alpha)\sigma(N-L_t)^{\vartheta}}{(1-\sigma)L_t\left(\varphi Z_t^{-1}+K_t^{-1}\right)}\left(\frac{\varphi K_t L_t^{1-\alpha}}{Z_t}+\delta_K\right)\right]^{\frac{1}{\theta}}.$

In general, even in the case in which $\theta=1$, i.e., in the case in which the preferences for the combination of consumer good and environmental quality, $x(C_t, S_t)$, are logarithmic, a BGP associated to the socially optimal path is characterized by $K_{t+1} = K_t = K^{OP}$, $S_{t+1} = S_t = S^{OP}$, $L_{t+1} = L_t = L^{OP}$ and $Z_{t+1} = Z_t = Z^{OP}$, entailing $g_Y^{OP} = g_c^{OP} = g_s^{OP} = g_k^{OP} = g_z^{OP} = 0$. Hence, the following proposition holds:

Proposition 7 *In general, if the household production function is given by Eq. (12b), the socially optimal path has a steady state where GDP growth—together with the accumulation of both capital and pollutants—ceases, differently than under laissez faire, where the economy can exhibit unbounded growth whenever $\theta=1$, thus leading to a climate apocalypse.*

The socially optimal path prevents the stock of pollutants to exceed the critical threshold M, thus avoiding a climate catastrophe, by sacrificing unbounded growth, with the exception of the case in which $\theta = \varphi = 1$. In this special case, the socially optimal path is governed by the following system of difference equations in L_t, z_t, g_{kt} and S_t: Eqs. (27, 29),

$$S_{t+1} - z_t^{-1}L_t^{1-\alpha} - (1-\delta_s)\,S_t = 0,\ S_0 \text{ given}, \tag{44}$$

$$\frac{\gamma\sigma M}{S_{t+1}^{2}}\left(\frac{M}{S_{t+1}}-1\right)^{-1}+\frac{\gamma\sigma(1-\delta_s)z_{t+1}}{c_{t+1}}-\frac{\gamma(1-\sigma)(1-\delta_s)z_{t+1}L_{t+1}^{\alpha}}{(1-\alpha)(N-L_{t+1})^{\vartheta}}-\frac{\sigma z_t}{c_t}+\frac{(1-\sigma)z_tL_t^{\alpha}}{(1-\alpha)K_t(N-L_t)^{\vartheta}}=0, \tag{45}$$

where $c_t \equiv C_t/K_t = f\,(L_t, z_t) = \frac{(1-\alpha)\sigma(N-L_t)^{\vartheta}}{(1-\sigma)L_t\left(z_t^{-1}+1\right)}\left(\frac{L_t^{1-\alpha}}{z_t}+\delta_K\right).$

In this special case, a BGP is characterized by $L_{t+1} = L_t = L^{OP}$, $z_{t+1} = z_t = z^{OP}$, $g_{kt+1} = g_{kt} = g_k^{OP} \gtreqless 0$ and $S_{t+1} = S_t = S^{OP}$, entailing $g_S^{OP} = 0$ and $g_Y^{OP} = g_c^{OP} = g_Z^{OP} = g_k^{OP}$. Hence, one can state the following proposition:

Proposition 8 *If the household production function is given by Eq. (12b), unbounded GDP growth can be socially optimal only in the special case in which the marginal utility of consumption is not affected by environmental degradation*

($\theta = 1$), and total emissions can be stabilized by letting the abatement efficiency grow at the same rate as productive capital and production, i.e. whenever the elasticity of emissions with respect to abatement capacity is one (φ=1).

Proposition 8 emphasizes that the socially optimal plan is consistent with unbounded GDP growth only in the special case in which the increase in abatement capital (the progress of green technologies) can stabilize the stock of pollutants in an ever growing economy.

4.3 The "Green-Policy" Path

Under the hypothesis that the household production function is given by Eq. (12b), the "green-policy" path of the economy is governed by the following five equations in K_t, S_t, L_t, Z_t and D_t: Eqs. (23, 24, 32, 33) and

$$\frac{\gamma\left(\frac{M}{S_{t+1}}-1\right)^{1-\theta}}{C_{t+1}^{\theta}}\left[\frac{\alpha L_{t+1}^{1-\alpha}\left(1-\tau_{t+1}Z_{t+1}^{-\varphi}\right)+(1-\delta_k)(1-v_{t+1})}{1-v_t}\right]-\frac{\left(\frac{M}{S_t}-1\right)^{1-\theta}}{C_t^{\theta}}=0,\ S_0 \text{ and } Z_0 \text{ given,} \tag{46}$$

where $C_t = C\,(K_t, S_t, L_t, Z_t) = \left[\left(\frac{M}{S_t}-1\right)^{1-\theta}\frac{(1-\alpha)\sigma K_t(N-L_t)^{\vartheta}\left(1-\tau_t Z_t^{-\varphi}\right)}{(1-\sigma)L_t^{\alpha}}\right]^{\frac{1}{\theta}}$, and the evolution of τ_t, v_t and b_t is determined by the government's policy rule.

Given the two policy rules outlined in Sect. 3.3, the five Eqs. (23), (24), (32), (33) and (46) in K_t, S_t, L_t, Z_t and D_t fully characterize the "green-policy" path of the economy, and the same considerations made in that subsection still apply.

In the special case in which $\theta = 1$, (23), (32), (33) and (46) can be rewritten as (34)–(37). Thus, supposing that the government policies are the same as the policy rules outlined in Sect. 3.3, the dynamics of L_t, g_{kt}, z_t and d_t is fully characterized by the system (34)–(37). In this case, the government policy can make unbounded growth consistent with the convergence of S_t toward a sustainable level (a level lower than M) if $\varphi = 1$, i.e., if the economy is governed by Eqs. (24) and (34)–(37).

4.4 Numerical Example 2

Assume the following parameter values: $\alpha = 0.25$; $\gamma = 0.92$; $\theta = 0.2$; $\vartheta = 1$; $\sigma = 0.5$; $N = 1.4$; $\varphi = \delta_k = \delta_s = 0.1$; $M = 70.597574$.

Given these values, the BGP values obtained under laissez faire are the following:

$L^{LF} = 0.6787879$; $C^{LF} = 6.11572Z_0^{0.1} - 1.1100296$; $K^{LF} = 9.4403744Z_0^{0.1} - 1.7134687$; $Z^{LF} = Z_0$; $S^{LF} = 70.597574 - 12.813764Z_0^{-0.1}$; $g_Y^{LF} = g_k^{LF} = g_c^{LF} = g_s^{LF} = g_z^{LF} = 0$; $U^{LF} = \frac{0.5}{0.8}(1.1100295)^{0.8} + 0.5\ln(0.7212121) = 0.5160235$.

Given the same parameter values, the BGP values obtained when the economy follows its optimal path are the following:

$L^{OP} = 0.6$; $C^{OP} = 2.4386869$; $K^{OP} = 4.1921169$; $S^{OP} = 26.199494$; $Z^{OP} = 2.3852783$; $g_Y^{OP} = g_k^{OP} = g_c^{OP} = g_s^{OP} = g_z^{OP} = 0$; $U^{OP} = \frac{0.5}{0.8}(4.1326377)^{0.8} + 0.5\ln(0.8) = 1.8331697$.

Supposing that, along the BGP total emission taxes as a fraction of GDP are $\tau^{OP}(Z^{OP})^{-0.1}$=0.7257623 and $d^{OP} = 4.8274205$.

Comparing the laissez-faire BGP to the socially optimal BGP, one can check that $U^{OP} > U^{LF}$, while $Y^{LF} > Y^{OP}$, $C^{LF} > C^{OP}$, $L^{LF} > L^{OP}$ and $S^{LF} > C^{OP}$ whenever $Z_0 > \frac{4.8011476}{1000}$. Hence,

Proposition 9 *Whenever the household production function is given by Eq. (12b) and $\theta \neq 1$, numerical examples show for reasonable values of Z_0 that steady-state values of output, consumption and stock of emissions are higher under laissez faire than when the government adopts the optimal policy rule, while the reverse is true for people's steady-state leisure and well-being.*

4.5 Numerical Example 3

Assume the following parameter values: $\alpha = 0.25; \gamma = 0.98; \theta = \varphi = \vartheta = 1; \sigma = 0.5$; $N = 2.3522222$; $\delta_k = 0.1$; $\delta_s = 0.005$; $M = 165.26103$.

Given these values, the BGP values obtained under laissez faire are the following:

$$L^{LF} = 1.1597921;\ c^{LF} \equiv C^{LF}/K^{LF} = 0.8617855;\ Z^{LF} = Z_0;\ g_z^{LF} = 0;$$

$$g_Y^{LF} = g_k^{LF} = g_c^{LF} = g_s^{LF} = 0.1558112;\ U^{LF} \to -\infty \text{ as } t \to \infty \left(\text{“climate apocalypse”}\right).$$

Given the same parameter values, the BGP values obtained when the economy follows its optimal path are the following:

$L^{OP} = 1$; $c^{OP} \equiv C^{OP}/K^{OP} = 0.8113331$; $z^{OP} \equiv Z^{OP}/K^{OP} = 6$; $S^{OP} = 33.3333$; $g_s^{OP} = 0$; $g_Y^{OP} = g_k^{OP} = g_c^{OP} = g_z^{OP} = 0.0126667$; $U^{OP} \to \infty$ as $t \to \infty$. Supposing that the government adopts the optimal policy rule, along the BGP total emission taxes as a fraction of GDP are $\tau^{OP}(Z^{OP})^{-1} = 0.7714286$ and $d^{OP} = 5.9266722$.

Comparing the laissez-faire BGP to the socially optimal BGP, one can check that $g_Y^{LF} > g_Y^{OP} > 0$, while $U^{LF} \rightarrow -\infty$ and $U^{OP} \rightarrow \infty$ as $t \rightarrow \infty$. Hence,

Proposition 10 *Whenever the household production function is given by (12b) and $\theta = \varphi = 1$, numerical examples show that—along a BGP—GDP growth is higher under laissez faire than when the government adopts the optimal policy rule, while people's well-being collapses under the former and grows forever along the socially optimal path.*

5 Conclusion

We presented a dynamic general equilibrium model where production emits pollutants whose accumulation negatively affects human well being. Within this framework, we explored both the hypothesis that there is no limit to the possibility for households to defend themselves against environmental degradation by increasing the use of manmade artifacts, and the hypothesis that there is a threshold beyond which the adverse effects of the accumulation of pollutants—such as greenhouse gases—cannot be offset by devoting increasing quantities of output to this scope, Under both hypotheses, we derived the balanced growth path (BGP) of the economy when there is no government intervention ("laissez faire") and when there is a benevolent social planner. Then, we studied how the socially optimal plan can be decentralized by using the policy instruments available to the government, whose policy choices are subject to its intertemporal budget constraint.

We showed that, if it is always possible to offset the harm that environmental degradation causes on people's well being by an increased use of manmade products, GDP growth can go on forever under laissez faire in spite of the growing environmental damage due to production. In this case, (i) laissez faire is consistent with unbounded growth, (ii) environmental degradation has never catastrophic effects on human well being, and (iii) human well being remains constant along the BGP. In contrast, under the same circumstances, a benevolent social planner would generally lead the economy towards a steady state where GDP growth—together with the accumulation of both capital and pollutants—ceases. The exception is whenever the households' preferences for consumption and environment quality are logarithmic: in this case, even along a socially optimal path one can have unbounded GDP growth. However, also in this case numerical examples show that in the long-run GDP growth is higher along a laissez-faire path than along a socially optimal path, while people enjoy more leisure and well-being along the latter. Finally, it is possible to decentralize the socially optimal plan by taxing the emission of pollutants and subsidizing private investment in productive assets on the part of the government, if the optimal policy rule is consistent with the sustainability of public debt. Otherwise, other suboptimal green policy rules should be considered.

Under the hypothesis that the accumulation of pollutants can reach a threshold beyond which efforts to compensate or offset the damage they cause to people's well being by using more manmade products are vain (which is consistent with our knowledge concerning the long-term effects of global warming), laissez faire is generally inconsistent with unbounded growth. Indeed, if the marginal utility of consuming manmade products is not any longer positive once that the stock of pollutants surpasses a certain threshold, there is no incentive for households to go on accumulating wealth in a scenario of progressive environmental degradation, and one cannot have unbounded growth under laissez faire. However, in the special case in which households' preferences for consumption and environmental quality are logarithmic, the marginal utility of consuming manmade products is not affected by the stock of pollutants, and laissez faire is consistent with unbounded growth even if there is a threshold beyond which the adverse effects of the accumulation of pollutants on people's well being cannot be offset by devoting increasing quantities of output to this scope. Hence, under these circumstances, laissez faire leads to a "climate catastrophe": the stock of pollutants is driven beyond its maximum compatible with life on earth, thus precipitating the collapse of individual's well being. Such a catastrophe is always avoided along a socially optimal path: unbounded GDP growth can be socially optimal only in the special case in which the marginal utility of consumption is not affected by environmental degradation and total emissions can be stabilized by letting the abatement efficiency grow at the same rate as productive capital and production (i.e., whenever the elasticity of emissions with respect to abatement capacity is one). Also when there is a threshold beyond which the damage caused by pollutants cannot be offset by manmade products, the social optimal path can be decentralized by a public agency that taxes emissions and subsidizes investment in productive assets. In the presence of this threshold, numerical examples show that—when both the laissez-faire path and the socially optimal path are not characterized by unbounded GDP growth—steady-state values of output, consumption and stock of emissions are higher under laissez faire than when the government adopts the optimal policy rule, while the reverse is true for people's steady-state leisure and well-being. These numerical examples show also that, when both the laissez-faire path and the socially optimal path are characterized by unbounded GDP growth, the latter is higher under laissez faire than when the government adopts the optimal policy rule, while people's well-being collapses under laissez faire and grows forever along the socially optimal path.

Additional steps in the direction to utilize the model presented here to evaluate the impact of the green policies undertaken in many economies include the analysis of the stability properties of the BGPs and numerical solutions for the transitional paths converging to these BGPs, to be conducted by calibrating the model's parameters in accordance with the evidence regarding these economies. Moreover, a natural extension of the model amounts to treat the evolution of the stock of pollutants as the result of the production activities of many independent countries, whose green policies are therefore interdependent. We believe that these developments can further improve the model's ability to assess the medium and long-term welfare effects of policies aimed at tackling climate change.

References

Acemoglu, D., Aghion, P., Bursztyn, L., & Hemous, D. (2012). The environment directed technical change. *American Economic Review, 102*, 131–166.

Barnett, J., & O'Neill, S. (2010). Maladaptation. *Global Environmental Change, 2*, 211–213.

Barro, R. J., & Sala-i-Martin, X. (1995). *Economic growth*. McGraw-Hill.

Bartolini, S., & Bonatti, L. (2002). Environmental and social degradation as the engine of economic growth. *Ecological Economics, 43*, 1–16.

Bartolini, S., & Bonatti, L. (2003). Endogenous growth and negative externalities. *Journal of Economics, 79*, 123–144.

Bartolini, S., & Bonatti, L. (2008). Endogenous growth, decline in social capital and expansion of market activities. *Journal of Economic Behavior & Organization, 67*, 917–926.

Bretschger, L., & Karydas, C. (2019). Economics of climate change: Introducing the Basic Climate Economic (BCE) model. *Environment and Development Economics, 24*, 560–582.

Dietz, S., & Stern, N. (2015). Endogenous growth, convexity of damage and climate risk: How Nordhaus' framework supports deep cuts in carbon emissions. *The Economic Journal, 125*, 574–620.

Frankel, M. (1962). The production function in allocation and growth: A synthesis. *American Economic Review, 52*, 995–1022.

Golosov, M., Hassler, J., Krusell, P., & Tsyvinski, A. (2014). Optimal taxes on fossil fuel in general equilibrium. *Econometrica, 82*, 41–88.

Hassler, J., & Krusell, P. (2018). *Environmental macroeconomics: The case of climate change* (Vol. 4). Elsevier B.V..

Leipert, C., & Pulselli, F. M. (2008). The origins of research on defensive expenditures: A dialog with Christian Leipert. *International Journal of Design & Nature and Ecodynamics, 3*, 150–161.

Matthews, H. D., Gillet, N. P., Stott, P. A., & Zickfeld, K. (2009). The proportionality of global warming to cumulative carbon emissions. *Nature, 459*, 829–833.

Nordhaus, W. D. (1994). *Managing the global commons: The economics of climate change*. MIT Press.

Schumacher, I. (2019). Climate policy must favour mitigation over adaptation. *Environmental and Resource Economics, 74*, 1519–1531.

Uzawa, H. (2003). *Economic theory and global warming*. Cambridge University Press.

Distributional Effects of Monetary Policy

Valentina Bonifacio, Luis Brandao-Marques, Nina Budina, Balazs Csonto, Chiara Fratto, Philipp Engler, Davide Furceri, Deniz Igan, Rui Mano, Machiko Narita, Murad Omoev, Gurnain Kaur Pasricha, and Hélène Poirson

1 Introduction

The debate on monetary policy and inequality is ongoing. Since the 1980s, income and wealth inequality have risen significantly in advanced economies. Accordingly, public interest in inequality has increased especially after the Global Financial Crisis (GFC). Some have argued that easy monetary policy is behind rising trends in inequality (e.g., Petrou, 2021) and that asset purchases and other unconventional monetary policies increased income or wealth inequality (Stiglitz, 2015). The onset of the COVID-19 crisis has brought further to the fore the contrast between the disparities in access to health and vulnerability to income and job loss, and the booming financial markets, again following extensive monetary easing. Against this backdrop, the period since the GFC has also been characterized by increasing public interest in what central banks do (Fig. 1).

What are then the channels through which monetary policy may have an impact on income or wealth inequality and is there evidence to support economically significant effects? To examine this issue, this paper first establishes some stylized facts about trends in the distributions of income and wealth, global interest rates, and monetary policy easing cycles. A key fact emerges: the increase in inequality and the decrease in interest rates have both been long-term phenomena, likely driven by structural factors (Dabla-Norris et al., 2015). Furthermore, this trend has coincided, since the GFC, with substantial monetary easing in many advanced economies.

V. Bonifacio · L. Brandao-Marques · N. Budina (✉) · B. Csonto · C. Fratto · P. Engler · D. Furceri · D. Igan · R. Mano · M. Narita · M. Omoev · G. K. Pasricha · H. Poirson
IMF, Washington, DC, USA
e-mail: VBonifacio@imf.org; LMarques@imf.org; NBudina@imf.org; BCsonto@imf.org; CFratto@imf.org; PEngler@imf.org; DFurceri@imf.org; DIgan@imf.org; RMano@imf.org; MNarita@imf.org; MOmoev@imf.org; GPasricha@imf.org; HPoirson@imf.org

L. Paganetto (ed.), *Economic Challenges for Europe After the Pandemic*, Springer Proceedings in Business and Economics,
https://doi.org/10.1007/978-3-031-10302-5_9

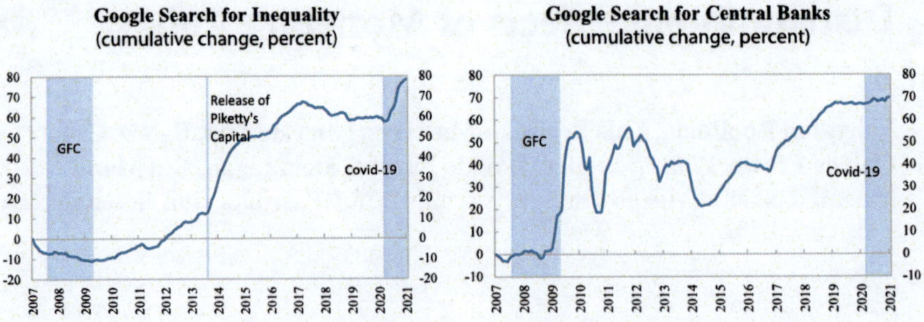

Fig. 1 Public Interest in Inequality and Central Banks. Sources: Google Trends and IMF staff calculations

Given the transient nature of its effects, can monetary policy be a significant driver of this rising trend in inequality? Or is the recent association between rising inequality and monetary easing likely spurious?

Through a critical survey of the literature, complemented with new micro-simulations and empirical and model-based analyses, the paper investigates whether monetary policy has worsened further the trend rise in inequality. Based on our reading of recent theoretical work on the role of agent heterogeneity in shaping macroeconomic dynamics (especially Kaplan et al., 2018), we set up a conceptual framework to explain how monetary policy can affect the distributions of income and wealth. Within the literature on macroeconomics and household heterogeneity, the studies that look specifically at monetary policy consider two types of channels: income channels and wealth channels. For the income channels, heterogeneity stems from households having diverse sources of income whereas for the wealth channels, it stems from either the dispersion of net worth across households or the heterogeneity of the composition of assets and liabilities in households' balance sheets. A key finding from the theoretical literature is that these two main channels have ambiguous implications for the net distributional effects of monetary policy.[1] This means that the determination of the effects of monetary policy on inequality remains an open empirical question.

When empirically analyzing the channels through which transitory monetary policy actions may affect the distribution of income and wealth, the paper focuses on within-country inequality mostly covering advanced economies, with available high-quality micro data. At the same time, the analysis and the discussion of the conceptual channels are relevant beyond advanced economies, particularly in the current context in which monetary policy was eased significantly in many emerg-

[1] For example, heterogeneity in the sources of household income could imply that, everything else equal, wealthier households (who rely relatively more on business income) benefit more from monetary policy easing than poorer households (more reliant on labor income). However, poorer households are also more likely to be able to participate in labor markets or avoid unemployment when monetary policy eases in response to reduced economic activity.

ing markets and the relevant literature surveyed here covers some nonadvanced economies. The pre-COVID-19 evidence on the effects of monetary policy on within-country inequality suggests that, once monetary policy shocks are properly identified, monetary accommodation reduces income inequality mostly by reducing unemployment (e.g., Coibion et al., 2017; Furceri et al., 2018). The evidence on the effects on wealth inequality, however, is less clear as it tends to rely on shorter time series.

Studies (pre-COVID-19) that put together several of the above channels (i.e., income and wealth channels) find mixed and often economically negligible net effects of transitory monetary policy easing actions on income inequality, with some variations across countries and between conventional and unconventional monetary policy. On the one hand, quantitative models featuring heterogeneity and a large fraction of hand-to-mouth consumers seem to find overall beneficial effects of monetary easing on inequality mostly because of general equilibrium effects (Ampudia et al., 2018; Kaplan et al., 2018). Similarly, studies using aggregate data seem to find an overall positive effect, or that monetary easing tends to reduce inequality (e.g., Auclert, 2019). In line with these studies, both the micro-simulations done for this paper and the simulation of a heterogeneous agent New Keynesian (HANK) model (Kaplan et al., 2018) confirm that pre-COVID, the net effects of monetary policy easing on inequality are small and temporary (i.e., they dissipate after about 8 quarters). On the other hand, recent work using Danish administrative household-level data finds that large asset price increases induced by monetary policy easing accrue much more to wealthier households and dwarf wage income gains to poorer households, thus raising inequality (Andersen et al., 2020).

Given the empirical and quantitative evidence that monetary policy has not been a meaningful driver of inequality, should central banks take distributional effects into account when formulating monetary policy? The answer is: yes and no. Yes, central banks should increase their communication to address the public's concerns about distributional issues and to clarify that countercyclical monetary policy can enhance welfare. Importantly, they should rely on counterfactuals to explain how monetary policy can improve outcomes. Central banks should also understand better and factor in differences among households within their existing policy frameworks, including by modelling and analysis of the distributions of income and wealth, as these affect monetary policy transmission. However, monetary policy should remain focused on macroeconomic stability as burdening monetary policy with other objectives risks reducing its effectiveness and may undermine central bank independence.

At the onset, several caveats apply. The paper does not cover the net welfare effects of monetary policy. In other words, it does not discuss the welfare impact of monetary policy easing relative to a counterfactual scenario, taking into account, in a unified framework, its aggregate effects on output, inflation, and unemployment as well as possible distributional effects. Also, the distributional effects of post-COVID extraordinary monetary policy measures are not covered here empirically. Notwithstanding the increased recourse to unconventional monetary policy measures, the limited time since the crisis outbreak and the current high degree of uncertainty would render any assessment of potential distributional effects premature. The effects of the secular decline in the natural rate of interest on inequality and the potential impact of inequality on the natural rate of interest are also not covered in this paper. Finally, the distributional effects of cross-border monetary policy spillovers are also not covered.

The rest of the paper is structured as follows: Section 2 highlights key stylized facts to motivate the discussion. Section 3 includes a discussion of the conceptual channels through which transitory monetary policy actions may affect the distribution of income and wealth, also illustrating their potential importance using data from the United States and Europe, with extensions to other OECD countries. Section 4 quantifies some of the channels and puts different channels together to assess the distributional impact of monetary policy. Section 5 concludes with policy implications.

2 Stylized Facts

Inequality moved center stage in the post-GFC era, and was further fueled by the COVID-19 shock. Inequality tends to increase during pandemics (Fig. 2),[2] and the severity of the COVID-19 crisis implied that close to 95 million more people have fallen into extreme poverty in 2020 (IMF, 2021). As such, it "has thrown into stark relief the high and rising economic inequality in the United States and elsewhere" (Qureshi, 2020). Corresponding evidence from the euro area also suggests the COVID-19 pandemic has worsened income inequality because its adverse consequences are particularly pronounced for young workers, women, and households with lower income (Schnabel, 2020; Dossche et al., 2020).

Major central banks have embarked on aggressive monetary easing in response to both the GFC and the COVID-19 crisis (Fig. 3). While easing mostly took the form of policy rate cuts at the peak of the GFC, the protracted nature of the crisis and, in some cases, the policy rate hitting the zero-lower bound, presented new challenges. As a result, many central banks had to resort to unconventional monetary policy. Another extensive round of monetary loosening was unleashed amidst the COVID-19 shock. The heavy reliance on monetary policy accommodation, including unconventional monetary policy, contributed to the sharp increase in public interest in central banks in the aftermath of the GFC and the steady increase since 2014 (see Fig. 1).

Decades of widening income and wealth disparities coincided at least in part with the prolonged monetary easing in the post-GFC era, particularly the unconventional measures. Within-country income inequality has been trending up in advanced

[2] The authors look at the evolution of inequality in the aftermath of SARS (2003), H1N1 (2009), MERS (2012), Ebola (2014), and Zika (2016).

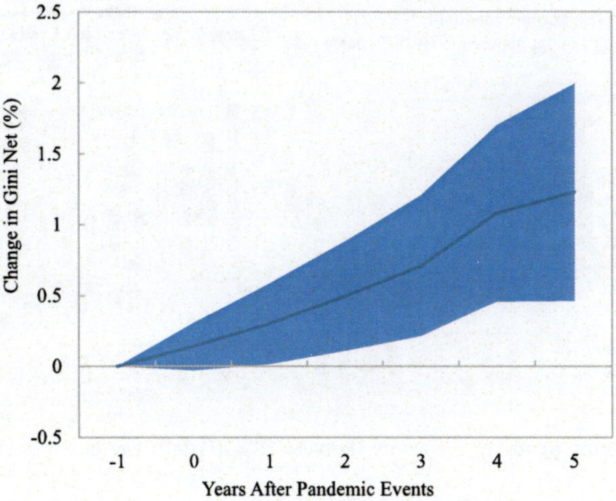

Fig. 2 Inequality in the aftermath of COVID-19. Source: Furceri et al. (2020)

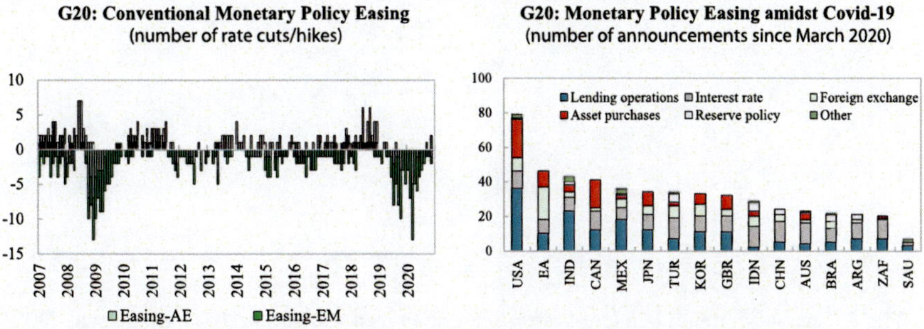

Fig. 3 Monetary policy: unconventional and conventional easing. Sources: Bloomberg for conventional easing and Cantú et al. (2021) for monetary policy easing measures

economies (AEs) over the last few decades. While the picture is mixed within the emerging markets (EMs), they started off from higher inequality levels. Wealth inequality has been on the rise as well. For example, in the G20 countries, the share of wealth of the top 1 percent has increased over the past two decades (Fig. 4).

Global real interest rates have also been on a declining trend over the past 30 years, though the decline in the real neutral rate accelerated after the GFC (F). The secular decline in interest rates implies that, irrespective of the business cycle, central banks have had to accommodate the lower level of interest rates. In other words, the decline in interest rates has also reflected a declining neutral rate.

Both long-term developments have been driven by several structural factors, such as trade and financial integration, automation, and demographics (Fig. 5).

For example, for a sample of almost 100 AEs and emerging market and developing economies (EMDEs) over the period of 1980–2012, Dabla-Norris et al. (2015)

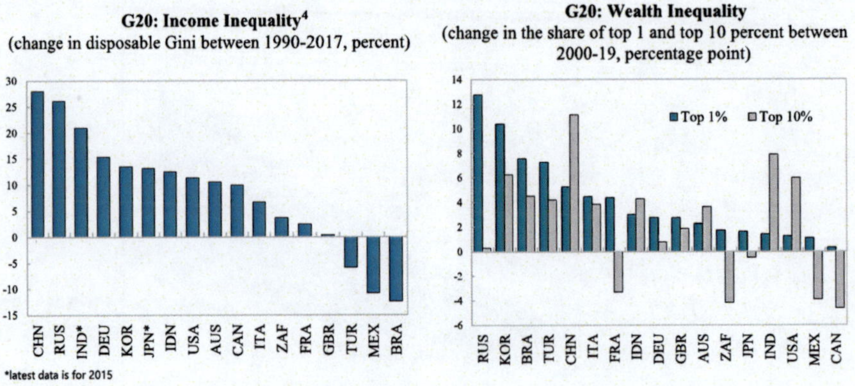

Fig. 4 Long-term trends in inequality. Sources: SWIID 9.0, Credit Suisse (2019), IMF staff calculations

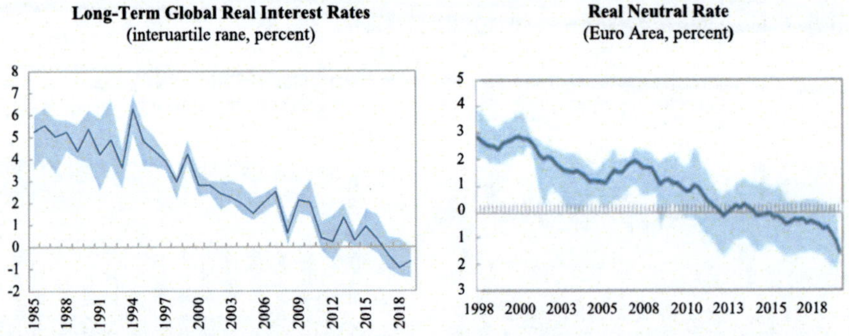

Fig. 5 Long-term trends in interest rates. Sources: Furceri and Tawk (2021), Brand et al. (2018)

found greater financial openness and technological progress and the easing of labor market regulations to be associated with rising within-country income inequality, while trade openness was found to have a negative relationship with inequality. At the same time, the authors show differential impacts of financial deepening across country groups. The decline in real interest rates has also been attributed to several factors, including globalization (Natal & Stoffels, 2019), potential growth (Pescatori & Turunen, 2015) and demographics (Han, 2019). These factors themselves are evolving in the current environment as COVID-19 not only lays bare some of the structural factors that drive inequality but might also put added pressure on interest rates if there are persistent changes to consumption and savings preferences (Jordà et al., 2020).

The secular rise in inequality and the (more) recent prolonged monetary accommodation have triggered a public debate about whether monetary easing exacerbated inequality. The debate has been made more intense by the public backlash against central banks, including the Occupy Wall Street protests. Most recently, the disconnect between buoyant financial markets (a boon for the rich) and a struggling real economy (bad news for everybody but particularly for poorer households) has reinvigorated the debate about the distributional effects of aggressive monetary easing policies in response to COVID-19 (Igan et al., 2020), with the potential to create political tensions, posing in turn risks to central bank independence. In response, central bankers have increased communications on distributional effects of monetary easing, pointing out that monetary policy easing led to more positive outcomes relative to the counterfactual.[3,4]

3 Channels for Distributional Effects of Monetary Policy

This section introduces a stylized yet comprehensive presentation of the channels through which monetary policy affects the distribution of income, wealth, and consumption, and highlights their potential importance using data from the United States and Europe, with extensions to other OECD countries.

3.1 A Stylized Framework

The literature has highlighted several channels for distributional effects, leaning on the newer theoretical models that integrate sticky prices, incomplete markets, and heterogeneity among households (and firms). Representative agent models make the implicit assumption that heterogeneity has little impact on aggregate macro dynamics. Further, many consider monetary policy to be "neutral" (or close to neutral) especially in the long run (Bernanke, 2015). In the discussion that follows, we focus on monetary policy shocks—that is, unexpected changes in the monetary policy stance. The aggregate transmission channels are standard: monetary policy alters interest rates, asset prices, and exchange rates.

The building blocks of all distributional channels of monetary policy are the various dimensions of household heterogeneity: income and wealth, age, skill level, sector of employment, marginal propensity to consume, access to finance, etc. These dimensions often overlap. For instance, skill level is correlated with income while wealth evolves through an individual's life cycle (and, hence, their age). Similarly, those in the lower end of the income distribution tend to have a higher marginal propensity to consume while those with more assets to use as collateral have easier

---

[3] "Bernanke chides Occupy Wall Street 'misconceptions'," CNN Money, November 3, 2011, https://money.cnn.com/2011/11/02/news/economy/bernanke_occupy_wall_street/index.htm, "Draghi Says ECB Policy Has Helped Reduce Inequality," Wall Street Journal, June 26, 2017, https://www.wsj.com/articles/draghi-says-ecb-policy-has-helped-reduce-inequality-1498499845

[4] Moreover, policymakers have often stressed that the increase in inequality and the decrease in interest rates are both long-term phenomena.

access to finance. One could thus think of income and wealth as the main channels reflecting and capturing various dimensions of heterogeneity.

As a result of these heterogeneities in the level and composition of income and wealth, different households can be affected differently by a given monetary policy action. In other words, they have different *exposures* to monetary policy shocks. Further, the same policy action can have potentially offsetting effects for the same household via different channels.

The distributional implications of these channels can vary across countries and through time. They may depend on country characteristics, such as reliance on capital markets versus banks; the initial composition of household balance sheets; labor bargaining powers and broader labor market flexibility; openness and the industrial structure of the economy. The time dimension over which the effects play out will also be shaped by these heterogeneities, in conjunction with rigidities like slow responses of prices and wages. The state of the business cycle may have a bearing on the various dimensions of heterogeneity and the strength of the related channels.

We next discuss the mechanisms through which different dimensions of heterogeneity generate distributional effects.

3.1.1 Income Channels

Households differ in terms of their primary source and level of income. Monetary policy can have distributional effects if these different sources of income and levels of earnings react differently to monetary policy shocks.

Income Composition Channel Richer households receive a larger share of their income from business and financial (capital) income, which is typically more responsive to monetary policy than labor income (Gornemann et al., 2016). As a result, under the *income composition channel*, monetary policy easing may benefit richer households more and increase income (and possibly consumption) inequality.

Earnings Distribution Channel Households also differ in terms of where their earnings fall in the overall distribution. Wages and employment prospects of low-income households are typically more sensitive to monetary policy and business cycles (Heathcote et al., 2010). For instance, less-skilled, lower-income workers are more likely to lose their job during a recession. Under the *earnings distribution channel*, monetary policy easing may reduce income and consumption inequality by stimulating economic activity and lessening the impact of an economic downturn.

3.1.2 Wealth Channels

Households differ not only by their wealth level (including whether their net wealth is positive or not) but also by what they own and what they owe (their wealth portfolio composition). By changing the value of the underlying assets and liabilities as well as inflation expectations, monetary policy may redistribute wealth among households.

Balance Sheet Composition Channel Household balance sheets can differ substantially both on the asset and the liability side. On the asset side, a fall in the interest rate affects different assets (real estate, bonds, stocks) differently, depending on their type and duration. On the liability side, how unexpected reductions in interest rates and their associated impact on exchange rates affect debt service and balance of loans also depends on these liabilities' type (including currency denomination) and maturity. The net effect of asset and liability side effects on wealth then is ambiguous. Under the *balance sheet composition channel*, monetary policy easing may decrease or increase wealth and consumption inequality.

Savings Redistribution Channel Households differ in terms of their level of wealth. Some households are borrowers with negative net wealth, others are savers with positive net wealth. Unexpected decreases in real interest rates favor borrowers and hurt savers. Further, borrowers typically are less patient and have a greater marginal propensity to consume. Under *the savings redistribution channel*, monetary policy easing may reduce wealth and consumption inequality.

A couple more specific channels are mentioned in the literature. One is the inflation channel whereby the relevant dimension of household heterogeneity is cash holdings and nominally fixed debt (Erosa & Ventura, 2002; Doepke & Schneider, 2006). The other is the interest rate exposure channel whereby the measure of a household's balance sheet exposure to interest rates is the difference between all maturing assets and liabilities at a given point in time (Auclert, 2019). In our simplified framework, these additional channels would be classified as wealth channels as they relate to differences across households in their assets and liabilities and their net wealth positions.

Figure 6 summarizes these dimensions of heterogeneity and illustrates how they generate different responses to monetary policy changes both *on impact* and through *general equilibrium feedback*. Note that the latter effects occur via consumption and investment, employment and labor income, as well as movements in the current and financial accounts. Such general equilibrium effects are likely to be observed over a longer time horizon and may offset over the business cycle. Their ultimate direction and size again depend on heterogeneities across households, and firms. As noted earlier, many of these heterogeneities are correlated with and are reflected in heterogeneity across income and wealth dimensions, as can be illustrated with some specific examples.

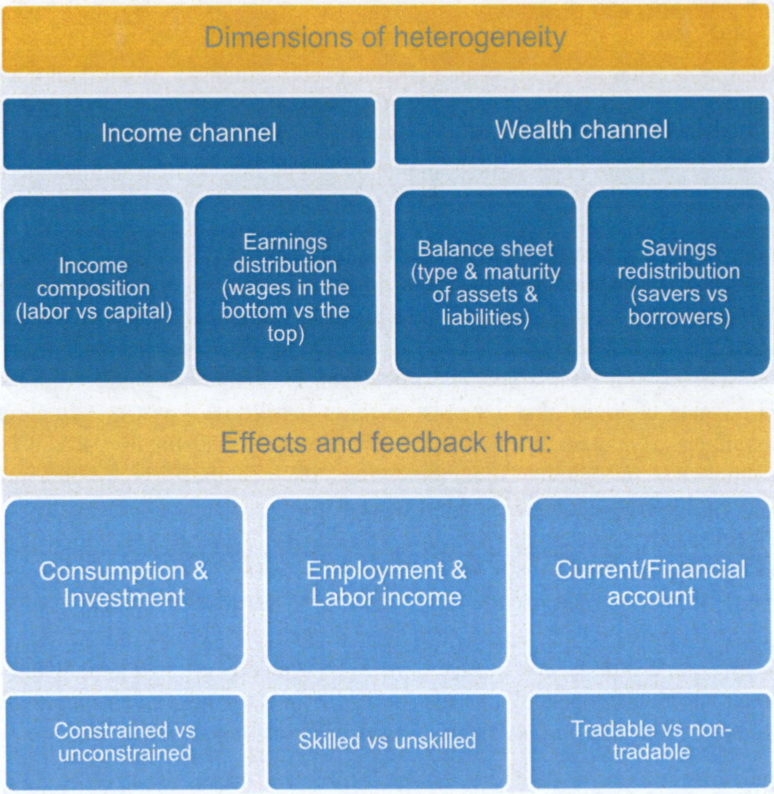

Fig. 6 Monetary Policy: channels for distributional effects

- Financial constraints of households and firms matter for their consumption and investment decisions. This then shapes their response to monetary policy changes.
- The incomes of skilled and unskilled workers face different sensitivities to monetary policy both on the extensive margin—captured by employment—and on the intensive margin—captured by wages.
- Tradable and non-tradable sectors respond differently to current account developments, with implications for their profits and the wages of households they employ.

In the rest of the paper, we first highlight the potential on-impact responses using measures of households' exposure to monetary policy. Then, we use a model to shed light on the general equilibrium feedback and the ultimate effects on inequality.

3.2 Exposures to Monetary Policy Shocks

Following the conceptual discussion about various distribution channels of monetary policy easing actions, this section illustrates the potential on-impact responses via household exposures to monetary policy shocks. Specifically, we illustrate the potential importance of the main income and wealth channels by documenting household exposures based on data from the United States and Europe, with extensions to other OECD countries.

As highlighted in the previous section, a monetary policy easing action can have distributional effects via the *income composition channel.* To gauge the intensity of this channel, we illustrate household exposures by the variations in the relative importance of labor and transfer income, and capital income across quintiles of disposable income distribution, using OECD's survey-based income distribution database (IDD) for OECD countries over 2014–2017.

On average for OECD countries, the share of labor income and transfers varies significantly across quintiles (Fig. 7). These variations reflect differences in the relative importance of capital income, and the concentration and composition of wealth. For instance, in the United States, capital income is especially concentrated at the very top, particularly at the top 1 and top 10 percent of the income distribution (Bivens & Mishel, 2013; Saez, 2019). In the euro area, rich households are also more likely to derive a higher share of income from capital, as they hold more financial assets (stocks, bonds), while households at the bottom benefit from relatively more generous transfer systems.[5] Other differences, including different cyclical positions, demographics, quality of labor market institutions, and the ability of fiscal policy to redistribute resources also contribute to these differences across countries.

A monetary policy easing action can also have distributional effects via the *earnings distribution channel*. In OECD countries, workers at the low end and middle of the earnings distribution face higher unemployment risk than those at the top. Over 2000–2019, unemployment among young workers, that earn less on average, has been much more volatile, compared to unemployment among old-age workers, that earn comparatively more, indicating that the young face much higher unemployment risk as their employment is more sensitive to economic cycles. Worse yet, countries whose youth unemployment is particularly volatile also have high average youth unemployment rates.[6] Through this channel, monetary policy easing mitigates the effects of recessions on unemployment, disproportionately benefiting younger, less experienced, and lower-paid workers, and thereby reducing

[5] See Lenza and Slacalek (2018), for 17 euro area countries, using HFCS (2016) and Amberg and others, 2021 for Sweden.

[6] For instance, in Italy, the youth unemployment rate among young workers was about 40 percent in 2014, above the national average and the unemployment rate among older workers (7 percent). As the economy recovered, the youth unemployment rate fell by 5 percentage points by 2016, while unemployment rate among older workers remained broadly unchanged over the same period (Marino & Nunziata, 2017).

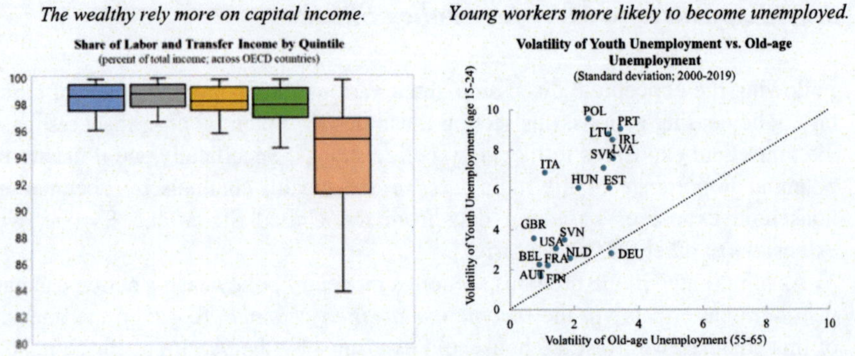

Fig. 7 Household exposures due to income composition and unemployment risk. Sources: OECD income distribution data, OECD unemployment by age groups; and IMF staff calculations. Notes: (1) Labor income also includes self-employed income, while capital and property income include income from financial assets (net of expenses), income from non-financial assets (net of expenses), and royalties. (2) The young, who typically earn less, face a higher risk of unemployment, because youth unemployment is more sensitive to economic cycles. Data labels use International Organization for Standardization (ISO) country codes

labor earnings disparities. In the absence of monetary policy easing, which boosts activity and reduces firms operating costs and thereby supports their employment, the low-income and low-skilled, particularly the young, would have been more likely to lose their jobs. This is the most powerful channel via which monetary policy easing actions can reduce inequality (e.g., Carney, 2016 for the United Kingdom, Draghi, 2016 for the euro area, and Amberg et al., 2021 for Sweden). However, monetary policy easing can also induce a skill-premium channel, which tends to offset in part the inequality reducing effect of earnings distribution channel, as high-skilled labor benefits relatively more due to capital-skill complementarity in production (Dolado et al., 2021, based on a New Keynesian Dynamic Stochastic General Equilibrium (DSGE) model).

A monetary policy easing action has distributional effects via the *balance sheet channel,* which we illustrate by assessing household exposures *due to composition of wealth* using the 2016 Survey of Consumer Finances (SCF) for the United States (US) and the 2016 Household Finance and Consumption Survey (HFCS) for the European Union (EU). Both surveys have a wealth of information on household balance sheets, which is used to illustrate variations in the composition of assets and liabilities across different wealth levels (Appendix 1). In the US and the EU, capital income tends to matter most for the wealthiest households because they hold more financial assets (Fig. 8). This is especially the case in the US, where almost two-thirds of the wealthiest 10 percent's assets are in bonds (16 percent) and stocks (46 percent). Except for this group, real estate accounts for the largest share of assets for most households in both the US and the EU. This means that monetary easing may have more equitable effects via house prices than through capital income, and households with mortgages also benefit from lower debt payments.

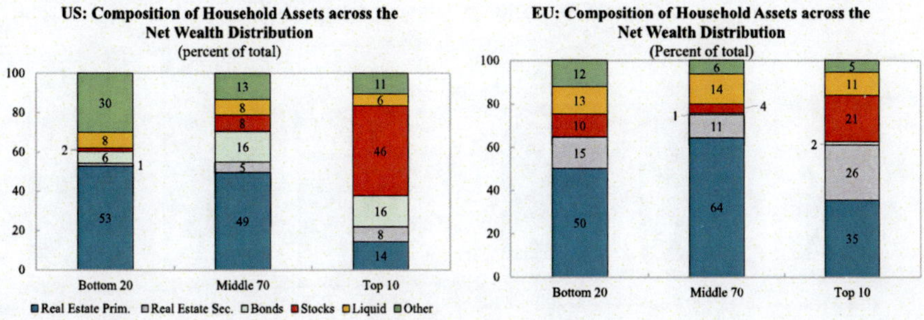

Fig. 8 Household exposures due to composition of assets. Sources: Survey of Consumer Finances (2016) for the United States; Household Finance and Consumption Survey (2016) for the European Union; and IMF staff calculations. Notes: The EU group comprises Austria, Belgium, Cyprus, Estonia, Finland, France, Germany, Greece, Hungary, Ireland, Italy, Latvia, Lithuania, Malta, Netherlands, Poland, Portugal, Slovak Republic, Slovenia, and Spain. See Appendix 1 for variable definitions

Differences in size and composition of household liabilities across the wealth distribution are important as well. Households' balance sheets are dominated by borrowing against real estate, which primarily takes the form of long-term nominal debt mortgages (Fig. 9). So, for example, by lowering debt service on mortgage debt, monetary policy easing directly affects household disposable incomes through this effect. The quality of the liabilities is also likely to vary across the distribution. For example, mortgage liabilities for the bottom 20 percent in the US are likely to be of subprime quality. Terms on these loans may be more sensitive to a tightening of financial conditions, e.g., because they are more likely to be adjustable-rate loans or lenders cut down on the marginal borrowers first as they become more risk averse. Since those in the bottom have higher marginal propensity to consume, a monetary policy easing shock that leads to lower debt service payments on lower-quality ARMs would actually lead to an increase in other types of loans such as car loans (Di Maggio et al., 2017).

How monetary easing affects income distribution will depend on the relative importance of these different channels, which in turn may vary based on different country characteristics. In countries with higher levels of financial inclusion, for instance, poor households have easier access to credit, and are more likely to be able to take out mortgages to buy houses—thereby benefiting from lower interest rates. In other countries, households tend to buy homes in cash and would not benefit from lower rates. In countries with bank-based financial systems, rich households who hold their savings in bank deposits and are not in debt could lose out from monetary easing through the savings redistribution channel (Sect. 4). In countries with more extensive social protection, the reduction of unemployment risk for lower-income workers from monetary easing may be more muted than in countries with less extensive social protection.

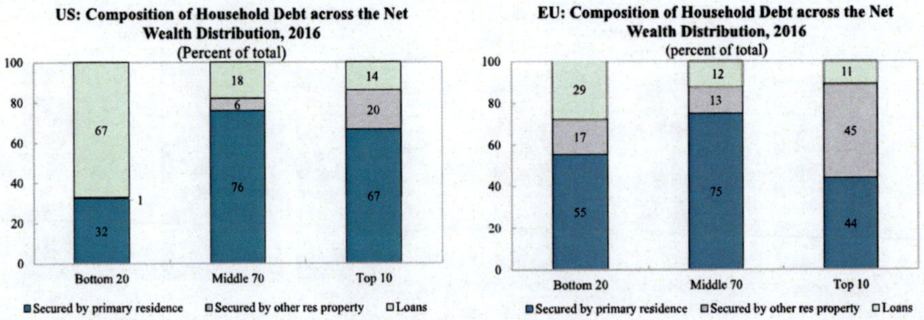

Fig. 9 Household exposures due to composition of liabilities. Sources: SCF (2016) for the US, HFCS (2016) for the EU, and IMF staff calculations. Notes: The EU group comprises Austria, Belgium, Cyprus, Estonia, Finland, France, Germany, Greece, Hungary, Ireland, Italy, Lithuania, Latvia, Malta, Netherlands, Poland, Portugal, the Slovak Republic, Slovenia, and Spain

4 Distributional Impact of Monetary Policy Shocks

The previous section has discussed exposures one at a time. However, the same household is typically exposed to several channels which may have offsetting effects. This section quantifies some of the channels and puts different channels together to assess the distributional impacts of monetary policy.

4.1 *Savings-Redistribution Channel: Microsimulations*

This section uses microsimulations to illustrate distributional effects of monetary policy shocks via the *savings redistribution channel*. Using a welfare metric capturing household exposures to changes in real interest rates, "unhedged interest rate exposures" (UREs), we simulate the impact of a monetary policy easing shock, equivalent to an interest rate fall of 100 bps to illustrate the hypothetical gains/losses across broad economic classes and age cohorts. Following Auclert (2019) and Tzamourani (2021), the URE metric is benchmarked using micro data for households from the United States and the European Union (Appendix 2). The findings are in line with the literature, but the precise magnitude is sensitive to the assumptions.[7]

Results confirm heterogeneities across broad social classes and age cohorts in the US, EU, and in selected euro area countries. The UREs vary across age cohorts

[7] While different maturity assumptions can lead to different results, our results are in line with those found in Auclert (2019) and Tzamourani (2021). By analyzing changes in net interest income, Dossche et al. (2019) find that due to the reduction in the interest rate an average euro area net borrower has gained close to EUR 2000 per year in lower interest payments during 2007–2017, whereas an average net saver has lost close to EUR 700 per year.

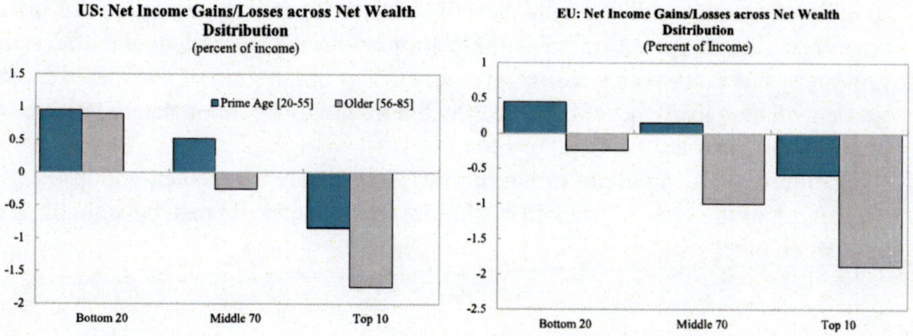

Fig. 10 Microsimulations: income effects from net interest rate exposures (an illustrative scenario: 100 bps fall in interest rate). Sources: SCF (2016) for the US, HFCS (2016) for the EU, and IMF staff calculations. Notes: The EU group comprises Austria, Belgium, Cyprus, Estonia, Finland, France, Germany, Greece, Hungary, Ireland, Italy, Lithuania, Latvia, Malta, Netherlands, Poland, Portugal, the Slovak Republic, Slovenia, and Spain

(prime age households (20–55 years old) and older households (56–85) and wealth levels (defined as bottom 20 percent, middle 70 percent, and top 10 percent of the net wealth distribution). These trends are broadly similar across the income distribution and more refined age groups.

Overall, poor and middle-class households with large debts and little financial assets tend to have larger negative UREs, therefore likely to benefit relatively more from a fall in interest rate. UREs tend to increase with income and age, with older, particularly rich households having the largest positive UREs, as documented by Auclert (2019). However, within the EU, cross-country variations are substantial with UREs positive across all income groups, on average for Germany and Austria, and negative for a substantial part of income and net wealth distribution in Cyprus, Ireland, Netherlands, Portugal, and Spain (Tzamourani, 2021, based on 2010 HFCS data).

Illustrative results for the income effects from a monetary policy easing shock, proxied by a fall in the real interest rate by 100 bps, reveal that gains/losses for the US and the EU vary by wealth levels and age cohorts, reflecting individual's life cycle (Fig. 10).

Our findings suggest that the poor, as well as the younger middle-class households with large debts (negative URE), benefit from a negative interest rate shock. However, these income gains could vary significantly within the EU, as they may not materialize in countries where net interest rate exposures are positive across all income groups (e.g., Austria and Germany), while in some countries these gains may be substantial across the wealth distribution, given that the UREs are negative for a substantial part of income and net wealth distribution in Cyprus, Ireland, Netherlands, Portugal, and Spain (Tzamourani, 2021, based on 2010 HFCS data).

The results also show that the wealthy and middle-income older households with little debt and large fixed income investments, e.g., bank savings, with positive UREs are disadvantaged by the negative interest shock. However, it is important to stress that the wealthy would benefit from the resulting rise in equity prices when real interest rates decline as these simulations do not include the effect of a prolonged monetary policy easing on equity prices in the form of unrealized capital gains, which typically benefit the wealthy but might not be immediately reflected in households' income.

Therefore, it is important to put the different channels together, and assess the net effects, as the same household might lose through one channel, but gain through another channel.

4.2 *Asset Price Channel: Microsimulations*

This section illustrates the impact of an asset price shock induced by expansionary monetary policy across the wealth distribution in the US and the EU. To this end, we simulate the impact of a 10 percent increase in asset prices (stocks, real estate, and bonds) on the distribution of capital gains relative to net wealth for the same three groups of households as in the previous section: bottom 20 percent, middle 70 percent, and top 10 percent. The methodology follows Adam and Tzamourani (2016), who study the distributional consequences of housing, bond, and equity price increases for EA households using data from the 2016 HFCS (Appendix 3).

Illustrative results show that a monetary policy easing action that leads to a 10 percent increase in asset prices has several partially offsetting effects on wealth distribution. Specifically: (i) higher equity prices favor wealthier households in both regions, (ii) increases in real estate prices favor mostly the bottom part of the distribution in the US and the middle part of the wealth distribution in the EU, while (iii) bond price increases leave the net wealth distribution largely unchanged. Capital gains on equities are the largest at the top of the distribution, though in the US the wealthy derive more than double the gains in the EU (7.4 and 3 percent, respectively; Fig. 11). In the US, the net wealth gains from housing price increases are skewed toward the poorer households with the bottom twenty percent gaining 13.6 percent, compared to a 5.8 percent gain in the EU. Overall, the wealthy in the US derive larger gains from equity holdings (7.4 percent), while the wealthy in the EU derive relatively larger gains from real estate assets (5.4 percent), which may reflect the relatively higher importance of capital markets in the US and/or preferences of the EU households for real estate.

Our results for the EU are broadly in line with the findings of Adam and Tzamourani (2016). In particular, equity prices benefit the top end of the net distribution, while housing prices show a hump shaped distribution of gains, with the middle class benefitting the most. That said, it is important to keep in mind that the magnitude of the results depends on the level of wealth (i.e., even tiny changes could look large in percentage terms for households with very low levels of net wealth). In this respect, the result for the US that the bottom 20 percent benefit

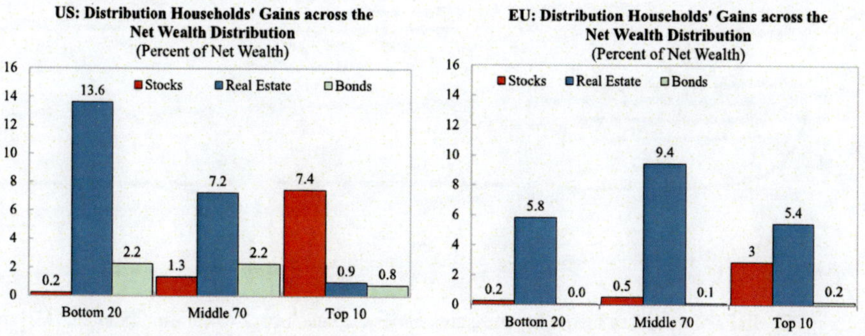

Fig. 11 Microsimulations: capital gains from asset shock (an illustrative scenario: 10 percent increase in asset prices). Sources: SCF (2016) for the US, HFCS (2016) for the EU, and IMF staff Calculations. Notes: The EU group comprises Austria, Belgium, Cyprus, Estonia, Finland, France, Germany, Greece, Hungary, Ireland, Italy, Lithuania, Latvia, Malta, Netherlands, Poland, Portugal, the Slovak Republic, Slovenia, and Spain

the most from monetary policy induced house price increases should be taken with caution.[8]

These findings suggest that the distributional impact of monetary policy varies across asset classes, with gains in different asset prices having different implications for the net wealth dispersion. The capital gains in equity co-vary with the households' net wealth position, while housing price increases significantly reduce net wealth inequality. The results also imply that different asset returns would affect household consumption differently, and, hence, have important distributional effects on welfare with often opposite signs.

4.3 A DSGE Model for the United States

This section uses Kaplan et al. (2018) model—KMV henceforth—to assess the distributional effects of conventional monetary policy shocks. In this model, portfolio effects are very strong and tend to dominate the responses of income and wealth inequality, while the responses of wages and fiscal policy affect primarily the distribution of consumption. These conclusions stem in part from the assumption of rigid prices but flexible wages. A detailed discussion of the model is in Appendix 4.

---

[8] This simple simulation focuses on within cohort heterogeneity. However, it is also important to note that, even though higher house prices benefit households at the bottom of the distribution, rising house prices may have negative effects on young and middle-aged households that plan to purchase or increase their housing stock to accommodate a growing family. These intergenerational aspects, not explicitly discussed here, matter for wealth inequality (Bielecki et al., 2022).

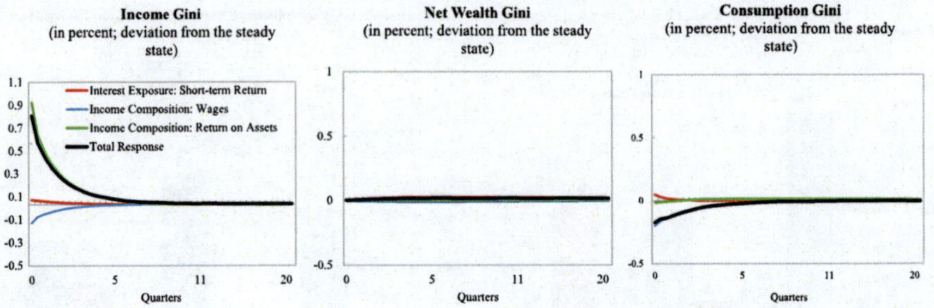

Fig. 12 IRFs of three key inequality measures under the benchmark calibration. Source: IMF staff calculations

When referring to a monetary policy loosening, we use an exogenous shock to the inflation-targeting Taylor rule of 100 bps in annualized terms. The distributional effects of such a shock are evaluated through impulse response functions (IRFs) of Gini indices of income, net wealth, and consumption. The benchmark calibration used here assumes that the fiscal space generated by a monetary policy easing shock is used to pay down debt,[9] which is not KMV's baseline specification.

As shown in Fig. 12, a monetary policy loosening under our benchmark calibration of KMV leads to:

- Higher *income* inequality as the rich benefit from higher total returns to assets (green line) and thus the portfolio effect outweighs any positive impacts on labor income.
- Roughly unchanged *wealth* inequality despite rising income inequality. This is due to wealth at the bottom being very responsive to increases in income, while wealth at the top is not. The average household holds assets worth 3 times their income. At the top of the wealth distribution, the assets-to-income ratio is larger than 12, while at the bottom it is essentially zero.
- Lower *consumption* inequality. Rising wages support the consumption of the poorest (blue line), while consumption of the rich barely moves because their permanent income is roughly unchanged.

The role of fiscal policy is assessed by comparing results from the benchmark specification above with a version of the model where the increased fiscal space generated by monetary loosening is used to adjust transfers.[10,11] KMV find that combining transfers and monetary loosening helps improve the aggregate transmission of monetary policy shocks.

Figure 13 shows that distributional outcomes are also better, particularly when measured in terms of consumption inequality, which is the most relevant measure

[9] See KMV, Table 8, column 4.

[10] This is the baseline specification in KMV.

[11] See Section IV.D for a detailed discussion.

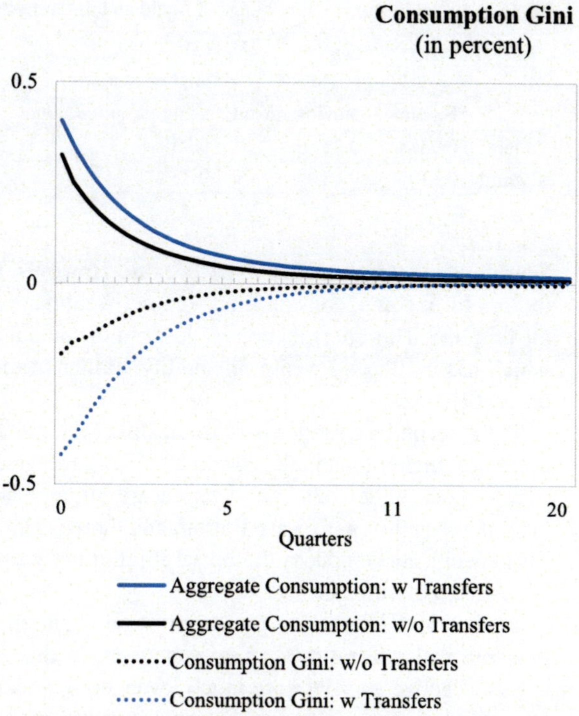

Fig. 13 IRFs when combining monetary policy loosening with fiscal transfers. Source: IMF staff calculations

of inequality from a welfare perspective. Higher transfers lead to increased demand, which raises wages. Both effects disproportionately support the poorest households and thus reduce inequality. It is hard to disentangle the wage and transfer channels separately as the two reinforce each other: higher wages themselves create fiscal space through higher tax revenues, which can then be further distributed through transfers.

We also explore the role of different initial wealth parametrizations. KMV calibrate wealth and income distributions to those of the US. To study the role of the initial wealth distribution in driving results, we adjust some underlying parameters that govern the steady-state distributions of liquid and illiquid asset holdings. Table 1 shows the degree of inequality of asset holdings in the baseline (column 1) and across three different alternative parametrizations (columns 2–4). The corresponding Gini indices for France and Germany, calculated using HFCS (2016), are presented for comparison (columns 5 and 6, respectively).

In the first alternative parametrization (column 2), we assume higher borrowing costs by increasing the wedge between lending rates and policy rates (8 percent compared to 4 percent in the baseline).[12] Under this specification, the distribution of liquid assets is understandably most affected, reducing sharply the fraction of

[12] See KMV Online Appendix, Table E.1, column 4.

Table 1 Initial inequality in holdings of liquid and illiquid assets (Gini index, in percent)

	(1)	(2)	(3)	(4)	(5)	(6)
	Baseline	Higher lending spread	Higher cost of using illiquid account	Higher neutral rate	France	Germany
Liquid	0.98	0.83	0.93	0.72	0.77	0.71
Illiquid	0.81	0.82	0.73	0.83	0.70	0.82

households that have negative net wealth. However, the IRFs of the different Gini indices for income, consumption, and net wealth are all very similar to the ones in the baseline. This specification is closer to the actual data for Germany (column 6), which has an illiquid wealth inequality similar to the US but lower liquid wealth inequality.

In the second alternative parametrization (column 3), the cost of using the illiquid account is higher than in the baseline.[13] The aggregate effects of the same monetary policy shock under this specification are slightly larger, while consumption and income inequality's IRFs are similar, and there is slightly less net wealth inequality. This specification reduces the initial illiquid net wealth inequality to closer to that of France (column 5).

In the third alternative parametrization (column 4), we raise the equilibrium long-run real interest rate, r*, to 4 percent. In this specification, monetary policy is less effective as MPCs are much lower because liquid wealth is higher, and few households borrow. The distributional impacts are similar regarding consumption and income inequality, but this specification produces larger net wealth inequality driven by the direct interest rate channel. This calibration is very close to the data for Germany (column 6).

Short of a full recalibration, we cannot take the above results as representative for either Germany or France, even if the Gini indices of net wealth in those countries may be similar to those under the alternative parametrizations we analyzed. Other measures of inequality beyond the wealth Gini would be critical to calibrate, like the share of households with negative net worth, the share of households with little or no liquid wealth or the distribution of labor earnings.

4.4 Labor Earnings Channel: Empirical Assessment

Labor market outcomes are key drivers of changes in income inequality (Bivens & Mishel, 2013). Displaced workers experience a 30 percent immediate loss in annual earnings compared to non-displaced workers, and 20 percent even after 15–20 years (Von Wachter et al., 2009). Hence, policy actions affecting labor market dynamics are bound to have large and long-lasting effects on inequality.

[13] See KMV Online Appendix, Table E.2, column 5.

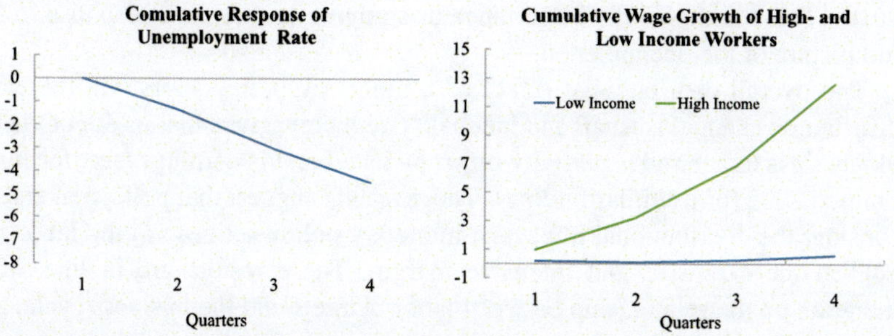

Fig. 14 Earnings distribution channel at the extensive and intensive margins (impact of monetary policy loosening of 100 bps in the US). Sources: Albrizio et al. (2021) and IMF staff calculations. Notes: High- and low-income workers defined as one-standard deviation below and one-standard deviation above average earnings, respectively

This section studies the distributional effects of monetary policy easing shocks via the labor market channel, disentangling the intensive from the extensive margin. Specifically, we decompose the overall effect into heterogeneous effects on employment status (drawing on Albrizio et al., 2021) and wages.[14] Such an assessment has important implications for policy as it can shed light on whether changes in labor market disparities reflect broadening the pool of workers by including those that are less productive, or changes in wage disparities within the same pool of workers (see Appendix 5 for the empirical framework and estimations).

Unemployment Effects Monetary policy easing mitigates the effects of recessions on unemployment, disproportionately benefiting younger, less experienced, and lower-paid workers. Figure 14 (left-hand side) presents the cumulative impulse response for unemployment rate after a monetary loosening of 100 bps. After four quarters, there is a 4 percentage-point drop in unemployment. These results are in line with recent reduced-form evidence from Germany (Broer et al., 2020) and the U.S. (Alves et al., 2019), estimating that individual with lower earnings are particularly sensitive to aggregate fluctuations or monetary policy shocks.

Wage Effects Using individual-level data from the Current Population Survey (CPS), we find that, for those who stay employed, wages at the top rise disproportionately more than those at the bottom of the distribution following monetary loosening, offsetting in part the unemployment effect (Fig. 14, right-hand side). Moreover, earnings at the top of the distribution are mainly affected by changes in hourly wages, while earnings at the bottom of the distribution are mainly affected by changes in hours worked and employment status (in line with Heathcote et al.,

[14] The effect on wages is analyzed separately for hourly wages and hours worked. We do not find evidence of an effect on hours worked. Hence, the latter results are not shown for sake of brevity.

2010). This highlights the importance of studying jointly their response to have a full picture of the phenomenon.

The overall distributional effect of a monetary policy shock via the earnings distribution channel is small and inequality-reducing, given that its effect via unemployment is larger and is partially offset by its effect via earnings (see, for instance, Shimer, 2005 for a similar finding). These results suggest that policymakers should consider the distributional impact of monetary policy actions via the labor market both at the extensive and intensive margin. These results are in line with the literature on the relationship between labor markets and the business cycle, and on the identification of the categories of workers that suffer the most during recessions (Hoynes et al., 2012; Hoynes, 2000; Devereux, 2001).

The results for earnings conditional on being employed allow us to abstract from issues connected to changes in the pool of workers, while the results for unemployment reflect a compositional effect. For instance, suppose that expansionary monetary policy makes it possible to hire less productive workers. If less productive workers are paid their marginal product, then the newcomers will be paid less than the incumbents. This is not monetary policy increasing inequality among existing workers, but rather the pool of workers now having more variation in terms of productivity and therefore becoming unequal in terms of pay.

Disentangling the composition effect from the effect conditional on remaining employed is also important to draw policy implications. In particular, increased earnings inequality may not be an undesirable outcome if this is the result of a more diversified labor force. If overall earnings inequality were to increase only as a result of the fact that the newcomers are less productive, the increase in inequality would be a good thing: the direct consequence of a larger, more inclusive, labor market.

4.5 Results from Other Studies in the Literature

Existing research investigating the distributional effect of monetary policy has relied on the three main approaches used so far in this paper: (i) micro-simulations; (ii) modeling; and (iii) empirical analyses.[15]

Before we summarize the literature results for each one of these approaches in detail, it is worth noting the challenges common to all. First, the measurement of inequality itself remains a difficult task hindered by the availability, quality, and timeliness of comprehensive, granular household surveys. Second, studies differ widely in how they measure monetary policy and most employ simple proxies rather than exogenous, well-identified shocks.

[15] See Colciago et al. (2019) for a more comprehensive stocktaking on the theoretical and empirical literature on monetary policy and inequality.

Micro-simulations These simulations combine the response of key macroeconomic variables to monetary policy shocks with household exposure to these macroeconomic variables. For instance, they identify winners and losers across net wealth distributions by assessing the sensitivity of capital gains on various assets (real estate, equities, and bonds) to a 10 percent increase in the prices of these assets, as a monetary policy easing shock would typically push up the prices of risky assets (see the exercises we present in Section 3B). Given data availability constraints, this type of studies tends to focus on a single or a few countries (typically, United States and the euro area). Looking at income inequality in 8 OECD countries between 2007 and 2012, O'Farrell et al. (2016) report that expansionary monetary policy reduced inequality in Canada, the Netherlands, and the United States but increased it in most European countries through the income composition and earnings distribution channels. But these effects are negligible in magnitude. By contrast, focusing on the earnings distribution channel in 4 European countries between 1999 and 2016, Lenza and Slacalek (2018, 2021) find a *negative* effect of expansionary policy on income inequality. For wealth inequality, they report negligible effects. Similarly, Adam and Tzamourani (2016) find a negligible impact of asset purchases on wealth inequality in the euro area. Others point to differences across countries and asset classes. Adam and Zhu (2016) find that an expansionary policy reduces wealth inequality in most of the euro area but increases it in Austria, Germany, and Malta. O'Farrell et al. (2016) report that increases in equity and bond prices in response to an accommodative monetary stance increase wealth inequality while house price increases reduce it, but, again, these effects are estimated to be small.

Macroeconomic Modeling Analyses These involve a large set of macroeconomic and financial variables calibrated to data from a particular country. They then employ scenario analyses to compare outcomes under different assumptions on monetary policy actions. Doepke and Schneider (2006) use data from the United States, Meh et al. (2010) from Canada, and Casiraghi et al. (2018) from Italy. Overall, they tend to report that: (i) income inequality increases in the short run but declines in the medium run, with insignificant effects in the long run, (ii) wealth inequality increases but this is short-lived, (iii) consumption inequality decreases both in the short and the medium run. When assessing the distributional implications of different strategies, Feiveson et al. (2020) find that the improvements in macroeconomic outcomes from adopting an inflation make-up strategy are potentially more significant in models that take distributional considerations more seriously. By reducing the severity of ELB recessions, alternative strategies have potential longer-run beneficial effects on economic inequality.

Empirical Analyses These estimate directly the reduced-form effects of exogenous monetary policy shocks on household income and consumption inequality (studies of wealth inequality are rare given even more binding data availability constraints). Commonly used techniques are multivariate time-series (vector autoregressions or local projections) and panel-data analysis. Expansionary monetary policy is reported to reduce inequality in the euro area (Guerello, 2018; Samarina

& Nguyen, 2019), Italy (Casiraghi et al., 2018), the United Kingdom (Mumtaz & Theophilopoulou, 2020, 2017), the United States (Coibion et al., 2017; Albrizio et al., 2021), and in a panel of advanced and emerging market economies (Furceri et al., 2018). This is consistent with the findings of earlier studies documenting the inequality-reducing impact of inflation (e.g., Albanesi, 2007). A few studies find adverse effects of monetary policy easing on inequality in Denmark (Andersen et al., 2020), the United Kingdom (Cloyne et al., 2016), and Japan (Saiki & Frost, 2014)[16] but caution that the analysis focuses on a single channel (e.g., the impact on mortgagors), that the time series they use are short, or that specific country characteristics could explain the findings. The ambiguity of the overall impact on inequality in these studies is in line with a U-shaped effect where monetary easing lifts both the low-end (through the earnings distribution channel) and the high-end of the income distribution (through the balance sheet composition channel).[17] The magnitude of the reported effects is similar for conventional and unconventional monetary policy (e.g., Albrizio et al., 2021)[18] and is generally small (except for those reported by Andersen et al., 2020).

The evidence in this paper is broadly in line with the results in the literature. While the literature is still evolving, and a consensus has not yet fully emerged, the key takeaways can be summarized as follows (Fig. 15):

(i) The magnitude of the net distributional effect is small compared to the trend evolution in inequality within countries.
(ii) Monetary policy easing may even reduce, not increase, inequality of income and consumption in the medium term.
(iii) In the short term, wealth and perhaps income inequality may rise in response to monetary policy easing.

Three additional points are noteworthy.

First, some empirical studies show that a reduction in the policy rate increases income inequality. The problem with at least some of those studies is that changes in policy rates capture both exogenous monetary policy actions and systematic response to economic conditions; so, what they are capturing is the response of inequality to both policy shocks and changes in economic conditions. As shown by Furceri et al. (2018), while expansionary exogenous shocks reduce inequality, the

---

[16] By contrast, Inui et al. (2017) find that monetary policy shocks do not significantly affect income and consumption inequality when using Japan's data during the 2000s.

[17] Amberg et al. (2021); also see Di Casola and Stockhammar (2021).

[18] Albrizio et al. (2021) investigate the distributional effects of U.S. monetary policy for the pre- and post GFC periods. In the latter period, monetary policy actions were mostly expansionary, took place in a period of weak economic activity, and were mostly unconventional measures. The results suggest that monetary policy expansion tends to increase employment and output and has small effects on income and consumption inequality and could even reduce inequality over the medium term. The effects are not statistically different between conventional and unconventional monetary policy, but tend to be larger for tightening than easing, confirming earlier results on asymmetric effects (Tenreyro & Thwaites, 2016).

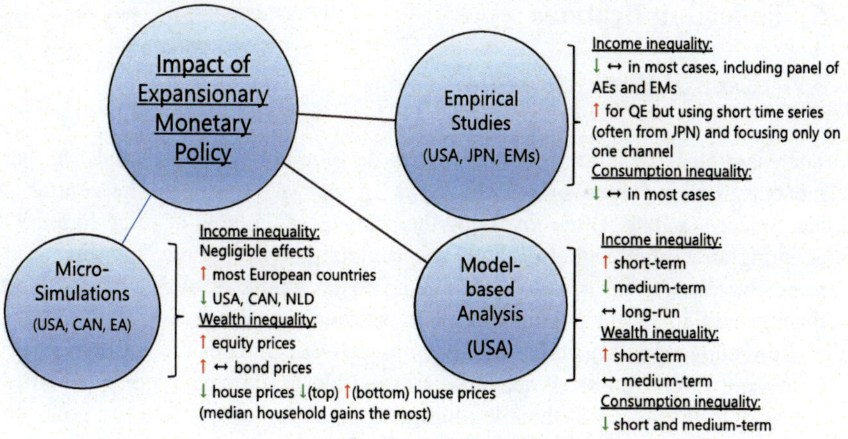

Fig. 15 Summary of findings in the literature on the distributional effects of Monetary Policy

systematic response of policy rates to worsening economic conditions is associated with increased income inequality. That said, some more recent, carefully executed analyses paying attention to endogeneity still find large adverse effects of monetary policy accommodation on inequality (e.g., Andersen et al., 2020). Thus, additional research is clearly needed.

Second, microsimulations offer only a partial equilibrium exercise primarily capturing on-impact distributional responses by combining reduced-form estimates of the effects of monetary policy shocks on key macroeconomic and financial variables with the sensitivity of the income and wealth distribution to these effects. Notably, rather than identifying a direct link between monetary policy and inequality, they offer insights on the potential distributional channels. And their validity, as that of empirical studies, relies on the ability to identify exogenous monetary policy actions in addition to the plausibility of the simplifying assumptions they make about the balance sheet composition of households and the response function of households to changes in interest rates and asset prices.

Last but not least, specific country cases may vary. Such differences may reflect structural issues such as labor market flexibility and constraints on mobility or the structure of credit markets (in particular, mortgages)—one of many country characteristics that could affect the distributional effects of monetary policy, as mentioned earlier in the conceptual framework discussion.

5 Policy Implications

5.1 Central Bank Mandate

There are clear benefits to central banks developing a coherent and transparent monetary policy framework (IMF, 2015). In such a framework, the central bank has a clear mandate. Often involving the primacy of the goal of price stability and adopting an explicit inflation target to promote macroeconomic stability. Adding more objectives to the central bank's mandate has a number of drawbacks, most of them general in nature and not specific to distributional concerns.

Burdening monetary policy with other objectives is not desirable as it may reduce its overall effectiveness. It may not be credible as monetary policy alone may not be able to effectively handle multiple goals, especially when the goals come into conflict. Under those circumstances, having a clear primary mandate for price stability will help anchor inflation expectations and facilitate the management of tradeoffs. Multiple goals may even be counterproductive, decreasing welfare, if other policies that are more likely to be effective at addressing distributional effects become less likely to be implemented as the result of central banks taking on the burden of achieving distributional objectives. Finally, multiple objectives raise a potential risk to central bank independence and can complicate communications of monetary policy (Box 1).

This is not to say that policymakers should ignore distributional considerations altogether in the conduct of monetary policy. Within the existing policy frameworks, central banks should factor in heterogeneity among economic agents, including by modeling the distributions of income and wealth in their analysis and disseminating the results, as these affect monetary policy transmission. For example, the transmission of monetary policy depends on the heterogeneity of household balance sheets, notably through the collateral effects of real estate wealth.[19] Income heterogeneity also affects monetary policy transmission because it gives rise to different marginal propensities to consume across agents (Auclert, 2019). In addition, accounting for heterogeneity increases the impact of forward guidance on aggregate consumption and inflation, particularly in a liquidity trap (Ferrante & Paustian, 2019).

Even for a central bank with a price stability mandate, distributional considerations could also guide the choice of monetary policy targets. For example, the redistributive effects of unanticipated inflation are different between inflation targeting and price-level targeting (Meh et al., 2010). In addition, for central banks with a dual mandate, when heterogeneity is taken into account, most households would prefer a larger weight on unemployment stabilization at the expense of price stability because it would increase the provision of consumption insurance (Gornemann et al., 2016).

[19] See, for example, Aladangady (2014), Kaplan et al. (2014, 2018), Cloyne et al. (2019), Gelos et al. (2019), and Dossche et al. (2021).

Still, monetary policy cannot be the only tool used for macroeconomic stabilization, provided there is room to use other tools. Countercyclical fiscal policy, in particular, has an important complementary role to play as it improves the tradeoffs faced by central banks, especially when interest rates are close to the effective lower bound (McKay & Reis, 2021).[20] Furthermore, the two policies can complement each other in other ways: monetary loosening creates fiscal space which, if used to provide targeted transfers, could improve both macro and distributional outcomes, as illustrated with model simulations in Fig. 13. This is particularly relevant in countries with weak social safety nets and/or limited fiscal space, where monetary policy can be a powerful complement to fiscal policy—a situation that has been borne out during the COVID crisis.

Box 1 Can Central Banks Handle Multiple Policy Objectives?

Monetary policy may not be able to effectively handle multiple goals as a single monetary policy instrument cannot achieve multiple independent policy goals (Tinbergen, 1962). While this concern can be addressed by increasing the number of instruments, adding additional goals to the central bank's mandate may reduce welfare in the context of multiple policymakers and multiple frictions. This is because making the central bank the residual claimant of all macroeconomic problems may make other policymakers, some of whom may be better placed to deal with distributional issues (e.g., fiscal policymakers), less likely to act or encourage them to engage in behavior that is not welfare enhancing (Davig & Gürkaynak, 2015).[21]

Multiple objectives may threaten central bank independence. An independent central bank has long been seen as an advantageous way of solving time inconsistency in monetary policy (Kydland & Prescott, 1977; Barro & Gordon, 1983; Rogoff, 1985). In theory, a central banker insulated from political pressure and who places a large (but finite) weight an inflation target should be able to overcome the inflationary bias that afflicts governments more concerned with short-term goals. In practice, there is substantive empirical evidence that credibly links central bank independence (with accountability) to lower inflation (Klomp & de Haan, 2010). Multiple objectives sap central bank independence because they make the central bank more susceptible to pressure from political or special interest groups.

(continued)

[20] More generally, even if monetary policy is unconstrained and can handle macroeconomic stabilization on its own, fiscal policy tools such as automatic stabilizers are useful as providers of social insurance.

[21] Even if it were impossible to add more instruments to the central bank's toolkit, it is fairly straightforward that assigning a loss function to the central bank that mimics the social loss function (i.e., one that could include a distributional term) would yield monetary policy that is optimal conditional on the toolkit and the state variables. However, the key point made by Davig and Gürkaynak is that "optimal monetary policy" may not be "optimal policy."

Having multiple objectives also complicates communication and makes the central bank less transparent and less accountable. A single quantitative objective for an indicator such as medium-term inflation—one that the central bank can to a large extent influence—for example, will be easy to monitor and can be used to benchmark the central bank's performance. Having one goal also simplifies central bank communication and makes it less likely that central bank announcements will foster confusion, hinder decision-making in the private sector, and lead to inferior outcomes (Eusepi & Preston, 2010; Reis, 2013).

Still, such objectives can often be complementary and even central banks that explicitly target inflation still care about economic growth, financial stability, and financial inclusion and development. Meeting complementary goals for real economic goals, for example, can be justified if there is a short-run tradeoff between inflation and unemployment that the central bank can exploit or in the absence of Blanchard and Gali's (2007) "divine coincidence" (Reis, 2013). However, a multiplicity of objectives is more likely to generate difficult tradeoffs when the objectives come into conflict.

Therefore, additional monetary policy targets must meet certain pre-conditions to be included in the central bank mandate (Reis, 2013). First, it needs to be measurable in an unambiguous way. Second, monetary policy must be useful in attaining it. Third, it must give rise to a tradeoff with the other goals in a way that achieving one (e.g., price stability) does not guarantee achieving the other (less inequality) and requires a change in policy.

While it is quite possible that tradeoffs exist between price stability and distributional objectives, it is difficult to argue that inequality can be unambiguously measured as it has many dimensions (e.g., consumption, income, and wealth inequality). Furthermore, as argued before in this paper, if any, monetary policy has weak effects on inequality.

Importantly, any distributional impact can be addressed with policies specifically designed for this purpose. Many of these policies can also address group-specific concerns arising from the cyclical impact of monetary policy. Well-targeted redistributive fiscal policies across households as well as across regions can reduce inequality of disposable incomes can best address group-specific concerns. Other government policies, including training and education reforms and labor market policies that can address skill gaps, can help reduce inequality (IMF, 2014, 2019).[22]

Central banks and financial regulators have other tools besides monetary policy which could have more targeted effects on inequality. For example, policies directed at fostering financial development and financial inclusion can have important

[22] The policies need to be designed carefully because some policies can rather have adverse distributional effects (Fabrizio et al., 2017). For example, making labor market flexible tends to increase inequality (e.g., Kahn, 2012; Ostry et al., 2021).

beneficial distributional consequences (Carstens, 2021). Reducing the costs of participating in capital markets can decrease wealth inequality (Favilukis, 2013). Increased access to payments, savings, and insurance also tends to be associated with reductions in inequality, but access to credit can either increase or reduce inequality, depending on the quality of regulation and supervision, and the relative importance of different channels (Cihak et al., 2020).

5.2 Central Bank Communication

Clear communication from central banks is needed to help fill the gaps in perception and to allow monetary policy to remain focused on macroeconomic stabilization. Regardless of the overall effects of monetary policy on distribution, persistently low interest rates can create the perception of increased inequality as counterfactuals are unobservable, while high asset prices, or low returns on savings are highly visible. As Bank of England's Haldane said (Haldane, 2018): "When it comes to evidence on the distributional impact of monetary policy, there are wide gaps in understanding and even wider gaps in perception." There are three things, in particular, that central banks can do.

First, central banks need to clearly state their objectives and mandate. They should also explain how their conduct of monetary policy helps achieve those objectives. Clarifying to the public what the central bank can and cannot do helps with accountability. A clear understanding of the objectives of monetary policy by the public fosters trust in the institution, and ultimately serves to reduce political pressure for central banks to take on additional objectives that could reduce the efficacy of monetary policy.

Second, central bankers can emphasize that monetary policy is a blunt tool to address group-specific concerns. This is not a new issue for central banks. For example, spikes in food and energy prices—when core inflation is low—can have disproportionate effects on certain groups. In addition, unemployment can be temporarily high for certain groups or regions due to sector-specific shocks.

Finally, central banks need to recognize and discuss public concerns of any distributional effects of monetary policy (see also Honohan, 2019). Given their access to data and research expertise, central banks are in a good position to measure and clarify the distributional effects of their policies on income and wealth. Some central banks have done this in recent years. For example, mentions of distributional effects or inequality were largely non-existent in ECB speeches prior to 2006, but in recent years these issues are increasingly discussed by ECB officials (Fig. 16; specific examples include Constâncio, 2017; Lane, 2019; Schnabel, 2020). The ECB has also tried to gauge how inequality shapes the transmission channel of monetary policy to consumption.[23]

---

[23] Slacalek et al. (2020) add the various income and balance sheet channels together and find that the effects on labor income benefit all households—particularly "hand-to-mouth households"—and quantitatively outweigh the effects on financial income.

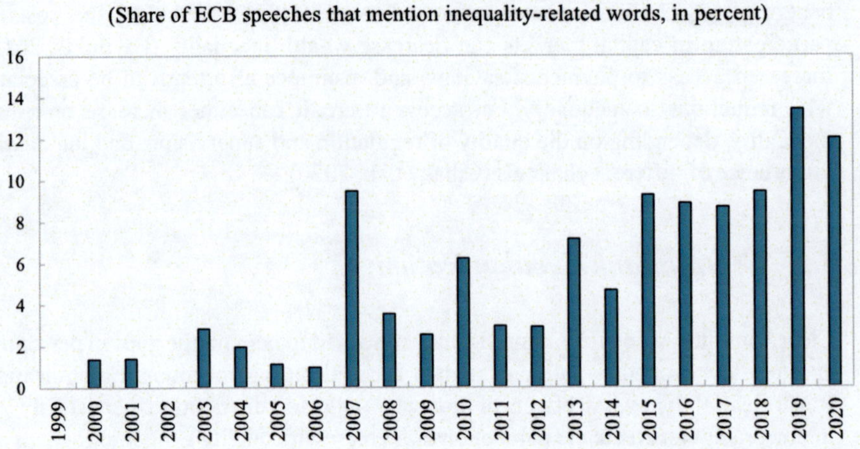

Fig. 16 ECB communication about distributional effects. Source: IMF staff calculations based on data from European Central Bank Speeches Dataset (23 April 2020) retrieved from: https://www.ecb.europa.eu/press/key/html/downloads.en.html. Notes: ECB speeches with any mention of (case-insensitive) "inequality" or "income distribution" or "distributional effects" or "income dispersion" or "distribution of income". The counts do not include 26 speeches which were presentations, and for which no text in English was available

One way to address the public concerns about distributional effects of monetary policy is to highlight counterfactuals. Central banks can mention inequality would likely have been worse without monetary policy accommodation. Importantly, they can argue that monetary policy actions are welfare increasing, notwithstanding possible distributional effects.[24] For example, former ECB President Mario Draghi said in 2016 (Draghi, 2016): "In short, monetary policy is today protecting the interests of savers by ensuring a faster closing of the output gap and preserving the economic potential on which savers' income depends." Another way to address public concerns about distributional effects of monetary policy is to emphasize that structural factors are behind the secular increase in inequality and long-run decline in interest rates.

Chile and Sweden provide two illustrative examples of how central banks have dealt with distributional concerns by employing different communications strategies (Box 2). In both countries, the central bank follows an inflation targeting framework. Still, Chile and Sweden have very different income distributions. Given Chile's historically high inequality, public debate on inequality has not focused on monetary policy but on structural reforms. In Sweden, historically low levels of inequality and

[24] Evidence from the United States suggests that, without quantitative easing in response to the GFC, unemployment would had been persistently higher through the end of 2018, hurting households at the lower end of the distribution the most (Eberly et al., 2019). Similarly, unconventional monetary policy evidently increased GDP through 2014–w18 in the euro area and potentially lowered the unemployment rate (Rostagno et al., 2019).

preference for equality, combined with rising prices of homes and other assets in a period of persistently negative policy rates after the global financial crisis, led to a robust policy debate on the impact of monetary policy on the distribution of income and wealth. Both central banks have emphasized the importance of monetary policy focusing on macroeconomic stabilization and highlighted counterfactuals, in their communication about distributional issues.

6 Conclusions

Monetary policy has not been a driver of the rise in inequality that many advanced economies have experienced in recent decades. Income and wealth inequality have steadily risen in the United States and Europe, for example, since the 1980s while monetary policy has gone through various tightening and easing cycles. Some structural factors driving the rise in inequality have also pushed the neutral real interest rate (r*) to very low levels, to which central banks had to respond by lowering policy rates. With the COVID-19 shock, monetary policy space has narrowed further, including in EMDEs. The low r* made it increasingly difficult for monetary policy to play its countercyclical role using conventional tools but the use of unconventional monetary policy tools after the GFC has been controversial in many circles. In part, the debate has centered on the association between easy monetary policy since 2007 and the observed increased in wealth inequality. This debate has gained new strength with the COVID-19 crisis and its disproportionate impact on health and economic security of the most disadvantaged segments of the population.

The existing literature reviewed in this paper is still evolving but mostly find small net effects of monetary policy on inequality. Monetary policy easing mostly reduces income inequality through the labor income channel. The beneficial distributional effects come from a reduction of unemployment and increased participation in the labor force by the unskilled and younger workers. The effects on the wealth distribution are less clear and depend on the composition of assets and liabilities of households' balance sheets. The size of the distributional effects of monetary easing depends on the relative importance of different channels and should vary based on country characteristics. The simulations presented in this paper are broadly in line with these findings, although more work is needed to calibrate the results to different countries and jurisdictions.

Although central banks have adapted their communication strategies to include distributional issues, our current state of knowledge indicates that these considerations should not change their mandates. Monetary policy should remain focused on macroeconomic stabilization and price stability remains an appropriate primary goal. An additional mandate for the central bank to reduce inequality could also have important adverse implications for central bank accountability and independence and reduce the effectiveness of monetary policy to achieve its primary target of price stability. We argue in this paper that other policies (e.g., fiscal policy) are better suited to address distributional issues and group-specific concerns.

At the same time, central banks should better understand and factor in differences among households within their existing policy frameworks, including through modeling and analysis of the distribution of income and wealth, which affects monetary policy transmission. The key role for central banks in the inequality debate—including during COVID-19—is to ensure clear communication through various outlets, including speeches by central bank officials, official reports, and community outreach events, addressing the public's concerns about the distributional effects of monetary policy actions.

Several aspects of the relationship between monetary policy and inequality require further study. The effects of unconventional monetary policy, including asset purchases by central banks, are less clearly understood than those of conventional tools and are not fully addressed in this paper. Furthermore, the unprecedented response of central banks around the world to the COVID-19 crisis may have different distributional effects than those previously observed or may work through different channels. The distributional consequences of monetary policy, if any, are also largely unknown for EMDEs where social safety nets are less robust and the exchange rate channel of monetary policy is more important. Finally, the ongoing review of the monetary policy frameworks of major central banks could have important implications for our understanding of how central banks should deal with inequality issues. Investigating some of these issues should be a fertile ground for further research.

Box 2 Central Bank Communication on Distributional Issues: The Cases of Chile and Sweden

Chile

Chile has historically had a high level of income inequality, in line with other countries in Latin America (Fig. 17), and similar levels of wealth inequality to that of some advanced economies (e.g., the United States or Germany). Chile has also seen a monetary policy easing cycle lasting several years: the monetary policy rate was at a historically low level of 0.5 percent in December 2020.

In October 2019, a raise in subway fares triggered a series of protests and violent demonstrations against high inequality, increased cost of living, and inadequate pensions and access to health and education. Central bank policies were not a target of the protestors, possibly because of the success of the Central Bank of Chile's (BCdC) inflation targeting framework in stabilizing inflation. Trust in the central bank to stabilize inflation remained high, as deviations of long-term inflation expectations from target were lowest among emerging economies and even some advanced economies. Following the start of the social unrest, the central bank provided liquidity and foreign exchange to the financial system and monetary stimulus to the extent allowed by its mandate of inflation targeting.

(continued)

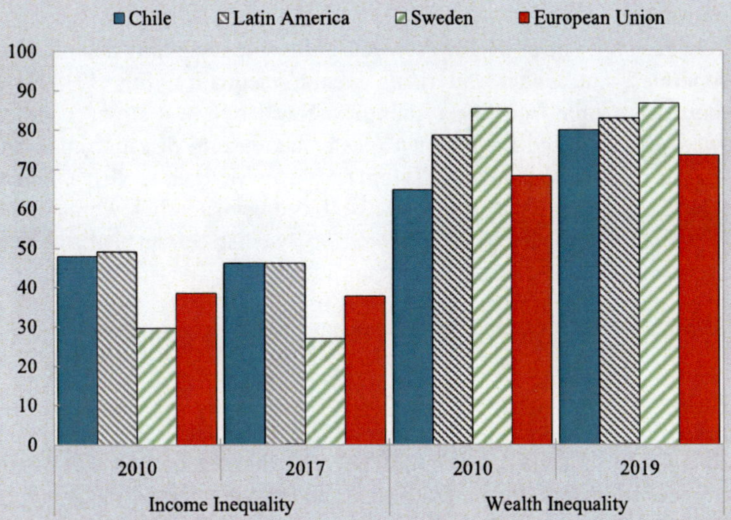

Fig. 17 Wealth and income inequality in Chile and Sweden (Gini coefficients). Sources: Credit Suisse, ECLAC - Economic Commission for Latin America and the Caribbean; WID, Word Inequality Database, and IMF staff calculations

The BCdC's communication has long been focused tightly on its core mandate of price stability. Within this mandate, the BCdC has communicated on the adverse impact of high inflation and unemployment on inequality, and therefore, on the importance of having monetary policy focus on macroeconomic stabilization. During his address to the Senate on December 5, 2019 following the release of the Monetary Policy Report, Governor Mario Marcel noted that high inflation and unemployment hurt the poor and increase inequality. The Governor provided a counterfactual of high inflation (6 percent) and unemployment (10 percent) and said that in this scenario, inequality would rise to levels not seen in 27 years, mostly through rising unemployment.

In its communications, the BCdC has also underscored that the conduct of monetary policy should consider heterogeneities in the labor market. In the December 2018 monetary policy report, the central bank published a special report on the labor market, which used disaggregated data to present some stylized facts on the Chilean labor market and analysis of the economic adjustment in response to macroeconomic shocks via the intensive margin (for example, via changes in composition between salaried and self-employed, changes in participation rates, wage flexibility in hired work, etc.).

(continued)

Sweden

Sweden has one of the lowest levels of income inequality among advanced economies, but higher and rising wealth inequality (Fig. 17). However, relative to people from other countries, Swedes have a stronger preference toward equality, and have shown greater increase in dissatisfaction withthe existing level of inequality (Bublitz, 2016; Medgyesi, 2013). Since the global financial crisis, Sweden has also faced persistently low inflation (even negative inflation) which has prompted the Swedish central bank, the Sveriges Riksbank, to keep interest rates extraordinarily low. The Riksbank cut its main policy rate to negative territory in February 2015 (where it remained until December 2019) and introduced an asset purchase program.

Rising prices of homes and other assets in a period of persistently negative policy rates, as well as a preference for greater equality, combined to lead to a robust policy debate on the impact of monetary policy on the distribution of income and wealth. The terms of reference, set in 2016, for the review of monetary policy framework and the Sveriges Riksbank Act by the Riksdag Committee on Finance included an assessment of whether monetary policy should take distributional considerations into account. The committee concluded that the distributional consequences of monetary policy since the global financial crisis have been small, and if anything, have ameliorated income differences through lower unemployment. It also concluded that the distributional effects of its own proposals were small.

Prior to the global financial crisis, the Riksbank made some references in public to the distributional effects of monetary policy (Fig. 18). However, the pre-2006 references highlighted the negative impact of high inflation on distribution of income and wealth. For example, in the Sveriges Riksbank Act of 1999, the price stability mandate of the central bank is also grounded on the beneficial effects of low inflation in terms of reducing arbitrary redistributions of income between savers and borrowers. Between the global financial crisis and 2016, the Swedish central bank did not communicate about the distributional effects of monetary policy (Fig. 18).

Starting in 2016, the Riksbank has included the distributional effects of monetary policy in its communications. This has been mostly through public statements from central bank officials, but not exclusively. For example, at the urging of the Riksdag Committee on Finance, since 2017 the central bank has also included a section on the distributional effects of monetary policy in its annual Accounts of Monetary Policy, which are submitted to the Committee. The November 2020 Monetary Policy Report also included an article on the distributional effects of the Riksbank's measures.

(continued)

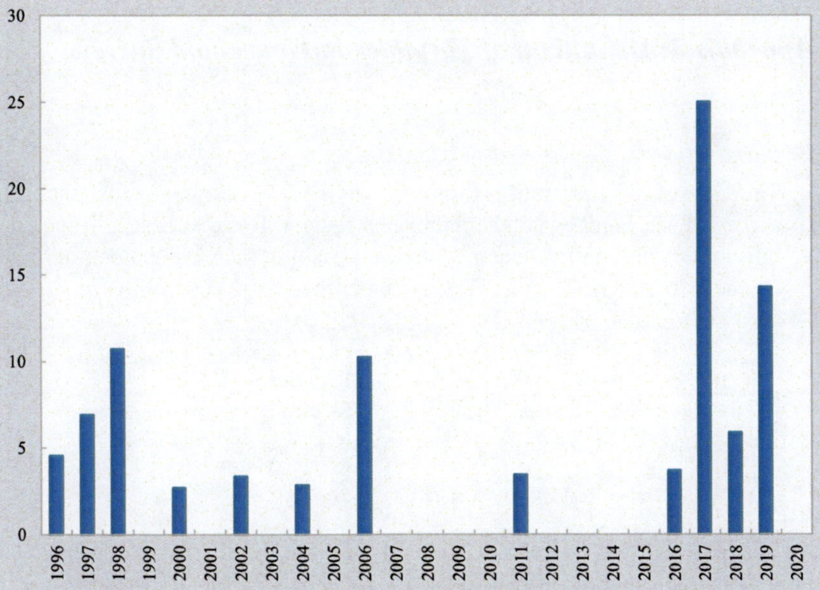

Fig. 18 Riksbank speeches mentioning distributional issues (percent of total). Sources: Sveriges Riksbank and IMF staff calculations. Notes: The analysis was performed on speeches available at https://www.riksbank.se/en-gb/press-and-published/speeches-and-presentations/, as of 31 Jan 2020. The chart plots the share of speeches by Riksbank officials per year that mention (case-insensitive) inequality, distributional effects, distribution of income, income dispersion or income distribution

The Riksbank's communications have emphasized that while expansionary monetary policy contributes to higher asset prices in the short term, benefitting certain groups more than others, it also leads to higher employment and stronger growth, which equalize incomes and wealth. It has also emphasized that high and volatile inflation has distributional effects, that a monetary policy focused on an inflation target counteracts. In addition, central bank officials highlighted the need to reform housing and tax policies to counteract the steep rise in housing prices and the redistribution of wealth between owners and rentals and existing homeowners and first-time buyers.

Appendices

Appendix 1: Definiti on of Variables in Household Surveys

The **Survey of Consumer Finances (SCF)** is a triennial cross-sectional survey of US families conducted by the Federal Reserve Board. It includes information on families' balance sheets, pensions, income, and demographic characteristics. The 2016 SCF covers more than 6500 households.

Assets	Liabilities
Real Estate Prim = Real Estate Primary Residence	Secured by Primary Residence: Mortgages Secured by Primary Residence
Real Estate Sec. = Real Estate Secondary Residence	
Stocks = directly held stock + stock mutual funds + other managed asset (50%) + Business	Secured by Secondary Residence: Mortgages Secured by Secondary Residence
Bonds = directly held bonds + bond mutual funds + savings bonds + other managed assets (50%)	Loans: Education loans + Vehicles loans + Other installments loans + Other loans
Liquid Assets = transaction accounts + CDs + Quasi-liquid retirement accounts (79%)	

The **Household Finance and Consumption Survey (HFCS)** is a survey coordinated by the European Central Bank. It collects information on assets, liabilities, income, and consumption of households. The survey is based on 84,000 interviews in 18-euro area countries (Austria, Belgium, Cyprus, Estonia, Finland, France, Germany, Greece, Ireland, Italy, Latvia, Lithuania, Malta, Netherlands, Portugal, Slovak Republic, Slovenia, and Spain) as well as Poland and Hungary.

To illustrate the decomposition of assets, we classify them into the following categories: real estate primary, real estate secondary, bonds, stocks, liquid, and others. Similarly, we classify liabilities into three categories: mortgages secured by primary residence, mortgages secured by other residence, and loans.

The SCF and the HFCS do not include the same variables. Hence, several simplifying assumptions are made in order to break down both assets and liabilities in the above broad categories. For example, for the US, we split the variable "other

Assets	**Liabilities**
Real Estate Prim = Real Estate Primary Residence	Secured by Primary Residence: Mortgages Secured by Primary Residence
Real Estate Sec. = Real Estate Secondary Residence	
Stocks = shares publicly traded + self-employment business + mutual funds (80%) + managed accounts (50%)	Secured by Secondary Residence: Mortgages Secured by Secondary Residence
Bonds = bonds + mutual funds (20%) + managed accounts (15%)	Loans: installment loans + credit line + credit card debt
Liquid Assets = deposits + money owed to households + voluntary/whole life insurance	

managed assets" equally into bonds and assets. Then we assume that 79% of the variable "quasi-liquid retirement accounts" is liquid assets. For the EU, we assume that 80% of the mutual funds are hold in stocks and the remaining 20% in bonds. Finally, for the variable "managed account," 50% was allocated to assets while 15% to bonds.

Then we rank households according to their position in the net wealth distribution and we divide them into three groups: households in the bottom 20% of the distribution (the poor), households in the middle 70% of the distribution (the middle class), and households in the top 10% of the distribution (the rich).

Appendix 2: Benchmarking "Unhedged Interest Rate Exposures"

Microsimulations are based on a welfare metric, "Unhedged Interest Rate Exposures" (UREs), capturing households' exposures to changes in real interest rates, which has been proposed by Auclert (2019) and applied for the United States and Italy. Tzamourani (2021) follow the same approach to derive the URE metric for euro area households. Their findings suggests that a fall in interest rate can affect income distribution, redistributing away from households with large positive UREs (e.g., with large share of short-term fixed-income investments such as certificates of deposits and/or fixed-rate mortgages) towards households with large negative UREs (e.g., with large share of long-term bond investments and/or adjustable-rate mortgage liabilities). Auclert (2019) defines URE as:

$$URE = Y - T - C + A - L \tag{1}$$

where Y-T is net annual disposable income, C is a consumption measure that includes durable and non-durable goods as well as interest and principal payments. A and L are the remaining assets and liabilities maturing in a year, respectively.

Data. We use micro data surveys of consumer finances for the US and the EU, namely, the 2016 Survey of Consumer Finances (SCF) for the US and the 2016 Household Finance and Consumption Survey (HFCS) for the EU (see Appendix 1 for details on coverage and data processing).

Caveats. The simulations are based on several simplifying assumptions related to the type and maturity of various assets and liabilities, as in Auclert (2019). For the US, simulations also use the 2016 Survey of Consumer Expenditures to benchmark household consumption in the 2016 SCF. For the EU, simulations use broadly similar assumptions, except that household consumption data are directly observable in the HFCS while household disposable income is proxied by gross income due to data availability. Simulations also do not include the effect of a prolonged monetary policy easing on asset prices resulting from unrealized capital gains from higher assets prices, which typically benefit the wealthy but might not be immediately reflected in households' income. Further, the simulations do not account for the effect of higher real estate prices on debt levels and home affordability, particularly at the bottom of the distribution. Also, given that our results are based on the 2016 survey data (latest available), potential changes in household income and finances since then can potentially alter the results. Finally, the results are subject to measurement error, a common caveat with survey data.

Given these caveats, the results are for illustration only, as different assumptions may lead to different results. Nevertheless, our broad findings are in line with Auclert's results for the US and Tzamourani's results for the EU.

Appendix 3: Benchmarking Distributional Implications of Asset Price Increases

Microsimulations are based on the 2016 Survey of Consumer Finances (SCF) for the US, and the 2016 Household Finance and Consumption Survey (HFCS) for the EU. We first compute household net wealth, defined as the difference between household asset and liabilities, using portfolio information available from the 2016 SCF for the US and the 2016 HFCS for the EU, and then scale household holdings of bond, real estate, and equities by their net wealth position. Further, we compute household capital gains on each asset by multiplying the relevant asset-to-net wealth ratio with a hypothetical 10 percent price increase.

For the EU, housing wealth includes households' real estate and holdings of mutual funds that predominately invest in real estate. Bond holdings are defined as the sum of the direct bond holdings, mutual funds predominantly investing in bonds and 79 percent of private pension holdings. Equity holdings are the sum of stocks and business wealth, and equity mutual funds, and 21 percent of private pension holdings. For the US, real estate includes primary residence, other residential property, and 16 percent of other assets. Bond holdings are defined as the sum of savings bonds, bonds, 20 percent of pooled investment fund, 79 percent of retirement accounts, and 15 percent of other assets. Equity holdings are the sum of stocks, business wealth, 80 percent of pooled investment funds, and 21 percent of other assets.

Capital gains are scaled by the net wealth in line with the broadly agreed, but not uncontestable, principle of scale invariance, which requires the inequality measure to be invariant to equi-proportional changes in initial net wealth. For example, assuming the net wealth of the original distribution to be 1 unit for one bracket and 20 units for another and multiplying both of these by a factor of 100, the resulting distribution of 100 and 2000 would imply that inequality did not change. However, the same result would also mean that the top bracket would receive more than 95 percent of total new wealth of 2079, i.e., the top bracket wealth would increase by 1980 units, while the bottom bracket—by 99 units).

Appendix 4: The Heterogeneous Agent New Keynesian Model of KMV

Main features. The Heterogeneous Agent New Keynesian (HANK) model of Kaplan et al. (2018) (KMV) combines a rich cross-sectional household heterogeneity under incomplete markets with standard New Keynesian features of price rigidities, monopolistic competition, and a Taylor rule. In the model, agents can save in two assets: a low-return short-dated asset and a high-return long-dated asset subject to transaction costs.

The model is calibrated to the US to match key micro data, including (i) net wealth inequality, with about 60 percent of households either in debt or holding close to zero cash; (ii) inequality in asset holdings, with the wealthiest decile holding 88 and 75 percent of all long- and short-dated assets respectively; and (iii) inequality in labor earnings, with 32 percent of labor earnings accruing to the wealthiest decile.

These features allow the model to create a large endogenous aggregate marginal propensity to consume (MPC), making consumption much more responsive to monetary policy shocks through general equilibrium effects, or what KMV call "indirect effects." A monetary policy loosening incentivizes an immediate increase in consumption, particularly for agents facing a borrowing constraint. Increased demand for goods leads to larger labor demand and wages, which reinforce the effects on consumption.

Caveats. In this model, the portfolio channel is very strong and typically swamps the direct and other channels through which monetary policy affects *income* inequality. That is because wages are assumed to be flexible but not prices, and thus profits contract after a monetary expansion which lowers the price of equity and thus raises the subsequent returns to equity. If wages were also rigid, households would not see a significant rise in their labor income following a monetary policy shock, which would suppress the *income* and *consumption* of the poorest the most. At the same time, profits could become procyclical under sufficient wage rigidity, and thus asset returns would not rise as much as under flexible wages. Thus, moving to wage rigidity would support the *wealth* of the rich but suppress their *income*, while their *consumption* would be roughly unaffected due to stable permanent income. The KMV model puts some channels together but like any model it does not capture all relevant channels. Gornemann et al. (2016) build a HANK model featuring the crucial employed-unemployed margin, not modeled in KMV. They find that looser monetary policy reduces not only consumption but also income inequality, the latter being the opposite of the response in KMV. Note that Gornemann et al. (2016) abstract from the liquid/illiquid assets dichotomy that KMV argue is crucial to understand monetary policy transmission.

Appendix 5: Empirical Strategy and Specification for the Results on Earnings

The empirical analysis of monetary policy easing on unemployment is based on Albrizio et al. (2021), who use the local projection method of Jordà (2005), augmented with the smooth transition regression approach of Granger and Teräsvirta (1993) to allow state-dependent responses. The analysis uses the US macro and household data at quarterly frequency over 1980–2016, which allows looking at monetary policy actions in the pre- and post-2008 periods to account for potential changes in distributional effects.

To quantify the effects of monetary policy shocks on wages, we estimate the following equation for labor market outcomes:

$$\begin{aligned} w_{i,t+4} - w_{i,t} = \alpha\, X_{it} + \sum_{q=1}^{4} \beta_q \left(FFR_{t+q} - FFR_{t+q-1}\right) + \\ + \sum_{q=1}^{4} \gamma_q \left(FFR_{t+q} - FFR_{t+q-1}\right) w_{it} + \delta w_{it} + \mathcal{E}_{it}, \end{aligned} \tag{2}$$

where w_{it} is demeaned earnings for individual i in quarter t and FFR_t is the Federal Fund Rate.[25] The vector X_{it} consists of the following controls: a second-order polynomial in age, state fixed effects, occupation fixed effects, industry fixed effects, education fixed effects (10 categories), seasonal fixed effects (12 categories), gender, race, individual relationship to the household's head (4 categories). The parameter γ_q are our parameters of interest. If large and significant, it suggests a heterogeneous impact of monetary policy shocks on labor market outcomes.

Monetary policy shocks (i.e., changes in the FFR) are identified by exploiting high-frequency variations in interest rate futures within a narrow time window around Federal Open Market Committee (FOMC) announcements, follow-

[25] Demeaned earnings are defined as log $wage_{i,t} - 1/N \sum_{i'} \log wage_{i',t}$.

ing Gertler and Karadi's (2015) framework. The response of futures to FOMC announcements is a proxy of the investors' surprise around monetary policy announcements. If the announcement was in line with investors' expectations, then future prices would not shift around the announcement. By contrast, surprisingly tighter or surprisingly looser monetary policy will result in shifts in future prices proportional to the size of the surprise. In the first stage, we regress changes in the FFR on surprises in futures in response to the FOMC announcements.

We use individual-level data on earnings and wages from the Current Population Survey (CPS). The CPS data is a well-established source of data for labor market indicators. However, it is important to note that data are top-coded. Therefore, we are not able to observe the dynamics at the upper end of the distribution.

The results of second stage regressions in response to changes in the FFR instrumented by surprises in futures are reported in Table 2. Both columns include the full set of control variables.[26] Column (1) reports the dynamic effect of an exogenous quarterly change in the FFR on the year-on-year (yoy) change in wages. In particular, a 100 bps increase in the FFR decreases yoy average wages by 0.6 percent in the first quarter after the monetary policy shock, compared to 1.1

Table 2 Second stage estimates of changes in earnings in response to changes in the FFR

	(1)	(2)
ΔFFR_{t+1}	−0.0058*** (0.0012)	−0.0058*** (0.0012)
ΔFFR_{t+1} * $wages_{it}$		−0.0050*** (0.0017)
ΔFFR_{t+2}	−0.0051*** (0.0011)	−0.0051*** (0.0011)
ΔFFR_{t+2} * $wages_{it}$		−0.0102*** (0.0015)
ΔFFR_{t+3}	−0.0082*** (0.0012)	−0.0082*** (0.0012)
ΔFFR_{t+3} * $wages_{it}$		−0.0076*** (0.0015)
ΔFFR_{t+4}	−0.0112*** (0.0017)	−0.0112*** (0.0017)
ΔFFR_{t+4} * $wages_{it}$		−0.0123*** (0.0023)
$wages_{it}$	−0.5401*** (0.0007)	−0.5430*** (0.0008)
N	1,553,880	1,553,880
R^2	0.3	0.3

Standard errors in parentheses
*p < 0.1, **p < 0.05, ***p < 0.01

[26] The inclusion of a linear trend among the controls does not alter the results.

percent in the fourth quarter. Column (2) reports the same regression introducing interaction terms for the initial level of wages (1 year ago). The results confirm significant heterogeneity in labor market outcomes in response to a monetary policy shock. Given that individual-level wages in the controls are demeaned using quarter-specific wage averages, the point estimate for coefficients on the change in the FFR is unchanged by construction.[27]

References

Adam, K., & Tzamourani, P. (2016). Distributional consequences of asset price inflation in the Euro area. *European Economic Review, 89*, 172–192.

Adam, K., & Zhu, J. (2016). Price-level changes and the redistribution of nominal wealth across the Euro area. *Journal of European Economic Association, 14*(4), 871–906.

Aladangady, A. (2014). *Homeowner balance sheets and Monetary Policy*. FEDS Working Paper No. 2014–98.

Albanesi, S. (2007). Inflation and inequality. *Journal of Monetary Economics, 54*(4), 1088–1114.

Albrizio, S., Estefania, J., & Furceri, D. (2021). *Non-linear macro and distributional effects of US Monetary Policy*. IMF Working Paper.

Alves, F., Kaplan, G., Moll, B., & Violante, G. (2019). *A further look at the propagation mechanism of Monetary Policy shocks in HANK*. Mimeo, Princeton University.

Amberg, N., Jansson, T., Klein, M., & Rogantini Picco, A. (2021). *Five facts about the distributional income effects of Monetary policy*. Sveriges Riksbank Working Paper No. 403.

Ampudia, M., Georgarakos, D., Slacalek, J., Tristani, O., Vermeulen, P., & Violante, G. (2018). *Monetary Policy and household inequality*. ECB Working Paper No. 2170.

Andersen, A. L., Johannesen, N., Jørgensen, M., & Peydró, J.-L. (2020). *Monetary policy and inequality*. CEPR Discussion Paper No. 15599.

Auclert, A. (2019). Monetary policy and the redistribution channel. *American Economic Review, 109*(6), 2333–2367.

Barro, R. J., & Gordon, D. B. (1983). Rules, discretion, and reputation in a model of Monetary Policy. *Journal of Monetary Economics, 12*(1), 101–121.

Bernanke, B. (2015, June 1). *Monetary Policy and inequality*. Brookings Blog.

Bielecki, M., Brzoza-Brzezina, M., & Kolasa, M. (2022). Intergenerational redistributive effects of Monetary Policy. *Journal of European Economic Association., 20*(2), 549–580.

Bivens, J., & Mishel, L. (2013). The pay of corporate executives and financial professionals as evidence of rents in top 1 percent incomes. *Journal of Economic Perspectives, 27*(3), 57–78.

Blanchard, O. & Gali, J. (2007). Real Wage Rigidities and the New Keynesian Model. *Journal of Money, Credit and Banking, 39*:35–65. https://doi.org/10.1111/j.1538-4616.2007.00015.x.

Board of Governors of the Federal Reserve System. (2016). Survey of Consumer Finances (SCF): scf2016.

Brand, C., Bielecki, M., & Penalver, A. (2018). *The natural rate of interest: Estimates, drivers, and challenges to Monetary Policy*. ECB Occasional Paper No. 217.

[27] A possible consideration is that the empirical specification above does not allow for enough flexibility in the functional form, restricting the heterogeneous effect to be linear in the wage, while it could have a different, possibly more complex, relationship. As a robustness check, we interact the change in the FFR with a dummy for people with a wage larger than the (year-specific) average. This alternative specification does not alter our conclusions. Results are available upon request.

Broer, T., Kramer, J., & Mitman, K. (2020). *The curious incidence of shocks along the income distribution*. Mimeo, Institute for International Economic Studies, Stockholm University.
Bublitz, E. (2016). *Misperceptions of income distributions: Cross-country evidence from a randomized survey experiment*. HWWI, Hamburg Institute of International Economics (HWWI) Research Papers No. 178.
Cantú, C., Cavallino, P., De Fiore, F., & Yetman, J. (2021). *A global database on central banks' monetary responses to Covid-19* (Vol. No. 934). Bank for International Settlements.
Carney, M. (2016, December 5). *The Spectre of monetarism*. Speech at the Roscoe Lecture, Liverpool John Moores University.
Carstens, A. (2021, May 6). *Central Banks and inequality*. Remarks at the Markus' Academy, Princeton University's Bendheim Center for Finance.
Casiraghi, M. E., Gaiotti, M. L. R., & Secchi, A. (2018). A "reverse Robin Hood"? The distributional implications of non-standard Monetary Policy for Italian households. *Journal of International Money and Finance, 85*, 215–235.
Cihak, M., Sahay, R., Barajas, A., Chen, S., Fouejieu, A., & Xie, P. (2020). *Finance and inequality*. IMF Staff Discussion Note No. 20/01.
Cloyne, J., Ferreira, C., & Surico, P. (2016). *Monetary Policy when households have debt: New evidence on the transmission mechanism*. Bank of England Staff Working Paper No. 589.
Cloyne, J., Huber, K., Ilzetzki, E., & Kleven, H. (2019). the effect of house prices on household borrowing: A new approach. *American Economic Review, 109*(6), 2104–2036.
Coibion, O., Gorodnichenko, Y., Kueng, L., & Silvia, J. (2017). Innocent bystanders? Monetary Policy and inequality. *Journal of Monetary Economics, 88*, 70–88.
Colciago, A., de Haan, J., & Samarina, A. (2019). Central Bank policies and income and wealth inequality: A survey. *Journal of Economic Surveys, 33*(4), 1199–1231.
Constâncio, V. (2017). *Inequality and macroeconomic policies*. European Economic Association.
Credit Suisse. (2019, October). *Global wealth databook*.
Dabla-Norris, E., Kochhar, K., Ricka, F., Suphaphiphat, N., & Tsounta, E. (2015). *Causes and consequences of income inequality: A global perspective*. IMF Staff Discussion Note No. 15/13.
Davig, T., & Gürkaynak, R. S. (2015). Is optimal Monetary Policy always optimal? *International Journal of Central Banking, 11*(4), 353–382.
Devereux, P. J. (2001). The cyclicality of real wages within employer-employee matches. *ILR Review, 54*(4), 835–850.
Di Casola, P., & Stockhammar, P. (2021). *When domestic and foreign QE overlap: Evidence from Sweden*. Sveriges Riksbank Working Paper No. 404.
Di Maggio, M., Kermani, A., Keys, B. J., Piskorski, T., Ramcharan, R., Seru, A., & Yao, V. (2017). Interest rate pass-through: Mortgage rates, household consumption, and voluntary deleveraging. *American Economic Review, 107*(11), 3550–3588.
Doepke, M., & Schneider, M. (2006). Inflation and the redistribution of nominal wealth. *Journal of Political Economy, 114*(6), 1069–1097.
Dolado, J. J., Motyovszki, G., & Pappa, E. (2021). Monetary Policy and inequality under labor market frictions and capital-skill complementarity. *American Economic Journal: Macroeconomics, 13*(2), 292–332.
Dossche, M., Hartwig, J., Pierluigi, B., & Velasco, A. (2019). *The Redistribution of Interest Income in the Euro Area, 2008-2018*. Mimeo, European Central Bank.
Dossche, M., Kolndrekaj, A., & Slacalek, J. (2020). *COVID-19 and income inequality*. Mimeo, European Central Bank.
Dossche, M., Slacalek, J., & Wolswijk, G. (2021). *Monetary Policy and inequality*. ECB Economic Bulletin Issue No. 2/2021.
Draghi, M. (2016, October 25). *Stability, equity, and Monetary Policy*. Text of the 2nd DIW Europe Lecture at the German Institute for Economic Research (DIW).
Eberly, J. C., Stock, J. H., & Wright, J. H. (2019). *The Federal Reserve's current framework for Monetary Policy: A review and assessment*. NBER Working Paper No. 26002.

Erosa, A., & Ventura, G. (2002). On inflation as a regressive consumption tax. *Journal of Monetary Economics, 49*(4), 761–795.

European Central Bank. (2016). *Household Finance and Consumption Survey, (HFCS)*, Household Finance and Consumption Survey (HFCS) (europa.eu).

Eusepi, S., & Preston, B. (2010). Central Bank communication and expectations stabilization. *American Economic Journal: Macroeconomics, 2*(3), 235–271.

Fabrizio, S., Furceri, D., Garcia-Verdu, R., Li, B. G., Lizarazo, S. V., Tavares, M. M., Narita, F., & Peralta-Alva, A. (2017). *Macro-structural policies and income inequality in low-income developing countries*. IMF Staff Discussion Note No. 17/01.

Favilukis, J. (2013). Inequality, stock market participation, and the equity premium. *Journal of Financial Economics, 107*(3), 740–759.

Feiveson, L., Goernemann, N., Hotchkiss, J., Mertens, K., & Sims, J. (2020). *Distributional considerations for Monetary Policy strategy*. FRB Finance and Economics Discussion Paper No. 2020-073.

Ferrante, F., & Paustian, M. O. (2019). *Household debt and the heterogeneous effects of forward guidance*. FRB International Finance Discussion Paper No. 1267.

Furceri, D., & Tawk, N. (2021). *Lower-for-longer: Challenges and opportunities for Asian economies*. IMF Working Paper.

Furceri, D., Loungani, P., & Zdzienicka, A. (2018). The effects of Monetary policy shocks on inequality. *Journal of International Money and Finance, 85*, 168–186.

Furceri, D., Loungani, P., & Ostry, J. D. (2020, May 11). *How pandemics leave the poor even farther behind*. IMF Blog.

Gelos, G., Grinberg, F., Khan, S., Mancini-Griffoli, T., Narita, M., & Rawat, U. (2019). *Has higher household indebtedness weakened Monetary Policy transmission?* IMF Working Paper No. 19/11.

Gertler, M., & Karadi, P. (2015). Monetary policy surprises, credit costs, and economic activity. *American Economic Journal: Macroeconomics, 7*(1), 44–76.

Gornemann, N., Kuester, K., & Nakajima, M. (2016). *Doves for the rich, Hawks for the poor? Distributional consequences of Monetary Policy*. International Finance Discussion Paper No. 1167.

Granger, C., & Teräsvirta, T. (1993). *Modelling non-linear economic relationships*. Oxford University Press.

Guerello, C. (2018). Conventional and unconventional Monetary Policy vs. households' income distribution: An empirical analysis for the Euro area. *Journal of International Money and Finance, 85*, 187–214.

Haldane, A. (2018, April 10). *How Monetary Policy affects your GDP*. Finch Lecture at the University of Melbourne.

Han, F. (2019). *Demographics and the natural rate of interest in Japan*. IMF Working Paper No. 19/31.

Heathcote, J., Perri, F., & Violante, G. (2010). Unequal we stand: An empirical analysis of economic inequality in the United States, 1967-2006. *Review of Economic Dynamics, Elsevier for the Society for Economic Dynamics, 13*(1), 15–51.

Honohan, P. (2019, October). *Should Monetary Policy take inequality and climate change into account?* PIIE Working Paper No. 19-18.

Hoynes, H. W. (2000). Local labor markets and welfare spells: Do demand conditions matter? *Review of Economics and Statistics, 82*(3), 351–368.

Hoynes, H., Miller, D. L., & Schaller, J. (2012). Who suffers during recessions? *Journal of Economic Perspectives, 26*(3), 27–48.

Igan, D., Kirti, D., & Martinez Peria, S. (2020, August 26). *The disconnect between financial markets and real economy*. IMF Research Special Notes Series on COVID-19.

International Monetary Fund. (2014). *Fiscal policy and income inequality*. Policy Paper.

International Monetary Fund. (2015). *Evolving Monetary Policy frameworks in low-income and other developing countries*. Policy Paper.

International Monetary Fund. (2019). *G-20 report on strong, sustainable, balanced, and inclusive growth.*

International Monetary Fund. (2021, April). *World Economic Outlook: Managing divergent recoveries.*

Inui, M., Sudo, N., & Yamada, T. (2017). *Effects of Monetary Policy shocks on inequality in Japan.* Bank of Japan Working Paper No. 17-E-3.

Jordà, O. (2005). Estimation and inference of impulse responses by local projections. *American Economic Review, 95*(1), 161–182.

Jordà, O., Singh, S. R., & Taylor, A. M. (2020). *Longer-run economic consequences of pandemics.* Federal Reserve Bank of San Francisco Working Paper No. 2020-09.

Kahn, M. L. (2012). Labor market policy: A comparative view on the costs and benefits of labor market flexibility. *Journal of Policy Analysis and Management, 31*(1), 94–110.

Kaplan, G., Violante, G., & Weidner, J. (2014). The wealthy hand-to-mouth. *Brookings Papers on Economic Activity, 1*, 77–138.

Kaplan, G., Moll, B., & Violante, G. L. (2018). Monetary policy according to HANK. *American Economic Review, 108*(3), 697–743.

Klomp, J., & de Haan, J. (2010). Inflation and Central Bank independence: A meta-regression analysis. *Journal of Economic Surveys, 24*(4), 593–621.

Kydland, E. F., & Prescott, E. C. (1977). Rules rather than discretion: The inconsistency of optimal plans. *Journal of Political Economy, 85*(3), 473–491.

Lane, P. (2019). *Households and the transmission of monetary policy.* Central Bank of Ireland/ECB Conference on Household Finance and Consumption.

Lenza, M., & Slacalek, J. (2018). *How does monetary policy affect income and wealth inequality? Evidence from the Euro Area.* ECB Working Paper No. 2190.

Lenza, M., & Slacalek, J. (2021). *How does monetary policy affect income and wealth inequality? Evidence from quantitative easing in the Euro Area.* Mimeo.

Marino, F., & Nunziata, L. (2017). *The labor market in Italy, 2000–2016.* IZA World of Labor, Evidence-based policy making.

McKay, A., & Reis, R. (2021). Optimal automatic stabilizers. *The Review of Economic Studies., 88*(5), 2375–2406.

Medgyesi, M. (2013). *Increasing income inequality and attitudes to inequality: a cohort perspective*, GINI Discussion Paper 94.

Meh, C., Rios-Rull, J., & Terajima, Y. (2010). Aggregate and welfare effects of redistribution of wealth under inflation and price-level targeting. *Journal of Monetary Economics, 57*(6), 637–652.

Mumtaz, H., & Theophilopoulou, A. (2017). The impact of Monetary Policy on inequality in the UK. An empirical analysis. *European Economic Review, 98*, 410–423.

Mumtaz, H., & Theophilopoulou, A. (2020). The impact of monetary policy on inequality in the UK. An empirical analysis. *European Economic Reviuew, 2017, 98*(C), 410–423. EconPapers: The impact of monetary policy on inequality in the UK. An empirical analysis (repec.org).

Natal, J.-M., & Stoffels, N. (2019). *Globalization, market power, and the natural interest rate.* IMF Working Paper No. 19/95.

O'Farrell, R., Rawdanowicz, Ł., & Inaba, K. I. (2016). *Monetary policy and inequality.* OECD Economics Department Working Paper No. 1281.

Ostry, D. J., Berg, A., & Kothari, S. (2021). Growth-equity trade-offs in structural reforms. *Scottish Journal of Political Economy, 68*(2), 209–237.

Pescatori, A., & Turunen, J. (2015). *Lower for longer: Neutral rates in the United States.* IMF Working Paper No. 15/135.

Petrou, K. (2021). *Inflation, Inequality, and the Problem This Time: Monetary Policy and Its Discontent.* Remarks Prepared for the Institute of International Economic Policy George Washington University Karen-Petrou-Remarks-Inflation_Inequality_and-the-Problem-This-Time_Monetary-Policy-and-Its-Discontent-IIEP-GWU.pdf (fedfin.com).

Qureshi, Z. (2020, November 17). *Tackling the inequality pandemic: Is there a cure?* Brookings Institution Report.

Reis, R. (2013). Central Bank design. *Journal of Economic Perspectives, 27*(4), 17–44.
Rogoff, K. (1985). The optimal degree of commitment to an intermediate monetary target. *The Quarterly Journal of Economics, 100*(4), 1169–1189.
Rostagno, M., Altavilla, C., Carboni, G., Lemke, W., Motto, R., Guilhem, A. S., & Yiangou, J. (2019). *A tale of two decades: The ECB's Monetary Policy at 20*. ECB Working Paper Series No. 2346.
Saez, E. (2019, March 2). *Striking it richer: The evolution of top incomes in the United States (updated with 2017 final estimates)*.
Saiki, A., & Frost, J. (2014). Does unconventional Monetary Policy affect inequality? Evidence from Japan. *Applied Economics, 46*(36), 4445–4454.
Samarina, A., & Nguyen, A. (2019). *Does Monetary Policy affect income inequality in the Euro area?* DNB Working Papers No. 626.
Schnabel, I. (2020). *Narratives about the ECB's monetary policy – reality or fiction?* Juristische Studiengesellschaft.
Shimer, R. (2005). The Cyclical Behavior of Equilibrium Unemployment and Vacancies. *American Economic Review, 95*(1), 25–49.
Slacalek, J., Tristani, O., & Violante, G. (2020). Household balance sheet channels of Monetary Policy: A back of the envelope calculation for the Euro area. *Journal of Economic Dynamics & Control, 115*(C), 103879.
Stiglitz, J. (2015). *New Theoretical Perspectives on the Distribution of Income and Wealth among Individuals:* Part IV: Land and Credit, NBER Working Paper Np 21192.
Tenreyro, S., & Thwaites, G. (2016). Pushing on a string: US Monetary Policy is less powerful in recessions. *American Economic Journal: Macroeconomics, 8*(4), 43–74.
Tinbergen, J. (1962). *Shaping the world economy: Suggestions for an international economic policy*, New York: Twentieth Century Fund.
Tzamourani, P. (2021). The interest rate exposure of Euro area households. *European Economic Review, 132*, 103643.
Von Wachter, T., Song, J., & Manchester, J. (2009). *Long-term earnings losses due to mass layoffs during the 1982 recession: An analysis using US Administrative Data from 1974 to 2004*, unpublished paper, Columbia University.

Covid-19 Shock and Fiscal-Monetary Policy Mix in a Monetary Union

Anna Bartocci, Alessandro Notarpietro, and Massimiliano Pisani

JEL Classification E31, E32, E58

> A strong, symmetric fiscal response that offsets the economic damage from the pandemic is in the economic interest of all countries in the eurozone.[1]

1 Introduction

The recessionary macroeconomic effects on the euro area (EA) economy of the Covid-19 shock are of particular interest from both a theoretical and a policy perspective. First, the shock affects most severely low-income households, as they typically have very imperfect or no access at all to financial markets and therefore cannot smooth consumption in response to an unexpected fall in income. The drop in their income originates a large reduction in their consumption demand, since these households typically exhibit a high marginal propensity to consume.[2] Second, all

[1] In: *Why we all need a joint European fiscal response.* Contribution by Fabio Panetta, Member of the Executive Board, European Central Bank, published by Politico on 21 April 2020.
[2] See Coenen et al. (2008).

The views expressed in this paper are those of the authors alone and should not be attributed to the Bank of Italy or the Eurosystem. We thank Fabio Busetti, Stefano Neri and two anonymous referees for useful comments. Any remaining errors are the sole responsibility of the authors.

A. Bartocci · A. Notarpietro · M. Pisani (✉)
Bank of Italy, Rome, Italy
e-mail: anna.bartocci@bancaditalia.it; alesssandro.notarpietro@bancaditalia.it; massimiliano.pisani@bancaditalia.it

L. Paganetto (ed.), *Economic Challenges for Europe After the Pandemic*, Springer Proceedings in Business and Economics,
https://doi.org/10.1007/978-3-031-10302-5_10

countries in the EA are resorting to expansionary fiscal policy measures to support aggregate demand, possibly with different intensities reflecting the availability of fiscal space at the time of the shock. While fiscal policy is conducted mainly at country level, cross-country spillovers associated with intra-EA trade integration may call for a coordinated fiscal response. Third, while the central bank stabilizes union-wide inflation, the effective lower bound (ELB) constrains the use of the monetary policy rate and requires the central bank to deploy non-standard monetary policy measures.[3] Thus, the analysis of cross-country spillovers, cross-country fiscal coordination, and macroeconomic interaction between monetary and fiscal policy is of paramount importance for an assessment of the policy response to the Covid-19 shock in a monetary union.

This paper evaluates the effectiveness of a monetary and fiscal policy mix in response to the Covid-19 shock by simulating a dynamic general equilibrium model of a monetary union calibrated to the EA. We use a New Keynesian, two-region monetary union model. For simplicity, we calibrate the two EA regions in a symmetric way. In particular, they have equal size and degree of openness. The remaining parameters of the model are calibrated in line with the literature.

The main features of the model are the following ones.

First, in each of the two regions, labelled Home and rest of the EA (REA), there are three types of households, called "Ricardian," "hand-to-mouth (HTM)," and "restricted." Ricardian households have access to domestic and international financial markets and own domestic producers of physical capital. HTM households consume their available wage income in every period. Thus, their consumption is heavily affected by the drop in current income following the pandemic shock. Restricted households have access only to the market for domestic long-term sovereign bonds (thus, their access to financial markets is "restricted"). Moreover, they own, jointly with domestic Ricardian households, the domestic producers of physical capital. The financial market segmentation generated by the presence of restricted households allows non-standard monetary policy measures such as central bank asset purchases to have real effects.[4]

Second, in each region, the domestic fiscal authority (the government) can make resources available to HTM households through an increase in targeted lump-sum transfers, financed by issuing (short- and long-term) public debt. The latter is stabilized around its long-run target by adjusting lump-sum taxes paid by Ricardian households.

Third, the central bank of the monetary union sets the monetary policy rate according to a standard Taylor rule subject to the ELB. Once the ELB is reached, the central bank can implement non-standard measures to achieve its price stability objective, buying Home and REA long-term sovereign bonds in the secondary markets.

---

[3] See Cova et al. (2017) and Neri and Gerali (2017) for an analysis of the low level of the natural interest rate in industrialized countries and its relation with the so called "secular stagnation".

[4] See Chen et al. (2012).

Fourth, in some simulations it is assumed that, following the debt-financed fiscal expansion, the sovereign spread exogenously increases in one region and induces a further rise in the long-term rate beyond the (mechanical) rise due to the increase in public debt. The exogenous rise in the sovereign spread captures in a stylized way concerns of investors about the regional fiscal space and public debt sustainability. Moreover, it assumed that the higher sovereign spread is fully passed-through to the interest rate paid by households and firms.[5] Alternatively, it is assumed that the fiscal expansion is financed by a sovereign bond issued by a monetary-union wide supranational fiscal authority and perceived by investors as a "safe" asset, i.e., different from the regional sovereign bond, it does not pay a spread over the risk-free rate.

We model the Covid-19 shock as a mix of cross-country symmetric demand and supply shocks. While the pandemic initially manifested itself as a supply contraction, the subsequent lockdown measures and the entailed large increase in uncertainty resemble a contractionary demand shock.[6] The shocks induce a recession in the EA and, thus, reduce the available income of HTM households and drive the policy rate to the ELB, under the assumption of no-fiscal policy response. We then study the fiscal policy response by alternatively assuming that (1) only the Home fiscal authority raises targeted, lump-sum fiscal transfers to domestic HTM households and public consumption; (2) both Home and REA fiscal authorities simultaneously raise transfers to their HTM households and public consumption; (3) the central bank, to favour the achievement of the inflation target, implements long-term sovereign bond purchases in the case of simultaneous fiscal response by both countries; (4) the increase in transfers to HTM households and public consumption in each region is financed by a safe bond issued by a supranational fiscal authority.

The main results are the following. First, higher lump-sum targeted fiscal transfers to HTM households and public consumption spending in one region (Home), financed by issuing public debt, reduce the recessionary effects both domestically and abroad (via trade channel). The implicit fiscal multiplier of Home GDP is 0.9, that of REA GDP is 0.2.[7] Second, the monetary union-wide recession is more effectively mitigated if both regions implement expansionary fiscal measures and the central bank limits the increase in long-term rates by purchasing sovereign bonds. The implicit multipliers of both Home and REA GDP are 1.1 and rise to 1.4 in the case of central bank intervention. Moreover, following the central bank intervention, Home and REA inflation rates would be 0.7% points higher than in the case of only fiscal stimulus. Third, cross-country simultaneous fiscal expansions are less effective if sovereign bond yields increase relatively more in one region (Home) because investors perceive the bond as risky (Home GDP multiplier decreases to

[5] See Corsetti et al. (2014) on the so-called "sovereign risk channel" of fiscal policy.

[6] Later in this section we discuss this point in detail.

[7] The implicit multiplier is computed as the difference, in the fourth quarter, between GDP with fiscal stimulus and GDP without fiscal stimulus, divided by the size of fiscal stimulus. In the fourth quarter the fiscal stimulus ends and, in the no-stimulus scenario, GDP achieves its trough.

0.8, REA multiplier to 1.0). Effectiveness can be regained if a supranational fiscal authority issues a safe bond.[8]

Our choice of modelling the pandemic as a mix of aggregate demand and aggregate supply shocks is grounded in the most recent literature on the macroeconomic effects of the Covid-19 shock. A growing number of contributions analyze the macroeconomic impact of the Covid-19 shock and the related policy options to counteract it, offering different views on the interpretation (and modelling) of the pandemic. Faria-e-Castro (2020) models the pandemic shock as a negative demand shock. According to Guerrieri et al. (2020), in the presence of nominal rigidities, supply shocks can trigger changes in aggregate demand that are larger than the initial supply shocks. Eichenbaum et al. (2020) suggest that an epidemic can be thought of as giving rise to negative aggregate demand and aggregate supply shocks. The aggregate demand shock arises because susceptible people reduce their consumption to lower their probability of being infected. The negative aggregate supply shock arises because susceptible people reduce their hours worked to lower their probability of becoming infected. However, the qualitative and quantitative responses of consumption, hours worked and investment depend very much on which shock dominates. Baqaee and Farhi (2020) use a parsimonious quantitative input-output model of the US economy to disentangle the contribution of demand and supply shocks and conclude that both are necessary to match the data, which features large reductions in real GDP but only mild deflation. More recently, IMF (2020) suggests that lockdowns and voluntary social distancing played a near comparable role in driving the economic recession. On the empirical side, Brinca et al. (2020) estimate a Bayesian VAR on US data to try to separate labor demand and labor supply shocks. Their estimates suggest that two-thirds of the drop in the aggregate growth rate of hours in March and April 2020 are attributable to labor supply. Balleer et al. (2020) study price-setting behavior in German firm-level survey data during the Covid-19 pandemic and conclude that supply and demand forces coexist, but demand shortages dominate in the short run.

Based on the findings of these contributions, we model the pandemic as a mix of aggregate demand and supply shocks affecting each EA region symmetrically. Different from these contributions, we focus on the EA, the role of cross-country spillovers and the interaction between fiscal and monetary policy responses under the assumptions of ELB and imperfect access to financial markets.

Our paper contributes to the literature on the monetary and fiscal policy mix in a monetary union. Bianchi et al. (2020) simulate a DSGE model of the US economy to assess the implications of a coordinated fiscal and monetary strategy aiming at creating a controlled rise of inflation to wear away a targeted fraction of debt. The coordinated strategy enhances the efficacy of the fiscal stimulus planned

[8] Asymmetric sizes and openness would modify the cross-country spillovers. The bigger and more open a region, the larger its spillovers to the other region. The cross-country asymmetry would not greatly alter the response of the EA variables to the cross-country symmetric pandemic shock and to the same fiscal measures simultaneously implemented in both regions.

in response to the Covid-19 pandemic and allows the Federal Reserve to correct a prolonged period of below-target inflation. Different from them, we focus our analysis on a monetary union and non-standard monetary policy measures. As in their case, we find that the policy mix has positive effects on inflation. Coenen et al. (2020) show that a combination of imperfectly credible forward guidance, asset purchases and fiscal stimulus is effective in undoing the distortionary effects due to the ELB, in particular when asset purchases enhance the credibility of the forward guidance policy. Different from them, we focus on a mix of two particular fiscal measures, i.e., fiscal transfers to HTM households and public consumption. Bayer et al. (2020) distinguish between transfers conditional on being unemployed (that mitigate income risk and the adverse impact of the lockdown ex ante) and unconditional transfers (stabilizing income ex post only). They find that for unconditional transfers, the multiplier ranges between 0.1 and 0.5, for conditional transfers between 1 and 2. Different from them, we focus on ex post transfers and their interaction with non-standard monetary policy measures. Burlon et al. (2017) evaluate the impact of accommodative non-standard measures in correspondence of a debt-financed increase in public investment in a monetary union. Pietrunti (2020) analyzes the impact of monetary and fiscal policy coordination in a closed-economy New Keynesian model of the euro area. We focus on public transfers and public consumption spending and monetary-fiscal policy mix within a monetary union.

Benigno (2004) shows how monetary policy should be conducted in a general equilibrium two-region, currency-area model with monopolistic competition and price stickiness. This framework delivers a simple welfare criterion based on the utility of the consumers that shows the usual trade-off between stabilizing inflation and output. Gali and Monacelli (2008) report that in the presence of country-specific shocks and nominal rigidities, the policy mix that is optimal from the viewpoint of the union as a whole requires that inflation be stabilized at the union level by the common central bank, whereas fiscal policy plays a country-specific stabilization role, one beyond the efficient provision of public goods. Farhi and Werning (2017) find that the benefits of a fiscal union are larger, the more asymmetric the shocks affecting the members of the currency union, the more persistent these shocks, and the less open the member economies. Different from these contributions, we provide a positive (i.e., not normative) analysis of monetary and fiscal policy interaction in a monetary union when the ELB holds and access to financial markets is incomplete.

Our paper is also related to the literature on fiscal multipliers in large-scale DSGE models used in policy institutions. Among the others, Coenen et al. (2012) find that there is agreement across models on both the absolute and relative sizes of different types of fiscal multipliers and, in particular, fiscal policy is most effective if it has moderate persistence and if monetary policy is accommodative. Different from this contribution, we focus on the EA and the interaction among regional fiscal policies and the EA-wide monetary policy.

The paper is organized as follows. The next section describes model setup and calibration. Section 3 illustrates the simulated scenarios. Section 4 reports the results. Section 5 concludes.

2 Model

We provide an overview of the model (Sect. 2.1), describe the different types of households (Sect. 2.2), the capital good producers (Sect. 2.3), the monetary policy instrument rule (Sect. 2.5), the fiscal sector (Sect. 2.6), and briefly discuss the calibration (Sect. 2.7).

2.1 Overview

The model represents the EA economy composed of two regions: Home, and the rest of EA (REA). The size of the EA economy is normalized to 1. Home and REA have sizes equal to n, and n^*, respectively (with $n > 0$, $n^* > 0$, and $n + n^* = 1$).[9]

Home and REA share the currency and the central bank. The latter sets the nominal interest rate, which reacts to EA-wide inflation and output according to a Taylor rule.

One crucial feature of the model is that the ELB is an endogenous constraint on the EA (short-term) monetary policy rate and that the central bank can purchase domestic long-term sovereign bonds in each EA region secondary market to try to stabilize inflation dynamics (in line with the medium-term inflation target).

Another key model feature is financial segmentation as in Chen et al. (2012), that allows central bank asset purchases to have real effects in our model.[10] In each EA region there are three types of households, labeled "restricted," "Ricardian," and "HTM." Restricted households have access only to the domestic long-term sovereign bond market and, joint with domestic Ricardian (see below), own shares of domestic "capital producers."

Ricardian households have multiple investment choices, because they invest in domestic short- and long-term sovereign bonds, and international short-term bonds, traded with Ricardian of the other country. Ricardian households own domestic firms operating in the final and intermediate sectors (other than the capital producers) and hold shares of the domestic capital producers. HTM households do not have access to financial markets and in each period consume all available labor income.

All households supply differentiated labor services to domestic non-financial firms (other than capital producers) and act as wage setters in monopolistically competitive labor markets, as they charge a wage markup over their marginal rate of substitution between consumption and leisure. Wage and labor decisions are taken by Ricardian households for all households. The overall wage income is equally distributed across all households.

---

[9] For each region, size refers to the overall population and to the number of firms operating in each sector.

[10] See also Bartocci et al. (2017).

On the production side, there are (1) capital producers, (2) firms that, under monopolistic competition, produce intermediate tradable goods, and (3) firms that, under perfect competition, produce two final goods (consumption and investment goods).

Capital producers are firms that optimally choose investment in physical capital to maximize profits under perfect competition, subject to the law of capital accumulation and quadratic adjustment costs on investment, taking prices as given. They rent capital to domestic firms producing intermediate goods and rebate profits to domestic restricted and Ricardian households.

Intermediate tradable goods are produced combining domestic capital and labor. Given the assumption of differentiated intermediate goods, firms have market power. Thus, they are price-setter and restrict output to create excess profits. Intermediate tradable goods can be sold domestically and abroad. It is assumed that markets for tradable goods are segmented, so that firms can set a different price in each of the two regions.

The two final goods are sold domestically and are produced combining all available intermediate goods using a constant-elasticity-of-substitution (CES) production function. The two resulting bundles can have different composition.

In line with other dynamic general equilibrium models of the EA (see, among the others, Warne et al. 2008 and Gomes et al. 2010), we include adjustment costs on real and nominal variables, ensuring that consumption, investment, and prices react in a gradual way to a shock. On the real side, consumption habits and quadratic costs prolong the adjustment of households consumption and investment, respectively. On the nominal side, quadratic costs make wages and prices sticky.[11]

In what follows, we report the equations describing main Home households' decisions (Sect. 2.2), Home capital goods producers (Sect. 2.3), Home intermediate sector (Sect. 2.4), monetary union-wide monetary policy (Sect. 2.5), and home fiscal policy (Sect. 2.6). Similar equations hold for REA households and fiscal policy (we state it when this is not the case). Finally, we report the calibration (Sect. 2.7).

2.2 Households

In each EA region there are three types of households: Ricardian, restricted, and HTM households. Each of them has a specific mass over a continuum: $0 < \lambda_{ric}, \lambda_{res}, \lambda_{HTM} < 1$ for Ricardian, restricted, and HTM households, respectively. Their sizes are such that their sum is equal to 1, so that the total mass of households is equal to the dimension of the country.[12] We consider a symmetric equilibrium. Thus there is a representative household and representative firm for each type of household and firm, respectively.

[11] See Rotemberg (1982).

[12] For instance, in the case of the Home country $n(\lambda_{ric} + \lambda_{res} + \lambda_{HTM}) = n$.

2.2.1 Ricardian Household

The representative Ricardian household maximizes her lifetime expected utility subject to the budget constraint. She invests in domestic short- and long-term sovereign bonds, riskless international short-term bonds, the latter are traded with Ricardian households of the other country. She owns domestic firms operating in the final and intermediate sectors (other than the capital producers), and holds (constant) shares of the domestic capital producer, together with restricted household and, thus, indirectly invests in domestic physical capital. The lifetime expected utility, in consumption C_{ric}, and labor L_{ric} is

$$E_t \left\{ \sum_{\tau=t}^{\infty} \beta_{ric}^{\tau} \left[\left(Z_{C,t} \frac{C_{ric,\tau} - bbC_{ric,\tau-1}}{1-\sigma} \right)^{1-\sigma} - \frac{L_{ric,\tau}^{1+\tau_L}}{1+\tau_L} \right] \right\}, \tag{1}$$

where E_t denotes the expectation conditional on information set at date t, $\beta_{ric} \in (0, 1)$ is the discount factor, $bb \in (0, 1)$ is the external habit parameter, $1/\sigma > 0$ is the elasticity of intertemporal substitution, $\tau_L > 0$ is the reciprocal of the Frisch elasticity of labor supply. The term $Z_{C,t}$ represents a consumption preference shock, that we use joint with other shocks to simulate the pandemic. The budget constraint is

$$\begin{aligned}
&B_{ric,t} + B_{ric,t}^{REA} + P_t^{long} B_{ric,t}^{long} \\
&= R_{t-1}^{B} B_{ric,t-1} + (1 - \Gamma_{B,t-1}) \left(R_{t-1}^{B,REA} B_{ric,t-1}^{REA} \right) \\
&+ \left(1 + \kappa^{long} P_t^{long} \right) B_{ric,t-1}^{long} + (1 - \tau_{w,t}) W_t L_t - \Gamma_{W,t} + \Pi_t^{prof} \\
&- (1 + \tau_{c,t}) P_{C,t} C_{ric,t} - TAX_t \\
&+ share_{k_{ric}} (1 - \tau_{k,t}) \left(R_t^K K_{t-1} - P_{I,t} I_t \right) \\
&- \frac{\phi_{ric,long}^{I}}{2} \left(P_t^{long} B_{ric,t}^{long} - share_{B_{ric}}^{long} \frac{\bar{P}^{long} \bar{B}^{long}}{n\lambda_{ric}} \right)^2 - \phi_{ric,long}^{II} P_t^{long} B_{ric,t}^{long},
\end{aligned} \tag{2}$$

where B_{ric}, B_{ric}^{REA}, and B_{ric}^{long} are the positions in domestic riskless one-period (short-term) nominal bonds, international riskless one-period (short-term) nominal bonds, and domestic long-term sovereign bonds, respectively. They are all denominated in euros. Bonds B_{ric} and B_{ric}^{REA} pay the (gross) the interest rates R^B and $R^{B,REA}$, respectively. The variable P^{long} is the price of domestic long-term domestic sovereign bonds. Following Woodford (2001), the bond is formalized as a perpetuity paying an exponentially decaying coupon $\kappa^{long} \in (0, 1]$. The implied gross interest rate is

$$R_t^{long} = \frac{1}{P_t^{long}} + \kappa^{long}. \tag{3}$$

The variable Π^{prof} represents profits, rebated to households in a lump-sum way, from ownership of domestic firms other than capital producers. The term P_C is the price of the final non-durable consumption goods. The variable $TAX > 0$ is lump-sum tax paid to the government. Parameters τ_c, τ_w, and τ_k are tax rates paid on consumption, labor and capital, respectively ($0 \leq \tau_c, \tau_w, \tau_k \leq 1$).

The parameter $share_{kric}$ is the share of capital goods producers held by the Ricardian households ($0 < share_{k_{ric}} < 1$). It multiplies profits rebated by capital producers (K is the domestic physical capital stock, R^K its return, I investment in physical capital and P_I its price).

The term Γ_B is the adjustment cost on the internationally traded bond, the parameters $\phi^I_{ric,long}, \phi^{II}_{ric,long} > 0$ in the budget constraint represent the adjustment costs on long-term sovereign bonds.[13]

The parameter $0 < share^{long}_{B_{ric}} < 1$ is the share of overall supply of domestic long-term sovereign bonds, $\bar{B}^{long}$, held in steady state by the Ricardian household, and $\bar{P}^{long}$ the price of the bond in steady state. The variables W and L_{ric} are the nominal wages and the labor supplied by the generic Ricardian household, respectively. The household sets the nominal wage under monopolistic competition, taking as given the demand for labor by domestic firms in the intermediate sector and subject to quadratic wage adjustment costs. The term Γ_W in the budget constraint is the wage quadratic adjustment cost paid in terms of the total wage bill.[14]

---

[13] Adjustment costs on asset positions of households are needed to make the model stationary, given the assumption of incomplete financial markets. The term Γ_B is defined as

$$\Gamma_{B,t} \equiv \phi_{B1} \frac{exp(\phi_{B2}[B^{REA}_{ric,t} - \bar{B}^{REA}_{ric}]) - 1}{exp(\phi_{B2}[B^{REA}_{ric,t} - \bar{B}^{REA}_{ric}]) + 1}, \tag{4}$$

where ϕ_{B1}, $\phi_{B2} > 0$ are parameters. The term $\bar{B}^{REA}_{ric}$ is the steady-state position of the representative Home Ricardian household in the market. See Benigno (2009).

[14] It is defined as

$$\Gamma_{W,t} \equiv \frac{\psi_W}{2} \left(\frac{W_t / W_{t-1}}{\Pi_{t-1}^{indw} \overline{\Pi}_{EA}^{1-indw}} - 1 \right)^2 W_t L_{ric,t}, \tag{5}$$

where the parameter $\psi_W > 0$ measures the degree of nominal wage rigidity, L_{ric} is the total amount of labor and $0 \leq ind_W \leq 1$ is a parameter that measures indexation to the previous-period (gross) price inflation and $1 - ind_W$ to the EA central bank (constant) gross inflation target.

The representative Ricardian household optimally chooses consumption, labor, short-and long-term bonds to maximize utility, subject to the budget constraint (Eq. 2) and to the demand for labor by firms in the intermediate sector. As the resulting first order conditions are standard, we do not report them to save on space.[15] Other households supply the same amount of working hours and get the same hourly wages as those of Ricardian households.

2.2.2 Restricted Household

The representative restricted household, with mass $0 \leq \lambda_{res} < 1$ in the Home population, maximizes a utility function similar to the one of the Ricardian households:[16]

$$E_t \left\{ \sum_{\tau=t}^{\infty} \beta_{res}^{\tau} \left[Z_{C,t} \left(\frac{C_{res,\tau} - bbC_{res,\tau-1}}{1-\sigma} \right)^{1-\sigma} - \frac{L_{res,\tau}^{1+\tau_L}}{1+\tau_L} \right] \right\}. \tag{6}$$

The restricted household invests in long-term sovereign bonds, holds constant shares of domestic capital goods producers and, thus, indirectly invests in domestic physical capital. The budget constraint is

$$\begin{aligned} P_t^{long} B_{res,t}^{long} &= P_t^{long} R_t^{long} B_{res,t-1}^{long} + (1-\tau_{w,t}) W_t L_{res,t} \\ &+ (1 - share_{k_{ric}})(1-\tau_{k,t}) \left(R_t^K K_{t-1} - P_{I,t} I_t \right) - (1+\tau_{c,t}) P_{C,t} C_{res,t} \\ &- \frac{\phi_{res,long}}{2} \left(P_t^{long} B_{res,t}^{long} - share_{B_{res}}^{long} \frac{\bar{P}^{long} \bar{B}^{long}}{n\lambda^{res}} \right)^2, \end{aligned} \tag{7}$$

where $(1 - share_{k_{ric}})$ is the share of capital goods producers held by the restricted households. The parameter $\phi_{res,long} > 0$ measures the adjustment cost on long-term sovereign bonds. The term $0 < share_{B_{res}}^{long} < 1$ is the share of (overall) long-term sovereign bonds held in steady state by the restricted household. She takes labor income as given, because both wage and hours worked are decided by the Ricardian household.

In the symmetric equilibrium the representative restricted household optimally chooses consumption and long-term sovereign bonds to maximize her utility subject to the budget constraint.

---

[15] They are available upon request. Asset choices imply no-arbitrage conditions, that, up to first order, equate the expected returns on the different assets. The optimization problem for the choice of the optimal amount of work offered is solved only by Ricardian households.

[16] The term $Z_{C,t}$ is the same consumption preference shock that enters the utility function of Ricardian households.

2.2.3 HTM Household

Following Gali et al. (2004), it assumed that there is a representative HTM household, with mass $0 \leq \lambda_{HTM} < 1$. She is subject to the budget constraint

$$(1+\tau_{c,t})P_{C,t}C_{HTM,t} = (1-\tau_{w,t})W_tL_t + TR_t. \tag{8}$$

In every period the household consumes the overall available income and gets lump-sum transfers ($TR_t > 0$) from the domestic government. She takes labor income as given, because both wage and hours worked are decided by the Ricardian household. In the simulated scenarios lump-sum transfers sustain HTM consumption when labor income decreases.

2.3 *Capital Goods Producers*

There is a continuum of capital producers having the same size as that of the regional economy and acting under perfect competition. The representative capital goods producer is owned by domestic Ricardian and restricted households. Its stochastic discount factor is therefore a weighted sum of the Ricardian and restricted households' stochastic discount factors, with weights equal to the corresponding shares of capital producers' ownership.

The capital accumulation law is

$$K_t = (1-\delta)K_{t-1} + Z_{I,t}\left(1 - AC_t^I\right)I_t, \tag{9}$$

where $0 < \delta < 1$ is the depreciation rate. The adjustment cost on investment, AC^I, is

$$AC_t^I \equiv \frac{\phi_I}{2}\left(\frac{I_t}{I_{t-1}} - 1\right)^2, \tag{10}$$

where $\phi_I > 0$ is a parameter. Investment I is a final non-tradable good, composed of intermediate tradable (domestic and imported) goods, its price is P_I.[17] Capital producers rent existing physical capital stock K_{t-1} in a perfectly competitive market at the nominal rate R_t^K to domestic firms producing intermediate goods. Profits are rebated in a lump-sum way to restricted and Ricardian households according to the corresponding shares $(1 - share_{k_{ric}})$ and $share_{k_{ric}}$, respectively.

[17] Because of the adjustment costs on investment, a "Tobin's Q" holds.

The representative capital producer optimally chooses the end-of-period capital K_t and investment I_t subject to the law of capital accumulation, the adjustment costs on investment, and taking all prices as given.

The presence of restricted households and capital producers introduces financial segmentation in the model and, thus, allows non-standard monetary policy measures, like the sovereign bond purchases by central bank, to have real effects.

Finally, the term $Z_{I,t}$ in the capital accumulation law is an investment-specific shock, one of the exogenous shocks that we use to model the direct effects of the pandemic on the economy.

2.4 *Intermediate Sector*

The intermediate goods are produced by firms under perfect competition, according to the production function

$$Y_t = K_{t-1}^{\gamma(1+Z_{\gamma,t})} L_t^{1-\gamma(1+Z_{\gamma,t})}, \tag{11}$$

where K_{t-1} and L_t are physical capital and labor respectively. The parameter γ, $(0 < \gamma < 1)$ is subject to a temporary positive shock, $Z_{\gamma,t}$ that represents a temporary change in technology conditions due to the government regulation in response to pandemic shocks. The interpretation is that firms are forced by the government to temporarily substitute capital for labor to adapt to the pandemic. For example, some workers are temporarily laid-off to respect imposed social distancing and those workers that continue to work have to receive additional equipment for safety reasons (safety devices, masks, glass or plastic screens, information technology equipment to work from home).

2.5 *Monetary Policy Rule*

We assume the following specification for the monetary-union wide monetary policy rule:

$$\frac{R_t}{\bar{R}} = max\left\{\frac{1}{\bar{R}}, \left(\frac{R_{t-1}}{\bar{R}}\right)^{\rho_r}\left(\frac{\pi_{EA,t}}{\bar{\pi}_{EA}}\right)^{(1-\rho_r)\rho_\pi}\left(\frac{y_{EA,t}}{y_{EA,t-1}}\right)^{(1-\rho_r)\rho_y}\right\}. \tag{12}$$

The rule describes how the central bank conducts its monetary policy. The variable R_t is the gross policy rate and $\bar{R}$ its steady-state value. The parameters $0 \leq \rho_r \leq 1$, $\rho_\pi > 0$, ρ_y measure the sensitivity of the policy rate to its lagged value, to (quarterly) gross inflation rate (in deviation from the target $\bar{\pi}^{EA}$), and to the quarterly gross growth rate of output $y_{EA,t}/y_{EA,t-1}$, respectively. The monetary union-wide CPI inflation rate $\pi_{EA,t}$ is a geometric average of Home and REA CPI inflation rates (respectively π_t and π_t^*) with weights equal to the correspondent country steady-state GDP shares. The monetary union output, denoted $y_{EA,t}$, is the sum of Home and REA GDP.[18] The *max* means that we take into account the (endogenous) ELB (R is the nominal monetary policy rate in gross terms, thus it is equal to 1 at the ELB).

2.6 Fiscal Sector

Fiscal policy is set in each bloc (Home and REA). The Home government budget constraint is

$$B_t - B_{t-1} R_{t-1}^B + P_t^{long} B_t^{long} - R_t^{long} P_t^{long} B_{t-1}^{long} = P_{H,t} G_t + TR_t - T_t - TAX_t \tag{13}$$

The variable G_t represents government purchases of goods and services (i.e. public spending for consumption). Consistent with the empirical evidence, G_t is fully biased towards the domestic intermediate good. Therefore, it is multiplied by the corresponding price index $P_{H,t}$.[19]

$TR_t > 0$ are lump-sum transfers to HTM households, and $TAX_t > 0$ are lump-sum taxes imposed on Ricardian households.

The same tax rates apply to every domestic Ricardian, restricted, and HTM household. Tax rates on labor income, capital income, and consumption are $\tau_t^w, \tau_t^k, \tau_t^c$, respectively ($0 \leq \tau_t^w, \tau_t^k, \tau_t^c \leq 1$). Total government revenues from distortionary taxation T_t are given by the identity

$$\begin{aligned} T_t \equiv\ & \tau_t^w W_t n L_t + \tau_t^k n R_t^k K_{t-1}((1 - share_{k_{ric}})\lambda_{res} + share_{k_{ric}} \lambda_{ric}) \\ & + \tau_t^c P_t n (\lambda_{ric} C_{ric,t} + \lambda_{res} C_{res,t} + \lambda_{HTM} C_{HTM,t}). \end{aligned} \tag{14}$$

The government follows a fiscal rule defined on lump-sum taxes TAX_t to bring the public debt as a percentage of domestic GDP, $b_G^s > 0$, in line with its long-run (steady-state) target $\bar{b}_G^s$. The fiscal rule is

$$\frac{tax_t}{\bar{tax}} = \left(\frac{b_{G,t}^s}{\bar{b}_G^s} \right)^{\phi_G}, \tag{15}$$

[18] The lagged interest rate ensures that the policy rate is adjusted smoothly and captures the idea that the central bank prefers to avoid large changes and reversals in its policy instrument.

[19] See Corsetti and Müller (2006).

where the parameter $\phi_G > 0$ calls for an increase (reduction) in lump-sum taxes as a ratio to GDP, tax, relative to its steady-state value $\bar{tax}$, whenever the current-period short-term public debt as a ratio to GDP, $b^s_{G,t}$, is above (below) the steady-state target, $\bar{b}^s_G$. Results somewhat depend on the fiscal instrument chosen to stabilize public debt and, in the case of taxation, on the extent to which it is distortionary. We choose lump-sum taxes to stabilize public finance as they are non-distortionary and, thus, allow for a "clean" evaluation of the macroeconomic effects of public transfers to HTM households and public consumption. Moreover, when simulating the model, the fiscal rule in each country is not active during the fiscal stimulus, i.e., the regional fiscal authorities keep lump-sum taxes paid by Ricardian households constant as a ratio to GDP. The rules are active after the discretionary stimulus, consistent with fiscal authorities stabilizing public debt in the medium and long run (after the stimulus is over). For simplicity, it is assumed that the changes in issued long-term sovereign bonds are proportional to the changes in issued short-term sovereign bonds. Moreover, all distortionary tax rates (τ^w, τ^k, τ^c) are kept constant at their corresponding steady-state levels in all simulations.

2.7 Calibration

The model is calibrated at quarterly frequency. For simplicity, it is assumed that the two regions are symmetric. The chosen calibration allows our model to adequately capture the dynamics of the main EA variables and is in line with those of Warne et al. (2008) and Gomes et al. (2010), that develop large-scale DSGE models of the EA. The only key departure from these contributions is the chosen value of the natural rate. In line with the low estimates for the EA natural rate reported by Neri and Gerali (2017), we calibrate the model so that the net natural rate is equal to 0 in steady state. The steady-state net annualized inflation rate is 2%. In our model, the (nominal) gross policy rate is, in steady state, equal to the ratio between gross inflation and the households' discount factor.[20] We set the discount factor of Ricardian households to 0.9998, as reported in Table 2. Thus, the (net) policy rate is around 2% as well.

Table 1 reports the (flexible-price) steady-state equilibrium. Private consumption, public consumption, investment, and imports are set to 59%, 21%, 20%, and 20% of GDP, respectively.[21]

Table 2 reports parameters regulating preferences and technology. The elasticity of intertemporal substitution is set to 1 (i.e., log preferences in consumption) The

[20] The economy gross growth rate is always set to 1.

[21] In our model, overall public spending is equal to the sum of public consumption, public transfers and interest payment on public debt. According to national accounting, public consumption is equal to the sum of purchases and public wages. In the model we do not distinguish among the last two items.

Table 1 Main variables

	Home	REA
Macroeconomic variables		
Private consumption	59	59
Public consumption	21	21
Investment	20	20
Imports	20	20
Imports of consumption goods	16	16
Imports of investment goods	4	4
Share of EA GDP	50	50
Inflation rate (%, annualized)	2	2
Financial variables		
Nominal short-term rate (%, annualized)	2	2
Nominal long-term rate (%, annualized)	2.3	2.3
Long-term public debt	100	100
Share held by Ricardian households	50	50
Share held by restricted households	50	50
Short-term public debt	6	6
Net foreign asset position	0	0

Note: REA = rest of the euro area. Public debt as % of annualized output; other variables are % of output

discount factor of restricted households is 0.999. The consumption habit parameter is set to 0.7. The Frisch labor elasticity is set to 0.5. The share of Ricardian, restricted, and HTM households are set to 0.55, 0.2, 0.25. Ricardian households hold a share of capital producers equal to 0.4, restricted households equal to 0.6.

For the production of intermediate goods, we assume a Cobb-Douglas production function. The elasticity of output to physical capital is 0.35 and the elasticity to labor is 0.65. The depreciation rate of physical capital to 0.025.

For final goods, the elasticity of substitution between domestic and imported intermediate goods is 1.5. The weight of the domestic intermediate good is 0.8.

Table 3 reports the markups and the elasticities of substitution among intermediate tradables and among labor varieties. They are set to 6 and 4.3, respectively, which correspond to steady-state mark-ups of 1.2 and 1.3.

Table 4 reports the adjustment costs. The investment adjustment cost is equal to 6. Concerning nominal rigidities, the parameter measuring the cost for adjusting the price of goods is set to 380. The one for adjusting nominal wages is set to 400. The parameter that measures the degree of indexation to previous-period inflation is set to 0.7 for both prices and wages.

Table 5 reports the parameters of the monetary policy and fiscal rule. For monetary policy, the response to inflation, ρ_π, is relatively large and equal to 1.7, consistent with the estimated value reported by Warne et al. (2008). The policy rate is adjusted slowly, given that the corresponding coefficient, ρ_r, is set to 0.87. The response to output growth, ρ_y, is set to 0.1. For fiscal policy, lump-sum taxes respond to public debt according to a coefficient set to 0.6.

Table 2 Preferences and technology

Parameter	Home	REA
Ricardian households discount factor $\beta_{ric}, \beta^*_{ric}$	0.9998	0.9998
Restricted' discount factor $\beta_{res}, \beta^*_{res}$	0.999	0.999
Intertemporal elasticity of substitution $1/\sigma$	1.0	1.0
Habit bb	0.7	0.7
Inverse of Frisch elasticity of labor supply τ	2.0	2.0
Share of households in population		
Ricardian households λ_{ric}	0.55	0.55
Restricted households λ_{res}	0.2	0.2
HTM households $1 - \lambda_{ric} - \lambda_{res}$	0.25	0.25
Share of households in capital producers		
Ricardian households $share_{k_{ric}}$	0.4	0.4
Restricted households $1 - share_{k_{ric}}$	0.6	0.6
Intermediate goods		
Depreciation rate of capital δ	0.025	0.025
Elasticity subst. btw. factors of production	1.0	1.0
Bias towards capital	0.35	0.35
Final consumption goods		
Elasticity subst. btw. dom. and imported goods	1.50	1.50
Bias towards domestic tradable goods	0.80	0.80
Final investment goods		
Elasticity subst. btw. dom. and imported goods	1.50	1.50
Bias towards domestic tradable goods	0.80	0.80

Note: REA = rest of the euro area. "*" refers to REA

Table 3 Gross markups

	Markups (elasticities of substitution)	
	Intermediate goods	Wages
Home	1.2 ($\theta_T = 6.0$)	1.33 ($\psi = 4.3$)
REA	1.2 ($\theta^*_T = 6.0$)	1.33 ($\psi^* = 4.3$)

Note: REA = rest of the euro area. "*" refers to REA

3 Simulated Scenarios

The first scenario simulates that both Home and REA are subject to the same Covid-19 shock, modelled as a combination of recessionary consumption-preference, investment-specific, and technology shocks lasting four quarters. The consumption-preference shock directly affects Ricardian and restricted households. The shocks are cross-country symmetric. The scenario is run under the alternative assumptions that the ELB does not constrain or, in the second scenario, constrains the monetary policy rate. The shocks are calibrated to obtain a decrease in Home and REA GDP of around 10% (trough level) if the ELB endogenously binds. In the third scenario, in response to the recessionary shocks, the Home fiscal authority raises

Table 4 Adjustment costs

Parameter	Home	REA
Ricardian households		
Long-term sovereign bond $\phi^{I}_{ric,long}$, $\phi^{I,*}_{ric,long}$	0.001	0.001
Long-term sovereign bond $\phi^{II}_{ric,long}$, $\phi^{II,*}_{ric,long}$	0.001	0.001
International bond ϕ_{B1}	0.05	–
International bond ϕ_{B2}	0.05	–
Resctricted households		
Long-term sovereign bond $\phi_{res,long}$, $\phi^{*}_{res\_long}$	0.001	0.001
Firms		
Physical capital ϕ_I, ϕ^*_I	6.0	6.0
Wage and prices		
Nominal wages κ_W, κ^*_W	400	400
Home intermediate tradable goods κ_H, κ^*_H	380	380
REA intermediate tradable goods κ_{REA}, κ^*_{REA}	380	380
Home price indexation to past inflation α_H, α^*_H	0.7	0.7
REA price index. to past inflation α_{REA}, α^*_{REA}	0.7	0.7
Wage indexation to past inflation α_W, α^*_W	0.7	0.7

Note: REA = rest of the euro area. "*" refers to REA

Table 5 Monetary and fiscal policy rules

Parameter	Home	REA	EA
Fiscal policy rule and tax rates			
ϕ_G, ϕ^*_G, ϕ^{EA}_G	0.6	0.6	0.6
τ_c, τ^*_c	0.2	0.2	–
τ_w, τ^*_w	0.4	0.4	–
τ_k, τ^*_k	0.3	0.3	–
Monetary policy rule			
Lagged interest rate ρ_r	–	–	0.87
Inflation ρ_π	–	–	1.70
Output growth ρ_y	–	–	0.10

Note: EA = euro area; REA = rest of the EA. "*" refers to REA

lump-sum transfers targeted to domestic HTM households and public spending for consumption for four quarters (in the fifth quarter, the fiscal items are newly set to their corresponding steady-state values). The increases in transfers and public consumption are financed by issuing public debt to domestic households. In the fourth scenario, both Home and REA fiscal authorities raise lump-sum transfers and public consumption for four quarters. The increases in transfers and public consumption are financed by issuing new public debt. We simulate, in the fifth scenario, that the fiscal authorities and the EA-wide central bank both respond to the shock. The central bank in the initial period of the simulation announces and implements a long-term sovereign bond purchase programme in the secondary market to keep the long-term interest rates close to their baseline levels. In the final two scenarios it is respectively assumed that the yield on Home sovereign bonds exogenously increases more than in the REA region (sixth scenario) and that the monetary union-wide fiscal response is implemented by a hypothetical EA-common fiscal authority (seventh scenario). Finally, in the sensitivity analysis, we simulate the policy mix under the assumption of a higher share of HTM households in the population.

In all scenarios the fiscal package is set, in each region, to 4% of baseline (steady-state) GDP, a value in line with the size of fiscal packages implemented in some EA countries. The increases in transfers and public consumption are, for simplicity, assumed to be 2% of baseline GDP each. The regional fiscal authorities keep lump-sum taxes paid by Ricardian households constant as a ratio to GDP during the first four quarters (the fiscal rules described by Eq. 15 are not active in those quarters). All scenarios are run under perfect foresight. Thus, all shocks but the initial one (i.e., the surprise) are perfectly anticipated by households and firms and the fiscal and monetary policy responses are fully credible.

4 Results

4.1 Recessionary Shock and the ELB

Figure 1 reports the responses of the main macroeconomic variables to the Covid-19 shock under the alternative assumptions on ELB constraining or not constraining the policy rate. Consumption and investment widely decrease in both Home and REA. Given the lower aggregate demand, firms reduce production and labor demand. Lower hours worked and real wage force HTM households to reduce their consumption that in each period is equal to wage income.[22] The presence of HTM households, thus, amplifies the negative effects of the shock on aggregate consumption. Lower aggregate demand in one region has negative spillovers to the other one, via lower imports.[23]

Moreover, lower aggregate demand induces firms to decrease prices in both regions. As a result, EA inflation decreases relative to the baseline. The central bank reacts to lower inflation and economic activity in the EA by reducing the policy rate, according to the Taylor rule (see Eq. 12). In the ELB-scenario, the policy rate hits the ELB.[24] The constant nominal policy rate and the lower expected inflation

[22] Absent the ELB, real wages mildly increase in the initial periods, then start declining and fall below their steady-state after around six quarters. The initial response reflects the relatively higher stickiness of nominal wages compared to prices. When the ELB binds, real wages immediately fall, because the recessionary effects of the shock are amplified.

[23] The overall effects are symmetric, given the nature of the shock and the calibration of the two regions.

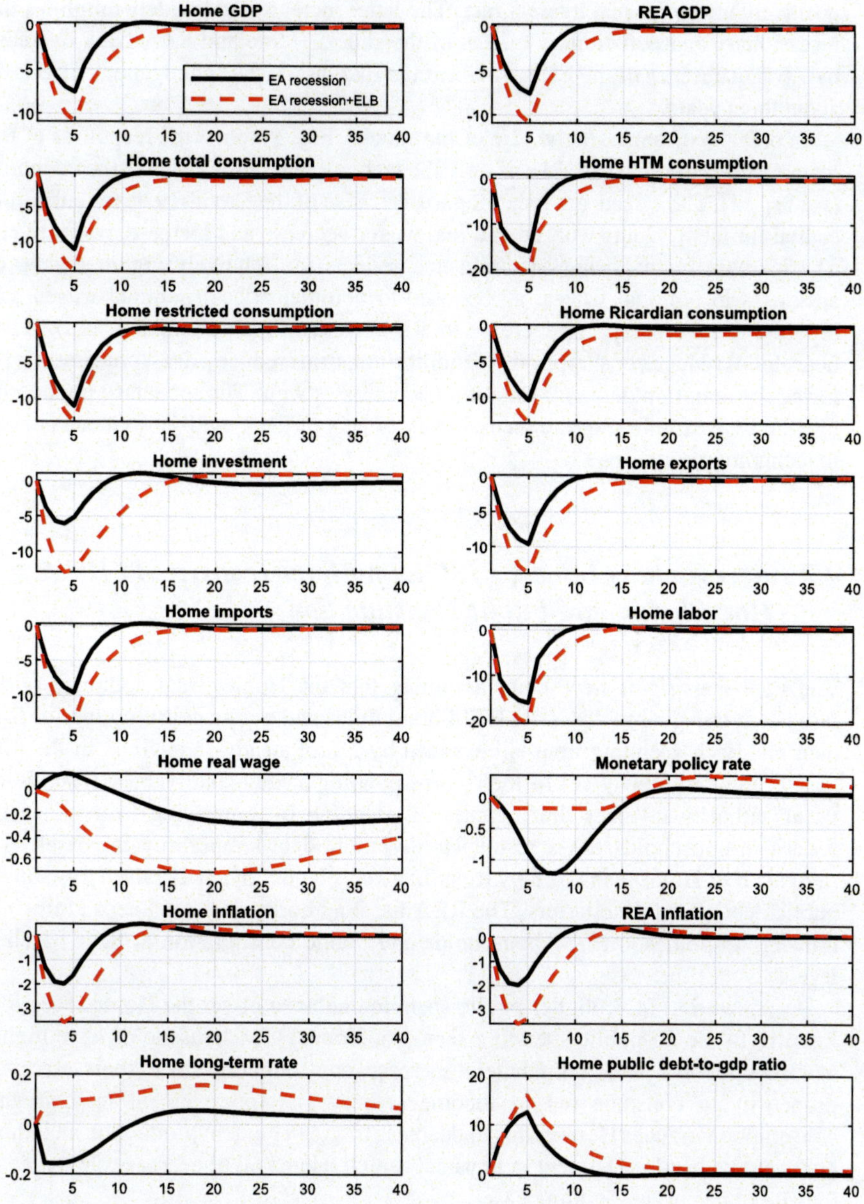

Fig. 1 Covid-19 shock and ELB. Notes: quarters on the horizontal axis; on the vertical axis, % deviations from the baseline; inflation and interest rate: annualized pp deviations; public debt: ratio of annualized GDP, pp deviations

positively affect the real interest rate. The latter increases and widely amplifies the recessionary and deflationary effects of the shock. Home and REA GDP decrease by 7.6% in absence of the ELB, 10.9% if the ELB binds. The endogenous ELB lasts about three years.

In order to disentangle the role of the shocks, Fig. 2 reports the responses of the main macroeconomic variables if only the technological shock affects the economy (see Eq. 11). The effects are recessionary. Because of the Covid-19, firms substitute capital for labor. Hours worked and real wages decrease and increase, respectively. The increase in real wages is mild and reflects the relatively higher degree of stickiness in nominal wages, as opposed to nominal prices (nominal wages, not reported to save on space, decrease to a lower extent than nominal prices). HTM households reduce consumption. In equilibrium, firms reduce prices, consistent with lower consumption demand. Inflation decreases as well. The monetary policy rate hits the ELB, amplifying the recessionary effects of the Covid-19-induced change in technology conditions.

4.2 *Recessionary Shock, ELB, Lump-Sum Transfers to HTM Households, and Public Consumption*

The ELB-scenario is newly run assuming that the Home fiscal authority raises lump-sum transfers to domestic HTM households and public consumption for four quarters. Each spending item is increased by 2% of steady-state GDP. In the fifth quarter they are newly set to their corresponding steady-state values. The Home fiscal authority finances the increase in spending by borrowing from domestic Ricardian households. As a result, Home public debt temporarily increases as a ratio to GDP. Home taxes paid by Ricardian households are newly raised to stabilize public debt after four quarters. The REA fiscal authority, instead, keeps lump-sum transfers to domestic HTM households and public consumption at their baseline levels.

As shown in Fig. 3, higher public spending helps to offset the Home recession. Relative to the no-public spending scenario, Home HTM households have higher available income and immediately increase consumption, since their marginal propensity to consume out of income is one. The improvement in aggregate consumption induces Home firms to decrease to a lower extent production and, thus, hours worked and investment in physical capital. Home GDP decreases less than in the no-Home public spending case.

The improvement in Home aggregate demand is matched not only by domestic production, but also by imports of goods and services produced by REA. Thus, the increase in Home public spending has positive spillovers to REA macroeconomic

[24] We assume that there is little space for the central bank to reduce the policy rate, consistent with the very low level of the EA policy rate at the moment of the pandemic shock.

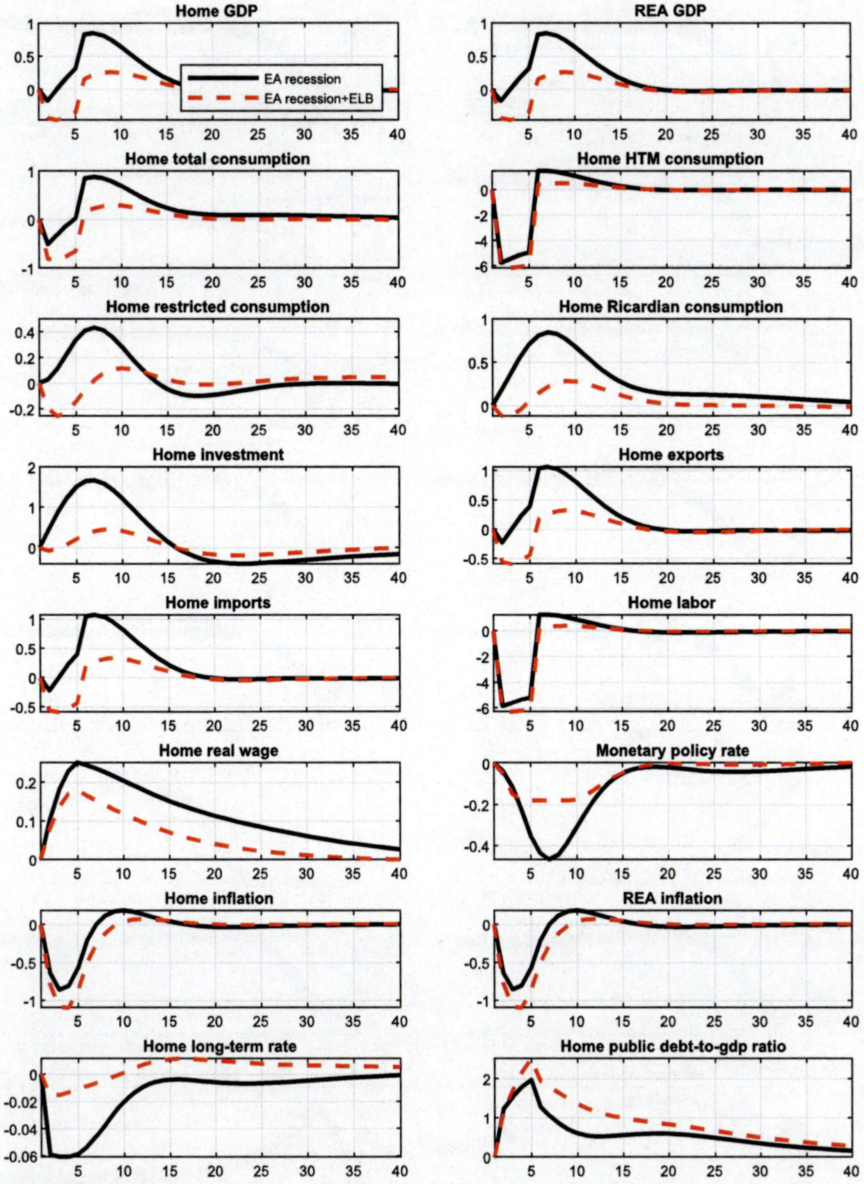

Fig. 2 Covid-19 shock and ELB: the role of the supply shock. Notes: quarters on the horizontal axis; on the vertical axis, % deviations from the baseline; inflation and interest rate: annualized pp deviations; public debt: ratio of annualized GDP, pp deviations

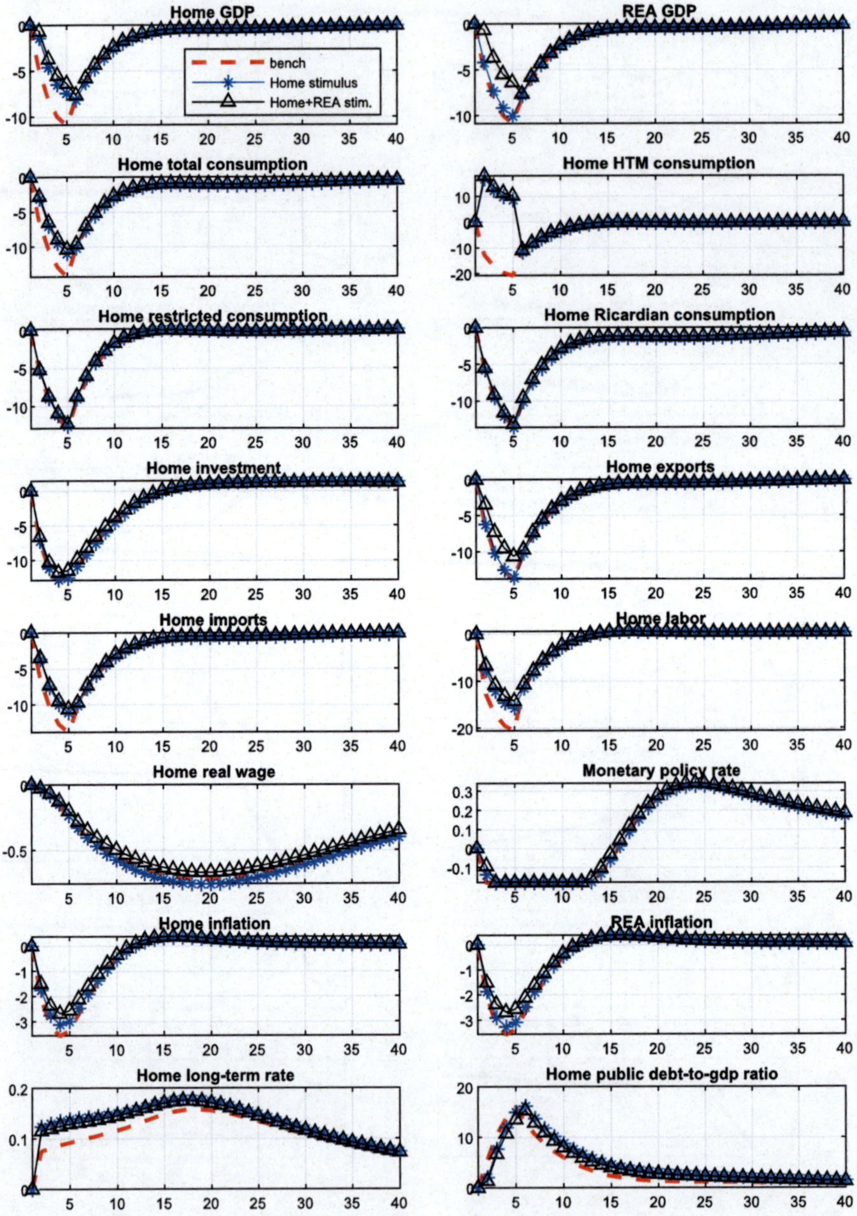

Fig. 3 Covid-19 shock and public spending. Notes: quarters on the horizontal axis; on the vertical axis, % deviations from the baseline; inflation and interest rate: annualized pp deviations; public debt: ratio of annualized GDP, pp deviations

Table 6 Implicit fiscal multipliers: real GDP response

Fiscal stimulus	Home multiplier	REA multiplier
Only Home	0.9	0.2
Home+REA	1.1	1.1
Home+REA+non-standard mon. pol.	1.4	1.4
Home+REA+increase in Home sovereign spread	0.8	1.0
Home+REA (supranational fiscal authority)	1.1	1.1

Note: REA = rest of the euro area
The implicit multiplier is computed as the difference, in the fourth quarter, between GDP with fiscal stimulus and GDP without fiscal stimulus, divided by the size of fiscal stimulus. In the fourth quarter the fiscal stimulus ends and, in the no-stimulus scenario, GDP achieves its trough

conditions. This is a consequence of the trade integration among the two regions (both Home and REA exports are set to 20% of the corresponding GDP). In the fourth quarter (last quarter of the stimulus implementation), Home GDP decreases by 7.4% and REA GDP by 10.1%, instead of 10.9% as in the case of no-stimulus. Thus, the implicit multipliers in the fourth quarter are 0.9 (Home GDP) and 0.2 (REA GDP), respectively (see Table 6).

Trade integration and the related expansionary spillovers could justify a simultaneous increase in both Home and REA transfers to domestic HTM households and public consumption implemented by the corresponding fiscal authorities. Figure 3 reports this case, i.e., it is assumed that also the REA fiscal authority exogenously targeted raises lump-sum transfers to domestic HTM households and public spending for consumption for four quarters. Relative to the Home-public spending case, REA GDP decreases to a lower extent, because of the expansionary impulse associated with domestic public spending and higher HTM households' consumption. The Home economy also benefits from the REA fiscal impulse. Home exports to REA decrease to lower extent, consistent with the lower decrease in REA aggregate demand. Home GDP and, thus, hours worked decrease less, inducing the Home fiscal authority to increase transfers and public debt to a lower extent. Home GDP decreases by less than in no-fiscal response and Home-fiscal response cases, respectively. In the fourth quarter, both Home and REA GDP decrease by 6.4%, instead of 10.9% (case of no fiscal stimulus). The implicit multipliers of Home and REA GDP are both equal to 1.1.

Overall, results suggest that a simultaneous cross-region fiscal response can somewhat offset the recessionary effects of the pandemic shock.

4.3 Long-Term Sovereign Bond Purchases by the Central Bank

We assess the interaction between fiscal and monetary policy at the ELB by assuming that both Home and REA fiscal authorities simultaneously increase fiscal transfers and public consumption spending and, at the same time, the central bank implements a long-term sovereign bond purchase programme to favour the achievement of the inflation target. The amount of purchases is calibrated to roughly keep the long-term rates unchanged at their baseline level. Purchases of Home and REA sovereign bonds are proportional to corresponding Home and REA (GDP) shares of EA GDP.[25]

Figure 4 shows the responses of the main variables. Home and REA GDP decrease to a much smaller extent than under the no purchase programme-case. In the fourth quarter, Home and REA GDP decrease by 5.2% instead of 10.9% as in the no-fiscal stimulus case. The implicit fiscal multiplier is 1.4 (see Table 6). The reason is that Home and REA long-term interest rates mildly decrease, because the prices of the bonds, inversely related to their yields, increase in correspondence of the higher demand by the central bank. Ricardian and restricted households sell their bonds to the central bank and, thus, substitute consumption and investment in physical capital, whose return is relatively high, for bonds. The additional monetary stimulus favors both Home and REA aggregate demand that increase relative to the case in which only the fiscal response to the Covid-19 shock is implemented. Trade intensity improves as well, in line with the higher aggregate demand. The expansionary fiscal and monetary policy mix, by providing a larger sustain to aggregate demand, also improves inflation dynamics. Inflation decreases to a lower extent in both regions. Following the central bank intervention, Home and REA inflation rates would be 0.7% points higher than in the case of only fiscal stimulus. Thus, the central bank starts to raise the policy rate out of the ELB earlier than in the other considered scenarios. Monetary policy normalization, i.e., the return to a standard Taylor rule away from the ELB, is faster.

Overall, the results suggest that, at the ELB, the expansionary fiscal and monetary policy mix is the most effective way to offset the effects of a large, symmetric EA-wide recessionary shock like the Covid-19.

4.4 Increase in Home Sovereign Spread

In the previous simulations, the increase in public debt to finance increased targeted transfers and public consumption spending was not accompanied by financial tensions. The interest rate on short-term public debt was at its baseline level, because it is equal to the monetary policy rate. The interest rate on long-term sovereign bond raised, consistent with the changes in fundamentals, i.e., the higher demand of funds by the government.

Our model features an endogenous spread (term-premium) between short- and long-term bonds, due to the adjustment cost on long-term bond positions paid by Ricardian households. However, the model does not explicitly feature sovereign risk. To introduce it, we now assume that the interest rate paid by the Home

[25] See Burlon et al. (2017) for a similar analysis applied to the increase in public investment in a monetary union.

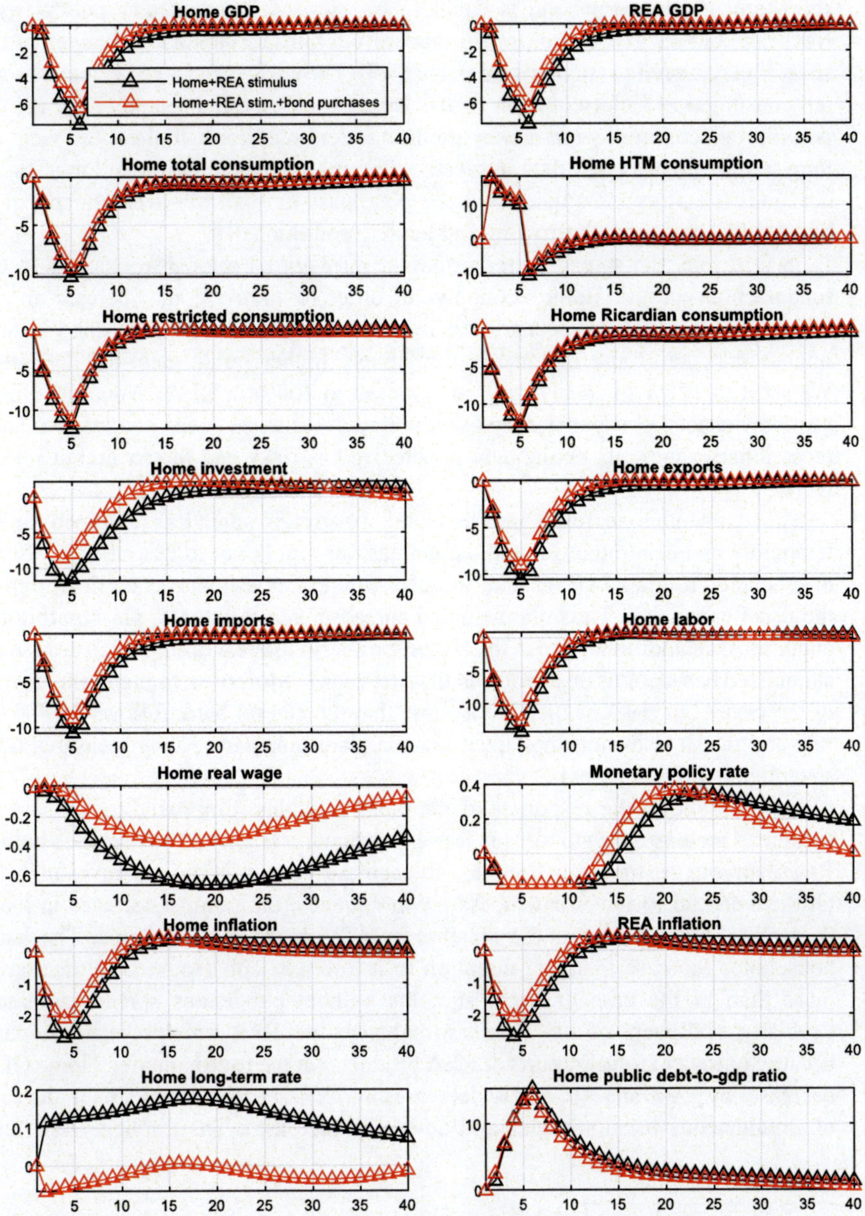

Fig. 4 Covid-19 shock, public spending, and sovereign bond purchases by central bank. Notes: quarters on the horizontal axis; on the vertical axis, % deviations from the baseline; inflation and interest rate: annualized pp deviations; public debt: ratio of annualized GDP, pp deviations

short-term government bond is equal to the sum of the monetary policy (risk-free) rate and an exogenous spread that we interpret as capturing changes in the sovereign risk premia (sovereign risk channel). The sovereign spread enters directly the consumption Euler equation of the Home Ricardian households and, via the no-arbitrage conditions implied by the first order conditions, it alters the yield on long-term bonds as well, thus indirectly affecting all consumption and investment decisions (i.e., there is a quick and complete pass-through of sovereign spread to households' and firms' borrowing and lending conditions).[26]

In principle, the spread increase may or may not be related to changes in the fundamentals of the Home economy. In order to motivate the increase in the sovereign spread, in this scenario we relax the symmetry assumption and instead impose that the Home region has a relatively higher public debt-to-GDP ratio. We set it to 125% in steady state, as opposed to 100% in REA. When the Home economy enacts an expansionary fiscal policy in response to the pandemic-related recessionary shock, its public debt is perceived as risky and the sovereign spread increases.

The exogenous increase in the Home sovereign spread is assumed to be temporary and of a rather limited amount, as our aim is not to describe the effects of a sovereign crisis but, instead, those of non-extreme financial tensions during the fiscal expansion. Thus, the assumed spread increase induces, via no-arbitrage conditions, an additional rise in the Home long-term interest rate equal to around 50 annualized basis points on average in the first year.[27] Moreover, to highlight the role of the sovereign risk channel, we assume that the central bank follows the Taylor rule and that it does not implement non-standard monetary policy measures (i.e., sovereign bond purchases).

Figure 5 shows the responses of the main variables. Compared to the case of no-spread increase, the stimulus is less expansionary. Higher Home spreads induce Ricardian and restricted households to increase consumption and investment in physical capital to lower extent. As a consequence, the relative increase in labor demand is lower and so is the increase in HTM households' income. The latter households increase their consumption to a lower extent. Home GDP decreases more than in the case of fiscal stimulus without exogenous spread increases. Crucially, spillovers of the Home stimulus to the REA are less expansionary, because of lower Home imports of REA products (in the fourth quarter, Home GDP decreases by 7.9% and REA GDP decreases by 7.1%, instead of 6.4% as in the case of simultaneous fiscal stimulus and no-spread increase). The implicit Home and

---

[26] Corsetti et al. (2014) propose a New Keynesian model of a two-region monetary union that accounts for the sovereign risk channel. They show that a combination of sovereign risk in one region and strongly procyclical fiscal policy at the aggregate level exacerbates the risk of belief-driven deflationary downturns.

[27] Laubach (2010) studies the dependence of the sovereign spread on the current level of fiscal indicators (such as the surplus-to-GDP or the debt-to-GDP ratios) for a panel of EA countries and finds that the elasticity is small or nil in non-crisis periods but increases rapidly and dramatically at times of financial stress.

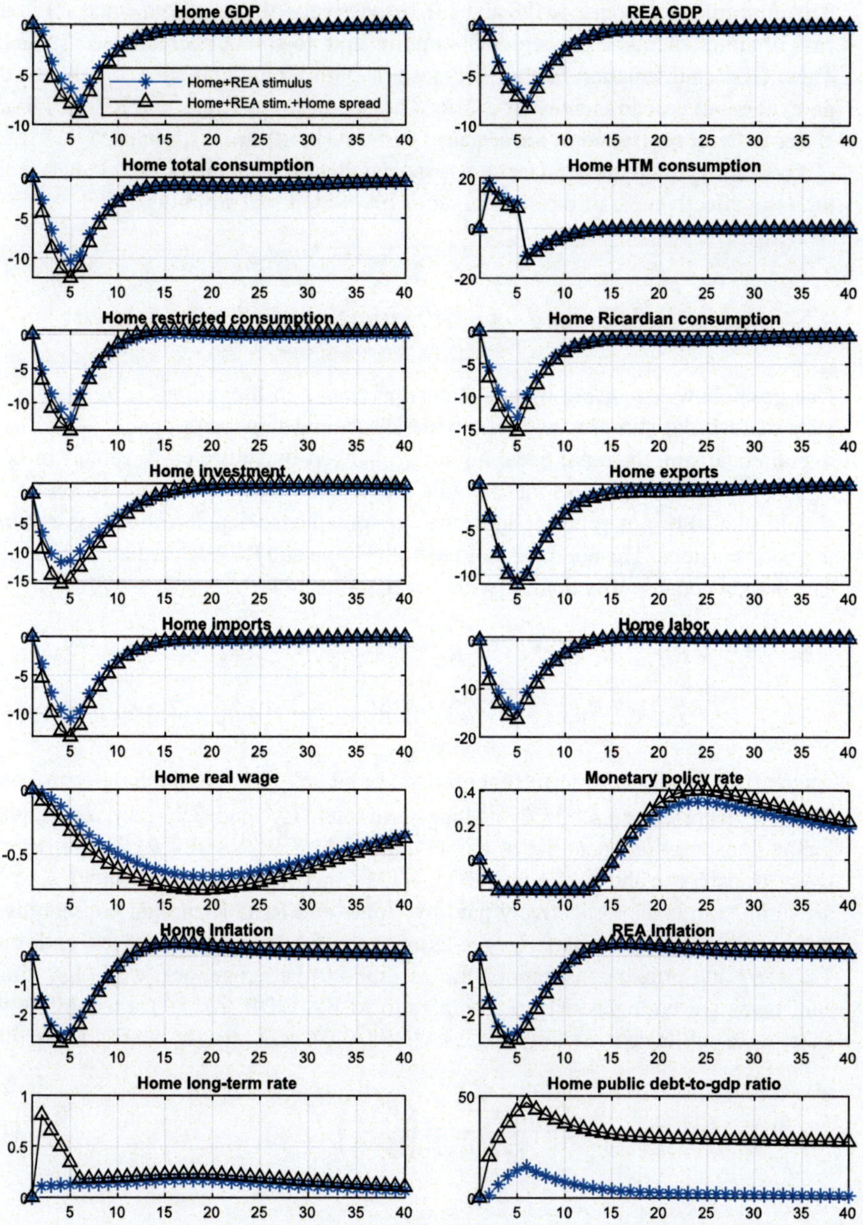

Fig. 5 Covid-19 shock, higher public spending, and spread. Notes: quarters on the horizontal axis; on the vertical axis, % deviations from the baseline; inflation and interest rate: annualized pp deviations; public debt: ratio of annualized GDP, pp deviations

REA multipliers decrease to 0.8 and 1.0, respectively (they are both equal 1.1 in the case of simultaneous cross-regional stimulus and no-spread increase, see Table 6). Thus, GDP and inflation further decrease in both Home and REA relative to the no-exogenous spread increase scenario. The decreases in Home and REA GDP are closer to those registered in the scenario without (joint) fiscal stimulus.[28]

Overall, regional financial tensions associated with local public debt issuance can limit the effectiveness of the simultaneous EA-wide fiscal stimulus.

4.5 Public Debt Issued by a Supranational Fiscal Authority

One possible way to avoid financial tensions in one of the regions is to finance the very same fiscal stimulus with EA-wide short- and long-term bonds, issued by a hypothetical supranational fiscal authority, backed by future tax revenues in both regions.[29] Thus, as long as these bonds are perceived as "safe" by investors, they should plausibly not generate increases in spread associated with region-specific financial tensions. The bonds are sold to both Home and REA Ricardian households. The budget constraint of the EA-wide fiscal authority is

$$B_{G,t}^{EA} - B_{G,t-1}^{EA} R_t + P_t^{EA,long} B_{G,t}^{EA,long} - P_t^{EA,long} R_t^{EA,long} B_{G,t-1}^{EA,long}$$
$$= TR_{H,t}^{EA} + TR_{REA,t}^{EA} + G_{H,t}^{EA} + G_{REA,t}^{EA} - TAX_{H,t}^{EA} - TAX_{REA,t}^{EA}, \quad (16)$$

where B_G^{EA} is the short-term (one-period) bond, $B_G^{EA,long}$ is the long-term bond, $P^{EA,long}$ its price and $R^{EA,long}$ its long-term rate, G_H^{EA} and G_{REA}^{EA} are respectively public consumption spending in Home and REA, TR_H^{EA} and TR_{REA}^{EA} are respectively transfers to the Home and REA HTM households, TAX_H^{EA} and TAX_{REA}^{EA} are lump-sum taxes respectively paid by Home and REA Ricardian households to their government and rebated by the latter to the EA-supranational fiscal authority. Transfers and public consumption are assumed to be exogenous, while EA lump-sum taxes are endogenously set, as a ratio to EA GDP (tax^{EA}), to stabilize the short-term public debt, as a ratio to EA GDP (b_G^{EA}), according to the following rule:

$$\frac{tax_t^{EA}}{\overline{tax}^{EA}} = \left(\frac{b_{G,t}^{EA}}{\bar{b}_G^{EA}} \right)^{\phi_G^{EA}}, \quad (17)$$

[28] The reduction in the fiscal multiplier would be larger with a larger and more persistent increase in the sovereign spread, as in the case of a sovereign crisis. See Gerali et al. (2018) for an evaluation of the sovereign-risk channel during the European sovereign crisis. See Locarno et al. (2013) for an analysis of the sovereign risk channel and fiscal multipliers.

[29] We do not consider the case of central bank intervening in the secondary markets for monetary policy purposes in response to financial tensions. Instead, we focus on the design of the supranational fiscal policy.

where $\overline{tax}^{EA}$ and $\bar{b}_G^{EA}$ are the steady-state values of the taxes and short-term public debt (ratio to EA GDP), respectively. Long-term bond issuance is such that the change in the value of long-term bonds is the same as the change in the value of short-term bonds, both as a ratio to EA GDP. All fiscal items of the EA supranational authority are set to zero in steady state. The term $\phi_G^{EA} > 0$ is a parameter, set to 0.6. Taxes are paid by each country according to the corresponding (GDP) share of EA GDP. The rule is not active during the four-quarter EA-wide fiscal stimulus and is calibrated like the national fiscal rules (see Eq. 15). Moreover, it is assumed that national fiscal authorities do not raise transfers to HTM and public consumption, since the expansionary fiscal policy response to the common shock is now delegated to the EA-wide fiscal authority.

Figure 6 shows the results. They are similar to those obtained if the transfers and public consumption are simultaneously raised by national fiscal authorities and the Home spread does not rise. The reason is that the amount and distribution of fiscal resources is the same in both cases and that Ricardian households have access to multiple financial markets to smooth the effects on consumption of the raise in taxation. Thus, the equilibrium is essentially the same. Macroeconomic conditions improve relative to the case of the stimulus financed by issuing national public debt when the Home spread increases.

All in all, a fiscal stimulus financed by issuing EA-wide bonds can be rather effective as long as the bonds are perceived as safe, i.e., the supranational fiscal authority makes a credible commitment to pay back its debt by raising future taxes.

4.6 Sensitivity: Higher Share of HTM Households

We assess the effectiveness of the mix of (1) non-standard monetary policy and (2) cross-region simultaneous fiscal policy under the assumption that the share of HTM households in each region is 50% of the population, instead of 25%.

Figure 7 reports the results. Home and REA GDP decrease to a slightly lower extent if the share of HTM households is higher. The higher share of HTM households implies that consumption of each HTM household increases by less, because the given amount of transfers is now distributed to a larger share of HTM households. However, aggregate demand decreases slightly less and so does economic activity. Inflation rate decreases to a lower extent and the ELB lasts less periods.

Overall, results suggest that the policy mix is effective in an environment, like the pandemic one, that is likely to be characterized by a high share of households featuring lack of access to financial markets.

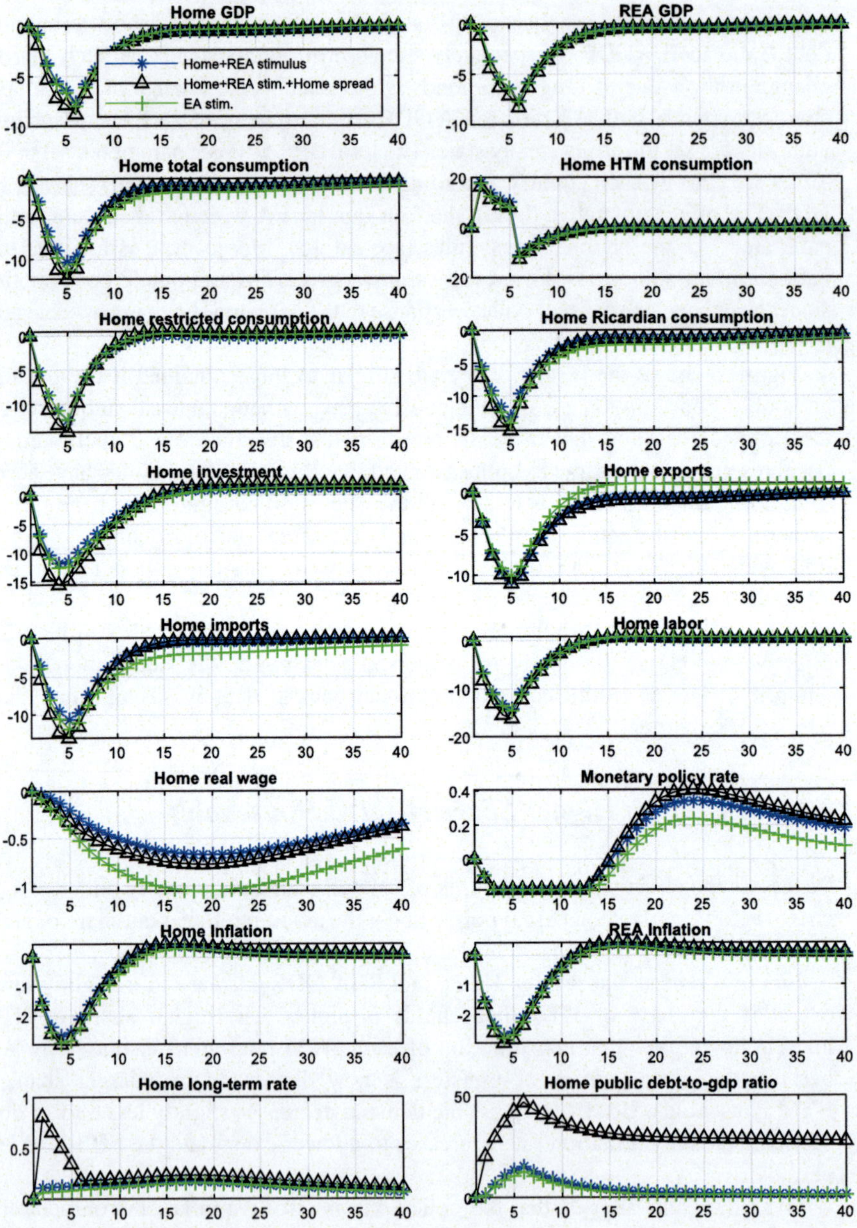

Fig. 6 Covid-19 shock and supranational fiscal authority's public spending. Notes: quarters on the horizontal axis; on the vertical axis, % deviations from the baseline; inflation and interest rate: annualized pp deviations; public debt: ratio of annualized GDP, pp deviations

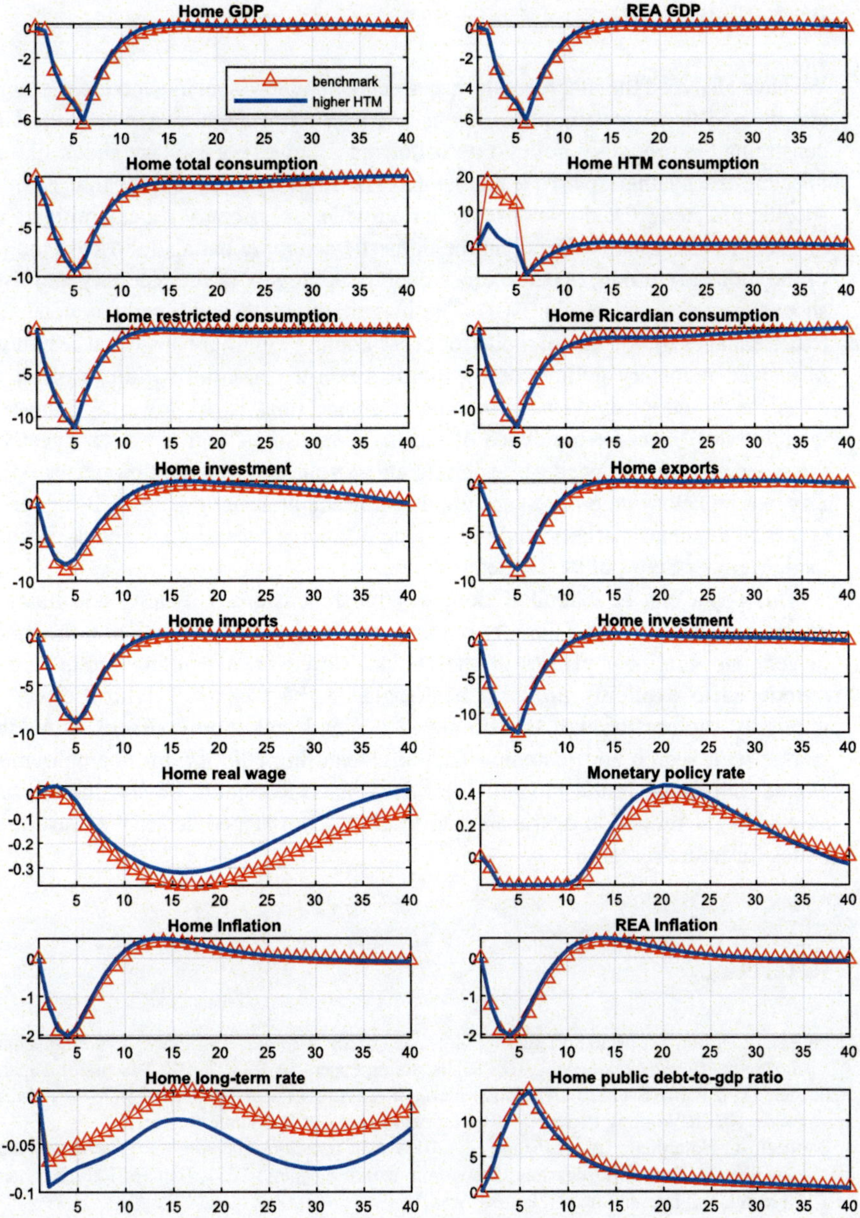

Fig. 7 Sensitivity: higher HTM households' share. Notes: quarters on the horizontal axis; on the vertical axis, % deviations from the baseline; inflation and interest rate: annualized pp deviations; public debt: ratio of annualized GDP, pp deviations

5 Conclusions

We have analyzed the macroeconomic effects of country-specific and cross-country coordinated fiscal and monetary measures in a monetary union where the ELB constrains the monetary policy rate following a large recessionary shock like the one implied by the Covid-19 pandemic. The main results suggest that country-specific unilateral fiscal responses to union-wide recessionary shocks mitigate not only the (recessionary) effects on the domestic economy but also those on the rest of the monetary union, because cross-country spillovers of recessionary and fiscal shocks are amplified by the ELB. The magnified size of spillovers, associated to trade-leakages in our model, calls for cross-country simultaneous fiscal responses. Moreover, monetary policy could provide a non-trivial contribution to offset the recession by adopting an accommodative stance (that is, by lowering long-term interest rates) in correspondence of the fiscal measures. Our results suggest that the relevance and the need of designing an appropriate fiscal and monetary policy mix in a monetary union are very important in the presence of the ELB, imperfect access to financial markets, and in the face of a large recessionary shock common to all Member States of the monetary union.

This paper can be extended along several dimensions. Liquidity and financial constraints, possibly occasionally binding, can be explicitly included in the model to generate nonlinear effects of the shock. Moreover, a banking sector can be introduced to explicitly model a bank balance sheet channel, whose effect we implicitly capture through the simulated demand and supply shocks.[30] A labor market with search and matching frictions, featuring equilibrium unemployment, can be introduced in the model. Other fiscal measures could be considered, such as a labor tax reduction or transfers to liquidity-constrained firms. We leave these issues for future research.

References

Balleer, A., Link, S., Menkhoff, M., & Zorn, P. (2020). *Demand or supply? Price adjustment during the Covid-19 pandemic*. CEPR Discussion Papers 14907, C.E.P.R. Discussion Papers.

Baqaee, D., & Farhi, E. (2020). *Nonlinear production networks with an application to the Covid-19 crisis*. NBER Working Papers 27281, National Bureau of Economic Research.

Bartocci, A., Notarpietro, A., & Pisani, M. (2019). *Non-standard monetary policy measures in the new normal*. Temi di discussione (Economic working papers) 1251, Bank of Italy, Economic Research and International Relations Area.

[30] Lower asset prices could amplify the propagation of the shocks via the banks' balance sheet, in particular if the policy rate is at the ELB, while, to the opposite, non-standard measures like central bank asset purchases could favor banks' balance sheet by sustaining asset prices. See Bartocci et al. (2019) for a model evaluating the impact of central bank asset purchases on the banking sector.

Bartocci, A., Burlon, L., Notarpietro, A., & Pisani, M.: *Macroeconomic effects of non-standard monetary policy measures in the euro area: The role of corporate bond purchases*. Temi di discussione (Economic working papers) 1136, Bank of Italy, Economic Research and International Relations Area.

Bayer, C., Born, B., Luetticke, R., & Muller, G. (2020). *The coronavirus stimulus package: How large is the transfer multiplier?*. Discussion Paper 14600, CEPR.

Benigno, P. (2004). Optimal monetary policy in a currency area. *Journal of International Economics, 63*(2), 293–320.

Benigno, P. (2009). Price stability with imperfect financial integration. *Journal of Money, Credit and Banking, 41*(s1), 121–149.

Bianchi, F., Faccini, R., & Melosi, L. (2020). *Monetary and fiscal policies in times of large debt: Unity is strength.*' NBER Working Papers 27112, National Bureau of Economic Research.

Brinca, P., Duarte, J. B., & Fariae-Castro, M. (2020). *Measuring sectoral supply and demand shocks during COVID-19*. Working Papers 2020-011, Federal Reserve Bank of St. Louis.

Burlon, L., Locarno, A., Notarpietro, A., & Pisani, M. (2017). *Public investment and monetary policy stance in the euro area*. Temi di discussione (Economic working papers) 1150, Bank of Italy, Economic Research and International Relations Area.

Chen, H., Cúrdia, V., & Ferrero, A. (2012). The macroeconomic effects of large-scale asset purchase programmes. *Economic Journal, 122*(564), F289–F315.

Coenen, G., McAdam, P., & Straub, R. (2008). Tax reform and labour-market performance in the euro area: A simulation-based analysis using the New Area-Wide Model. *Journal of Economic Dynamics and Control, 32*(8), 2543–2583.

Coenen, G., Montes-Galdon, C., & Smets, F. (2020). *Effects of state-dependent forward guidance, large-scale asset purchases and fiscal stimulus in a low-interest-rate environment*. Working Paper Series 2352, European Central Bank.

Coenen, G., Erceg, C. J., Freedman, C., Furceri, D., Kumhof, M., Lalonde, R., Laxton, D., Lindé, J., Mourougane, A., Muir, D., Mursula, S., de Resende, C., Roberts, J., Roeger, W., Snudden, S., Trabandt, M., & in't Veld, J. (2012). Effects of fiscal stimulus in structural models. *American Economic Journal: Macroeconomics, 4*(1), 22–68.

Corsetti, G., & Müller, G. J. (2006). Twin deficits: squaring theory, evidence and common sense. *Economic Policy, 21*(48), 597–638.

Corsetti, G, Kuester, K., Meier, A., & Müller, G. J. (2014). Sovereign risk and belief-driven fluctuations in the euro area. *Journal of Monetary Economics*, 2014, *61* (C), 53–73.

Cova, P., Pagano, P., Notarpietro, A., & Pisani, M. (2017). *Secular stagnation, R&D, public investment and monetary policy: A global-model perspective*. Temi di discussione (Economic working papers) 1156, Bank of Italy, Economic Research and International Relations Area.

Eichenbaum, M. S., Rebelo, S., & Trabandt, M. (2020). *Epidemics in the neoclassical and new Keynesian models*. NBER Working Papers 27430, National Bureau of Economic Research.

Farhi, E., & Werning, I. (2017). Fiscal unions. *American Economic Review, 107*(12), 3788–3834.

Faria-e-Castro, M. (2020). *Fiscal policy during a pandemic*. Working Papers 2020-006, Federal Reserve Bank of St. Louis.

Gali, J., & Monacelli, T. (2008). Optimal monetary and fiscal policy in a currency union. *Journal of International Economics, 76*(1), 116–132.

Gali, J., Lopez-Salido, J. D., & Valles, J. (2004). *Rule-of-thumb consumers and the design of interest rate rules*. NBER Working Papers 10392, National Bureau of Economic Research.

Gerali, A., Locarno, A., Notarpietro, A., & Pisani, M. (2018). The sovereign crisis and Italy's potential output. *Journal of Policy Modeling, 40*(2), 418–433.

Gomes, S., Jacquinot, P., & Pisani, M. (2010). *The EAGLE. A model for policy analysis of macroeconomic interdependence in the Euro area*. Working Paper Series 1195, European Central Bank.

Guerrieri, V., Lorenzoni, G., Straub, L., & Werning, I. (2020). *Macroeconomic implications of COVID-19: Can negative supply shocks cause demand shortages?*. NBER Working Papers 26918, National Bureau of Economic Research.

IMF. (2020). *Chapter 2: Dissecting the Economic Effects* . World Economic Outlook, International Monetary Fund.

Laubach, T. (2010). Fiscal policy and interest rates: The role of sovereign default risk. In *NBER International Seminar on Macroeconomics 2010*. NBER Chapters, National Bureau of Economic Research (pp. 7–29).

Locarno, A., Notarpietro, A., & Pisani, M. (2013). *Sovereign risk, monetary policy and fiscal multipliers: A structural model-based assessment*. Temi di discussione (Economic working papers) 943, Bank of Italy, Economic Research and International Relations Area.

Neri, S., & Gerali, A. (2017). *Natural rates across the Atlantic*. Temi di discussione (Economic working papers) 1140, Bank of Italy, Economic Research and International Relations Area.

Pietrunti, M. (2020). *The impact of a coordinated monetary and fiscal policy reaction to a pandemic shock*. mimeo.

Rotemberg, J. J. (1982). Monopolistic price adjustment and aggregate output. *Review of Economic Studies*, *49*(4), 517–31.

Warne, A., Coenen, G., & Christoffel, K. (2008). *The new area-wide model of the euro area: a micro-founded open-economy model for forecasting and policy analysis*. Working Paper Series 944, European Central Bank.

Woodford, M. (2001). Fiscal requirements for price stability. *Journal of Money, Credit and Banking*, *33*(3), 669–728.

Policy Mix During a Pandemic Crisis: A Review of the Debate on Monetary and Fiscal Responses and the Legacy for the Future

Giuseppe Ferrero, Massimiliano Pisani, and Martino Tasso

JEL Classification: E52, E58, E62, F01

1 Introduction and Main Policy Messages[1]

At the beginning of 2020, COVID-19 started spreading around the world. The consequences of the global health crisis have been dramatic. So far, more than 150 million people have fallen ill and about 3.2 million have died. The pandemic and the related lockdown measures enforced by governments depressed both aggregate demand and supply. In most countries, economic activity fell sharply in the first half of 2020, triggering severe increases in unemployment, a collapse of business sales and severe liquidity strains, which disproportionately affected small and medium-sized enterprises and brought important financial market segments to the verge of collapse (Visco, 2020). GDP partially recovered in the summer of 2020, as restrictions on economic activity and mobility were progressively eased, but it decreased in the final part of the year. At the time of writing this paper, the shock is

[1] The views expressed in this paper are those of the authors and do not necessarily reflect those of the Bank of Italy. We would like to thank Fabrizio Balassone, Andrea Brandolini, Fabio Busetti, Giacomo Caracciolo, Francesco Caprioli, Paolo Del Giovane, Silvia Delrio, Pietro Rizza, and Stefania Zotteri for their useful suggestions. All remaining errors are our own. The cutoff date for data used in this paper is April 2021. Lucia Esposito, Sergio Santoro, and Stefania Villa contributed to the boxes contained in this paper.

G. Ferrero · M. Pisani · M. Tasso (✉)
Banca d'Italia, Rome, Italy
e-mail: giuseppe.ferrero@bancaditalia.it; massimiliano.pisani@bancaditalia.it; martino.tasso@bancaditalia.it

L. Paganetto (ed.), *Economic Challenges for Europe After the Pandemic*, Springer Proceedings in Business and Economics,
https://doi.org/10.1007/978-3-031-10302-5_11

not over yet. Even if vaccines continue to be rolled out during 2021, the uncertainty is still high and constitutes a drag on a sustained recovery in the near future.

The extraordinary worsening of the economic outlook required policymakers to intervene in a timely and comprehensive manner. Governments introduced measures to relieve household and firm liquidity needs—such as debt moratoriums and temporary wage supplementation schemes—and to facilitate their access to new financing—such as loan guarantee programmes. The crisis came at a time when interest rates were persistently low in all the advanced economies, thus leaving limited scope for conventional monetary policy to counter deep deflationary shocks. Central banks dusted off and extended, both qualitatively and quantitatively, the toolkit developed during the global financial crisis and, in the euro area, the sovereign debt crisis. To support the essential role of banks in financing the real economy, bank supervisors used the flexibilities embedded in regulation and accounting standards to allow banks to use the capital and liquidity buffers.

The need to contrast the economic effects of the pandemic sparked an intense public debate, focusing on two questions: what are the most appropriate responses of monetary and fiscal policy in order to preserve income, consumption, investment, employment, production and price stability in the short and medium term? What are the implications of the measures adopted, in terms of independence of monetary policy, financial stability, and sustainability of public debt in the medium to long term?

The objective of this paper is to review the debate on the measures taken in response to the pandemic shock and the implications these measures could have for central banks and governments in the future. In doing this, we take into account how the previous crises—the global financial crisis and, in the euro area, the sovereign debt crisis—had already shaped the academic and policy debate about the role of monetary and fiscal policy.

Our logical starting point is that the worldwide macroeconomic environment was already changing toward a "new normal", when the COVID-19 crisis broke out. Both (i) structural changes in technology, preferences, and demographics and (ii) factors related to the global financial and the sovereign debt crises in Europe contributed to the progressive reduction of real interest rates and, especially in the last decade, to historically low growth and inflation rates in many advanced economies.

According to the empirical evidence and rapidly growing theoretical literature, the COVID-19 pandemic adds further downward pressure on aggregate demand and, thus, economic activity, income, inflation, and interest rates. Firms and households could face binding income and liquidity constraints, which would greatly limit their investment and consumption choices, respectively. Moreover, uncertainty about epidemiological developments and therefore economic prospects, fuelling households' and firms' anxiety, reduces their propensity to consume and invest and increases their precautionary savings. The longer the contraction in employment and investments lasts, the higher the probability that hysteresis effects materialize: the slowdown in human and physical capital accumulation may persistently reduce aggregate supply, productivity and, thus, potential output and the natural interest rate (which could be defined as the real short-term interest rate that equates the demand and supply of funds when output is at its potential).

Several policy messages can be inferred from the literature and from the analysis of the macroeconomic effects of the pandemic shock.

First, the combined effort of monetary and fiscal policies across the advanced economies was a key element of the emergency phase of the COVID-19 crisis in order to limit the economic damages by sustaining aggregate income, liquidity, and, thus, aggregate demand. These policies also set the stage for a subsequent recovery. The multi-front policy response to the COVID-19 crisis prevented the drying-up of liquidity and a credit crunch that could have led to a large wave of defaults, thus warding off a deflationary spiral with probable profound consequences for economic and financial stability.

Second, within their respective mandates, both fiscal and monetary authorities have an interest in cushioning the blow of the crisis and fostering the recovery. Thus, their incentives are currently aligned. This is reinforced by important complementarities. As discussed in the text of this paper, for example, the liquidity provided by central banks and the government loans guarantees programmes reinforce each other, supporting the flow of credit to hard-hit firms. Expansionary monetary policies, implemented with the aim of countering deflationary risks, avert market tensions and reduce funding costs not only for households and firms but also for governments. Therefore, they indirectly favour bold public supports, which could be properly targeted towards those most vulnerable to the consequences of the health crisis and with tighter borrowing and liquidity constraints.

Third, once the emergency phase is over and the spread of the vaccine is sufficiently wide, the recovery needs to be strong and persistent in order to swiftly reduce unemployment and potential vulnerabilities in the sovereign, financial and corporate sectors. It should be a global recovery that positively affects both aggregate demand and aggregate supply (i.e. potential output). In this phase, fiscal and monetary authorities should continue to provide support, readily adapting their action to the evolving situation. Withdrawing support too early and failing to act promptly, if needed, could jeopardize the recovery, exacerbate social disruptions and, ultimately, frustrate the efforts made so far to contain the economic damage caused by the pandemic.

Fourth, in order to achieve a strong global recovery, it is crucial that policymakers implement a policy mix based on accommodative monetary policy measures (if consistent with central bank targets) and a re-modulation of public spending towards public investment. The worldwide increase in public investment in infrastructure, human capital, and in research and development is the most effective measure to be implemented, in particular if, as it seems to be the case, real (and nominal) interest rates will remain at low levels for a prolonged period of time. Higher public investment in specific sectors could, among other things, contribute to improving health conditions and help reduce the environmental problems associated with carbon emissions, and favour greater digitalization of the economy around the globe.

Fifth, cross-country fiscal coordination could help to maximize the impact on the global recovery if countries with lower public debt exploit their larger fiscal space to provide additional stimulus to the domestic economy and, via trade spillovers, to the economy of their trading partners.

Sixth, there should not be any complacency about high private and public debt. The increase in both private and public borrowing in response to the pandemic was necessary. A solid recovery will favour private sector deleveraging. Once the recovery is firmly under way, those governments facing a large public debt and little fiscal space should implement, gradually, plans to achieve primary fiscal surpluses, and exploit the high growth rate of the economy and low interest rates to curb public debt. Reducing government current expenditure in favour of higher public investment and lower taxation of productive factors could be an appropriate strategy to induce both an increase in growth and the reduction of public debt. Given the different levels of national public debt and the different degrees of fiscal spaces, international coordination is necessary to maximize global growth and minimize global financial risks.

The remaining parts of the paper are organised as follows. Section 2 focuses on the macroeconomic implications of the COVID-19 shock. Section 3 describes the monetary and fiscal policy responses implemented at global level to increase resilience during the emergency phase. Section 4 discusses the legacy of the COVID-19 shock on the monetary and fiscal policy mix and how this mix should be designed in order to sustain the worldwide recovery once the emergency phase has come to an end. Section 5 concludes.

2 Macroeconomic Effects of the COVID-19 Global Health Crisis: Its Sectoral Propagation and Hysteresis Effects

The COVID-19 shock is a global health crisis that has simultaneously and abruptly affected all countries, causing a large contraction in economic activity.

A key distinctive factor of the COVID-19-induced recession is its sectoral composition, because the pandemic negatively affects some sectors more than others. Moreover, it is likely to reduce accumulation of human capital and knowledge, because of both the job destruction and of the obstacles to the normal operation of schools and universities to contain the diffusion of the virus. Because of slower knowledge and capital accumulation, the shock, even if it is transitory, can have negative long-run effects on potential output (hysteresis or "scarring" effects) and the natural interest rate. These effects can slow down the return to the pre-crisis macroeconomic conditions.

In what follows it is initially described how the COVID-19 shock propagates from the most hit sectors to the rest of the economy. Subsequently, possible hysteresis mechanisms induced by the pandemic are illustrated.

2.1 Cross-Sector Propagation of the COVID-19-Induced Recession

The contact-intensive services sectors have been greatly hit by the pandemic, in particular those associated with mobility and social gathering (e.g., tourism, transportation services, catering). This is due to contagion fears and social distancing measures imposed by the authorities.

Nevertheless, the recessionary effects are confined to the services sector only in the very initial phase. They spread to the rest of the economy via cross-sector interlinkages. Guerrieri et al. (2020) show that the immediate effect of a lockdown is to stop activity in contact-intensive businesses. Subsequently, the recession spreads to the rest of the economy if the complementarity relationships across sectors are strong enough, because lower spending in the contact-intensive services would imply lower spending for complement goods and services. Moreover, if financial market are incomplete and income cannot be fully insured, workers in shut-down sectors face a reduction in their income and, thus, reduce spending for other sectors' products. Thus, there are negative spillovers between the supply and the demand side of the economy: negative supply shocks may cause demand shortage when they trigger changes in aggregate demand larger than the shocks themselves. Closing down contact-intensive sectors (i.e., through public health policies) and providing full insurance payments to affected workers can achieve the first-best allocation for the utilitarian social planner.

The sectoral dimension of the shock and its spreading to the rest of the economy is also emphasized by Baqaee and Farhi (2020). They model COVID-19 as a combination of supply and demand shocks in a multi-sector New Keynesian model. These shocks propagate through supply chains, causing different sectors to become demand-constrained or supply-constrained. The contraction of the demand generates a large slack, initially concentrated in certain sectors of the economy. Income support to credit-constrained households can limit the drop in aggregate demand and output.

2.2 Lower Knowledge and Capital Accumulation

There is large pre-COVID-19 literature showing that temporary recessionary shocks can produce permanent damages to the economy through long-run "scarring" (or hysteresis) effects.[2] These effects of the pandemic shock can be non-trivial as well, given that the pandemic shock affects, directly and/or indirectly, workers, students, and firms.[3]

---

[2] See Cerra et al. (2020).

[3] Jordà et al. (2020) study major pandemics using the rates of return on assets stretching back to the fourteenth century. Significant macroeconomic after-effects of pandemics persist for decades,

Recessions can have long-lasting effects on unemployment by slowing human capital accumulation. There is evidence that poor market conditions at labour market entry cause workers to accept lower paid jobs, and that this has permanent effects for the careers of some. This could be true in the case of the pandemic shock, given that it has negatively impacted services, which are more labour-intensive.[4]

Unemployment has a negative impact on human capital accumulation, as unemployed workers' skills could deteriorate and their attachment to the labour force may weaken. The slower human capital accumulation could have negative long-lasting feedback effects on unemployment. Before COVID-19 shock the literature provided some attempts to quantify the impact of these scarring effects on future employment. Arulampalam et al. (2001) and Tumino (2015) find, for unemployed, a lasting wage penalty and an employment penalty, relative to workers with similar characteristics.

The long-run consequences for hardly-hit workers' human capital can be dramatic not only because of unemployment but also because the job loss can imply a possible mismatch of competence and skills. Human capital is job-specific and it cannot be taken for granted that in the new job the worker will be as productive as in the lost one.[5]

Human capital accumulation is also negatively affected by lower education, because governments have been forced to close schools to limit the spread of the virus. There is some evidence suggesting that a relatively short period of missed school will have consequences for skill growth of young cohorts. Carlsson et al. (2015) show that even just 10 days of extra schooling significantly raises scores on tests of the use of knowledge by 1% of a standard deviation.[6]

Moreover, the impact of the pandemic has been uneven among workers, with job losses concentrated mainly in low-skilled and low-paid areas of the workforce and it is especially severe on women and the young people.[7]

---

with real rates of return substantially depressed. Their results are consistent with the neoclassical growth model: pandemics may induce relative labor scarcity and/or a shift to greater precautionary savings.

[4] Manufacturing-led recessions can also induce hysteresis effects; Ruggles and Ruggles (1977) report evidence based on US data; Oreopoulos et al. (2012) evaluate evidence based on Canadian data; Brugiavini and Weber (2014) assess the longer-term consequences of the Great Recession on the European economy.

[5] See Portes (2020).

[6] Burgess and Sievertsen (2020) discuss how the global lockdown of education institutions is going to cause major (and likely unequal) interruption in students' learning.

[7] Mongey et al. (2020) use US data to show that employees in lockdown sectors typically have lower levels of education, lower incomes, and lower savings than employees outside of the sectors directly affected by these measures. ILO (2020) states the danger of a "lock-down generation": young workers are also concentrated in sectors which are most heavily impacted by the economic recession provoked by the pandemic; moreover, as new vacancies are heavily restricted, young jobseekers are facing increasing difficulties to transition to decent jobs. According to Georgieva et al. (2020), COVID-19 had disproportionate effects on women because they are more likely than men to work in social sectors "such as services industries, retail, tourism, and hospitality" that are hit hardest by social distancing and mitigation measures. In particular, pandemics put women at

Unequal access to education worsens the impact of the shock among young generations, in particular among the poorest students. Unequal access can be magnified by the fact that some teaching has moved on line and not all student have equal access to digital technology (e.g., availability of high-speed connection and computers at home).[8]

Moreover, persistent changes in consumption composition (for example, lower consumption of tourism services) or in labor organization (e.g., a structural increase in working-from-home arrangements) could make past investments non-productive. High debt and financial constraints can induce firms to reduce spending in investment. Similarly, corporate debt overhang may create "zombie firms", which have lesser incentives to invest in productive capital.

Low demand may have scarring effects on the economy by inducing firms to reduce investment in innovation. Fornaro and Wolf (2020) show that there are complementarities between aggregate demand and aggregate supply. High expected growth in the future induces more consumption and employment now, due to inter-temporally optimizing households; more consumption and employment today induce more firm investment and therefore more growth. In this economy, the coronavirus shock might reduce aggregate supply to such an extent that multiple equilibria become possible. The context of secular stagnation and liquidity trap might imply that the COVID-19 shock ends up triggering "stagnation traps induced by pessimistic animal spirits" and persistent underinvestment, which can lead to a lower natural rate and a ("L" like) non-recovery. According to these authors, to avoid such stagnation trap there is little that conventional monetary policy can do, but fiscal policy—most notably, productive public investment—can be of help.[9]

greater risk of losing human capital. Alon et al. (2020) use US data to show in a macroeconomic model that during the pandemics the ratio of labour hours supplied by women relative to men falls much more sharply than in "normal" recessions.

[8] UNICEF (2020) suggests that inherent inequalities in access to tools and technology threaten to deepen the global learning crisis (that already existed before COVID-19 hit). European Commission (2020a) reports that children who lack resources and support were already lower performers before the crisis and they are likely to have lost further ground during the COVID-19 school closures.

[9] The pandemic shock can not only induce pessimistic expectations but also raise uncertainty simultaneously in every country. Ercolani (2020a) points out that since the outbreak of COVID-19 the marked increased in uncertainty regarding the developments of the pandemic has determined an unprecedented spike of household savings in many advanced economies. Improved accessibility and efficiency of health systems not only enhance the health and quality of life of citizens, but can also attenuate the precautionary savings associated with increased uncertainty regarding health outcomes and hence spur households' demand. Dietrich et al. (2020), using a survey of US households interviewed on the 20th of March 2020, show that the average expected 12-month output loss amounted to 6.8%, surrounded by a high level of uncertainty with answers spanning from 1 to −15%. According to Ercolani (2020b), in the US most of the accumulated saving during the pandemic shock was undoubtedly generated by the social distancing and lockdown measures imposed by the government; however, part of it may also have been driven by precautionary motives due to grim labour prospects.

2.3 Main Takeaways

There are several important takeaways from the literature on the macroeconomic effects of the pandemic shock.

First, the pandemic transmission mechanism to the overall economy has a relevant sector-specific component: it directly and mainly affects some sectors and workers' categories (young and women in particular) and propagates to the rest of the economy via the increase in unemployment and (across-sector) complementarity relations. i.e., lower aggregate demand by households and firms in some sectors could negatively affect other sectors and, thus, the overall economic recovery. The negative shock on the demand side of the economies will likely dominate the negative shock on the supply side, and add disinflationary pressures on top of those due to the secular stagnation.

Second, the COVID-19 shock can produce costs also in the long run, given the interaction between cyclical and long-term growth factors (i.e., hysteresis effects on human capital and knowledge accumulation).

Third, from a policy perspective, non-standard monetary policy, liquidity-support measures, and targeted fiscal policy measures to sustain households' and firms' income can greatly help to alleviate the COVID-19-induced crisis.

All in all, the pandemic is a global health shock with deflationary effects affecting simultaneously all countries and, within each country, different households and firms in different ways, introducing large pessimism and uncertainty waves. Even if the multifaceted nature of the shock implies that its ultimate impact on the economic system is very difficult to predict (Caracciolo et al., 2020a, b; Locarno & Zizza, 2020), the risks associated with the shock-induced recession are extremely serious. Uncertainty and pessimistic expectations could give rise to negative spillovers between real and financial conditions in the economy. Uncertainty about the recovery from the pandemic, as it will depend on the virus resurgence, could induce households to increase their precautionary saving and, similarly, induce firms to exit from the market, in particular if they are overburdened with high debt. A muted recovery could have negative implications for financial conditions, given the high level of both public and corporate debt. A liquidity crisis could evolve into a solvency crisis. The deterioration in corporate creditworthiness could reduce the ability of firms to borrow funds. Without appropriate policy responses, a perverse and harmful loop between real and financial conditions could emerge and negatively affect macroeconomic conditions.

Being the COVID-19 a health shock simultaneously affecting all countries, it is rather implausible that some economies can exit from the emergency if, at the same time, some other do not. According to Biancotti et al. (2020), international coordination in the policy response to COVID-19 is key. Disagreements between countries as to the measures to be adopted to contain the spread of the virus and mitigate the economic costs, as well as any uncertainty about the way out of the crisis, risk worsening the negative impact of COVID-19 from both a healthcare and an economic standpoint.

These considerations can be used to assess the mix of measures adopted by fiscal and monetary authorities across the world in response to COVID-19 during the emergency phase and to design policy measures to support recovery once the emergency phase is over.

3 Policy Responses to the COVID-19 Shock: The Monetary and Fiscal Policy Mix in the Short-term

According to large part of the economic literature, in a "*normal*" environment, the roles of monetary and fiscal policies are clearly distinct, with the former having the task of preserving macroeconomic stability and the latter with the objective of maximizing long-term growth, subject to an intertemporal budget constraint, and implementing redistributive policies (see Box 1).

However, as described in the previous section, the COVID-19 pandemic is a global health crisis and, thus, it is not a "conventional" contractionary shock. The shock itself, the shutting down of businesses and the limits to mobility determined by the containment measures have a negative direct impact on economic activity. Moreover, they have a negative impact also through higher uncertainty. Households are uncertain about future employment and wage dynamics, firms are uncertain about future demand for their products and face weakened balance sheets, leading to cancellations and delays in investment plans (Lane, 2020). Economic activity in many sectors contracts and precautionary savings increase, regardless of the level of the interest rates.

Box 1 Monetary and Fiscal Interactions: A Conceptual View[10]

History and economic literature have taught us that the role and the interactions of monetary and fiscal policy depend on the economic environment (Bassetto & Sargent, 2020). This, in turn, is determined both by *structural factors* that tend to remain relatively fixed over time, or change at a very low frequency, and by *temporary factors,* that make main macroeconomic variables fluctuate along long-run trends.

Structural factors concern, for example, technology and technological progress, consumer preferences, the institutional structure, the distribution of households and firms in terms of age, labour participation, wealth and income, and productivity. All these factors contribute to determine potential growth, the level of long-term real interest rates and employment, the transmission of monetary and fiscal policy decisions within the economy.

Temporary factors, on the other hand, originate from unexpected changes in the economic environment (economic shocks), which tend to temporarily

(continued)

[10] Prepared by G. Ferrero and S. Santoro.

affect the demand or the supply of goods, services, credit, and financial assets and the degree of uncertainty that agents face when they have to take economic decisions. These factors determine economic fluctuations of both real and monetary variables.

Sometimes changes that initially appear temporary become permanent, due to *hysteresis effects* (see also Sect. 2). For example, economic shocks that lead to an increase in unemployment or a reduction in the supply of credit may determine a permanent reduction in income, economic growth, and technological progress. Workers who become unemployed may have difficulty in finding a job similar to the one they had and for which they had accumulated human capital. The longer this difficulty lasts, the greater the loss of human capital that had been accumulated and the more difficult it will be to find a job similar to the one that has been lost. Innovative and young, and therefore risky, firms may find it difficult to obtain bank credit, especially when a crisis hits the economy. The longer this difficulty persists and the fewer firms of this type are able to obtain funds, the less technological innovation and future economic growth.

Temporary factors and structural factors characterize "*normal*" and "*changing*" economic environments in different ways. The former is characterised by a relatively stable economic structure and contained economic fluctuations, which do not generate hysteresis phenomena. To describe the movements over time of the main economic variables in the "normal" environment, the economic theory refers to cyclical changes around a steady state (or long-run equilibrium). A "*changing*" economic environment, instead, can originate from strong unexpected variations originated in the financial sector (for example, the global financial crisis and the sovereign debt crisis) or in the real sectors (for example the pandemic crisis), or from structural changes in the economy. Structural changes may involve the demographic structure of the society (i.e., in terms of dependence ratio), the process of technological innovation (i.e., the transition to the digitalization of society), preferences (i.e., in terms of risk aversion of households), the institutional environment (i.e., the appearance of new business models that replace the old ones). When the changing environment is caused by a large strong shock, hysteresis effects may occur and the economy achieves a new long-run equilibrium (the "new normal" equilibrium), after the temporary effects fade away. In a changing environment, economic agents may need time in order to adapt to the "new normal".

The distinction between these two environments ("*normal*" and "*changing*") is important because it also affect the role that monetary and fiscal policy play within the economy.

According to large part of the economic literature, in a "*normal*" environment, the roles played by monetary and fiscal policies are clearly distinct.

(continued)

Monetary policy, not being able to permanently influence long-term real variables, should counteract cyclical fluctuations, specifically to preserve price stability and to keep growth in line with potential. On the contrary, countercyclical discretionary fiscal policies are considered ineffective (Eichenbaum, 1997; Feldstein, 2002). Two main reasons motivate this position. First, discretionary fiscal policy inevitably suffers from implementation lags and thus may not be the most appropriate policy tool in the midst of a "normal" recession. Second, theory and available econometric evidence on the effect of a fiscal stimulus in "normal times" point to fiscal multipliers below one: in other words, increasing public deficit by one euro begets less than one euro of additional output.[11] One of the prominent explanations of this finding is related to households being forward-looking: when deciding how much to consume and save, they take the flow of all their expected future incomes into account. Hence, if they receive a higher net transfer from the government today, they understand that it has to be backed by a lower net transfer at some point in the future, to ensure that the government fiscal policy remains sustainable. Consequently, households do not consume all the additional resources (this is the so-called *Ricardian equivalence* result). As in "normal times" a relatively higher fraction of households have access to credit than in a deep financial crisis, the concept of Ricardian equivalence offers a more realistic, albeit stylized, picture of their behaviour. An additional reason behind muted fiscal multipliers is related to the crowding-out of private investments: if the government increases its debt, it would need to pay a higher interest rate on it to induce investors to buy it, hence making the financing of private investment plans less attractive. Fiscal policy, instead, must be concerned with maximizing long-term growth and implementing redistributive policies, in such a way that debt sustainability is always preserved (or, in a more formal way, fiscal decisions are subject to the intertemporal budget constraint of the fiscal authority). Furthermore, economic theory and practice attribute the conduct of the two policies to two separate and independent institutions.

In a "*changing*" environment, this distinction might not be clear-cut. In some extreme circumstances the effectiveness of monetary policy in supporting the aggregate demand is put to the test, while some fiscal measures

(continued)

[11] In a survey on the pre great financial crisis literature, Ramey (2011) concluded that the empirical evidence on US temporary, debt-financed, increases in government purchases would have pointed to multipliers between 0.8 and 1.5. Blanchard and Perotti (2002) in a study based on post-WWII data find US peak multipliers around one; Hall (2009), studying the effects of government purchases during war episodes, finds values ranging from 0.7 to 1.0; Mountford and Uhlig (2009) find peak effects of public expenditures around 0.7. Also estimated structural DSGE models for the case of a temporary stimulus and no monetary policy accommodation pointed to rather low multipliers (in the range of 0.3 to 0.5; Coenen et al., 2012).

that redistribute resources across time become more effective since the Ricardian equivalence becomes less relevant even if firms and households are perfectly aware that today's higher fiscal deficit implies negative net transfers in the future.[12] The difficulties for conventional monetary policy in managing demand stem from the combination of different factors, both temporary and structural. A prominent example is given by the interaction between the reduction of real interest rates (arguably due to structural factors) and the presence of an effective lower bound on nominal interest rates. When policy rates reach their effective lower bound, they cannot be deployed to counteract the effects of a recession. Hence, unconventional instruments such as large securities' purchase programmes and forward guidance can be necessary to further lower interest rates in the economy and stimulate consumptions and investments. However, also these unconventional measures could result less effective than necessary. The high uncertainty about the "new normal" is an additional feature of a "changing" environment that may make the private sector less respondent to measures that mainly operates through interest rate changes.[13] In this environment, the limits to monetary policy effectiveness raise the concern that hysteresis effects can materialize, converting a temporary recessionary shock into a long-lasting stagnation. To avoid this outturn, fiscal policy should temporarily extend its role above the redistributive and the long-term growth ones.[14]

[12] Households can be severely constrained in their possibility to access credit, distorting their saving decisions in the direction of consuming more of fiscal transfers than they would do otherwise; high uncertainty might compress firms' investments below what would be warranted, hence requiring public investments to step in, reducing the risk of a crowding-out effect.

[13] Moreover, in a changing environment in which structural factors modify the behaviour of households and firms, the probability of rapidly reaching the effective lower bound may increase even if the changes do not affect the natural rate of interest. This is related to the fact that, in this context, also the policymakers could be uncertain about some aspects of the economic structure. In a "normal" environment in which changes occur very slowly and the shocks affecting the economy are not very persistent, the literature has shown that the central bank should adopt the so-called "Brainard principle", whereby policy responses should be relatively more gradual and prudent. Instead, in an environment of rapid changes and where the effects of shocks are more persistent, the Brainard principle may be reversed (Ferrero et al., 2019b). A gradual reaction would increase the risk of de-anchoring of long-term inflation expectations, and so it pays to be more aggressive. As a result, the effective lower bound is reached quickly even in those cases in which the level of official rates is initially relatively high.

[14] An additional argument in favour of a more active role for fiscal policy when the probability that policy rates reach the effective lower bound is relatively high is related to the existence of multiple equilibria: sharp drops in aggregate demand, driven by self-fulfilling pessimistic prophecies of households and firms, can trap the economy in a "bad" equilibrium, featuring low growth and inflation. Under these circumstances, having a fiscal policy that stands ready to adjust government spending can help avoiding the pessimistic beliefs to be confirmed.

Moreover, the shock has materialised in an environment in which most economies were characterised by historically low nominal and real interest rates, low inflation, and growth (the so-called "low interest rate environment").

The trend decline of nominal interest rates started (at least) in the eighties. It was part of a global phenomenon and coincided with the slow but persistent decline in real interest rates, a structural reduction of inflation in many advanced countries and a period of low macroeconomic volatility (the "Great Moderation"; Kim & Nelson, 2001; McConnell & Perez-Quiros, 2000).[15] According to the economic literature, a number of demand and supply factors have led to structural imbalances between the demand for investment and the supply of saving at a global level and consequently to lower global equilibrium real rates. Factors include: (*i*) demographic developments, such as the increase in life expectancy and the decline in population growth (Carvalho et al., 2016; Ferrero et al., 2019a; Aksoy et al., 2019); (*ii*) falling (relative) price of investment goods (Karabarbounis & Neiman, 2014; Thwaites, 2015); (*iii*) lower pace of technological innovation (Gordon, 2016); (*iv*) increase in wealth and income inequality (Summers, 2014); (*v*) rising savings rates in developing countries and the consequent increase in the demand for assets issued by advanced economies (Bernanke, 2005).

The decline accelerated with the outbreak of the global financial crisis and, in the euro area, with the sovereign debt crisis. Compared with a "normal" recession, in a "balance sheet recession" (Koo, 2008), such as the one that characterised the global financial crisis, monetary policy needs to be more accommodative, as traditional transmission channels that operate through intertemporal substitution turn out to be less effective (Mian & Sufi, 2014). Moreover, the increase of risk aversion and precautionary savings lead to the scarcity of relatively safer and long-term assets (Vayanos & Vila, 2020; King, 2019), further compressing the term premiums, inflation expectations and real and nominal interest rates.

Even though the debate on the overall effects of the COVID-19 shock on economic behaviours is still open, a consensus is emerging on the view that the contraction of the demand of investment and consumption and the increase of precautionary savings will exacerbate the low interest rate environment (see Box 2).

Box 2 COVID-19 and the Low Interest Rate Environment[16]

A number of factors and mechanisms set in motion by the COVID-19 shock may strengthen the downward trend of nominal and real interest rates in advanced economies. As long as the negative effects on aggregate demand

(continued)

[15] For a description of the low interest rate environment, its causes, and its implications for monetary policy see Ferrero and Neri (2017).

[16] This box is largely based on the ESRB-ECB Report on "Lower for longer—Macroprudential policy issues arising from low interest rates", to which Giuseppe Ferrero contributed.

are larger than those on aggregate supply, inflation is expected to decline, thus putting downward pressure on nominal interest rates (since the central banks would react by lowering policy rates, as long as they are not constrained by the effective lower bound and implementing quantitative and qualitative easing measures). To the extent that expected inflation does not decline by as much as nominal interest rates, real interest rates also fall (McKibbin & Fernando, 2020). Moreover, the presence of market frictions and borrowing and liquidity constraints, which limit the degree of completeness of financial markets, would exert downward pressure on equilibrium real interest rates even when the size of the supply shock initially dominates the size of the shock on aggregate demand (Guerrieri et al., 2020). The population slowdown and social distancing measures reduce the effective labour supply and, according to the neoclassical growth model, lessen investment demand, thus depressing the real natural rate (Rachel & Smith, 2017). At the same time, increased uncertainty over the pace and timing of the recovery may induce households to react to the shock by increasing saving, either to replace wealth used up during the peak of the calamity (Jordà et al., 2020) or through the surge in precautionary motives that is common in bad and uncertain times (Malmendier & Nagel, 2011). The precautionary saving boost could become particularly persistent when it is reinforced by "scarring of beliefs", i.e. a persistent change in the perceived probability of an extreme, negative shock in the future (Kozlowski et al., 2020).

Other factors, however, may exert a positive effect on real interest rates and thus avert (or limit) a further downward trend. First of all, if negative effects on aggregate supply are larger than those on aggregate demand, inflation would be expected to increase over the medium term horizon. Nominal interest would increase at short maturities because of the increase in policy rates that would likely be implemented by the monetary authorities in response to higher inflation. At longer maturities, higher nominal yields are driven by savers and investors who would require higher compensation for their funds to compensate for higher (expected) inflation (Goodhart & Pradhan, 2020); the effect on real interest rates would depend on the relative size of the increases in expected inflation and nominal interest rates. However, real interest rates may increase even in a scenario in which aggregate demand falls by more than aggregate supply. In particular, if the effective lower bound on nominal interest rates became binding and asset purchase programmes were ineffective in lowering long-term nominal interest rates, inflation expectations could decrease more than nominal interest rates (Fornaro & Wolf, 2020). The issuance of large amounts of safe government

(continued)

debt to finance government expenditure and mitigate the consequences of the pandemic crisis may reduce the saving surplus, and thereby, lead to a rise in interest rates (Rachel & Summers, 2019; Goy & Van den End, 2020). If the expansion of government expenditure is directed toward structural reforms and investments in technology, the transformation into a digital economy could raise productivity growth, exerting a positive effect on real interest rates in the long-run. Moreover, the high level of uncertainty created by pandemic shocks should put upward pressure on the risk premia component of interest rates (McKibbin & Sidorenko, 2006).

Overall, most of the analyses that use very long time-series to trace back to episodes similar to those of the COVID-19 pandemic, or model in a more structured way the economic interactions driven by the pandemic shock and the policy responses to it, conclude that the COVID-19 shock has added further downward pressure on the market real interest rates and the natural real rate of interest—which could be defined as the real short-term interest rate that equates the demand and supply of funds when output is at its potential, unemployment is at its natural rate and inflation is on target.

For the time being, advanced economies are still fighting the COVID-19 pandemic, so it is not possible to have sound empirical evidence on its long-term macroeconomic effects. As a consequence, recent analyses on the issue rely on academic research based on models of previous similar pandemics. Jordà et al. (2020) use a very long time series for Europe (starting in the fourteenth century) to estimate the effect of a pandemic shock on the natural real rate using a local projection model. The authors conclude that following a pandemic, the natural real rate of interest declines for years, reaching a minimum about 20 years later, with the natural real rate about 150 bps lower than if the pandemic had not taken place. About four decades later, the natural real rate returns to the level it would be expected to have reached if the pandemic had not taken place. The effect is still significant but smaller in the estimates of Holston et al. (2020), which modify Holston et al. (2017) to take into account the particular characteristics of the COVID-19 shock (which is not a Gaussian shock).

In a low interest rate environment the ability of the central bank to fulfill its mandate using policy rates may be frequently constrained by the presence of the effective lower bound on policy rates, which would be reached more frequently the lower the natural rate of interest.[17] In this case monetary policy should turn toward other instruments to lower interest rates in credit and financial markets.

The peculiar macroeconomic environment implies that monetary policy should not be "the only game in town", as it has been in the past in some countries (see Box 3). As illustrated in the following sections, a stimulating role for both monetary and fiscal policies is required to stabilise and sustain macroeconomic conditions (Bartsch et al., 2020). Thus, in the current circumstances, the incentives of monetary and fiscal authorities—within their respective mandates—are aligned. Moreover, as we will discuss in the next sections, some important complementarities arise too.

Box 3 Measuring the Degree of Fiscal and Monetary Accommodation[18]
It is widely accepted that since the Great Financial Crisis central banks have displayed an ample degree of monetary accommodation, while fiscal policy has been at times loose, at times tight. This concept is underlined by recent analyses and commentaries stating that in the euro area monetary policy has been the "only game in town" (e.g. Gopinath, 2019). But which are the appropriate instruments to measure the degree of monetary and fiscal accommodation?

The European Commission computes a *monetary condition index*, which is a weighted average of the real short-term interest rate and the real effective exchange rate relative to their value in a base period, where the weights assigned to the two variables reflect their relative impact on GDP after 2 years. A *financial condition index* is computed, among others, by the International Monetary Fund (IMF), as a combination of interest rates, asset prices, exchange rate and volatility. Fiscal stance is usually measured through the change in the *cyclically-adjusted primary balance* (e.g. by the IMF in percent of potential output). However, until the work by Batini et al. (2020), the literature had not offered a *combined monetary and fiscal index*, that dynamically tracks the policy stance.

In particular, Batini et al. (2020) builds an index that provides an estimate of the overall stance of monetary and fiscal policies in the euro area and its

(continued)

[17] The possibility of holding cash, whose nominal yield is zero, prevents the nominal yield on any financial asset from going significantly negative. When this constraint—the effective lower bound–binds, real interest rates are determined solely by inflation expectations. Once the effective lower bound is reached, the central bank is no longer in a position to counter the decline of inflation below the objective by lowering official interest rates. In these circumstances there may be a heightened risk of a de-anchoring of inflation expectations from the central bank's objective and of a further increase of real interest rates. The probability of a deflationary spiral or at least of a prolonged period of low growth both in economic activity and in prices increases (see Casiraghi & Ferrero, 2015).

[18] Prepared by Stefania Villa, co-author of the paper Batini et al. (2020).

three largest member countries (France, Germany, and Italy), by quantifying the impact of conventional and unconventional monetary and fiscal policies on aggregate demand. Each index is derived by estimating the impact of monetary and fiscal policy on output in a regression based on data obtained by simulating a rich estimated dynamic stochastic general equilibrium model of the EA economy (or of the individual EA member countries), and combining these estimates with historical data. The resulting *Dynamic Monetary and Fiscal Conditions index* (DMFCI) provides a synthetic measure of the stance that can be more easily conveyed to the public, compared to model-centric tools, such as the results of an estimated dynamic general equilibrium model. In addition, the DMFCIs allows assessing the overall degree of policy accommodation/restriction in the euro area and in individual countries, while the two components of the DMFCI (monetary and fiscal) help disentangle the contribution of the area-wide monetary policy and the collection of the individual countries' fiscal policies. It is worth clarifying that while indicators based on monetary and fiscal instruments (e.g. the shadow monetary policy rate and the cyclically-adjusted primary balance) reflect policy actions, the DMFCI captures the effects that these policy actions have on output. Finally, the DMFCI is constructed to represent the joint effect of the two policies, while its dynamic nature takes into account the delays with which policies affect economic activity. In other words, the value of the index for a given quarter also captures policy actions adopted in a relatively recent past. The level of the index shows the degree of tightening or loosening in monetary and fiscal conditions from a given base year.

The index computed by Batini et al. (2020) co-moves with other existing indices or measures that proxy the policy stance. When they do not, it is because the DMFCI captures some important feature not included in other indices, such as so-called unconventional monetary policies, crucial to provide a more precise assessment of the policy stance.

The main results of the work by Batini et al. (2020) show that the overall policy of the euro area became looser in the aftermath of the global financial crisis, but not before the recession was in full swing, with most of the loosening manifesting itself between 2009 and 2011. The stance was then tightened during the sovereign debt crisis before being loosened again around 2014 when the European Central Bank (ECB) embraced more drastic accommodative policy actions. Moreover, the patterns observed looking at the aggregate euro area DMFCI do not tally one to one with changes observed at the national level, where the evolution of the overall stance since the global financial crisis was, in fact, quite heterogeneous due to different fiscal stances. These results carry the policy implication that, having the ECB played the lion's share of the economic stimulus for several years, a more expansionary fiscal policy—assisted by interventions at the EU level especially in countries

(continued)

with more limited fiscal space—could play an important role in boosting economic activity in the EA. This is particularly relevant for dealing effectively with the economic consequences of the COVID-19 pandemic.

3.1 The Monetary Policy Responses

Monetary policy stepped in, not only to prevent a severe financial crisis in the first months after the shock, but also to stimulate aggregate demand, deploying a wide array of measures. These measures can be grouped into three types: expansionary measures, liquidity provision measures, and currency swap measures.

3.1.1 Expansionary Monetary Policy Measures

First, measures aimed at providing the expansionary monetary impulse. Beyond the reduction of policy rates in those countries where policy rates were still above the effective lower bound, expansionary measures include forward guidance and different forms of asset purchase programmes, to lower interest rates in the economy also at the medium-to-long-term horizons and stimulate consumption and investment. Here we briefly describe the main channels through which those measures operates.

Changes in Official Interest Rates They mainly affect short-term nominal interest rates. To the extent that nominal prices adjust slowly and short-term inflation expectations are well anchored, short-term real interest rates are also affected. The transmission to households' and firms' consumption, saving, and investment decisions and to inflation dynamics mainly relies on the intertemporal substitution effect and the cost of credit, although recent strands of the literature have emphasised the role of wealth effects (see Kaplan et al., 2018). A decrease in real interest rates affects households and firms decisions also via indirect channels: for example, the net worth and creditworthiness of household and firms can improve, inducing positive balance-sheet effects on the banking sector (Breckenfelder et al., 2016), which help lower lending rates even further. In addition, it can relax firms and households borrowing constraint by increasing the value of assets used as collateral in credit contracts (e.g., for firms, Bernanke & Gertler, 1989; Kiyotaki & Moore, 1997; Caballero & Krishnamurthy, 2003; Brunnermeier & Sannikov, 2014; for households, Eggertsson & Krugman, 2012; Korinek & Simsek, 2016; Farhi & Werning, 2016). The fiscal position of sovereign borrowers can also strengthen, making their recourse to debt financing both easier and cheaper. In open economies, an exchange-rate channel also operates, by which current and future expected movements in the domestic interest rate tend to appreciate or depreciate the (nominal) foreign exchange rate and, via short-run price rigidities, the real exchange rate, which affects international trade and, ultimately, economic activity and inflation. Since the pass-through from changes in official rates to long-term interest rates is not complete, the slope of the term structure is also affected. This in turn influences the profitability of financial institutions that operate maturity transformation, their attitude toward risk and the supply of credit.

Negative Interest Rate Policies When official interest rates are lowered to negative territory, two additional channels put downward pressure also on the longer-term components of the yield curve. The signalling channel, that, by removing the tightening bias, alleviates the substantial upward asymmetry in the distribution of forward rates close to zero, thus reducing also interest rates at longer maturities. The portfolio-rebalancing channel, which investors with strong aversion to negative nominal returns (either because of myopic behaviour or because of institutional constraints) activate by rebalancing their portfolios towards assets with longer maturities and with higher risk.

Forward Guidance It consists of announcements about future settings of policy instruments used to signal the monetary policy stance, in order to modify the current monetary policy conditions. It mainly operates through the signalling channel: by providing information about its future policy stance, the central bank is able to frontload the effects of expected future policy decisions and to lower the medium to longer component of the yield curve. Its effectiveness depend on the degree of commitment perceived by economic agents and the amount (and precision) of information that they already have in their information set when the forward guidance is implemented.

Purchase of Public and Private Securities Programmes such as the Quantitative Easing (QE) of the Federal Reserve and the Asset Purchase Programmes (APPs) and the Pandemic Emergency Purchase Programme (PEPP) of the European Central Bank (ECB), aim at stimulating the aggregate demand via several channels. The central bank "extracts duration" from the market (i.e. reduces the outstanding amount of medium and long-term securities in the market) by purchasing assets with medium and long-term maturities (so-called *duration channel*; see Vayanos & Vila, 2020). This, in turn, lowers term premia and medium- and long-term interest rates. The theoretical and empirical literature suggests that the effect on this yield component depends on certain characteristics of the assets, including the maturity and the issuer. Since some investors have a preference for long-term low-risk assets, a reduction in the volume of such assets available on the market will lower the yield that investors demand for holding them. For instance, institutional investors such as pension funds might want to hold a fixed amount of ten-year government bonds in their portfolios. In this case, a reduction in the volume of securities with a 10 year residual maturity will generate what can be dubbed a "local scarcity" (*the scarcity channel*). This reduction is transmitted also to other classes of assets by investors who want to maintain a higher return in their portfolios and rebalance their investments into riskier asset classes (*portfolio-balance channel*). The overall effect is a reduction of interest rates also on those assets that are not directly purchased by the central bank. The decline in safer asset returns also reduces banks' cost of funding on wholesale markets, strengthening their ability to lend (*bank-lending channel*). Through these financial effects, QEs and APPs affect households and firms decisions, sustaining aggregate demand and inflation, via a multiplicity of transmission channels, qualitatively similar to those activated by changes on official interest rates.

3.1.2 Liquidity Provision Measures

A second type of measures implemented by central banks in response to the pandemic shock aimed at preventing market dysfunction in order to preserve the correct functioning of the monetary policy transmission mechanism and to support the flow of funds to the economy. Given the different role played by individual segments of financial and credit markets in different countries, these measures have been very heterogeneous across countries and include asset purchase programmes targeted to specific segments of financial markets, emergency liquidity facilities, as well as funding facilities to support the essential role of banks in financing the real economy. In some countries, measures taken to ensure firms' liquidity have been more direct, in others less so. For example, in the United States, the Federal Reserve introduced the Paycheck Protection Program (PPP) Lending Facility and the Mainstreet Lending Program (MLP) in order to sustain liquidity to small and medium sized firms, non- profit organizations and self-employed workers. Both programmes operate by providing funding to financial institutions that evaluate the financial soundness of the debtors. The MLP provides that the Federal Reserve buys 95% of new or existing loans to qualified employers, while the issuing bank will keep 5% to discourage irresponsible lending. In exchange for the loan, employers must make reasonable efforts to maintain payroll and retain workers.

In the euro area, where the banking system plays a central role in financing businesses, the ECB has taken measures qualitatively similar to those implemented in recent years to counter deflationary risks, such as the Targeted and the Pandemic Emergency Long Term Refinancing operations (T-LTRO and PELTRO). Those measures provide favourable conditions in terms of both the maturity and the cost that banks pay for the liquidity in the refinancing operation, albeit conditional to satisfying some lending requirements. By binding its benefits to the fulfilment of certain requirements on lending performance these measures enhance the transmission of the favourable conditions of banks' funding to the credit supply and ultimately to aggregate demand.

3.1.3 The Global Dimension of Monetary Policy Measures

A third type of measures, crucial to address the global liquidity dimension of the crisis, are the currency swap lines between central banks. Given the international role of the dollar, the Fed expanded its existing swap lines with five other central banks (Bank of Canada, Bank of England, Bank of Japan, ECB, and the Swiss National Bank) and reduced, for these countries, the spread on the swap line over overnight indexed swap (OIS) from 50 to 25 basis points. Moreover, a new program with nine other central banks was created. In addition the Fed announced a new temporary repurchase facility for foreign and international monetary authorities, which allow approved holders to temporarily exchange their U.S. Treasury securities with the Fed for U.S. dollars. The Eurosystem reactivated its previous swap line agreements, and established new precautionary swap lines. In addition, it set up bilateral repo agreements with several other non-euro area central banks and, to further broaden the access to the Eurosystem's liquidity arrangements, it established the Eurosystem repo facility for central banks, which provides a precautionary backstop facility to address euro liquidity needs that might arise outside the euro area.

Two additional considerations could be done on the international dimension of the monetary measures adopted in response to the pandemic crisis.

First, according to some economists the swap network can be viewed as a step in the direction of a global financial safety net (Bordo, 2020). However, on this regard, it should be noted that a number of countries do not have access to the swap network. Some commentators suggested that the International Monetary Fund (IMF) and the World Bank should play a larger role in improving global liquidity and financial conditions. According to O'Neil and Lombardi (2020), Special Drawing Rights should be used to back swap access, while Collins et al. (2020) suggest to increase the IMF's financial resources to fight the pandemic and that the major central banks should link their swap lines to it.[19] According to Levy Yeyati (2020), the IMF should act as the dealer between the funding central bank and the borrowing country. Velasco (2020) suggests that the IMF, the World Bank, and the regional development banks should establish a special purpose vehicle that would issue bonds to be purchased by leading central banks to prevent an emerging market meltdown.

Second, non-standard monetary policy measures produce non-trivial international spillovers. Large asset purchase programmes (such as the QE in the US and APP in the euro area) have large and persistent effects on the exchange rate. According to Dedola et al. (2020), the announcement by the ECB of a LSAP, which increases the relative size of the balance sheet of the Eurosystem by about 20%, implies a persistent depreciation of the €/$ exchange rate by about 7%. The same effect is obtained in the $/€ exchange rate if the programme is announced by the Fed. However, the macroeconomic international spillovers of unconventional

[19] See also Reis (2019) on the cooperation between IMF and central banks to resolve financial crises.

monetary measures are not only transmitted through the exchange rate channel of monetary policy (Bluwstein & Canova, 2016). The impact on output and inflation of unconventional policies adopted by the ECB or the Fed are larger in foreign countries with more advanced financial systems. According to Dedola et al. (2013) under a high degree of financial integration country-specific shocks with a financial origin result in a much greater degree of macroeconomic synchronization across countries than real shocks.

All in all, central banks have had a crucial role in the response to the pandemic emergency, by providing global liquidity and by further enhancing monetary and financial conditions, to avoid a liquidity and financial crises of devastating dimensions and to contribute to sustain aggregate demand at worldwide level.

Box 4 A Review of the Debate on (Quasi-)Fiscal Monetary Policies[20]

In the weeks after the first wave of the COVID-19 pandemic, there has been an intense debate on what monetary policy can do in response to a shock such as the COVID-19 one. Two responses emerged from the debate: we will call them the "*orthodox*" and the "*heterodox*" view.

According to the "*orthodox*" response central banks should immediately intervene (and, in fact, they did) by dusting off (and in some cases extending both qualitatively and quantitatively) the armamentarium developed during the global financial and the sovereign debt crises. The type of measures considered are those described in Sect. 3.1.

Against this view, more "*heterodox*" proposals have re-emerged (helicopter drops, MMT, MP3, SEFF, etc.).[21] These proposals differ one from the other for important *institutional aspects*, but they start from the same *premises* and reach similar *general conclusions*. The first premise is that in response to the COVID-19 shock the effectiveness of monetary policy measures that rely on the interest rate channels are ineffective in stimulating aggregate demand. The second one is that expansionary fiscal policies financed in deficit by issuing and selling government bonds to the private sector may result *unsustainable* in the medium term and *ineffective* in increasing aggregate

(continued)

[20] This Box is largely based on Bank of Italy (2020), "COVID-19 and Economic Analysis: a Review of the Debate", Literature Review Issues 1 and 2, to which Giuseppe Ferrero contributed.

[21] Modern monetary theory (MMT), Monetary Policy 3 (MP3) and Standing Emergency Fiscal Facility (SEFF) are different proposals, appeared in the economic debate in the recent years, to implement monetary financing in order to stimulate aggregate demand. For a description of MMT see for example, Wray, L. Randall (Randall Wray, 2015). MP3 has been promoted by Ray Dalio, founder and CIO of Bridgewater investment fund. See for example Dailo (2019). The SEFF has been promoted by Elga Bartsch, Jean Boivin, Stanley Fischer and Philipp Hildebrand, who wrote a report for BlackRock Investment Management Company. See Bartsch et al. (2019).

demand in the short term. While the former is related to the fact that when the crisis will be over governments will find themselves with much higher public debt than before the crisis, with possible negative effects in terms of the cost of debt and limits to the ability to pursue expansionary fiscal policies in the future (Giavazzi & Tabellini, 2020), the latter is due to Ricardian equivalence effects: "*people may be more inclined to save rather than spend tax cuts (or monetary transfers) when they know that the cuts and transfers increase future government interest costs and thus raise future tax payments for themselves or their children*" (Bernanke, 2003). The conclusion is that in order to "*strengthen the effects of fiscal policy, by breaking the link between expansionary fiscal actions today and increases in the taxes that people expect to pay tomorrow*" (Bernanke, 2003), expansionary fiscal policies should be financed with a State liability that does not expire, public money (e.g. monetary financing).

While originally the expression 'helicopter drop' was coined by Friedman in 1969,[22] the policy prescription of a fiscal expansion financed by printing money in order to fight deflationary risks became popular with a speech of Ben Bernanke in 2002. Since in most countries the Treasury and the Central bank are two distinct institutions, the implementation of this policy would reduce to the following steps: to finance its expansionary fiscal policy the government issues irredeemable bonds that are purchased by the central bank, which returns the yields on those bonds to the Treasury in the form of seigniorage. From an accounting perspective, there is no difference between the direct distribution of money by the Central bank to economic agents and its indirect distribution channeled through the Treasury.[23]

The COVID-19 crisis has spurred again the debate on helicopter drops and on different ways to implement it. The debate revolves around what mostly affects its effectiveness (Ricardian equivalence, targeted transfers and the role of price rigidities), what are usually considered as the main limits (legal feasibility and central bank credibility/independence) and, finally, what are

(continued)

[22] Friedman proposed the following experiment: a helicopter flies over an economy that is growing at its potential dropping bills so that each citizen suddenly (and unexpectedly) has twice the cash he held before. A crucial assumption is that this is a unique event, which will never be repeated, and citizens know it. According to Friedman since the economy was already at its long-run equilibrium economic agents would not decide to save this additional amount of money: they will just spend it. Moreover, since the economy is running at its potential, there is no idle production capacity: production remains unchanged. The result is that after a transition period, the only change observed would be in terms of prices, which would double, without a permanent change in any of the real variables.

[23] A similar proposal, the "overt money finance", was proposed among others by Turner (2013), former Chairman of the UK Financial Services Authority, in response to the deflationary risks coming from the global financial crisis and the sovereign debt crises.

the differences between asset purchase programmes (such as QEs and APPs) and helicopter drops.

Ricardian equivalence. In order to have real effects on the economy (in terms of aggregate output and employment), it is not sufficient that the expansionary policy is financed by issuing money. It is also necessary that people spend the money they receive. According to some economists it is, therefore, necessary that agents perceive that the money injection is permanent, in the sense that money transfers will not be reversed in the future by the central bank or by the government. To this end, some claims that governments should issue a perpetuity and the central bank should buy it (Tabellini, 2020); others that the central bank should commit to permanently rollover government bond purchases once the bond matures (Barwell et al., 2020); some others that the central bank should credit directly the Treasury account and contemporaneously reduce its net worth (Galì, 2020a).

Targeted transfers. Many economists stress that in order to be effective such transfers should be targeted to groups of households and firms that face tighter constrains in terms of consumption, investment and production (Gaspar & Mauro, 2020; Simmons et al., 2020).

Price rigidities. The impact on prices and output would depend on the slope of aggregate supply, which in turn is affected by the degree of price and nominal wage rigidities. In the extreme case in which they are fully flexible (and this would be the case when the economy is growing at its potential), a shift in aggregate demand would merely imply a one-off jump in the price level; should output be below its potential, instead, a boost in aggregate demand would translate into an increase in output and inflation. To this end, Galì (2020b) compares quantitatively helicopter drops to conventional debt-financed stimulus in a New Keynesian model. The main results are: (i) helicopter drops provide a way to boost economic activity effectively, as long as prices are reasonably sticky, since "*when prices are sticky, aggregate demand and output are a function of current and expected real interest rates, which in turn are affected by the paths for the money supply and nominal interest rates. Those paths differ across financing methods* (money-financed vs debt-financed)"; (ii) money-financed tax cuts also appear to be more effective countercyclical policies than their debt-financed counterparts when the effective lower bound on policy rate is binding.

Legal feasibility. Reichlin and Shoemaker (2020) stress that the main limit of helicopter drops still remains, especially for the euro area, in the institutional framework and claim that "*this [quasi-fiscal monetary policy] poses a problem of legitimacy since the central bank does not directly respond to taxpayers and implies a lack of response by the political authorities. Ultimately, this would harm its effectiveness*". Buiter (2020a) claims, instead, that not implementing the institutional changes necessary to implement

(continued)

helicopter drops would be much more costly than implementing them and "*it would be criminally negligent to allow a design flaw in existing treaties to inhibit the appropriate use of helicopter money at a time of existential crisis*". Others, claim that helicopter drops could be implemented inside the current institutional frameworks (Yashiv, 2020; Tlaib, 2020; Bartsch et al., 2019).

Central bank credibility issues. Some authors focus on the credibility issue and the risks that once a central bank enter into helicopter drops, it will lose control over price stability in the future. Goodhart and Pradhan (2020) argue that since COVID-19 is mostly a supply shock which does not affect the future amount of capital in the economy, once the effects of the shock will be over, the effects of expansionary policies will remain and inflation will surge; Farmer (2020) stresses that if such a measure is temporary such a risk does not exist ("*This is a temporary helicopter drop that will, and should, cause a once and for all price increase. As long as it is temporary and does not lead to a permanent money financed deficit, it will not lead to inflation*").

Quantitative easing (QE) vs Helicopter drops (HD). From an accounting point of view, there is no difference if the central bank purchases the government bonds in the primary or in the secondary markets.[24] But if the purchases are made in the secondary market, what would differentiate a helicopter drop measure from a quantitative easing one? Differences are not in term of their final goals: both measures aim at stimulating aggregate demand. The differences lie in (i) the main channels which are activated, (ii) the degree of coordination of the actors involved and (iii) the "duration" of the programmes. QE aims at influencing aggregate demand primarily by reducing medium and long-term interest rates. To do so, the central bank buys low-risk securities (such as government bonds) with medium and long-term maturities. By making them relatively scarce it is able to increase their price and reduce, as a consequence, their returns. The reduction of the returns on the asset purchased is then transmitted to other financial assets and activates other channels that indirectly stimulates households' consumptions and firms' investments.[25] The duration of the programme is temporary and there is no need of "formal" coordination between the central bank and the government.

HD aim instead at influencing aggregate demand directly. What matters is not that the purchased securities become relatively scarce, but that the money created by the central bank is transferred by the government to households and firms that effectively use it to increase their consumptions and investments. Its effectiveness, therefore, rests on one of two (sufficient)

(continued)

[24] See for example Barwell et al. (2020).

[25] For a description of the main channels activated by quantitative easing programmes, see Cova and Ferrero (2015).

conditions. Either (i) agents perceiving the money injection as permanent (money transfers will not be reversed in the future by an equivalent increase in taxes), or (ii) if such injections will be reversed in the future, they should be targeted to agents with a relatively low discount factor (i.e. who care relatively little about future disbursements, either because of their preferences or because they are currently facing liquidity or borrowing limits). Given these requirements, the recent debate has emphasized two ways to implement HD-like policies starting from existing measures. The first consists in making QE permanent. Permanent purchases of government bonds can occur either (i) by issuing and purchasing irredeemable government bonds or (ii) by issuing redeemable bonds that the central bank (credibly) commits to repurchase every time that they matures. Many economists have been debating about this possibility. Some suggested just converting the bonds that central banks already purchased in QE programmes into irredeemable bonds (Vihriälä, 2020); some say that assets purchased in the context of QE programmes will inevitably be repurchased when they will expire[26]; others say that this is still an open option but the central banks at this stage should remain silent about it (Blanchard & Pisani Ferry, 2020). The main issue with permanent QE is that it implies a loss of capital for the central bank. While this has no implications in the short term since central banks are not subject to the same rules as private individuals and firms in accounting terms (Buiter, 2020b), if the capital shortfall is sufficiently large and it is not recovered in the medium to long term, the monetary authority could lose credibility in its ability to maintain price stability. Therefore, if the loss of capital is not replenished in the future, it will increase the risk of price instability; this is in fact the main argument against permanent QE according to opponents of this measure (Dowd, 2018). This has led to consider the second possibility, a non-inflationary permanent QE with targeted transfers. The idea is that capital should be replenished in the future with the central bank withholding part of the seigniorage that would otherwise have been transferred to the Treasury. The recent proposal by Galì (2020a), for example, suggests a conversion of actual QE programmes into permanent QEs, but at the same time, he suggests that the central banks and the governments agree on "*a permanent reduction in the transfer of ECB profits to governments in proportion to the effective debt cancellation*". However, since the reduction in revenues for the Government would imply a lower spending capacity and, other things equal, an increase in future taxes

(continued)

[26] In an article, the editorial board of the Financial Times claims that "*Central bankers say asset purchases under QE are temporary, meaning the newly-created money will one day be removed from the economy. But it is hard to bind the hands of their successors, who could one day make them permanent.*", Financial Times, 6 April 2020.

(Ricardian equivalence), for the effectiveness of such a program it would be crucial that monetary transfers are targeted to agents with a relatively low discount factor.

3.2 *The Fiscal Policy Responses in Advanced Economies*

In the course of 2020, fiscal policy across advanced economies operated through three groups of tools: automatic stabilizers, discretionary measures (with an impact on the budget balance), and other instruments to favour liquidity for firms and households. The first two sets of measures explain the extraordinary worsening of primary balances, by almost 9 percentage points of GDP on average, according to the latest IMF's estimates (IMF, 2021).[27]

The deep recession—with an average contraction of real GDP of almost 5 per cent—automatically reduced tax revenues and increased spending related to some income support schemes. According to the April 2021 IMF's estimates, this cyclical component is responsible for about one third of the worsening of primary balances in advanced economies. Additionally, all governments undertook a series of important discretionary support measures. As suggested by the IMF, among others, in the spring of 2020, the size and the characteristics of the shock called for a large, timely, and targeted fiscal support. According to the latest estimates by the IMF, advanced economies indeed implemented expansionary measures worth about 6 percentage points of GDP on average in 2020.[28] Moreover, many governments provided firms with further liquidity support, without an impact on the budget balances, for example in the form of tax deferrals, loans, and equity injections. Finally, in many instances, governments extended their guarantees to loans by commercial banks to businesses. This latter form of intervention is especially relevant in the United Kingdom and in many EU countries (see Box 5). In the last few months, as the spread of the virus continued and the need for strict mobility restrictions resurfaced, many governments passed new pieces of legislation to extend significant fiscal support to 2021 as well. In the fall of 2020, the IMF was expecting a relatively rapid unwinding of measures in the current year (IMF, 2020a). On the contrary, it

[27] Fiscal forecasts in real time in 2020 were surrounded by a relatively high degree of uncertainty. First, they reflected uncertainties related to the infra-annual evolution of the contagions and of macroeconomic variables (Locarno & Zizza, 2020). Second, the implementation of announced new fiscal measures and the normal operating of the public administration may have been slowed down by the pandemic itself. Third, new measures were introduced during the year and might have not been anticipated in previous forecasts.

[28] It should be stressed that the exact quantification of the expansionary fiscal stance for 2020—especially in real time—is a difficult exercise also because of uncertainties related to the estimation of the output gap.

now projects the cyclically-adjusted primary balance for the average of advanced economies to stay broadly constant in 2021 at the level of the previous year (IMF, 2021).

Given the size of the shock and its highly heterogeneous impact across different parts of the population, a bold fiscal stimulus was needed. As described by Elmendorf and Furman (2008), in those cases when a discretionary fiscal action is required, the stimulus should ideally be timely, temporary, and targeted. Timeliness is needed to make sure that the support is delivered at the right moment in time, also to ease liquidity constraints. In principle, a temporary shock requires a temporary response, not to increase the cost of public debt and endanger the balance of the public accounts in the longer term. Finally, proper targeting would be needed to maximize the short-term output effect of any public support. In most cases, this means directing resources towards the most vulnerable, who are also those with the highest propensity to consume out of government transfers.[29] Understandably, in the context of the current crisis, difficulties and constraints often prevented actual policies to adhere to these ideal criteria. Moreover, the need for social distancing to curb the spread of the virus arguably poses new challenges for the design of fiscal measures to sustain consumption and aggregate demand.

While there are many differences in the specifics of the fiscal support measures across countries, some commonalities emerge. In particular, as recognized by the OECD (2020a), many governments resorted to wage supplementation and job retention schemes widely and to an unprecedented extent. Both mandated business closures and the drop in demand for contact-intensive services increased the role of such instruments with respect to normal times or other recessions. In general, through these schemes the governments shoulder some of the firms' labor costs, thus limiting the likely surge in unemployment and the long-term consequences for the career perspectives of workers. Ultimately, by cushioning the fall in net incomes of interested workers, these schemes foster aggregate demand. Firms avoid losing experienced personnel through the recession and both the costly separation and re-hiring processes.

[29] According to the literature, targeted-transfers to liquidity-constrained households can be rather effective in sustaining aggregate demand during a large recession and if the effective lower bound holds. For example, Coenen et al. (2012) find that a 1 percent of GDP increase in targeted transfers raises US output by 1 to 1.5 percent if monetary policy remains accommodative for 2 years, roughly twice as large as under normal conditions. The importance of proper targeting of the government transfers in the context of the current crisis is also highlighted in the work by Bayer et al. (2020). In the framework of a heterogeneous agent (HANK) model, this paper finds multipliers of transfers to unemployed to be in the order of 1 to 2. Unemployment insurance-like transfers are the most effective fiscal policy tool to sustain household consumption also in the two-agent DSGE model by Faria-e-Castro (2020). Thus, there is a strong case for using targeted transfers to mitigate recessions, in particular if the recessions, as the COVD-19-induced one, affects different classes of households and firms in a different way.

At the same time, targeted liquidity support (in forms of tax deferrals, equity injections, and loan guarantees) are useful in preventing bankruptcies of hard-hit, but otherwise viable, firms reducing the risk of long-term damages for the growth potential of the economies. Obviously, discriminating firms in real time during a crisis could be difficult. In such circumstances, the possibility that government support ends up financing very low-productivity (zombie) firms is a legitimate concern. On the other hand, inaction can have important repercussions too. Indeed, bankruptcy events can have large and cascade effects given the weak macroeconomic conditions. In the midst of the crisis, withdrawing support to any firm could have huge costs, because of possible Keynesian multiplier effects (mainly related to the associated job losses and to the externalities for other sectors). Nevertheless, when the most critical phase of the emergency ends, the risk posed by the possible financing of zombie firms should be addressed. In the recovery phase, public support should prioritize firms with higher chances of long-run viability, while preserving affected workers' livelihood. To this aim, the Group of Thirty (2020) has advised governments to both improve the targeting of their credit-related policies and to design measures to encourage firms' capitalization. For instance, as suggested also by Blanchard et al. (2020), in that phase, governments could consider converting some of their liquidity-support measures into some form of equity.

It is probably too soon to properly empirically assess the effectiveness of many of the governments' programmes implemented in the early stages of the crisis. Nevertheless, thanks to the availability of high quality high frequency data, some authors have attempted some preliminary analysis. Baker et al. (2020) study the marginal propensity to consume of a large sample of US recipients of cash transfers from the federal government (through the so-called CARES act). They find that the stronger responses are those of households with lower incomes, greater income drops, and, in particular, lower levels of liquid assets, thus confirming the importance of the proper targeting of the support in the first phase of the crisis. While both Autor et al. (2020) and Chetty et al. (2020) find that the US loan program for small business which maintain their labor force through the recession (the Pandemic Paycheck Program) had a positive impact on employment, the size of the effect (and thus, ultimately, the desirability of the scheme) is still contentious. According to the ECB (2020a), government guarantees on loans played a crucial role in supporting the financing needs of firms in the early phases of the crisis. In this respect, as argued by Gobbi et al. (2020), the exit from the emergency phase should be carefully planned to avoid a possible loan foreclosure wave.

As far as Italy is concerned, there is some evidence that some of the policy measures adopted by the government in 2020 played a significant role in reducing the additional liquidity needs caused by the pandemic for corporations (De Socio et al., 2020). This extraordinary support to firms together with the adoption of a special wage supplementation scheme and of a layoffs abeyance is assessed to have been instrumental in avoiding about 600,000 layoffs in the last year (Viviano, 2020). Nevertheless, the shock—while attenuated by these policy measuresin 2020—is likely to have some negative carryover effects also in the medium run. For example, according to some estimates by Giacomelli et al. (2021), the size of the downturn in the past year, the only gradual recovery expected for 2021–2022 and the delayed effects of the crisis in 2020 could significantly increase the annual number of firms' bankruptcies in the medium run.

A special mention should be devoted to the euro area. Being a common currency area without a central fiscal capacity, the euro zone has been particularity put to the test by the pandemic. Indeed, in normal circumstances, the governance framework of the area assigns the bulk of the burden of macroeconomic stabilization to the common monetary policy and to the proper functioning of de-centralized automatic stabilizers, while national-level fiscal authorities are expected to be somewhat constrained in their discretionary actions. Moreover, the EU-wide budget is neither meant to support demand at the aggregate level, nor is large enough for it. The shock induced relevant changes, in terms of the size of the fiscal response, of the degree of coordination among countries and of the creation of new shared instruments. First, the so-called general escape clause of the Stability and Growth Pact (i.e. the set of fiscal rules) was activated to allow individual countries to implement additional support measures in both 2020 and 2021. Second, European authorities and governments agreed on the institution of a new set of common tools to provide financial support to hard-hit countries in the European Union. This list includes a centralized loan-based program to provide financing for country-level wage supplementation and short-term work schemes (SURE), an enhancing of the European Investment Bank fund for small and medium sized enterprises, and the creation of a new precautionary financial assistance facility with the European Stability Mechanism (the Pandemic Crisis Support). Most importantly, in July 2020 the European Council agreed on a common exceptional temporary recovery instrument, the so-called "Next Generation EU" (NGEU). To this aim, the European Commission will issue bonds worth up to 750 billion euros on behalf of whole Union and will use the resulting resources to provide loans and grants to individual countries in 2021–2026. While the specific uses of the program and the exact timing of disbursements are not fully specified yet, the program has the potential to provide a non-negligible macroeconomic support for the area as a whole. Moreover, the grant component of the scheme is particularly valuable for high public debt beneficiaries, by providing fiscal support without directly weighting on national budget balances. The fact that the euro area managed to arrange for a common response is important not only for its intrinsic political meaning, but also for the likely non-negligible cross-country spillovers of fiscal measures. Bartocci et al. (2020) simulate a two-region monetary union model of the euro area. They find that if one country responds to the pandemic shock by raising lump-sum fiscal transfers to "poor" households then the recessionary effects of the pandemic shock are reduced, both domestically and abroad via trade channel in the euro area.

3.2.1 COVID-19, the Design of Automatic Stabilizers, and Public Safety Nets

The size of the recessionary shock due to the pandemic and the highly heterogeneous effects of the crisis across economic sectors call for an assessment of the functioning of fiscal automatic stabilizers and the appropriate design of the public safety nets in terms of both generosity and coverage.

Indeed, the first fiscal line of defense in case of a downturn is obviously what can be automatically triggered by the swings of the economy, without the need for (possibly long) decisions. Even before the COVID-19 crisis, the proper design of automatic stabilizers in the presence of aggregate shocks was indeed the subject of a series of theoretical studies (Landais et al., 2018; McKay & Reis, 2016; McKay & Reis, 2021). While this literature is vast and hence difficult to reduce to a few homogenous messages, in general the presence of aggregate risks increases the optimal degree of generosity of some safety-net measures, in particular of the unemployment insurance schemes.

The mobility restrictions introduced to fight the spread of the virus and the drop in the demand for contact-intensive services increase the heterogeneity of the impact of the crisis. They also pose new challenges for the social safety nets of many advanced economies. People with temporary employment contracts, in general with low education levels, or those employed in sectors interested by lockdown measures clearly suffered higher-than average consequences (e.g. Bitler et al., 2020; Blundell et al., 2020; Casarico & Lattanzio, 2020; Rondinelli & Zanichelli, 2020; Carta & De Philippis, 2021). The pre-existing safety net is not always and not everywhere adequate to cope with this new environment. As found by the OECD (2020a), in many countries social protection schemes in general work much better for employees with stable work histories than for the rest of the population. Indeed, a common element of much of the government intervention in many advanced economies has been the extension of the coverage of social protection schemes to previously un-protected groups, such as the self-employed.

In order to draw firm conclusions, more data are needed on the distribution of the economic distress brought about by the pandemic, the actual implementation of support measures, and the medium-term effect on inequality. Nevertheless, the COVID-19 crisis is likely to push for a rethinking of public safety nets in many countries in terms of magnitude, coverage and timeliness (e.g. Moffitt & Ziliak, 2020 for a series of proposals for the United States).[30]

---

[30] The size and the length of the current shock is likely to renew the policy debate on the most adequate form of the safety net. On the one hand, different options to close the coverage gaps uncovered by crisis will probably be discussed. On the other hand, the possible difficulties of proper targeting income support in the midst of the crisis might reignite calls for unconditional and universal transfers (Francese & Prady, 2018). Weighting pros and cons of different structures for a hypothetical renewed social safety net, *once the crisis is over*, would be an interesting topic, but it is outside the scope of the current report.

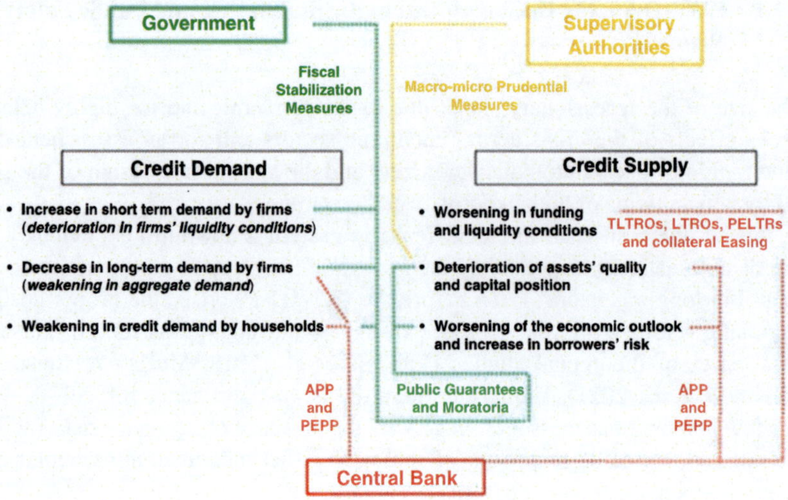

Fig. 1 Impact of COVID-19 shock on credit demand and supply and measures adopted by the authorities

Box 5 Fiscal, Monetary and Regulation Complementarities: Credit Provision and Public Guarantees[31]

While the lockdown measures do not affect directly the credit market, they indirectly do so. The fall in economic activity and the heightened uncertainty have a strong and negative effect on both demand and supply of credit through different channels, as shown in Fig. 1. In advanced economies a bold mix of measures undertaken by the governments, the central banks, and the micro- and macro-prudential authorities have contrasted the transmission of the shock to the credit market.

Following a shock like the COVID-19 pandemic, credit demand by non-financial corporation increases in the short term and falls in the medium term. The lockdown measures determine a strong contraction in economic activity, a deterioration of firms' liquidity conditions, and a halt of investments. While the liquidity shortage implies an increase of credit demand by firms, the reduction of investments is associated with a contraction in credit demand. In the short term the positive effect of the former likely dominates the negative effect of the latter.[32] In a longer perspective, the opposite holds.

(continued)

[31] Prepared by L. Esposito.

[32] Firms' needs to build long-term liquidity buffers in light of the ongoing uncertainty (Backer et al., 2020) and to refinance and restructure their debt sustain credit demand.

Credit demand by households for mortgages and consumer credit weakens in the short term reflecting the fall in consumer confidence, the contraction of spending on durable goods, and the deterioration of housing market prospects; households' demand recovers only when the uncertainty related to their financial conditions decreases.

As for credit supply, the COVID-19 shock hinders banks' willingness to lend through three main channels[33]: (*i*) Borrowers' risk increases. The contraction in revenues caused by the lockdown measures and the associated drop in aggregate demand hamper firms' financial position and creditworthiness. Households' financial conditions also weaken as a consequence of the drop in disposable income and wealth stemming from the fall in financial assets' prices.[34] (*ii*) Banks' assets' quality and capital position deteriorates. The reduction in firms' and households' ability to fulfil current obligations increases the expected flow of non-performing loans (NPLs) in banks' balance sheets. Furthermore, expectations of a rapid worsening of public finance balances, due to the massive fiscal measures undertaken, reduces government bonds prices and increases banks' losses on their portfolio. Both NPLs and government bonds depreciation erode bank capital. (*iii*) Banks' funding and liquidity conditions become vulnerable. Financial market tensions, mainly stemming from the spike in uncertainty, determine an increase of the cost of borrowing for banks. Share prices fall sharply, bond yields rise and credit default swap (CDS) premia increase.[35]

At the end of February 2020, financial market tensions caused a deterioration of banks' funding conditions. Such developments in financial markets were mitigated by the timely implementation of monetary policy measures, such as the pandemic emergency purchase programme (PEPP) announced by

(continued)

[33] The impact of the COVID-19 shock on credit demand and supply is likely to be heterogeneous across borrowers and banks. The impact on the demand will depend on firms' initial liquidity buffers, on their funding mix (bank or market based), the intensity of relationship lending, households' disposable income, borrowing constraints, and financial wealth; for banks the impact will vary depending on the intensity of relationship lending, on bank's business model and collateral availability.

[34] More generally, the COVID-19 shock causes a sharp deterioration in growth prospects. Furthermore, the subsequent recovery of the economic activity hinges, besides the duration of the pandemic, on a number of uncertain variables: the repercussions on people's confidence and spending decisions, the trend in households' propensity to save, the capacity of firms to stay in the market despite the losses suffered while their activity was suspended (see Box *The transmission of the effects of the pandemic to the Italian economy*, Bank of Italy Economic Bulletin, N.2/2020).

[35] Retail funding could also record a halt. While wealthy households may decide to rebalance their portfolios towards more liquid assets, poorer households and SMEs' deposits may fall reflecting their liquidity constraints.

the ECB on 18 March. In general, in absence of prompt policy interventions by national and international authorities, the COVID-19 shock would have likely generated on impact a shortage of credit supply in most countries, especially those where the supply of funds is intermediated by banks, and the leading in the medium term to a generalised weakness of credit dynamics. The rationale behind the policy measures undertaken was twofold: (i) sustaining firms' and households' liquidity conditions (both directly and by supporting banks' willingness to lend) in response of the extraordinary increase of liquidity needs due to the lockdown; (ii) contrasting the deterioration of the economic outlook, thus sustaining credit demand and supply both in the short and in the medium term. To fully achieve these objectives and counteract the pervasive impact of the COVID-19 crisis on the economy, policy responses were built to mitigate not only the direct impact of the shock but also the endogenous risk stemming from possible amplification effects, spirals, run, and non-linearities (Brunnermeier & Sannikov, 2016).[36] To this end, the following features of the policy mix were crucial: (*i*) they were aimed to support the economy decisively in the short term and committed to do so in the medium term; (*ii*) they were coordinated to gain efficacy and safeguard financial stability.

Crucially, public guarantees and central banks' liquidity provision feature a high level of complementarity. On the one hand, the provision of liquidity by the central bank is ineffective in absence of a broad-based public guarantees scheme because banks' willingness to lend would be constrained by the increase in perceived borrowers' riskiness. On the other hand, public guarantees are ineffective if banks' funding and liquidity conditions deteriorate. At the same time the success of these complementary measures and the pursuit of financial stability is underpinned by the central banks public sector purchase programmes, which help to counter the spreading of pessimistic expectations about the sustainability of public debt, especially in countries with limited fiscal space. Public guarantees—as compared to other categories of public spending—have the advantage of being state-contingent liabilities. As such,

(continued)

[36] In particular, spirals may stem from the presence of strategic complementarities between borrowing and lending decisions (Albertazzi & Esposito, 2017). These complementarities may weaken considerably credit dynamics generating a self-fulfilling loop in which the weakest side of the credit market creates a persistent demand/supply shortage. In general, the COVID-19 shock has the potential to trigger a self-fulfilling spiral where aggregate supply and demand suddenly fall (Galeotti & Surico, 2020; Fornaro & Wolf, 2020). Furthermore, when goods are not too close substitutes across sectors, the COVID-19 shock might look like a "Keynesian supply shock" where aggregate demand contracts more than the initial supply shock, creating a supply shortage (Guerrieri et al., 2020).

they have an indirect and limited impact on government debt.[37] Nevertheless, if financial markets coordinate on a bad equilibrium, which reflect investors' self-fulfilling expectations of debt unsustainability, the resulting increase in sovereign spreads would reduce ex-ante the efficacy of public guarantees in unlocking banks' credit supply, thus failing to address firms' liquidity needs and prevent their default. Moreover, if such equilibrium materializes, the increase in sovereign spreads would increase ex-post the riskiness of banks' assets, possibly activating an adverse sovereign-bank nexus.[38] In this context, monetary policy measures that ensure ordinate liquidity conditions in the sovereign market become a crucial instrument to preserve an efficient transmission of expansionary policies.

4 Looking Forward: The Legacy of the COVID-19 on Monetary and Fiscal Policy and the Road to the Global Recovery

4.1 High Public Debt and Contingent Liabilities

During 2020 governments of advanced economies acted boldly to counteract the effects on the economic activity of the pandemic and of the ensuing mobility restrictions. A strong discretionary fiscal support was indeed needed. Nevertheless, the combined effect of the stimulus and the recession will inevitably leave most economies with a much higher level of government debt.

Across advanced economies, average general government debt stood slightly above 100 percent of GDP at the end of 2019. According to the October 2019 IMF Fiscal Monitor (IMF 2019) this ratio would have followed a broadly flat profile in the following 5 years. The COVID-19 crisis dramatically changed this picture. Indeed, according to the April 2021 edition of the Fiscal Monitor IMF (2021), the

[37] According to the European framework for national accounts (ESA2010), in the case of 'standardised' guarantees - i.e. issued in large numbers, usually for fairly small amounts, along identical credit lines—the impact of guarantees on government deficit should be recorded at inception depending on the probability of default of the debtor.

[38] Following the collapse of Lehman Brothers in September 2008, a great many, in particular European, countries also issued guarantees but, at that time, they were adopted against default on bank bonds to help banks retain access to wholesale funding. Between 2009 and 2012, as argued by many authors, because of bank liabilities' guarantees, a negative feedback loop between sovereign and banking risk materialized and became the distinctive feature of the financial instability that spread out in the periphery of the euro area (Cooper & Nikolov, 2013; Acharya et al., 2014; Konig et al., 2015; Leonello, 2017).

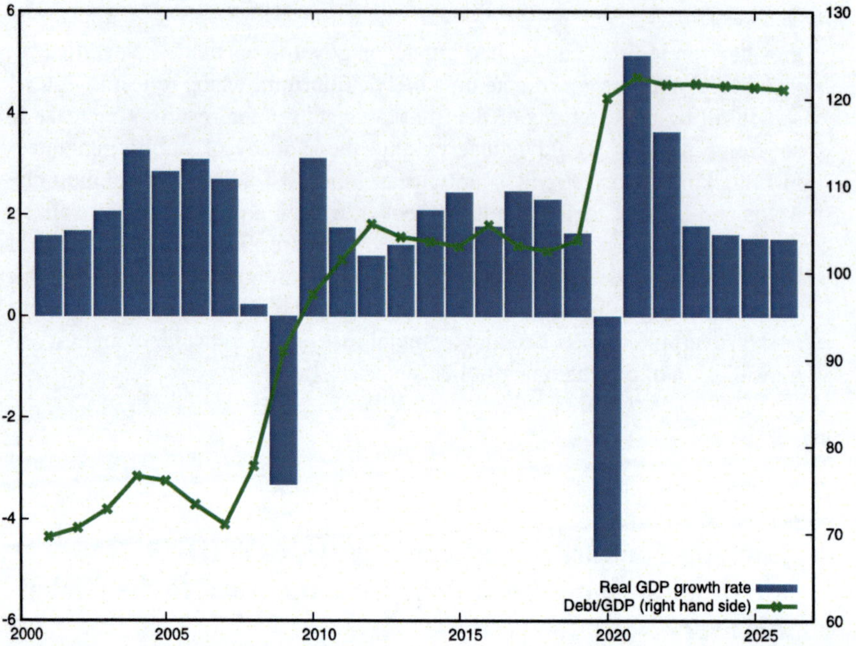

Fig. 2 Debt ratio and growth rate of real GDP in advanced economies. Source: IMF, World Outlook Database, April 2021

average debt-to-GDP ratio in advanced economies should have increased by about sixteen percentage points in 2020 and should stay at similar, elevated, levels in the medium term too (Fig. 2). While any forecast is surrounded by considerable uncertainty at this point in time in particular because of the unknown epidemic path and the strength of the recovery, there is little doubt that the current crisis will have deep and long-lasting effects on public finances across the world. While the extent of the worsening of public accounts in 2020 was heterogeneous across countries, only a few large advanced economies escaped a double-digit increase in their debt ratios, also because of the decline in the nominal product.

Moreover, as described above, many governments reacted to the COVID-19 crisis with the extension to the private sector of extremely large amounts of public guarantees on loans. As argued before, the rationales for this kind of intervention rely on its possible rapid implementation, its limited short-term costs for the public purses, and its effectiveness in mitigating liquidity issues for firms. By shielding private lenders from a share of the risk, these programmes can be instrumental in avoiding the occurrence of a credit crunch in a moment when many firms lack cash flow. The extent of the impact of these measures on the public accounts in 2020 is very heterogeneous across countries and depends, inter alia, on the specifics of the guarantee programmes and their actual use. In general, though, only a portion of the expected costs of these programmes has an immediate impact on the public accounts. For the most part, these measures thus constitute a contingent liability for governments. The timing and the extent of the transformation of these contingent debts into actual ones will depend on the speed and strength of the recovery. Thus, at this juncture, they are both surrounded by large margins of uncertainty.

The increase in public indebtedness—either in an explicit or in a contingent way—adds to already elevated risks for government accounts in many countries either because of the legacy of the Great Financial and Sovereign Debt crises or because of the expected effects of ageing populations. While long-term projections are notoriously difficult to make and are highly sensible to assumptions, in many countries debt-to-GDP ratios were expected to be on an upward trend even before the COVID-19 crisis hit. For instance, according to the Congressional Budget Office's 2019 long term budget outlook, the US federal debt held by the public would have increased from slightly less than 80 percent of GDP in 2019 to about 145 percent in 2049 (CBO, 2019). According to the European Commission 2019 Debt Sustainability Monitor, member states in the Union (including the United Kingdom) would have had to increase their primary structural balance by about 2.4 percentage points of GDP on average, just to guarantee the stability of their debt-to-GDP ratios by 2070 in the face of expected mounting ageing-related expenditures. The computed required adjustment for the euro area on average stood instead at 1.8 percentage points of GDP (European Commission, 2020b).[39]

High public debt ratios will thus most likely be the norm for the foreseeable future across many advanced economies. Even when governments fulfill their intertemporal budget constraints and, thus, in the absence of any sustainability concern, high public debt ratios can be a source of vulnerability. First, while the empirical assessment of a causal relation between debt and dismal growth performances may be contentious, high levels of public debt arguably can increase both borrowing costs for the private sector and uncertainty in the economy as a whole. They can also reduce the fiscal space for future counter-cyclical policies (Visco, 2017). Indeed, for instance, Romer and Romer (2019), using a panel of 30 OECD economies since 1980, find that countries with lower debt ratios implemented much more expansionary fiscal policies in response to financial crises and suffered less severe economic consequences. Second, a high debt ratio increases the potential for financial stability issues. For example, elevated annual gross borrowing needs exposes countries to increased risks due to the possible volatility in market sentiment. Therefore, while, as recommended by the IMF (2020a), governments should be wary of withdrawing their fiscal support too soon in the current circumstances, they should nevertheless start envisaging a strategy for dealing with high debt and rebalancing the public accounts in future better times.

[39] Notwithstanding the effect of the crisis, the most recent update of this analysis, also because of the expectation of a gradual improvement of the primary balance in the aftermath of the pandemic and of more favorable assumptions about the future evolution of real interest rates (based on the experience of the last decades), shows smaller adjustment needs both the EU and the EA (European Commission, 2021).

Risks related to high debt ratios can be partially mitigated by a number of factors, common to major advanced economies. In particular, the current low interest rate environment eases the refinancing costs of public debt. Because of this and because of the expected growth rate of the economies, Blanchard (2019) suggested that, under some circumstances, public debt might even have "no fiscal cost".[40] This paper shows that, when the growth rate of nominal product is larger than the implicit yield on debt, there are instances when the debt can be simply rolled-over without implying the need for increasing the primary balance in the future. Moreover, as shown by the October 2020 Fiscal Monitor (IMF, 2020a), many central banks across the world have largely increased their holdings of public debt securities since the onset of the COVID-19 crisis. From February to the time of the October 2020 Fiscal Monitor publication, the central banks of Japan, the Euro area, the US, and the UK bought marketable securities of their central government for an amount equal, respectively, to 75, 71, 57, and 50 percent of those issued in the same period. Ceteris paribus, this contributes to a further easing of the financial conditions in the short term. The purchases of the last few months accelerated a pre-existing trend since the Great Financial Crisis and further increased the role of central bank as major investors in sovereign debt. According to the OECD, at the end of 2020, the central bank held about 45 percent of national government securities in Japan and Sweden, above 20 percent in most European countries and in the US (OECD, 2021). In Italy, about one fourth of government securities was owned by the national central bank at the end of 2020, up from almost one fifth at the end of the previous year and from almost 6 percent at the end of 2014 (Bank of Italy, 2021).

Three factors drive the dynamics of the debt ratio: the differential between the growth rate of the economy and the implicit interest rate on public liabilities, the primary balance, and any (usually residual) adjustment to the stock of debt. This decomposition suggests a comprehensive approach towards gradual debt reduction over time. Clearly, even if a common theme could be traced, there are important country-specific circumstances that may warrant a somewhat differentiated approach both in terms of appropriate speed of adjustment and of selection of policies (IMF, 2020a).

In many countries, the implicit interest rate on debt is expected to keep falling in the next few years as old high-yield securities are gradually replaced by new low-yield ones (Fig. 3). Even with increasing yields over time, this reduction process will continue until the cost of the new debt will match the average one. Just as an example, the average implicit interest rate on existing debt in the euro area stood at about 1.9 percent in 2019. At the time of writing Euro-area governments could incur 10-year debts by paying an extremely limited yield on average (close

[40] Blanchard's contribution should not be considered as a normative one. It also explicitly considers the relevance of multiple equilibria in high public debt regimes where investors' expectations about the government's inability to fully repay its debt could foster self-fulfilling crises. This piece of research, delivered as the American Economic Association 2019 presidential address, stirred a large controversy. For example, Lian et al. (2020) note that high debt ratios are empirically associated to a higher probability of an increase in borrowing costs following a fiscal expansion.

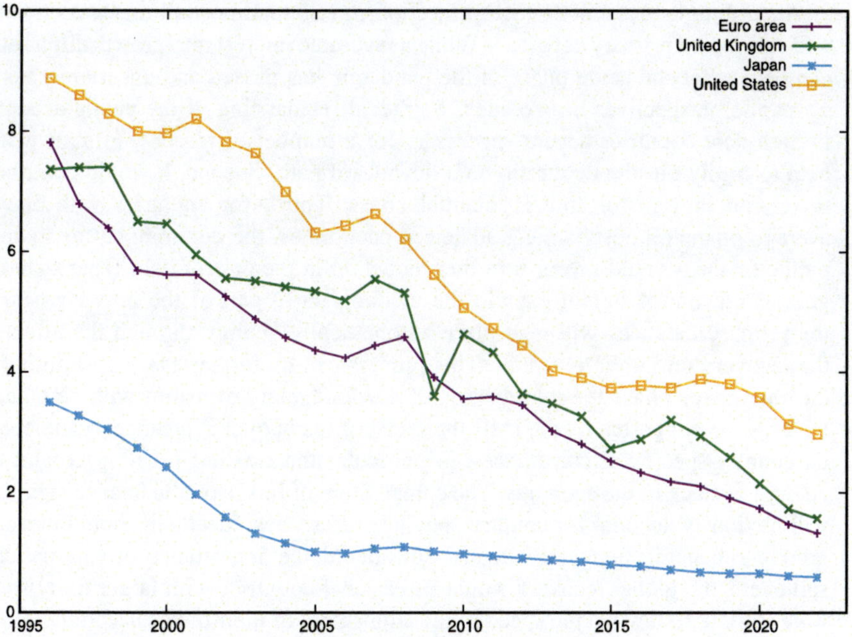

Fig. 3 Implicit interest rate on government debt in selected advanced economies. Source: European Commission Autumn 2020 fiscal forecast, AMECO database

to zero, in many instances). Governments can also take advantage of the current circumstances and adapt their issuance policies. In order to reduce rollover risks and increase resilience against future rate increases, they could lean towards longer-dated securities. Of course, this strategy implies a trade-off between relative costs and hedging features of different maturity structures of new issuances (OECD, 2020b). Indeed, as shown in the October 2020 Fiscal Monitor, advanced economies followed this strategy in the past few years: from 2002 to 2019, the average maturity on government bonds increased by about 2 years, to around seven on average.

Fiscal policy can also play a role in fostering long-term growth of the economies. First, it can be instrumental to the implementation of structural reforms, by easing possible short-term costs through redistributive policies. Second, it can play a direct role by prioritizing targeted budget measures with the largest multipliers (IMF, 2020a), by removing existing distortions in the tax-and-benefit structures, and by favouring productive investments (see Sect. 4.2). In general, the return to high rates of growth will be key in putting the debt ratio on a steady downward path. Thus, the quality of the selection of the public policies for the medium term is extremely important for the longer-term perspectives.

According to April 2021 IMF projections, in 2026 almost all major economies will still record primary deficits.[41] While a favorable interest rate-growth differential can help, after the acute phase of the pandemic has passed and uncertainty about economic perspectives has receded, a gradual rebalancing of the public accounts in high-debt countries appears necessary for a number of reasons. First, it would help to firmly put the debt ratio on a downward path. Second, it would contribute to rebuild buffers for future potential crises. Third, for countries with above-average financing costs among advanced economies, the commitment to sounder public finances could favour a further reduction in the cost of debt. Thanks to the gradual closure of output gaps in the medium term, part of the improvement in the primary balances will take place automatically, mainly through the effect of the recovery on public revenues. This process can be further eased by limiting in the emergency phase the introduction of new budgetary measures with permanent features. As suggested by the IMF, the speed of the budget adjustments can depend on country-specific circumstances, in particular the existing fiscal space and the amount of slack in the economy. The composition of future public finance measures will obviously account for country-specific preferences; ideally, it should preserve growth-enhancing budgetary items. Considered the importance of international spillovers, the global recovery would be easier if countries with larger fiscal space were to slow somewhat the speed of the adjustment of their public accounts.

4.2 *High Debt and the Conduct of Monetary Policy*

As reported in previous sections, the monetary policy decisions in reaction to the COVID-19 crisis reinforced the pre-existing trend towards large central banks' balance sheets. Moreover, the monetary authorities in the main economies are now among the largest holders of government debt. While these factors are a consequence of necessary steps to fulfil the monetary authorities' mandates, they nonetheless entail some risks.

First, a large balance sheet can increase interest risks for the central bank. Indeed, when fixed-term long-maturity bonds constitute a large share of the central bank's assets, a hypothetical future rate increase could generate a loss (e.g. Hall & Reis, 2015). In the short-term financial or capital losses are not an issue for central banks, since they are not subject to the same rules as private individuals and firms in accounting terms (see for example Buiter, 2020b). However, if the losses and the capital shortfall are sufficiently large and they are not recovered in the medium to long term, the monetary authority could lose credibility in its ability to maintain price stability. Therefore, if the loss of capital will not be replenished in the future, the risk of price instability will increase.

[41] The expected primary balances are −3.0, −0.6, −2.0, −2.1 percent of GDP respectively for the US, the euro area, Japan, and the UK.

Second, the exit from asset purchase programmes could end up putting some upward pressure on the implicit cost of government debt in many advanced economies. In principle, the concern of damaging debt sustainability or financial stability could influence the conduct of monetary policy once the recovery has terminated and the economic activity is again in line with potential output. Nevertheless, a few considerations can greatly attenuate this fear. While the refinancing costs of governments would be likely higher during the exit from unconventional measures, the relatively long average maturity of government debt can smooth the impact. Moreover, as discussed in Sect. 4.1, while the implicit cost of debt is relevant, the key driver of the debt-to-GDP dynamics is rather the difference between this value and the nominal growth rate of the economy. To the extent that the exit from the current regime of accommodative monetary policy signals improved economic perspectives (including higher inflation), the risks for the path of the debt ratio would be somewhat attenuated.

4.3 *Monetary Accommodation and Financial Stability*

As highlighted by the October 2020 IMF Fiscal Monitor, even before the COVID-19 crisis, private sector debt as a share of GDP was on the rise, reaching about 150 percent in 2019 across G20 countries. The pandemic obviously worsens this picture and will lead to a significant increase of non-financial firms' indebtedness (Visco, 2020). As discussed above, the extraordinary emergency policy support deployed during 2020 mitigated the liquidity pressures on the corporate sector. Nevertheless, over a somewhat longer horizon, in particular if the recovery is not sustained, firms' potential insolvencies could become an issue (IMF, 2020b). Small and medium sized enterprises, in particular in contact-intensive sectors, appear to be more likely to be relatively less well-equipped to weather the storms of the pandemic and the structural transformation of the economies. Thus, in some instances, corporate debt could have important repercussions both for governments (through the channel of public guarantees) and for banks. This contingency would further penalize the prospects for banking sector's profitability (ECB, 2020b), and, more in general, for financial stability.

At the same time, a long period of low interest rates could have some downsides too. In an environment in which interest rates remain low for a prolonged period of time, their beneficial effects in terms of reduced funding costs, greater easiness to borrow for consumption and investment, and increased asset prices may be reduced. They could even be dominated by the buildup of vulnerabilities in the financial system due to the presence of "distortions", "imperfections", and "institutional constraints" that may become "active", "economically more relevant" or "binding" when interest rates remain very low for a protracted period of time, favouring the building up of bubbles, excessive risk-taking, inefficient resource allocation, and debt overhang. Vulnerabilities may be favoured by money illusion,[42] myopic behaviour,[43] agency problem, and moral hazard.[44] The possible subsequent impairment of the provision of financial services and credit would affect the path of real economic activity.

In order to avoid the emergence of those financial stability issues, some measures could be taken. First, and foremost, the strength of the post-pandemic output growth is key. The sooner the recovery consolidates and activity returns in line with potential, the less likely the mentioned financial stability risks are to emerge. In such more favorable environment firms' recapitalizations, the reduction of leverage and the rebuilding of buffers against future crises would be easier. In this regard, it is important that the removal of the current expansionary fiscal and monetary policies is gradual and calibrated on the state of the economy (see also Sect. 3.2 on the risks of an early withdraw of support). Second, the use of appropriate regulatory and supervisory instruments will be crucial to limit behaviors by financial intermediaries that could lead to financial instability in the medium term.

4.4 *Towards a Knowledge-Based, "Green", and Digital Global Recovery: The Role of Public Investment*

As illustrated in previous sections, high public and private debt and an uncertain recovery are the main legacies of the pandemic shocks. To avoid financial instability, public and private finances have to be on a sustainable path in the medium run, and sustained economic growth is a key factor.

A contribution to achieving this goal can come from public investment. Like many other forms of government intervention, public spending in investment has the traditional expansionary effect in the short term. However, an increase in public investment—unlike most forms of current spending—is also expected to positively affect potential output. These positive effects at different horizons depend on many factors. In the short term, implementation lags are an obvious potential

---

[42] Agents focus on nominal variables, even though economic decisions should be based on real variables. Investors are unable to look through inflation and focus on the real return on investment. Agents may feel frustrated by the low level of nominal rates and decide to irrationally overcome these through search for yield.

[43] Agents are often short-sighted and focus on the short term, neglecting the future. Low rates may induce households to take on floating-rate mortgages without considering that interest rates could increase in the future, and to borrow excessively.

[44] A low interest rate environment may undermine agents' incentives to use resources efficiently, by weakening market controls and reducing the probability of default. Managers benefit from the rents associated with their positions (the agency problem), and have ex ante incentives to manage the firm successfully to maintain their position and to prevent a default: persistently low interest rates by reducing profitability of financial intermediaries operating the maturity transformation could increase moral hazard problems and may lead to a less efficient use of resources.

treat. Over longer horizons, the growth-enhancing impact of this kind of public expenditure depends on the extent of the untapped potential in the public capital stock and on the complementarity between these initiatives and future private activity (Ramey, 2020). Indeed, public investments can be effective in fostering long-term growth in particular if they are instrumental in favouring private activities (as in the case of some infrastructure, energy, digital economy, and R&D projects) and the accumulation of human capital (including measures for the health sector). Therefore, a careful selection of the projects—while challenging—appears to be key.

The literature suggests that, in the current and foreseeable circumstances, a world-wide increase in public investments could contribute to make the global recovery sustainable and durable, i.e., in restoring the pre-crisis level of output and in improving public and private debt sustainability.[45] The reasons are several.

First, when medium and longer term perspectives are far from clear and when private economic agents may display some lack of confidence in the future, public investments may provide a signal about the recovery. As suggested by the IMF (2020a), in the current circumstances, public investments can encourage firms' hiring and investments plans, which would otherwise be postponed. Of course, public investments and incentives for private ones could also be complement. Nevertheless, in some circumstances and depending of their design, incentives for private activities might fail to stimulate additional investments. Moreover, public investments can directly provide cash flow to firms and indirectly sustain their market value and access to credit markets.

Second, the complementarity between expansionary monetary and fiscal policy measures can be fully exploited to maximize the size of public investment multiplier (see Box 6).

Third, given that the shock is global, a coordinated symmetric cross-country response would generate positive spillovers. There would be no leakages associated with implementation by a single country in isolation. International coordination should also help those countries having greater financial needs. Spillovers would be magnified by the accommodative stance of monetary policy at global level.

While, as just discussed, there are several potential benefits of an increase in public investments, there are risks too. In this regard, it is important to note that the quality and efficiency of the decision processes for public investment projects appear to be crucial to minimize implementation lags in both the programming and actual realization phases. The resulting reduction in the uncertainty could be instrumental in fostering private activity. Conversely, inefficiencies in the selection and the realization of the projects could severely lower their positive output effect.

At the same time, the decision on which type of public investment that should be implemented is crucial. As discussed above, public investment should not necessarily be directed to increase only the stock of physical infrastructures. For

---

[45] For the euro area, the case for higher public investment has been debated at the policy level even before the COVID-19 crisis (Buti, 2020).

instance, investment in health can be extremely relevant to avoid new waves of the pandemic. Moreover, investment in human capital can be effective too, in particular in some countries featuring low levels of spending in education and in research and development. Finally, investment in "green" economy and in digitalization should also be considered. On the one hand, lowering the carbon footprint of the economic activities would be instrumental in reaching international environmental goals and in paving the way for a more sustainable growth. On the other hand, while the exact direction of the future production structure is hard to predict, a more digitalized economy would undoubtedly offer many new opportunities. While there seems to be some consensus in policy circles around the desirability of these broad priorities for many advanced economies, the selection of the actual projects will be a challenge. A microeconomic perspective based on cost-benefit analyses should support the decision process of allocating the resources among the different possible uses.

In conclusion, it is also important to recall that some of the benefits potentially brought about by new public investments in the fields of health, human capital, digitalization and green economy would likely go far beyond what is captured by the standard metric of GDP. Indeed, whether our measure of domestic product has even been (Bureau of Foreign and Domestic Commerce and Kuznets, 1934) or will be the most appropriate proxy for assessing the welfare of a society is an area of very active debate (Stiglitz et al., 2009; Dynan & Sheiner, 2018).

Box 6 Public Investment Multipliers[46]

Public investment multipliers can be large. This is particularly true during recessions and in periods of high uncertainty, when monetary and financial conditions remain accommodative, under the assumptions that investment projects are carried out efficiently without wastes of resources. Coordinated fiscal expansions can further amplify the effects. The exact definition of public investments used in the literature could differ across studies. Moreover, in practice, public investments could be quite heterogeneous in terms of nature and quality. However, some general lessons could be learned from empirical and simulation-bases inquiries.

According to the October 2020 IMF Fiscal monitor, in periods of high uncertainty, increasing public investment by 1 percent of GDP could strengthen confidence in the recovery and boost output by about 2.7 percent, private investment by 10 percent, and employment by 1.2 percent over a two-year horizon. These responses are contingent on the high quality of the investment projects and on the fact that existing public and private debt burdens do not weaken the response of the private sector to the stimulus.

(continued)

[46] Prepared by M. Pisani and M. Tasso.

Similarly, the October 2014 IMF World Economic Outlook reports that public investment shocks have statistically significant and long-lasting effects on output. In countries with high efficiency of public investment, the multiplier can be as large as 2.6 after 4 years (against a multiplier slightly lower than one under the case of low efficiency). The way the stimulus is financed is also relevant. The output effects are larger when public investment shocks are debt financed than when they are budget neutral.

The monetary policy stance matters for the size of the multipliers. According to the model-based simulations reported in the October 2014 World Economic Outlook, in advanced economies when monetary policy rates stay close to zero for 2 years, a 1 percent of GDP permanent increase in (fully efficient) public investment increases output by about 2 percent in the same year and by about 2.5 percent in the long run. The increase in short-run output would instead be smaller under normal conditions of less slack and with an immediate monetary policy response. Qualitatively similar conclusions are reported in Coenen et al. (2012), where public investment multipliers are compared across several different models for different monetary policy responses. For the euro area, Burlon et al. (2017) evaluate the macroeconomic impact of a (temporary) programme for public infrastructure spending under alternative assumptions about funding sources and the monetary policy stance. The quantitative assessment is made by simulating a dynamic general equilibrium model of a monetary union with region-specific fiscal policy. Results suggest that EA-wide stimuli are more effective than unilateral (region-specific) stimuli (Cova et al., 2017 find qualitatively similar results in the case of a simultaneous increase in public investment in advanced economies). Under EA-wide stimulus, the fiscal multiplier is close to 2 if the forward guidance on the short-term policy rate holds. If, in addition, the monetary authority keeps down also the long-term interest rates (with quantitative easing), the fiscal multiplier is even larger. Debt financing of the spending projects, particularly under an accommodative monetary policy stance and if the sovereign spreads do not increase, is more growth-friendly than financing through distortionary taxes. Busetti et al. (2019) stress that the effectiveness of the fiscal stimulus is larger if government spending is directed towards productive goods and its implementation occurs efficiently and without delays.

As in the case of other kinds of fiscal expansion, also an increase in public investments can have beneficial effects for other countries. Some results about these cross-country spillovers are available for the case of the euro area. In't Veld (2016) shows that when monetary policy does not offset the expansion, public investment in some core countries of the EA could have significant positive GDP spillovers to the rest of the Eurozone. If borrowing costs are low, the increase in government debt of core country would be modest, while

(continued)

debt ratios in the rest of the Eurozone could be somewhat improved. These simulations consider the illustrative case of a hypothetical rise in public investment in Germany and the Netherlands of 1 percent of baseline GDP for 10 years, while the monetary policy rate is kept constant for 2 years. This stimulus package increases GDP in Germany and in the Netherlands on impact by about 0.7–0.9 percent, and by about 1.3 percent after 10 years. Spillovers to the rest of the Eurozone are non-negligible, as higher demand from the expanding countries and a depreciation of the euro boost output. GDP in the rest of the Eurozone is around 0.3 percent higher. The study finds larger multipliers and spillovers for investment projects with a higher ability to raise the productivity of other productive factors in the economy. Elekdag and Muir (2014) also find similar results: in the case of the EA, cross-country spillovers of higher public investment are expansionary and non-trivial, in particular if the monetary stance is accommodative.

Alloza et al. (2019) use the EAGLE macroeconomic model of the euro area to simulate an investment-based fiscal stimulus of 1 percent of nominal GDP over 2 years in one large euro area country. Under the assumption of reactive monetary policy, the spillovers (computed as the ratio of GDP reactions of the destination country to the origin country) are below 0.1 on average in the 2 years after the shock. Similarly, spillovers in one country from a simultaneous fiscal stimulus of 1 percent of GDP over 2 years in all the other countries are small. Cross-country effects are instead larger under the assumption that the policy rate is kept constant at its baseline level during the first 2 years of the simulation. In this second case, for instance, the spillover to the rest of the area from an increase in German public investment is in the order of 0.25.

5 Conclusions

COVID-19 is probably the worst social and macroeconomic shock to be faced by the global economy since WWII. The path towards the recovery is uncertain and will most likely be long. The structure of the economy will probably be affected permanently by this crisis. Some sectors will inevitably suffer more and the transition towards the new equilibrium could imply significant costs.

With their decisions policy-makers can influence both the transition to the new equilibrium and the new equilibrium of the global economy.

Therefore, in the near future, policy-makers will face several tough choices and tradeoffs. Accompanying the necessary changes to the economic structure, while cushioning the blow to the most vulnerable, maintaining macroeconomic stability and avoiding the risks discussed in the paper will indeed be the challenge of the next few years.

The policy mix will be crucial to determine tradeoffs and, at the same time, to foster a sustained recovery and to improve health, environmental, and human capital conditions across the world. International cooperation is key to achieving these improvements in an efficient, effective, and inclusive way.

References

Acharya, V., Drechsler, I., & Schnabl, P. (2014). A pyrrhic victory? Bank bailouts and sovereign credit risk. *The Journal of Finance, 69*(6), 2689–2739.

Aksoy, Y., Basso, H. S., Smith, R. P., & Grasl, T. (2019). Demographic structure and macroeconomic trends. *American Economic Journal: Macroeconomics, 11*(1), 193–222.

Albertazzi, U., & Esposito, L. (2017). *Credit demand and supply: A two-way feedback relation*. Bank of Italy Working Paper Series.

Alloza, M., Cozmanca, B., Ferdinandusse, M., & Jacquinot, P. (2019). Fiscal spillovers in a monetary union. *ECB Economic Bulletin, 1*, 6.

Alon, T. M., Doepke, M., Olmstead-Rumsey, J., & Tertilt, M. (2020, April). *The impact of COVID-19 on gender equality*. NBER Working Paper Series, Working Paper No 26947, National Bureau of Economic Research.

Arulampalam, W., Gregg, P., & Gregory, M. (2001). Unemployment scarring. *The Economic Journal, 111*(475), F577–F584.

Autor, D., Lutz, B., Cho, D., Crane, L., Goldar, M., Peterman, W., Ratner, D., & Villar, D. (2020). *An evaluation of the paycheck protection program using administrative payroll microdata*. mimeo.

Backer, S., Bloom, N., Davis, S., & Terry, S. (2020). *COVID-induced economic uncertainty and its consequences*. VoxEU.

Baker, S. R., Farrokhnia, R. A., Meyer, S., Pagel, M., & Yannelis, C. (2020). *Income, liquidity, and the consumption response to the 2020 economic stimulus payments (No. w27097)*. National Bureau of Economic Research.

Bank of Italy. (2020). *Economic Bulletin No. 2/2020*.

Bank of Italy. (2021, April). *The public finances: Borrowing requirement and debt, Statistics series*.

Baqaee, D., & Farhi, E. (2020). *Supply and demand in disaggregated Keynesian economies with an application to the COVID-19 crisis. CEPR DP 14743*.

Bartocci, A., Notarpietro, A., & Pisani, M. (2020). COVID-19 shock and fiscal-monetary policy mix in a monetary union. In *Tema di Discussion n 1313 Bank of Italy Working Paper Series*. Bank of Italy, Economic Research and International Relations Area.

Bartsch, E. J., Boivin, S. F., & Hildebrand, P. (2019). *Dealing with the next downturn: From unconventional monetary policy to unprecedented policy coordination. SUERF Policy Note, Issue No 105*. Retrieved from https://www.suerf.org/policynotes/8209/dealing-with-the-next-downturn-from-unconventional-monetary-policy-to-unprecedented-policy-coordination/html

Bartsch, E., Bénassy-Quéré, A., Corsetti, G., & Debrun, X. (2020). It's all in the mix. How monetary and fiscal policies can work or fail together. In *Geneva Report on the world economy* (p. 23). PIIE.

Barwell, C., Chadha, J., & Grady, L. (2020). *COVID-19 crisis: Fiscal policy should lead and the Bank of England should follow for the duration of the crisis*. Retrieved from https://voxeu.org/article/COVID-19-crisis-fiscal-policy-should-lead-and-bank-england-should-follow

Bassetto, M., & Sargent, T. (2020). Shotgun weddings between fiscal and monetary policies. *Annual Review of Economics, 12*, 659–690.

Batini, N., Cantelmo, A., Melina, G., & Villa, S. (2020). How loose, how tight? A measure of monetary and fiscal stance for the euro area. In *Temi di discussione (Economic working papers) 1295*. Bank of Italy, Economic Research and International Relations Area.

Bayer, C., Born, B., Luetticke, R., & Müller, G. J. (2020). *The Coronavirus Stimulus Package: How large is the transfer multiplier?* mimeo.

Bernanke, B. (2003, May). *Some thoughts on monetary policy in Japan*, speech.

Bernanke, B. (2005). *The global saving glut and the U.S. current account deficit*. Remarks at the Sandridge Lecture, Virginia Association of Economists.

Bernanke, B., & Gertler, M. (1989). Agency costs, net worth, and business fluctuations. *The American Economic Review, 79*(1), 14–31.

Biancotti, C., Borin, A., Cingano, F., Tommasino, P., & Veronese, G. (2020, March 18). *The case for a coordinated COVID-19 response: No country is an island*. Retrieved from https://voxeu.org/article/case-coordinated-COVID-19-response-no-country-island

Bitler, M., Hoynes, H. W., & Whitmore Schanzenbach, D. (2020). *The social safety net in the wake of COVID-19, No. w27796*. National Bureau of Economic Research.

Blanchard, O. (2019). Public debt and low interest rates. *American Economic Review, 109*(4), 1197–1229.

Blanchard, O., & Perotti, R. (2002). An empirical characterization of the dynamic effects of changes in government spending and taxes on output. *The Quarterly Journal of Economics, 117*(4), 1329–1368.

Blanchard, O., & Pisani Ferry, J. (2020, April 10). *Monetisation: Do not panic*. Voxeu. Retrieved from https://voxeu.org/article/monetisation-do-not-panic

Blanchard, O., Philippon, T., & Pisani-Ferry, J. (2020). *A new policy toolkit is needed as countries exit COVID-19 lockdowns*. Peterson Institute for International Economics Policy Brief.

Blundell, R., Costa Dias, M., Joyce, R., & Xu, X. (2020). COVID-19 and inequalities. *Fiscal Studies, 41*(2), 291–319.

Bluwstein, K., & Canova, F. (2016). Beggar-thy-neighbor? The international effects of ECB unconventional monetary policy measures. *International Journal of Central Banking, 12*(3), 69–120.

Bordo, M. D. (2020, October). *Monetary policy cooperation/coordination and global financial crises in historical perspective*. NBER Working Paper, N. 27898.

Breckenfelder, J., De Fiore, F., Andrade, P., Karadi, P., & Tristani, O. (2016). *The ECB's asset purchase Programme: an early assessment, Working Paper Series 1956*. European Central Bank.

Brugiavini, A., & Weber, G. (2014). *Longer-term consequences of the great recession on the lives of Europeans*. Oxford University Press.

Brunnermeier, M., & Sannikov, Y. (2014). A macroeconomic model with a financial sector. *American Economic Review, 104*(2), 379–421.

Brunnermeier, M., & Sannikov, Y. (2016). *The I theory of money, Working Paper*.

Buiter, W. (2020a). *The helicopters are coming, project syndicate*. Retrieved from https://www.project-syndicate.org/commentary/helicopter-money-coronavirus-response-by-willem-h-buiter-1-2020-03

Buiter, W. (2020b). *Central banks as fiscal players: The drivers of fiscal and monetary policy space*. Cambridge University Press.

Bureau of Foreign and Domestic Commerce, & Kuznets, S. (1934). *National Income, 1929-1932*. U.S. Government Printing Office.

Burgess, S., & Sievertsen, H. H. (2020). *Schools, skills, and learning: The impact of COVID-19 on education*. Retrieved from https://voxeu.org/article/impact-COVID-19-education

Burlon, L., Locarno, A., Notarpietro, A., & Pisani, M. (2017). Public investment and monetary policy stance in the euro area. In *Temi di discussione (Economic working papers) 1150*. Bank of Italy, Economic Research and International Relations Area.

Busetti, F., Giorgiantonio, C., Ivaldi, G., Mocetti, S., Notarpietro, A., & Tommasino, P. (2019). Capital and public investment in Italy: Macroeconomic effects, measurement and regulatory weaknesses. In *Questioni di Economia e Finanza (occasional papers) 520*. Bank of Italy, Economic Research and International Relations Area.

Buti, M. (2020, January). *Economic policy in EMU: What role for fiscal and monetary policy? Which has more scope left? How to combine them?* SUERF Policy Note Issue No 124.

Caballero, R. J., & Krishnamurthy, A. (2003). Excessive dollar debt: Financial development and underinsurance. *The Journal of Finance, 58*(2), 867–893.

Caracciolo, G., Cingano, F., Ercolani, V., Ferrero, G., Hassan, F., Papetti, A., Savini, A., & Tommasino, P. (2020a) *COVID-19 and economic analysis: A review of the debate. COVID-19 and economic analysis: A review of economic analysis*. Banca d'Italia Literature Review Issue no. 3. Retrieved from https://www.bancaditalia.it/media/notizie/2020/COVID-literature-newsletter-n3.pdf

Caracciolo, G., Cingano, F., Ercolani, V., Ferrero, G., Hassan, F., Papetti, A., Savini, M., & Tommasino, P. (2020b). *COVID-19 and economic analysis: A review of the debate*. Banca d'Italia Literature Review Issue no. 1. Retrieved from https://www.bancaditalia.it/media/notizie/2020/COVID-literature-newsletter-n1.pdf

Carlsson, M., Dahl, G. B., Öckert, B., & Rooth, D. (2015). The effect of schooling on cognitive skills. *Review of Economics and Statistics, 97*(3), 533–547.

Carta, F., & De Philippis, M. (2021). *The impact of the COVID-19 shock on labour income inequality: Evidence from Italy, no. 606*. Bank of Italy, Economic Research and International Relations Area.

Carvalho, C., Ferrero, A., & Nechio, F. (2016). Demographics and real interest rates: Inspecting the mechanism. *European Economic Review, 88*, 208–226.

Casarico, A., & Lattanzio, S. (2020). The heterogeneous effects of COVID-19 on labor market flows: Evidence from administrative data. *COVID Economics, 52*.

Casiraghi, M., & Ferrero, G. (2015). *Is deflation good or bad? Just mind the inflation gap, Questioni di Economia e Finanza (occasional papers) 268*. Bank of Italy, Economic Research and International Relations Area.

CBO. (2019, June). *The 2019 long-term budget outlook*.

Cerra, V., Fatas, A., & Saxena, S. C. (2020). *Hysteresis and business cycles*, CEPR Discussion Paper No. DP14531.

Chetty, R., Friedman, J. N., Hendren, N., & Stepner, M. (2020). *How did COVID-19 and stabilization policies affect spending and employment? A new real-time economic tracker based on private sector data (no. w27431)*. National Bureau of Economic Research.

Coenen, G., Erceg, C. J., Freedman, C., Furceri, D., Kumhof, M., Lalonde, R., Laxton, D., Lindé, J., Mourougane, A., Muir, D., Mursula, S., de Resende, C., Roberts, J., Roeger, W., Snudden, S., Trabant, M., & In't Veld, J. (2012). Effects of fiscal stimulus in structural models. *American Economic Journal: Macroeconomics, American Economic Association, 4*(1), 22–68.

Collins, C., Potter, S., & Truman, E. (2020). Enhancing central bank cooperation in the COVID-19 pandemic. In M. Obstfeld & A. S. Posen (Eds.), *How the G20 can hasten recovery from COVID-19*. Peterson Institute for International Economics PIIE BRIEFING 20-1.

Cooper, R., & Nikolov, K. (2013). *Government debt and banking fragility: The spreading of strategic uncertainty*, Working Paper.

Cova, P., & Ferrero, G. (2015). *The Eurosystem's asset purchase programmes for monetary policy purposes*. Banca d'Italia, Occasional Papers N. 270.

Cova, P., Pagano, P., Notarpietro, A., & Pisani, M. (2017). Secular stagnation, R&D, public investment and monetary policy: A global-model perspective. In *Temi di discussione (Economic working papers) 1156*. Bank of Italy, Economic Research and International Relations Area.

Dailo, R. (2019). *It's time to look more carefully at "monetary policy 3 (MP3)" and "modern monetary theory (MMT)"*. Retrieved from https://www.linkedin.com/pulse/its-time-look-more-carefully-monetary-policy-3-mp3-modern-ray-dalio/

De Socio, A., Narizzano, S., Orlando, T., Parlapiano, F., Rodano, G., Sette, E., & Viggiano, L. (2020). *Gli effetti della pandemia sul fabbisogno di liquidità, sul bilancio e sulla rischiosità delle imprese*. Bank of Italy.

Dedola, L., Karadi, P., & Lombardo, G. (2013). Global implications of national unconventional policies. *Journal of Monetary Economics, 60*, 66–85.

Dedola, L., Georgiadis, G., Gräb, J., & Arnaud, M. (2020). Does a big bazooka matter? Quantitative easing policies and exchange rates. *Research Bulletin, 76*.

Dietrich, A., Kuester, K., Müller, G., & Schoenle, R. (2020, March 24). *News and uncertainty about COVID-19: Survey evidence and short-run economic impact*. mimeo. Retrieved from https://voxeu.org/article/news-and-uncertainty-about-economic-fallout-COVID-19

Dowd, K. (2018). *Against helicopter money*. Retrieved from https://www.cato.org/cato-journal/winter-2018/against-helicopter-money

Dynan, K., & Sheiner, L. (2018). *GDP as a measure of economic well-being, working paper, 43*. The Brookings Institution.

ECB. (2020a). Public loan guarantees and bank lending in the COVID-19 period. *Economic Bulletin, 6*.

ECB. (2020b, November). *Financial stability review*.

Eggertsson, G. B., & Krugman, P. (2012). Debt, deleveraging, and the liquidity trap: A Fisher-Minsky-Koo approach. *The Quarterly Journal of Economics, 127*(3), 1469–1513.

Eichenbaum, M. (1997). Some thoughts on practical stabilization policy. *American Economic Review, 87*(2), 236–230.

Elekdag, S., & Muir, D. (2014). *Das public Kapital: How much would higher German public investment help Germany and the Euro area? WP 14/227*. International Monetary Fund.

Elmendorf, D. W., & Furman, J. (2008). *If, when, how: A primer on fiscal stimulus*. The Brookings Institution.

Ercolani, V. (2020a, November 5). *Strengthening national health systems and dampening precautionary attitudes, COVID-note*. Bank of Italy.

Ercolani, V. (2020b, July 8). *COVID-induced precautionary saving in the US: The role of the unemployment rate, COVID-note*. Bank of Italy.

European Commission. (2020a). *Educational inequalities in Europe and physical school closures during COVID-19, Fairness Policy Brief Series*.

European Commission. (2020b, January). *Debt sustainability monitor 2019, Institutional Paper 120*.

European Commission. (2021, February). *Debt sustainability monitor 2020, Institutional Paper 143*.

Farhi, E., & Werning, I. (2016). A theory of macroprudential policies in the presence of nominal rigidities. *Econometrica, 84*(5), 1645–1704.

Faria e Castro, M. (2020). *Fiscal policy during a pandemic*. Federal Reserve Bank of St. Louis Working Paper 2020-006.

Farmer, R. (2020). *COVID-19: Economic policy response*. Retrieved from https://cfmsurvey.org/users/roger-farmer

Feldstein, M. (2002). *Commentary: Is there a role for discretionary fiscal policy? Rethinking stabilization policy*. A symposium sponsored by The Federal Reserve Bank of Kansas City, Jackson Hole Wyoming.

Ferrero, G., Gross, M., & Neri, S. (2019a). On secular stagnation and low interest rates: Demography matters. *International Finance, 22*(3), 262–278.

Ferrero, G., & Neri, S. (2017). *Monetary policy in a low interest rate environment*. Occasional Papers, N. 392. Bank of Italy.

Ferrero, G., Pietrunti, M., & Tiseno, A. (2019b). *Benefits of gradualism or costs of inaction? Monetary policy in times of uncertainty*. Economic working papers, N. 1205. Bank of Italy.

Fornaro, L., & Wolf, M. (2020). *COVID-19 coronavirus and macroeconomic policy, CEPR discussion papers 14529*. C.E.P.R. Discussion Papers.

Francese, M., & Prady, D. (2018). *Universal basic income: Debate and impact assessment, no. 2018/273*. International Monetary Fund.

Galeotti, A., & Surico, P. (2020). *A user guide to COVID-19*. Retrieved from https://voxeu.org/article/user-guide-COVID-19

Galì, J. (2020a, March 17). *Helicopter money: The time is now*. Voxeu. Retrieved from https://voxeu.org/article/helicopter-money-time-now

Galì, J. (2020b). The effects of a money-financed fiscal stimulus. *Journal of Monetary Economics, 115*, 1–19.

Gaspar, V., & Mauro, P. (2020). *Fiscal policies to protect people during the coronavirus outbreak*. IMF blog. Retrieved from https://blogs.imf.org/2020/03/05/fiscal-policies-to-protect-people-during-the-coronavirus-outbreak/

Georgieva, K., Fabrizio, S., Lim, C. H., & Tavares, M. M. (2020). *The COVID-19 gender gap*. Retrieved from https://blogs.imf.org/2020/07/21/the-COVID-19-gender-gap/

Giacomelli, S., Mocetti, S., & Rodano, G. (2021). *Fallimenti d'impresa in epoca COVID, Note COVID-19, 27 gennaio*. Bank of Italy.

Giavazzi, F., & Tabellini, G. (2020, March 24). *COVID perpetual Eurobonds: Jointly guaranteed and supported by the ECB*. Voxeu. Retrieved from https://voxeu.org/article/COVID-perpetual-eurobonds

Gobbi, G., Palazzo, F., & Segura, A. (2020). *Unintended effects of loan guarantees during the COVID-19 crisis*. VoxEU.

Goodhart, C., & Pradhan, M. (2020). *Future imperfect after coronavirus*. VoxEU.org.

Gopinath, G. (2019, October). *World Economic Outlook, Global manufacturing downturn, rising trade barriers (foreword)*. International Monetary Fund.

Gordon, R. J. (2016). *The rise and fall of American growth: The U.S. standard of living since the civil war*. Princeton University Press.

Goy, G., & Van den End, J. W. (2020). *The impact of the COVID-19 crisis on the equilibrium interest rate*. VoxEU.org.

Group of Thirty. (2020). *Reviving and restructuring the corporate sector post-COVID. Designing public policy interventions*.

Guerrieri, V., Lorenzoni, G., Straub, L., & Werning, I. (2020). *Macroeconomic implications of COVID-19: Can negative supply shocks cause demand shortages? NBER WP 26918*.

Hall, R. E. (2009). *By how much does GDP rise if the government buys more output? Brookings papers on economic activity, economic studies program* (Vol. 40, pp. 183–249). The Brookings Institution.

Hall, R. E., & Reis, R. (2015). *Maintaining central-bank financial stability under new-style central banking (No. w21173)*. National Bureau of Economic Research.

Holston, K., Laubach, T., & Williams, J. C. (2017). Measuring the natural rate of interest: International trends and determinants. *Journal of International Economics, 108*(1), S59–S75.

Holston, K., Laubach, T., & Williams, J. C. (2020). *Adapting the Laubach and Williams and Holston, Laubach, and Williams models to the COVID-19 pandemic*. Federal Reserve Bank of New York Note.

ILO. (2020). *The impact of the COVID-19 pandemic on youth, and what to do about it*. Retrieved from https://www.ilo.org/brussels/information-resources/news/WCMS_759403/lang%2D%2Den/index.htm

IMF. (2019, October). *Fiscal monitor*.

IMF. (2020a, October). *Fiscal monitor*.

IMF. (2020b, October). *Global financial stability report*.

IMF. (2021, April). *Fiscal monitor*.

In't Veld, J. (2016, August). *Public investment stimulus in surplus countries and their euro area spillovers*. ECFIN European Economy Economic Brief 016.

Jordà, O., Sanjay, R. S., & Taylor, A. M. (2020). *Longer-run Economic Consequences of Pandemics, Working Paper Series 2020-09*. Federal Reserve Bank of San Francisco.

Kaplan, G., Moll, B., & Violante, G. L. (2018). Monetary policy according to HANK. *American Economic Review, 108*(3), 697–743.

Karabarbounis, L., & Neiman, B. (2014). The global decline of the labor share. *Quarterly Journal of Economics, 129*, 61–103.

Kim, C. J., & Nelson, C. (2001). A Bayesian approach to testing for Markov switching in univariate and dynamic factor models. *International Economic Review, 42*, 989–1013.

King, T. B. (2019). Expectation and duration at the effective lower bound. *Journal of Financial Economics, 134*(3), 736–760.

Kiyotaki, N., & Moore, J. (1997). Credit cycles. *Journal of Political Economy, 105*(2), 211–248.

Konig, P., Anand, K., & Heinemann, F. (2015). Guarantees, transparency and the interdependency between sovereign and bank default risk. *Journal of Banking and Finance, 45*, 321.

Koo, R. (2008). *The holy grail of macroeconomics: Lessons from Japan's great recession*. Wiley.

Korinek, A., & Simsek, A. (2016). Liquidity trap and excessive leverage. *American Economic Review, 106*(3), 699–738.

Kozlowski, J., Veldkamp, L., & Venkateswaran, V. (2020). *Scarring body and mind: The long-term belief-scarring effects of COVID-19*. National Bureau of Economic Research Working Papers, No 27439.

Landais, C., Michaillat, P., & Saez, E. (2018). A macroeconomic approach to optimal unemployment insurance: Theory. *American Economic Journal: Economic Policy, 10*(2), 152–181.

Lane, P. (2020). *The ECB's monetary policy in the pandemic: Meeting the challenge*. Speech by Philip R. Lane, member of the executive board of the ECB, at the 62nd NABE annual meeting "global reset? Economics, business, and policy in the pandemic".

Leonello, A. (2017). Government guarantees and the bank-sovereign nexus. *ECB Research Bulletin, 35*.

Levy Yeyati, E. (2020, March 31). *COVID, fed swaps and the IMF as lender of last resort*. VoxEU. Retrieved from https://voxeu.org/article/COVID-fed-swaps-and-imf-lender-last-resort

Lian, W., Presbitero, A. F., & Wiriadinata, U. (2020). *Public debt and r-g at risk*. IMF Working Paper 20/137.

Locarno, A., & Zizza, R. (2020). *Previsioni ai tempi del Coronavirus, note COVID-19, 11 maggio*. Bank of Italy.

Malmendier, U., & Nagel, S. (2011). Depression babies: Do macroeconomic experiences affect risk taking? *The Quarterly Journal of Economics, 126*(1), 373–416.

McConnell, M., & Perez-Quiros, G. (2000). Output fluctuations in the United States: What has changed since the early 1980s? *American Economic Review, 90*, 1464–1476.

McKay, A., & Reis, R. (2016). The role of automatic stabilizers in the US business cycle. *Econometrica, 84*(1), 141–194.

McKay, A., & Reis, R. (2021). Optimal automatic stabilizers. *Review of Economic Studies., 88*(5), 2375–2406.

McKibbin, W. J., & Fernando, R. (2020). *The global macroeconomic impacts of COVID-19: Seven scenarios*. The Australian National University Centre for Applied Macroeconomic Analysis Working Papers, No. 19/2020.

McKibbin, W. J., & Sidorenko, A. A. (2006). *Global macroeconomic consequences of pandemic influenza*. The Australian National University Centre for Applied Macroeconomic Analysis Working Papers, No 26/2006.

Mian, A., & Sufi, A. (2014). *House of debt*. Chicago University of Chicago Press.

Moffitt, R. A., & Ziliak, J. P. (2020). COVID-19 and the US safety net. *Fiscal Studies, 41*, 3.

Mongey, S., Pilossoph, L., & Weinberg, A. (2020). Which workers bear the burden of social distancing policies? *COVID Economics, 12*, 69–86.

Mountford, A., & Uhlig, H. (2009). What are the effects of fiscal policy shocks? *Journal of Applied Econometrics, 24*(6), 960–992.

O'Neil, J., & Lombardi, D. (2020, April 28). *How to use the SDR*. Project Syndicate. Retrieved from https://www.project-syndicate.org/commentary/imf-sdr-vehicle-to-finance-COVID19-mitigation-by-jim-o-neill-and-domenico-lombardi-2020-04?barrier=accesspaylog

OECD. (2020a). *Supporting livelihoods during the COVID-19 crisis: Closing the gaps in safety nets*.

OECD. (2020b). *Sovereign borrowing outlook for OECD countries 2020*. Special COVID-19 Edition.

OECD. (2021). *Sovereign borrowing outlook for OECD countries 2021*.

Oreopoulos, P., von Wachter, T., & Heisz, A. (2012). The short- and long-term career effects of graduating in a recession. *American Economic Journal: Applied Economics, 4*, 1–29.

Portes, J. (2020). *The lasting scars of the COVID-19 crisis: Channels and impacts*. Retrieved from https://voxeu.org/article/lasting-scars-COVID-19-crisis

Rachel, L., & Smith, T. D. (2017). Are low real interest rates here to stay? *International Journal of Central Banking, 13*(3), 1–42.

Rachel, L., & Summers, L. H. (2019, March 7–8). *On falling neutral real rates, fiscal policy, and the risk of secular stagnation*. Brookings Papers on Economic Activity Conference Drafts.

Ramey, V. A. (2011). Can government purchases stimulate the economy? *Journal of Economic Literature, American Economic Association, 49*(3), 673–685.

Ramey, V. A. (2020). *The macroeconomic consequences of infrastructure investment*. National Bureau of Economic Research, Working Paper, No. 27625.

Randall Wray, L. (2015). *Modern money theory: A primer on macroeconomics for sovereign monetary systems*. Palgrave Macmillan.

Reichlin, L., & Shoemaker, D. (2020, March 26). *Fault lines in fiscal-monetary policy coordination*. Voxeu. Retrieved from https://voxeu.org/article/fault-lines-fiscal-monetary-policy-coordination

Reis, R. (2019, June). *A solution to sudden stops: The IMF and central banks should work together to resolve financial crises*. IMF Finance and Development. Retrieved from https://www.imf.org/external/pubs/ft/fandd/2019/06/imf-and-central-banks-working-together-reis.htm

Romer, C. D., & Romer, D. H. (2019). *Fiscal space and the aftermath of financial crises: How it matters and why (No. w25768)*. National Bureau of Economic Research.

Rondinelli, C., & Zanichelli, F. (2020). *Principali risultati della seconda edizione dell'indagine straordinaria sulle famiglie italiane nel 2020, Note COVID-19*. Bank of Italy.

Ruggles, N. D., & Ruggles, R. (1977). The anatomy of earnings behavior. In F. T. Juster (Ed.), *Distribution of economic well-being* (pp. 115–162). National Bureau of Economic Research.

Simmons, R., Littera, G., Culkin, N., Dini, P., Fantacci, L., & Amato, M. (2020). *Helicopter, Bazooka or Drone?* Retrieved from https://www.politico.eu/article/helicopter-bazooka-drone-economic-policy-coronavirus-crisis-money/

Stiglitz, J., Sen, A., & Fitoussi, J. (2009). *Report of the commission on the measurement of economic performance and social progress*.

Summers, L. H. (2014). U.S. economic prospects: Secular stagnation, hysteresis, and the zero lower bound. *Business Economics, 49*, 65–73.

Tabellini, G. (2020, March 20). *Eurobond con cura*. Il Foglio.

Thwaites, G. (2015). *Why are real interest rates so low? Secular stagnation and the relative price of investment goods*. Bank of England Working Paper No. 564.

Tlaib, R. (2020). *Automatic BOOST to communities act*. Retrieved from https://tlaib.house.gov/sites/tlaib.house.gov/files/Automatic%20Boost%20to%20Communities%20Act%20.pdf

Tumino, A. (2015). *The scarring effect of unemployment from the early '90s to the great recession*. Institute for Economic and Social Research Working Paper 2015-5.

Turner, A. (2013, February 6). *Debt, money and mephistopheles*. Speech at Cass Business School.

UNICEF. (2020, June). *Unequal access to remote schooling amid COVID-19 threatens to deepen global learning crisis*. Press release 4. Retrieved from https://www.unicef.org/press-releases/unequal-access-remote-schooling-amid-COVID-19-threatens-deepen-global-learning

Vayanos, D., & Vila, J. L. (2020). A preferred-habitat model of the term structure of interest rates. *Econometrica*. Previously published in 2009 as NBER Working Paper, No. 15487.

Velasco, A., (2020). *Preventing an emerging-market meltdown*. Project Syndicate. Retrieved from https://www.project-syndicate.org/commentary/international-funding-can-prevent-emerging-market-meltdown-by-andres-velasco-2020-06?barrier=accesspaylog

Vihriälä, V. (2020, April 15). *Make room for fiscal action through debt conversion*. VoxEU.

Visco, I. (2017). *"Sviluppo dell'economia e stabilità finanziaria: il vincolo del debito pubblico", relazione presentata al 63° Convegno di studi amministrativi su "La tutela degli interessi finanziari della collettività nel quadro della contabilità pubblica: principi, strumenti, limiti"*, Varenna.

Visco, I. (2020, November 16–17). *The G20 under Italy's leadership in 2021*. Keynote speech by Mr Ignazio Visco, Governor of the Bank of Italy, at The Global Foundation - Rome Roundtable 2020 "Which way the world after the pandemic? Our inclusive human future", Virtual meeting.
Viviano, E. (2020). *Alcune stime preliminari degli effetti delle misure di sostegno sul mercato del lavoro, Note COVID-19*. Bank of Italy.
Yashiv, E. (2020, March 26). *Breaking the taboo: The political economy of COVID-motivated helicopter drops*. Voxeu. Retrieved from https://voxeu.org/article/political-economy-COVID-motivated-helicopter-drops

Next Generation EU, Green Deal and Sustainable Growth

Luigi Paganetto

The Covid crisis caused a negative supply and demand shock with many sectors of services, from culture to tourism, but also in commerce and retail, hit to death and others not touched or even benefited by the crisis.

Under these conditions the fall in demand implies an unprecedented accumulation of savings by lockdown consumers and an equally unprecedented loss of receipts from their non-suppliers. This effect, which leads to an increase in the stock of savings on the one hand and poverty on the other, is equivalent to a massive transfer of wealth. The impact on employment is particularly worrying in the current situation also because of the decoupling between public capital, where the process of accumulation, which has long been slowed down, and private capital (Scandizzo, 2021).

The post Covid crisis has added up to the slowdown trend of the growth rate of total productivity in the euro area.

From an accounting point of view, the slowdown is mostly due to 'traditional' capital (non-ICT physical capital), while ICT capital and 'intangibles' have also contributed to the productivity slowdown. Changes to human capital—as measured in growth accounting—have not been significant contributors to the productivity slowdown as the composition of the labor force changes slowly, at least in most countries. Ned Phelps argues in his recent book on dynamism (Phelps et al., 2020) that the shortcomings of traditional neoclassical economics include the failure to take into account the non-pecuniary aspects of work, such as self-realization and job satisfaction, and that this results in a view of economic growth that fails to account for the dynamism of modern economies—specifically, the way in which they innovate (Phelps, 2015).

L. Paganetto (✉)
Economics Foundation, University of Rome Tor Vergata, Rome, Italy
e-mail: luigi.paganetto@uniroma2.it

L. Paganetto (ed.), *Economic Challenges for Europe After the Pandemic*,
Springer Proceedings in Business and Economics,
https://doi.org/10.1007/978-3-031-10302-5_12

Education, skills, migration, aging, and labor market institutions may also contribute to the long run growth. Europe needs to adopt policies that can effectively limit the impact of the aging of its population on productivity and welfare costs investing at the same time on technology and innovation.

In this context the European Union has launched an intervention plan of 750 billion euro based for more of 50% on green and digital investments and an energy transition program putting the EU on track for a 55% reduction in carbon emissions by 2030, and net-zero emissions by 2050.

The United Nations Energy Transition Report (2021) assumes that energy transition can no longer be limited to incremental steps. It must become a transformational effort, a system overhaul, based on the rapid upscaling and implementation of all available technologies to innovate for the future.

Indeed, no green growth comes without innovation (Aghion et al., 2009).

But innovation has not been at the heart of the economic policies for energy transition.

IEA Report 2021 pointed out that technologies currently available to the market at scale will not be sufficient to effect a global clean energy transition to net-zero emissions, and a continued and strong focus on R&D is essential to the transition.

The Report concludes that clean energy innovation needs faster progress. The challenge of climate change cannot be tackled without technological advances.

The main question is to establish the role of innovation in supporting energy efficiency and power generation in renewables.

The green growth policy is taking place until now largely disregarding the innovation factor.

The EU declaration on A Green and Digital Transformation of the EU (March 2021) is the first step planning to deploy and invest more in green digital technologies to achieve climate neutrality and accelerate the green and digital transitions in priority sectors in Europe, using the Next Generation and InvestEU funds.

This policy choice must however deal with the decline in patenting activities that, since 2012, in Europe has gone hand-in-hand with a drop in the share of startups and scale-ups in the energy and sustainability sectors. The decline raises some questions, given that start-ups are important drivers of aggregate investment activities and significant carriers of innovation (Acemoglu et al., 2012; EIB, 2019).

In the case of solar photovoltaics (PV), the downward trend seems to be fully consistent with a technology entering its maturity stage. It is important that Europe maintains its competitive advantage in these different technologies, ensuring that the market does not shift to another region, as was the case with solar PV. Energy storage technologies are crucial.

The European Union spends 0.05% of GDP on climate-related R&D. Investment varies widely between EU members, depending on their national priorities. France and Germany each account for approximately 20% of EU government expenditure on climate-related R&D, followed by Italy with 12%.

Investing in digital smart power grids is a priority for the green policy. While Europe is at the forefront of green technologies, its position in digital adoption or innovation is less encouraging.

Not only are digital adoption rates of European firms lower than those of their US counterparts, innovation in digitalisation is also lower. Patent data reveal that Europe is lagging behind both the United States and China for patent applications relevant to industry 4.0.

"Investments in infrastructure projects could prove largely beneficial in keeping the green innovation engine running. Infrastructure is a critical component of the innovation system and largely determines the feasibility of the adoption and diffusion of new technologies. In addition, recent calculations suggest that public infrastructure investments have the potential to offer high returns by driving down the costs of the clean energy transition. Public infrastructure investments in renewable energy are good for the workforce by curbing job losses resulting from the coronavirus pandemic" (EIB, 2021).

The European Union's "energy efficiency first" principle is behind improvements in energy intensity. According to the latest available data (2017), Europe is a champion in decoupling its economy from energy use, investing around 60 billion of euro. Italy is a champion in Europe and boasts the lowest energy intensity with respect to the USA and China. Italy is a champion in Europe. Energy efficiency is a priority in climate options policy aiming for substantial growth of the electrification of energy end-uses and the transmission and distribution of energy through smart power grids.

Enabling activities are necessary for reducing emissions, though they act only indirectly. Investment in transport infrastructure allows fossil fuels to be substituted by electricity, as traffic is switched from oil-based road transport to electric trains.

In Italy transports account for 22% of total CO2 emissions. 90% of which are linked to road transports. Energy efficiency implementation is mainly linked to the buildings that are responsible for around 10% of total CO_2 emissions. The Italian Government plan to produce in 2030 70–72% of electrical energy by wind and photovoltaic plants is an ambitious goal coherent with EU guidelines and implies a giant investment of 70 gigawatts in the next 10 years bringing renewables to 120 gigawatts.

The past successes of Italy in increasing the renewables plants was, however, largely linked to the hydroelectric sector that today is no longer able to increase its size. Italy's achieved over the past few years an average of less than 1 GW per year in renewables that implies an annual increase of 0.8%. At this rate, our 2030 targets won't be met until 2090.

To avoid this negative result, the priority is to adopt new administrative procedures as envisaged by the Italian Recovery Plan, in order to overcome permitting bottlenecks for renewables projects. Environmental authorizations require an unpredictable length of time to be released. The government approach aims to simplify permitting rules and build an efficient governance system for investments made under Next Generation EU. The main challenge is the temporal profile of events and policies. Both public intervention and private initiatives are needed to redirect market forces toward cleaner energy Current approaches to green growth policies are ignoring that the portfolio of technologies available tomorrow depends on what is done today. Aghion conclusion is we need a wider portfolio of back stop technology turning the green innovation machine (Aghion et al., 2021).

Public infrastructure investments in renewable energy are good for the workforce by curbing job losses resulting from the coronavirus pandemic. At the same time digitalisation and the green transition will seriously impact EU labor markets. Both will change the kind of skills required, creating and potentially destroying jobs. The phenomenon of labor market polarization increasingly concerns the industrial sector of the most advanced economies (Paganetto & Lucio Scandizzo, 2018).

There is a risk that people will not possess the right mix of skills needed for the jobs to be created, which could have profound social and economic consequences. A lack of sufficient skills limits the ability of individuals to respond to the new post Covid scenario and to a changing job market.

Transition costs will be significant also in the optimistic outlook of energy transition (Blanchard & Tirole, 2021). The contrast between winners and losers in the climate and innovation policy will tend to create new inequalities (Paganetto & Lucio Scandizzo, 2017) UE recently proposed to create a Social Fund of 72 billion of euro to face this challenge.

Reforms in learning systems and new social shocks absorbers are needed to deal with the consequences of energy transition and climate policies realizing a sustainable growth in Europe.

References

Acemoglu, D., Aghion, P., Bursztyn, L., & Hemous, D. (2012). The environment and directed technical change. *American Economic Review, 102*(1), 131–166.

Aghion, P., Hemous, D., & Veugelers, R. (2009, November). *No green growth without innovation*. Bruegel Policy Brief, Issue 2009/2007.

Aghion, P., Benabou, R., Martin, R., & Roulet, A. (2021). *Environmental preferences and technological choices: Is market competition clean or dirty?* Harvard University.

Blanchard, O., & Tirole, J. (2021). *Major future economic challenge*. Republique Francais, International Commission chaired by Olivier Blanchard and Jean Tirole, Juin.

EIB. (2019). *Investment Report 2019/2020 Accelerating Europe's Transformation.*

EIB. (2021). *EIB investment report 2020/2021: Building a smart and green Europe in the Covid-19 era, report.*

IEA. (2021). *World Energy Outlook, Report.*

Paganetto, L., & Lucio Scandizzo, P. (2017). Innovation, inequality and growth. In L. Paganetto (Ed.), *Sustainable growth in the EU - Challenges and solutions*. Springer.

Paganetto, L., & Lucio Scandizzo, P. (2018). Skill polarization and inequality: Are they real and inevitable? In L. Paganetto (Ed.), *Getting globalization right. Sustainability and inclusive growth in the post Brexit age*. Springer.

Phelps, E. S. (2015). *Mass flourishing: How grassroots innovation created jobs, Challenge, and change*. Princeton University Press.

Phelps, E., Bojilov, R., Hoon, H. T., & Zoega, G. (2020, May). *Dynamism: The values that drive innovation, job satisfaction, and economic growth*. Harvard University Press.

Scandizzo, P. L. (2021). *Creating an epistemic community: The experience of the Villa Mondragone International Economic Seminar*. Springer.

United Nations. (2021). *Energy transition report.*